Members of the Tihāmah Expedition 1982

Anderson Bakewell, leader
Antony Bream
Keith Brockie
Steven D. Ehrlich
John Nankivell
Dr. Selma Al-Radi
Francine Stone

Frontispiece **Bāb Mishrif, Hodeida**
Antony Bream 170×135mm (lifesize) reversed image, line etching and dry point

STUDIES ON THE
TIHĀMAH

The Report of the Tihāmah Expedition 1982 and Related Papers

Edited by Francine Stone

Longman

Longman Group Limited
Longman House, Burnt Mill, Harlow,
Essex CM20 2JE, England
and Associated Companies throughout the world.

First published in 1985

ISBN 0 582 78387 9

British Library Cataloguing in Publication Data

Tihamah Expedition (1982)
Studies on the Tihāmah: the report of the
Tihāmah Expedition 1982 and related papers.
1. Tihāma (Yemen)
I. Title II. Stone, Francine
953'.32 DS247.Y4

ISBN 0-582-78387-9

Maps by Swanston Graphics, Derby, England.

Set in 10/10 pt Linotron 202 Bembo
Printed in Great Britain by William Clowes Limited, Beccles and London

CONTENTS

Note: Specialised glossaries appear at the end of each chapter

Plate 0.1 **Village Views I** near Bājil Nankivell *505×380mm pencil drawing courtesy of Collection Baudrand*

FOREWORD

To the majority of the public, Yemen is synonymous with its mountain realm, "The Switzerland of the Middle East," "Another Tibet".... And to be sure, much of what has been written in recent years has unveiled to Westerners the marvels of the exuberant architecture of Ṣan'ā', the stone villages perched on razorback ridges, the petticoat contours of terraced fields, in short the Yemen of the Zaydī, mountain tribesmen. It was high time to introduce the world to the treasures of this exceptionally beautiful country shut away upon itself until the Revolution of 1962. Yet in all that has been said, some of it in works of the highest quality, little has come to the fore about the coastal region of the Tihāmah: a market bazaar, a white-washed façade, a sambuk's prow pointing out to sea, a few fleeting glimpses....

In the domain of scholarly research, one finds the same preference for the mountains or the upland plateau regions. During the last ten years, the Yemen has opened its doors to considerable numbers of researchers but few have taken the Tihāmah as their field of study.

As for tourists attracted by the growing appeal of the Yemen, they usually content themselves with the standard Ṣan'ā'-Ta'izz-Hodeida road triangle, a loop that lets them while away a brief hour in the narrow streets of Zabīd, stretch their legs in the marvellous Wednesday *sūq* of Bājil or the Friday *sūq* at Bayt al-Faqīh. Mingling amid the throngs of straw hats, they can sense that the Tihāmah teems with life, but they will hardly come to appreciate the milieu in which these people exist, the framework wherein they conduct their lives. The remainder of their trip to the Tihāmah will be spent, apart from these furtive forays, on the Chinese and Soviet-built tarmac road, following a route which is as dull as it is straight. The heat will always confront them, and thanks to it and possibly a sand storm, our tourists will take away with them an image of the Tihāmah as an overridingly inhospitable place.

The Tihāmah Expedition, to its great credit, has rectified this impression which is as unfair as it is overgeneralised. The organisers of the Expedition, Anderson Bakewell and Francine Stone marshalled the means and launched a multi-disciplinary enterprise, capable of portraying life on the Tihāmah through a variety of complementary programmes. This approach of looking at things from all angles brings to mind many traits of the Carsten Niebuhr expedition of 1762 which was carried out under the aegis of the Danish crown. Only Niebuhr survived the climatic conditions of the Tihāmah and was able to bring back the fruits of the expedition and assemble them in the invaluable *Description de l'Arabie*. Anderson and Francine, when they conceived of the Tihāmah Expedition, doubtless took Niebuhr's endeavour as a model, it being the first modern expedition. And if one senses more than just a desire to emulate, it is this decided influence on the 1982 expedition version which gives it an air of "harkening back", a quality not in the least devoid of charm. The word "expedition" has come to imply a certain risk. Yet in a Yemen catapulted into the 20th century, where a Boeing 737 takes you within hours to the staging place for your work, when electricity and television have preceded you into the villages, where the Toyota has supplanted the humble donkey, can one really speak of an expedition? However, we prefer to understand the term not for its adventure or its risk, but for what it connotes of an attitude, a frame of mind, a rhythm, a cadence, a wisp of nostalgia, if you will.

But let us not fool ourselves: the style of the Tihāmah Expedition is accompanied by a determined scientific rigour, the contributions on the geology, the flora and the fauna of the Tihāmah, for instance, furnishing all the technical proficiency that could be desired. In reading the description of the Tihāmah vegetation by John Wood, how can one not think of the great Swedish botanist, Peter Forsskal, one of the first victims on the Niebuhr expedition, one who was motivated by a scientific drive remarkable for the era.

Yet not even Niebuhr in his *Description de l'Arabie* could cover the subject of history, for the history of Yemen was in those days practically a blank page, a few semi-mythical figures, legends and not more. But here in three concise papers, this book gives us a synthesis of what is now known about the Tihāmah's past, particularly in the contribution of John Baldry, the authority on the modern history of the region. Thanks to Robert Wilson, we comprehend the amazing transmutations of such mediaeval towns as al-Mahjam and al-Kadrā', once important centres and now little more than hummocks of rubble stretching for kilometres. Coupled with the archaeological finds presented by Dr. Selma Al-Radi, the fresco allows us to reconstruct a picture of the rich historical background of the Tihāmah, a picture which is indispensable to a firm understanding of the Tihāmah of the 20th century.

The presentation of Tihāmah architecture, an art of powerful originality, does homage to man's genius for adapting to the gruelling conditions of his life, homage to the management of space, the utilisation of scant resources, the capacity to play with light and shadow: the facades capture the blaze of light; the interiors tame it. Granted that the techniques of craftsmanship differ from those in the highlands, the architectural creativity of the Tihāmah tribes is every bit the equal of that of the mountain people.

It took the commitment and the competence of Anderson Bakewell to speak of the music of the Tihāmah and to record for posterity the melodies, the songs, the rhythms and the distinctive instruments there, something that the outsider does not often have the good fortune to hear.

But the most original – and perhaps the most audacious – aspect of the Expedition was the concept of bringing artists to describe and document the Tihāmah. From the window of a Toyota, the rapacious lens of an Instamatic or a Canon can grab and carry off a portrait, a bit of scenery – a theft and sometimes a violation at a 1/100th of a second. A drawing, a watercolour require a whole other approach. The artist has to give up any appetence or aggression and submit to a rite: take out his materials, sit down, contemplate, allow the ambiance to permeate him.... It is only by paying this price of admission that an artist can enter into and realise a gesture, can recreate the atmosphere in a mosque, can transmit a sense of the terrain, of a bird feeding. In this book, one appreciates the variety of artistic techniques: the effect of an etching, the precision of a pencil drawing, the reverie of a watercolour. One will above all savour the individual approach of each artist: Antony Bream who is particularly interested in landscapes and figures; Keith Brockie who has dedicated his life to wildlife and natural history painting; John Nankivell whose talent lies in architectural drawings. One cannot fail to value the fidelity to the grand Orientalist Art tradition that brought the exoticism of the East to an avid 19th century Europe. One thinks of the *Description of Egypt* but also of Lane, of Roberts, and of course one remembers Baurenfeind, the Niebuhr Expedition member who, before Yemen could claim his life, bequeathed to science a wealth of fine drawings.

Undoubtedly, the contributions in the present book will at last do justice to the Tihāmah. Leafing through its pages, one is struck by the power with which these studies evoke the place: there is the wide expanse of shore where aquatic birds squabble and preen with only the sun and the wind as witness; there are those scenes glimpsed at the turning of an alley-way; the strobic play of light and shadow; the solitary dome of a mosque, the sea in front and the encroaching sands behind, its precinct offering the alms of a little shade to the memory of an unknown saint; there are the reception rooms, profuse in their decorations over which the eye wanders for hours in the languid, beaded heat of an afternoon *qāt* session, the body reposing on a high angareb; there are the song cycles of the foothills and the clamour of the weekly *sūq*, that universe of straw and hemp and clay, wherein are jumbled together the wares and the human affairs that go back and forth between the mountains and the plain.

Yes, he who knows and loves the Tihāmah will find himself supremely at home amongst these pages. But more than a powerful description, *Studies on the Tihāmah*, is also an invitation, an invitation to Yemenis to protect their cultural patrimony and to hold it in esteem; an invitation to conserve the physical environment and to protect its flora and fauna. The researcher also will find an invitation in the form of encouragement to study one or another aspect which the Expedition and guest contributors could not pursue, such as the linguistic questions, the religious and sociological heritage embodied in the festivals at saints' tombs, the tribal organisation, the customary laws. Furnished with the Expedition portfolio the amateur artist is similarly encouraged to complete the harvest so richly begun here.

For everyone, this book is an invitation to travel. But for those who lack the opportunity, it will remain an unforgettable evocation of a region which, no less so than the highlands, constitutes an integral part of the land known as Arabia Felix.

Etienne Renaud
Rome, April 1984

PREFACE

This volume of collected papers has grown out of the Tihāmah Expedition, an independent research project that in early 1982 surveyed the wildlife, archaeology, architecture, music and ethnography on the coastal plain of North Yemen.

The Expedition grew out of an original intention to investigate the music of the region, a subject which had aroused my own particular interest in previous visits there. But persistent and often basic questions on a number of different aspects of the Tihāmah and its inhabitants kept presenting themselves. Though some fine work had been done of late in several specific fields, a ground of information was lacking, and it seemed to Francine Stone and myself that a broader based survey, an expedition, involving other disciplines was needed.

A seven member team, we approached the Tihāmah as a geographical and cultural entity which, though in no sense isolated, was quite distinct from highland and interior Arabia. Niebuhr's expedition was a model in its quality of observation and documentation, and the same multi-disciplinary format offered us the opportunity of collaboration between seemingly disparate disciplines. An exchange was encouraged throughout the fieldwork, and a picture of the Tihāmah emerged that emphasised the interdependent elements there, from the obvious mutual effect of the flora and the fauna, to the interrelationship of the architecture and the crafts, or the natural materials and the musical instruments, or the historical placement of ports and the changing terrain, and so on. This exchange was a source of immense satisfaction both at the time and as the material was being prepared for publication.

The decision to include artists rather than photographers was inspired by the work of Rupert Kirk whose watercolours of coastal scenes in the British Somaliland of the 1830s I happened to see on view at the Royal Geographical Society. Far from being mere picturesque studies in an obsolete medium, these hand-rendered pieces communicated to me a great sense of place, and coincidentally much the same sense that I had previously experienced on the Yemen Tihāmah. Given this manifest richness of information, it seemed wholly appropriate to choose to take artists there.

The challenge of working with artists in the field was difficult to imagine beforehand. Though it was at times necessary to accommodate one's own perceptions to a subtle and often idiosyncratic vision of the artist, who is after all not an illustrator, the realignment was nearly always rewarding. The shortcomings of the artistic media were obvious – the lack of rapidity of documentation, the occasional lack of cooperation from the weather or the subject or the onlookers or the artist himself. Despite these shortcomings, however, I very much appreciated the skill and the eloquence with which the artist can accentuate details of specific interest and produce highly informative, lasting records. Certainly the "event" of the documentation process was in its impact considerably lessened as the artist became, over a period of hours or even days, a part of the landscape or village scene. The Tihāmīs themselves absolutely delighted at the attentions of the artists, and their excited posturing quickly gave way to appreciative accommodation. They were in fact so pleased to be presented with sketches and paintings as gifts that we had to exercise some restraint in the early stages of the Expedition if any portfolio were to be brought back at all.

The limitations of the fieldwork will be obvious to anyone consulting a map of South Arabia. The Tihāmah is of course not exclusively of North Yemen, and any subsequent work should take into account that portion that lies in Saudi Arabia. Logistical constraints prevented visits to the outlying islands (notably Kamarān, Zuqar, and the Ḥanīsh group) and travel in the border zones (south of Mawzaʿ and north of ʿAbs), surveys of which would surely contribute towards a fuller picture of the archaeology and natural history of the region. Above all, studies of the Tihāmah dialect and tribal structure, important subjects only touched upon in the field, merit considerably more attention.

That more questions are ultimately posed than are answered by these surveys will not, it is hoped, detract from their usefulness, nor impede the material, however fragmentary, from stimulating further, deeper studies.

The pleasures of the fieldwork, and they were many, stemmed equally from the excellent company of the Expedition members who bore the stiff pace of an ambitious programme with remarkable stamina and good humour, and from the Tihāmīs themselves who, while bemused by our countless queries, welcomed us with every ready assistance, tact and graciousness.

Anderson Bakewell,
Expedition leader
Shillingford, April 1984

ACKNOWLEDGEMENTS

The Tihāmah Expedition, which only began with its work in the field, subsequently encompassed an art exhibition, public exhibitions on the theme of "Studies on the Tihāmah," a recording of Tihāmah music, publication of limited edition prints, an Expedition report, and finally the editing of the field surveys and related papers into the present volume. It is therefore fitting and proper that acknowledgement be given here to the individuals and institutions which provided support to these several phases of the Expedition, and without which an independent, multifaceted project such as this could never have taken place.

First and foremost, we wish to express our gratitude to Rothmans of Pall Mall (Overseas) Ltd for the financial contributions that made the fieldwork possible, and for the unconditional backing that encouraged work which would benefit the people of the Yemen Arab Republic. Yemenia (Yemen Airways) provided generous assistance, and the Tihāmah Expedition was further sponsored by the Explorers Club (New York), the American Foundation for the Study of Man, Turner Wright & Partners Ltd, and by patrons Mr. Malcolm Horsman, Miss Irena Knehtl and Mr. D.H. Gates, to whom the organisers are extremely grateful.

The Expedition's affiliations with the American Institute for Yemeni Studies and the Royal Geographical Society furnished logistical and administrative assistance which was invaluable. In particular, Prof. Abbas Hamdani, president, and Dr. Leigh Douglas, resident director of AIYS in 1982, extended themselves greatly on behalf of the programme, as have the subsequent officers of AIYS, an institution which is an asset to foreign researchers in Yemen. The director of the Royal Geographical Society, Dr. John Hemming, and Keeper of the Map Room, Brigadier G.A. Hardy, brought their distinguished good offices to bear on the Expedition projects, while Nigel and Shane Winser of the RGS Expedition Advisory Centre were both midwives and god parents, personally concerned for the Expedition's success at every major stage of preparation and implementation. It would not have happened without them.

In Yemen, the Expedition had the honour of working under the guidance of the Yemen Centre for Research and Studies, where Dr. 'Abd al-'Azīz Maqāliḥ, director, and Bilqīs al-Ḥaḍrānī, assistant, facilitated the field programme. To them we are thankful, and to Dr. 'Abd al-Karīm al-'Iryānī, prime minister, and to Qāḍī 'Alī Abū al-Rijāl, governor of Hodeida, for their gracious permission to conduct our work on the Tihāmah in 1982. The many individuals who offered aid, expertise and information to the programme while in Yemen included Jon Bjornson, James Callahan of USIS, Barbara Crocken, 'Abd al-Raḥmān al-Muḥsin al-Dhamrān, Ibrahim El-Domi of the Tihama Development Authority, Werner Dubach, James Dunlop of the British Embassy, Dr. Ed Keall of the Royal Ontario Museum, Irena Knehtl, Shaykh Muḥammad 'Alī al-Mazarīyah of Bājil, Dr. P. Patterson of USAID, Thomas Scotes, Muḥammad 'Alī Sulaymān of al-Mu'tariḍ, Carol Taylor, Sheila Unwin, Aḥmad 'Abduh al-Wāqidī of Zabīd, Dr. Claire Willington, David Wilson of the National Tobacco and Match Co., Mr. & Mrs. Charles Young, and the countless good people of the Tihāmah who welcomed us, hosted us and informed us.

Of those who have taken an active interest in the artistic aspect of the Expedition, we have first to thank Ian Fleming, director of the Brotherton Gallery, for his admirable energies as art advisor to the Expedition. Dalu Jones, co-editor of AARP, put herself behind every aspect of the project from the outset. Our thanks go equally to those who responded to the results with more than mere appreciation, doing what they could to further the creative work and bring it to a wider public. Among them are Dick Temple of the Temple Gallery, Fred Allen, Primrose Arnander, Mr. and Mrs. H.G. Balfour-Paul, Mr. and Mrs. Antonin Besse, Mr. and Mrs. F. Carlton Colchord, Naomi Collins of Islam Centennial Fourteen, Alistair Duncan of the World of Islam Festival Trust, Dale Egee, W. Facey, Dolores Fairbanks of the Aga Khan Program for Islamic Architecture, Sarah Graham-Brown, Vanessa Harrison of the BBC, Ragnar Johnson, George Kassis, Trevor Mostyn of MEED, Andrew McIntosh Patrick, Venetia Porter, Marjorie Ransom and Tessa Sayle.

The research work, before during and after the Expedition, has been fructified by the suggestions and contributions of numerous scholars and informed individuals. While specific data are credited in the pages which follow, it gives us pleasure to reiterate here our gratitude to those who repeatedly made their knowledge available to us, demonstrating the great spirit of cooperation which prevails amongst those interested in the Yemen today. Above all, our thanks go to John Baldry, the Expedition's principal advisor and team member who could not at the last moment join in the fieldwork, but who throughout has furnished information and insight into the region he so profoundly knows. Etienne Renaud generously gave, as he has to many who have worked in the Yemen, of his knowledge and of his accumulated wisdom. Others who have served in various ways to enrich the material, and whom we wish to thank warmly are Dr. Yūsuf 'Abdullāh, Sayyid Maḥmūd 'Abdullāh al-Ahdal, Dr. Gus W. Van Beek, John Burton of the Fauna Preservation Society, Dominique Champault, Sir Hugh F.I. Elliott, Dr. Claudie Fayein, John Gasperetti, Prof. S.D. Goitein, Rosalind W. Haddon, F. Nigel Hepper, Fr. Albert Jamme, Michael Jennings, Dr. Harmut Jungius of the International Union for Conservation of Nature and Natural Resources, Dr. Jack King, Jr., Eric Macro, Derek H. Matthews, Martha Mundy, Dr. Cynthia Myntti, Alain Saint-Hilaire, Sayyid Aḥmad al-Shāmī, Fernando Varanda, Shelagh Weir and O. Wright.

Finally, we want to extend heart-felt thanks to the contributors of the guest papers for making it possible to expand the scope of this volume beyond the field surveys carried out by the Expedition members, and to the publishers and editors at Longman for seeing the value of the work and for focussing their skills on its publication. We are also fortunate to have been assisted by Yamini Patel who, as our architectural draftswoman and graphic artist, designed the public exhibitions, prepared the architectural material for publication, and shaped the book from its inception. Lastly, the editor wishes to thank Robert Wilson for reviewing and proofreading, with the most amenable wit and acumen, portions of the manuscript; notwithstanding, any errors which may occur herein are to be laid at the editor's doorstep.

LIST OF ILLUSTRATIONS

We are grateful to the artists Antony Bream, Keith Brockie and John Nankivell, as well as to Steven D. Ehrlich and Kiki Larsen, for their kind permission to reproduce their works of art which appear in this volume. We also thank the various owners of original paintings and drawings from the Expedition, both those who are named herein and those who have wished to remain anonymous, for their courtesies extended in the course of producing the book.

INTRODUCTION

Along the apron of the south western Arabian Peninsula, facing the Red Sea, lie the coastal lowlands known as the Tihāmah. Backing up to the foothills of the Arabian highlands, the Tihāmah extends from below Jiddah in Saudi Arabia, down the length of the North Yemen coast, and some would say, onto the shores of the Indian Ocean. The portion of the Tihāmah which is situated within the region called the 'Asīr is traditionally designated Tihāmat al-'Asīr. However, modern political boundaries now divide the plain, and that which comprises the Saudi Arabian Tihāmah forms two sections, the Tihāmat al-Shām from al-Līth to Birk at the lava field north of Jīzān, and the Tihāmat al-Janūb thence to the present North Yemen border. The North Yemen stretch, known as the Tihāmat al-Yaman, takes Hodeida as the dividing line between two segments which are commonly referred to as the northern and the southern Tihāmah.[1]

The word *tihāmah* is an ancient Semitic one, familiar to many of us from the Bible where its Hebrew phonetic variation, *tehōm*, occurring in the Book of Genesis, is translated "the *Deep*" ("the darkness above the Deep", Gen 1:2). It is found in Akkadian with the meaning of ocean depths or lowest reaches of the earth, and it is usually associated with the myth of creation.[2] In Arabic, as in the Epigraphic South Arabian form *T-h-m-t* which preceded it, the term *Tihāmah* is confined to the designation of a specific geographical region, although the cognate *taham* carries the more general meaning of a "land descending to the sea",[3] and *tahamah* further connotes "a vehemence of heat", "stillness of wind", and "having a foul odour".[4]

The actual geographical region meant by *Tihāmah* differs according to different sources. Al-Hamdānī, the 10th-century Yemeni historian and geographer, uses it to refer to "the maritime lowlands south of Makkah [Mecca]",[5] and the lexicographer E.W. Lane elaborates on this, adding "a certain land well known commencing from Dhát 'Irk toward Nejd and extending to Mekkah [Mecca] and beyond it to the distance of two days journeys and more, then uniting with the Ghowr, and extending to the sea; some say it adjoins the land of El-Yemen."[6]

Ibn Khaldūn, the 14th-century historian, states that "the name *tihāmah* denotes the low country of Yaman adjoining the sea-coast and extending from as-Sirrayn on the borders of the Hijāz, to the extremity of the province of Aden, round by the Indian Ocean";[7] whereas J.W. Redhouse, translator of medieval Yemeni texts, understood that it runs "from near Bábu'l-Mendeb in the south to the frontier of the territory of Mekka [Mecca]".[8] Carsten Niebuhr, leader of the 1762-3 Danish Expedition to Arabia, took it that the Tihāmah "begins at Suez, and extends round the whole peninsula to the mouth of the Euphrates",[9] an uncharacteristic overstatement which indicates that Niebuhr took the word literally to mean "coastal strip". H. Wehr is perhaps wisest in keeping his definition to the most general of terms, giving the Tihāmah as a "coastal plain along the south-western and southern shores of the Arabian Peninsula".[10]

The Tihāmah Expedition 1982 worked between 'Abs and Mawza', a distance of some 200km, all of which is contained within the boundaries of the Yemen Arab Republic (North Yemen). The papers of this book deal primarily, but not exclusively, with this sector of the plain. Added to the field surveys carried out by members of the Tihāmah Expedition are guest papers which were invited to supplement the Expedition's work, the aim being to publish a symposium of recent information on the salient features of the Tihāmah.

To the reader who is largely unfamiliar with the Tihāmah, it might be desirable to have a broad picture of the region and a summary of its history, before embarking on the specialised texts of this volume. While such an introduction necessitates a gambit of generalisations which do little justice to the subject, it is hoped that the reader will go forward into the book comfortable enough to make the best use of the monographs to be found there.

---

1. See H. St. John Philby, *Arabian Highlands*, Ithaca, 1952; and W. Thesiger, "A Journey Through the Tihama, the 'Asir, and the Hijaz Mountains," *Geographical Journal*, Vol. 110, 1947, pp. 188-200. I am also grateful to John Gasperetti for discussions regarding the demarcations of the Saudi Arabian Tihāmah regions.
2. Prof. S.D. Goitein has very kindly supplied me with background information on the word *tehōm*, citing the large body of literature on the subject which exists in dictionaries of biblical and ancient Near Eastern studies.
3. E.W. Lane, *Arabic-English Lexicon*, London, 1863-74, Bk. I, p. 320. For further information about the Epigraphic South Arabian *T-h-m-t*, see G. Lankester Harding, *An Index and Concordance of Pre-Islamic Arabian Names and Inscriptions*, Toronto, 1971, p. 140.
4. E.W. Lane, ibid.
5. See J.W. Redhouse's translation of al-Khazrajī's *The Pearl Strings; a history of the Resúliyy dynasty of Yemen*, Leiden-London, 1906-18, Vol. III, p. 17, n.47.
6. E.W. Lane, op. cit.
7. See H.C. Kay, *Yaman Its Early Mediæval History*, London, 1892, p. 165.
8. J.W. Redhouse, op. cit., p. 44, n.257.
9. C. Niebuhr, *Travels Through Arabia and Other Countries in the East*, Edinburgh, 1792, Vol. II, p. 318.
10. H. Wehr, *Arabic-English Dictionary*, ed. J.W. Cowan, Ithaca, 3rd edition, 1976, p. 98. Without first-hand knowledge of the region south of Mawza', I cannot confirm nor can I disavow the notion that the Tihāmah extends onto the shores of the Indian Ocean, as the mediaeval sources indicate. Hugh Leach and John Shipman however have both very kindly offered their impression that Ṣubayḥī territory, west of Aden, is not considered by those who live there to be a part of the Tihāmah. The question remains then: where in the south does the coastal strip cease to be the Tihāmah?

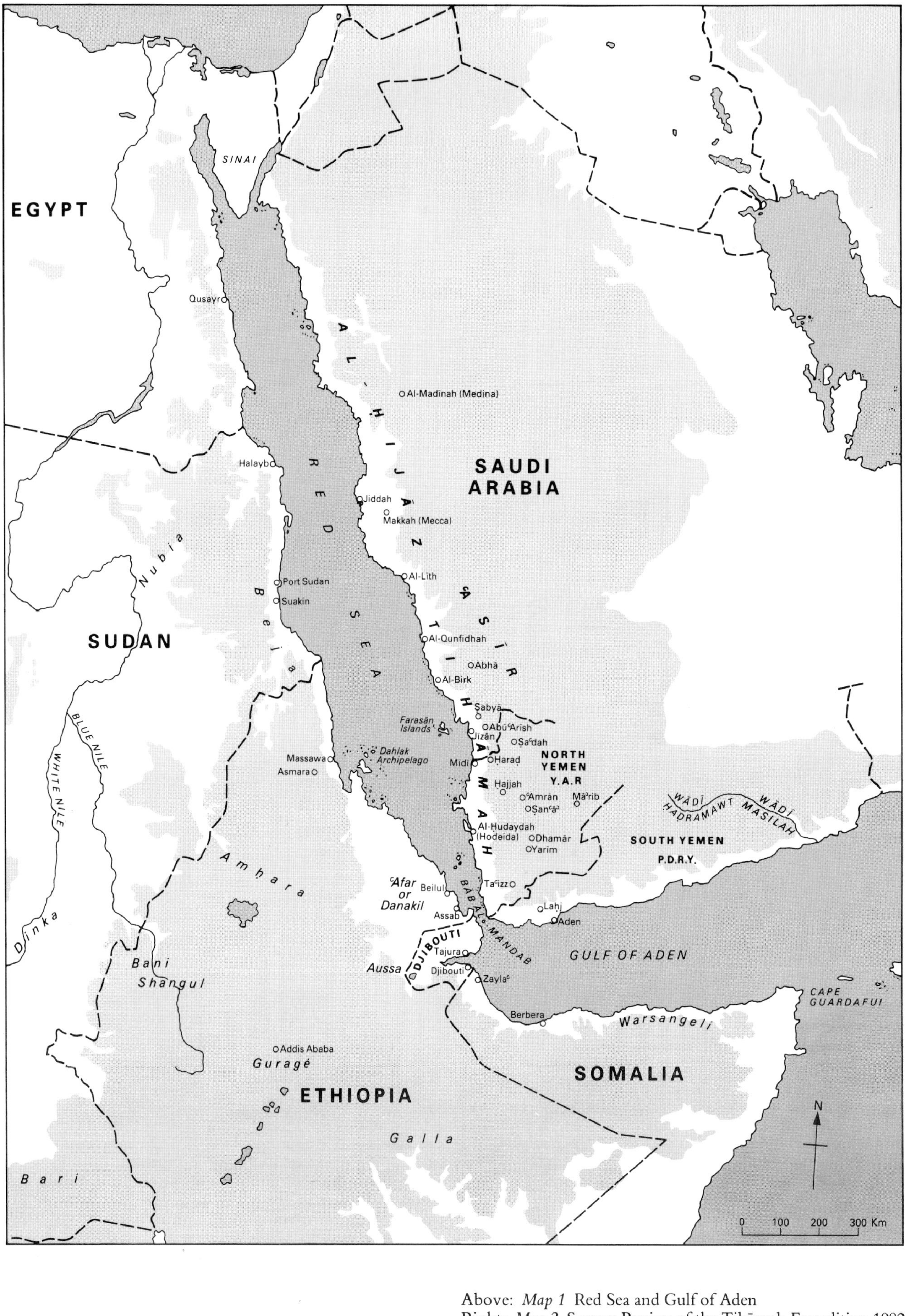

Above: *Map 1* Red Sea and Gulf of Aden
Right: *Map 2* Survey Region of the Tihāmah Expedition 1982

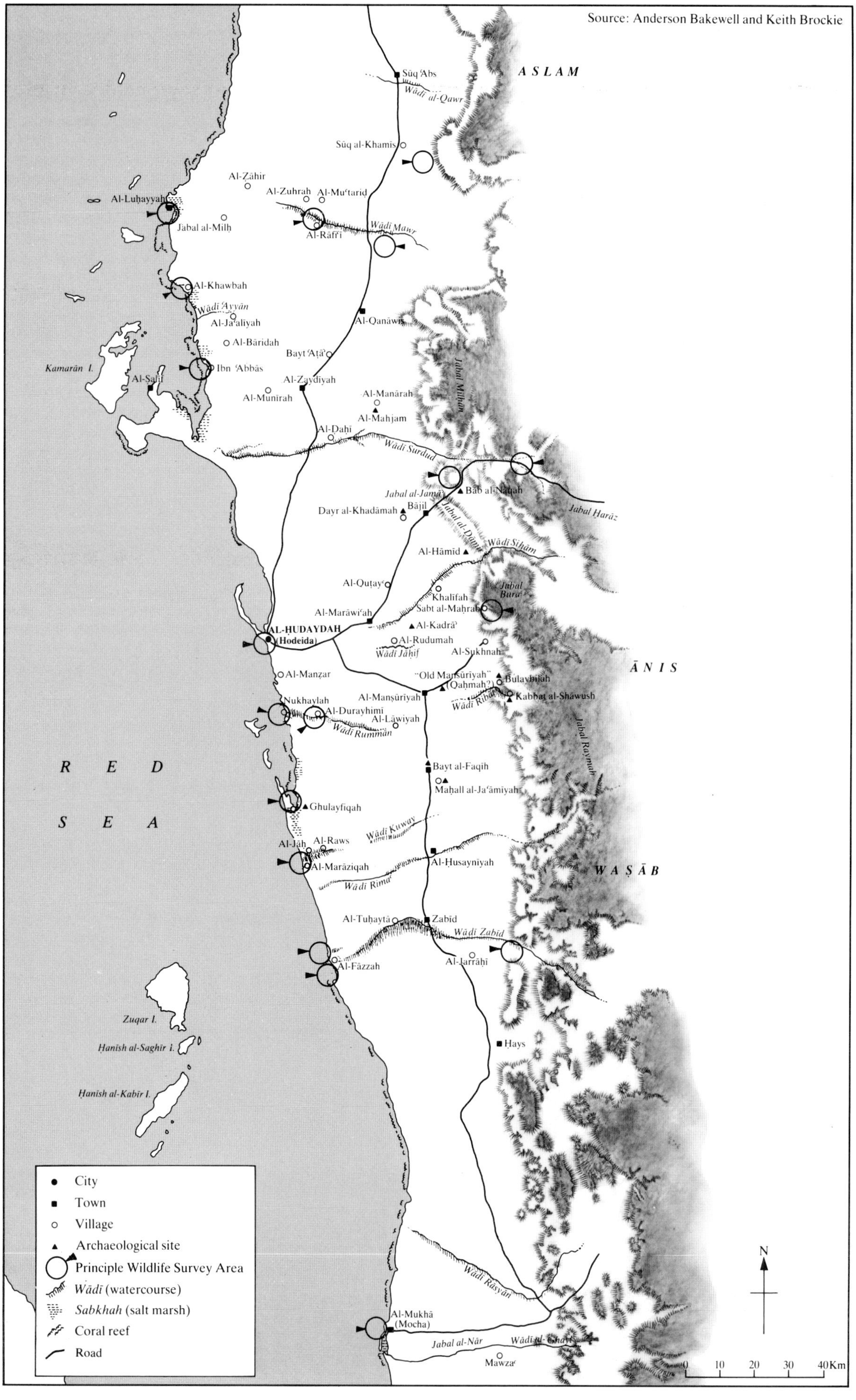
Source: Anderson Bakewell and Keith Brockie
ASLAM
Sūq ʿAbs
Wādī al-Qawr
Sūq al-Khamīs
Al-Zāhir
Al-Zuhrah
Al-Muʿtarid
Al-Luḥayyah
Jabal al-Milḥ
Wādī Mawr
Al-Rāfiʿī
Al-Khawbah
Wādī ʿAyyān
Al-Jaʿāliyah
Al-Qanāwiṣ
Al-Bāridah
Bayt ʿAṭā'
Kamarān I.
Al-Ṣalīf
Ibn ʿAbbās
Al-Zaydiyah
Al-Munīrah
Al-Manārah
Al-Mahjam
Jabal Milḥān
Al-Ḍaḥī
Wādī Surdud
Jabal al-Jamīʿ
Bāb al-Nāqah
Dayr al-Khadāmah
Bājil
Jabal al-Dāmin
Jabal Ḥarāz
Wādī Sihām
Al-Ḥāmid
Al-Quṭayʿ
Khalīfah
Jabal Burāʿ
Sabt al-Maḥrab
Al-Marāwiʿah
Al-Kadrā'
AL-ḤUDAYDAH (Hodeida)
Al-Rudumah
Wādī Jāḥif
Al-Sukhnah
ĀNIS
Al-Manẓar
"Old Manṣūriyah" (Qaḥmah?)
Bulaybilah
Al-Manṣūriyah
Wādī Ribāṭ
Kabbat al-Shāwush
Nukhaylah
Al-Durayhimī
Al-Lāwiyah
Wādī Rummān
Jabal Raymah
RED SEA
Bayt al-Faqīh
Maḥall al-Jaʿāmiyah
Ghulayfiqah
Wādī Kuway
Al-Jāḥ
Al-Raws
Al-Marāziqah
Al-Ḥusayniyah
WAṢĀB
Wādī Rimaʿ
Al-Tuḥaytā
Zabīd
Wādī Zabīd
Al-Fāzzah
Al-Jarrāḥī
Zuqar I.
Ḥanīsh al-Saghīr I.
Ḥays
Ḥanīsh al-Kabīr I.
City
Town
Village
Archaeological site
Principle Wildlife Survey Area
Wādī (watercourse)
Sabkhah (salt marsh)
Coral reef
Road
N
Wādī Rasyān
Al-Mukhā (Mocha)
Jabal al-Nār
Wādī al-Ghayl
Mawzaʿ
0 10 20 30 40Km

On first sight the Tihāmah appears a flat desiccated plain, averaging 20-40km wide, too narrow for drama of its own but too broad for the spectacle of the mountains to be seen through the haze from the coast. A second look reveals an undulating terrain, set off by isolated rock outcrops, stands of sorghum, skylines of palm trees and thin mirages that shimmer over the seaboard crusts of salt. Steep canyons slash the foothills where seasonal rivers (*wādīs*) flow out onto the plain, laddering its narrow length with arable cropland and date groves. The intervals between the *wādīs* are given over to zones of desert sand in the west and boulder-strewn scrub in the east. Coral reefs fringe the coastal waters and good harbours are few. Everywhere, access to fresh water is crucial.

Life on the plain is undeniably harsh. Rain falls in a scant 110mm per year, coming in two unreliable monsoon spates of late summer and early spring. Apart from a mid-winter respite, the heat does not dip below sweltering, with temperatures well exceeding 40°C. by July and the humidity adding its oppression. Although malaria is the greatest natural hazard on the Tihāmah, other endemic sub-tropical diseases join in giving the Tihāmah a justly deserved reputation for unwholesomeness'. We know that two-thirds of the Jewish population of the highlands, banished to Mawza' on the southern Tihāmah, mainly in 1679, perished there within two years;[11] and only Niebuhr survived the fevers that befell all six men of his expedition. Ancient soothsayers, before the coming of Islam, singled out the Tihāmah as one of the four cursed and inauspicious places of the Yemen,[12] and they were right in many ways, as Niebuhr ably describes:

> In these desarts, diversified here and there only by bare rocks, and in these flat plains, there is nothing to soften the force of the sun's rays, but all vegetables are burnt up, and the soil is everywhere reduced to sand. The drought is so extreme, that whole years will pass without rain; and the torrents which fall from the hills are lost among the sands long before they can reach the sea. Were it not for these river-waters, which being swelled in the rainy season, are drained off to fertilize the lands, the husbandman would be unable to raise even those scanty crops which his harvests at present afford. By observations made with good thermometers, we found, that in these plains, as, for instance, at Loheya [al-Luḥayyah], Mokha [Mocha], and Maskat [Muscat, Oman], the heats were as intense as in any other hot country whatever.[13]

Geologically, the Tihāmah forms a part of the deep tectonic trench of the Red Sea that is itself an extension of the Rift Valley system of Africa. Many trees and plants of the savannah and sahara regions of Africa grow here. Dune grasses and scrub, acacia trees and succulents do their best to fasten the loose soils of the plain and lend a paltry shade. In this habitat, hyaena, mongoose, fox and feral cat stalk for food. The lovely gazelle is now rare, and the stately Arabian bustard badly over-hunted, but waterbirds and waders abound in the coastal lagoons, and the foothills ring with the raucous cries of parrots, baboons and hornbills.

What strikes one immediately about the Tihāmah is its contrast to highland Arabia. Coming down out of the mountains, the Tihāmah culture begins where straw hats and conical thatch huts first appear. Skins darken. Stone terraces give way to earthen bunds that surround fields of millet, maize, sesame, cotton and tobacco along the *wādī* banks. Here religious preferences change to the Sunnī branch of Islam which accommodates the veneration of local saints and miracle workers, unlike the Shī'ah practices of the Zaydī sect in the highlands. The veil is not strictly required, and rural women often dispense with modesty in deference to the heat. The sway of tribal confederations is not as palpably felt as in the mountains, and symbols of the tribesman, the *jambīyah* dagger and the firearm, are not as frequently seen.

Although Arabic is the language of the Tihāmah, it is spoken in an idiosyncratic dialect that is often unintelligible to other Yemenis. An anecdote from mediaeval history illustrates how the Tihāmī tongue has been effected by the disparate strains of society there, making pronunciation a give-away to one such as al-Mukarram, the Ṣulayḥid ruler who in 1089 A.D. carried out a bloody sack of Zabīd, the capital city of the Tihāmah:

> His heralds now proclaimed his orders to unsheathe the sword against the people of the captured town. But he warned the army that the Arabs of the Tihāmah begat children by black concubines, and that a black skin was common to both slave and free. "But if ye hear a person pronounce the word *aẓm*, AZM (as if it were written with the letter *z* [ز]), know that he is an Abyssinian [slave] and slay him. If he pronounce it AẒM (with the letter *ẓ* [ظ]), he is an Arab, and ye shall spare him."[14]

Despite the apocryphal ring to the story, it is certain that the Tihāmah dialect contains not only accents but loan-words of African origin brought by slaves and merchants over the centuries from across the Red Sea.[15]

Indeed the peoples of the Tihāmah are a fascinating racial mix. Placenames such as Ḥārat al-Hunūd (Place of the Indians), elements of costume from the Danakil tribes of Ethiopia, grandfathers who were Ottoman soldiers, sailors familiar with Zanzibar and Ḥaḍramawt, ex-slaves who retain their master's name, pearl divers possessed of pidgin Italian or French, these are not uncommon elements in Tihāmī society, features which co-exist with tribesmen of pure Arab stock who trace their ancestry back to pre-Islamic Ḥimyar clans. Facial types on the Tihāmah vividly reflect these and other origins.

The people make their living mostly from the sea and the soil. To farming and herding are added the coastal economies of fishing, date palm growing, salt production and (formerly) pearl diving. Goods are bought and sold in open-air weekly markets. Weaving, indigo dyeing, pottery and brick making, although in decline, are still practised by the men. The womenfolk are accomplished at basketry, embroidery and painted decoration. Many traditional life styles persist among the plain dwellers, certain modern amenities not withstanding.

11. See S.D. Goitein, *From the Land of Sheba*, New York, 1973, p. 119. Prof. Goitein describes the expulsion to Mawza' as "in many ways the most decisive event in their [the Yemenite Jews] later history". (Ibid.)
12. Al-Hamdānī, *The Antiquities of South Arabia, being a translation... of the 8th Book of al-Hamdānī's AL-IKLĪL*, trans. N.A. Faris, Princeton, 1938, repr. Westport, 1981, pp. 69-71.
13. Niebuhr, op. cit., Vol. II, p. 312.
14. Kay, op. cit., p. 36.
15. We collected (thanks to A. al-Rudaynī) the following loan-words of alleged African origins: *kurtah* (Galla) = clothes; *gorgorah* (Galla) = *fūṭah* or sarong; *būddah* (Ethiopic) = a change from animal to human form; *yallim* (Amharic) = not any; and in the work of Henry Cassels Kay we find mention of *dayba'* being a Nubian word for "white". (Op. cit., p. xviii.)

Four major styles of architecture typify the Tihāmah. The merchant houses of the port towns, with their latticed wood balconies and coral masonry are quintessentially "Red Sea" in style. Inland, Zabīd has produced a brick and plaster work that renders the façades and interiors of the houses in whitewashed patterns as intricate as lace. Burnt brick is the fabric of the massive, castellated forts that were erected in the early part of this century; but by their very impermanence, the thatch huts of the northern Tihāmah achieve perhaps the most remarkable architectural expression of all, fashioned from loam and hemp and elaborately hand-painted as they are.

Music on the Tihāmah plays an important role in daily life. The most characteristic, and that which best evokes the spirit of the place, is the music performed by professional itinerant musicians at nearly all public gatherings – weddings, circumcision ceremonies, weekly markets, healing sessions, saint's day and date harvest festivals. Highly rhythmic, it features pipes, lyres and a variety of drums, and it accompanies dances of the most extraordinary nature. This is very much "Red Sea" music, and it shares much in instrumentation and technique with the tradition found up and down the Red Sea coast on both sides.

For everyone, the heat governs the patterns of the day, obliging strenuous activity to cease in the noontime blaze, when shade, liquid and the reclining posture are requisite. Family living takes place in walled compounds or courtyards open to the sky, and at night, rope-strung beds are pulled out under the stars to catch the slightest breeze. Overhead, palm trees susurrate, mingling the night-time scents of jasmine, hemp, tobacco and incense. But today, one must wait for the throb of diesel pumps and the crackle of television to fall silent before the beauty of the Tihāmah night can reign as it did before man and his improvements ever arrived on the plain.

Evidence of the earliest human history of the Tihāmah still lies buried under its sands and scattered amongst its boulders. While it seems to be a fertile site for prehistoric settlements, knowledge of this period is woefully lacking. Traces of the pre-Islamic era are, however, beginning to emerge. Al-Hāmid, the only pre-Islamic site on the Tihāmah as yet to produce inscriptions, stands at the mouth of a major access valley which leads to the highlands where the ancient kingdom of Ḥimyar, also known as Saba, stood. From here, trading concerns with Africa must have entailed way-stations on the plain as early as the 5th century B.C., and al-Hāmid may have been one of these, although probably of later date.

Graeco-Roman writers give us a vivid picture of the Tihāmah coast and hinterland in the 1st and 2nd centuries A.D. when luxury goods from the interior, incense and myrrh and alabaster, as well as locally made weapons, were exported from Musa, a roadstead on the southern Tihāmah which much later developed into the well-known coffee port of Mocha. As the power of the Ḥimyar kingdom waned, the Tihāmah fell prey to incursions from the Christian kings of Abyssinia whose armies invaded briefly in the 4th and 6th centuries A.D.

The coming of Islam, however, initiated an era of prosperity which was to bring the Tihāmah to the forefront of Yemen history. In 822 A.D., Zabīd was created the capital city of the country, from which rule was extended over the highlands. Zabīd continued with minor breaks as the first city of Yemen through the early mediaeval period. It became the centre of culture and learning, a university town of great renown.

In 1229 A.D., a dynasty named for its rulers, the Rasūlids, began an age of prolific building activity on the Tihāmah. Forts, mosques, roads and water systems were constructed with elegance and durability. Pottery and textile industries flourished, and the fields came under maximum cultivation. Scores of towns sprang up, many more than exist today. By the 15th century, however, overtaxation and tribal disorders had all but exhausted the resources of the plain; its produce dwindled, and the blowing sands began their destruction....

Although the Tihāmah ceded its political importance in the late mediaeval period to other regions of Yemen, it never ceased to function as the mercantile portal of the country. In fact most of what outsiders, from the Romans onward, have known of the Yemen has been the Tihāmah. Sixteenth-century trade in textiles and coffee created enviable wealth that attracted first the marauding Portuguese and subsequently the Mamluks from Egypt and then the Ottomans, both of whom sought to carve out lucrative holdings for themselves on the Tihāmah. It was not until 1636 A.D. that the Zaydī Imām from the highlands succeeded in driving out the Turkish invaders, leaving in their place his own equally unpopular overseers.

The following two centuries saw an almost continual process of intrusion, misrule or misalliance, and eventual expulsion of outside forces – mostly Ottoman Turks but also Egyptians, Idrīsī followers from the 'Asīr, Sharīfs of Abū 'Arīsh, Sa'ūds, soldiers of the Imām and even the English and the Italians who managed to bomb every major port of the Yemen Tihāmah in a series of misbegotten and self-serving ventures.

The nearly constant warfare which prevailed, coupled with tribal reluctance to accept the central authority of the ruling Imām, accelerated the decline of many towns in the Tihāmah. Mocha and al-Luḥayyah slowly fell into disuse; while conversely the newly established port of Hodeida gained ascendancy. In 1809, al-Luḥayyah was devastated by vengeful tribes, and Mocha ceded its commercial vitality to Aden when the British took control there in 1839 A.D.. Up and down the Tihāmah, factious local tribes were causing havoc. When G. Wyman Bury wrote in 1919 that "the whole of the Tihama, except the garrison towns and their immediate neighbourhood, is out of control",[16] he described Tihāmah affairs of long standing.

It was not until the last twenty years, since the Revolution which created the Yemen Arab Republic in 1967 A.D., that the revival of the Tihāmah region could begin, a tarmac road system be built, the port of Hodeida modernised, and an efficient irrigation system refurbished. Today the Tihāmah is at peace and once more shows the promise of economic vitality with benefits for all of the Yemen.

Notes on presentation

Because this book seeks to provide information both to readers with general interests and to those with specialised knowledge, it has been necessary to devise a system of presentation whereby the content of the volume would be accessible to those with little or no Arabic training, at the same time as it would offer substantive material to specialists. Accordingly, Arabic words are followed by a brief English translation where they first appear in each paper, and full glossaries are provided at the end of each chapter. The 1956 BGN/PCGN system

16. G.W. Bury, *Arabia Felix*, London, 1915, p.40.

of transliteration, recommended by the UN Conference of 1967, has been adopted with certain modifications which will be explained below. This system was chosen over other equally workable ones because it conforms to that of the published maps utilised by the Expedition in the field. The system has been modified to the extent that the definite article *al-* does not change in front of words beginning with the Sun letters, and a subscript dot is used instead of the cedilla under the *ḥ*, *ṭ*, *ḍ*, *ṣ* and *ẓ*.

An effort has been made to trim the kind of scholarly thickets which make Arabic studies very hard-going for general readers, myself included. The singular form of Arabic words has been used as a rule, rather than encumbering the untrained reader with the somewhat gymnastic plurals of the language, even though this has in turn given rise to the awkwardness of the English "s" added to Arabic words used in a plural context, thus *imāms* for *a'immah*, *wādīs* for *audiyah*, *sūqs* for *aswāq*, and so on.

Likewise, the transliteration scheme has been relaxed where words and placenames are mentioned which are likely to be familiar to the ordinary reader in their anglicised forms. Such words as Aden, Dhofar, Hodeida, Iraq, Islam, Mecca, Medina, Mocha, pasha, Saudi Arabia, sufi, Yemen and Yemeni have been spared the diacriticals. However, all other placenames, proper names and Arabic words including *al-Qur'ān* (the Koran), *wādī*, *shaykh* and *imām* have been treated formally; furthermore, where the placenames Hodeida and Mocha are cited in the history papers, which were written largely from primary sources, these too have been systematically transliterated as al-Ḥudaydah and al-Mukhā'.

Where source material which employs some other system of transliteration is cited but not quoted directly, the notation [sic] follows Arabic words with discrepant spellings. In other instances, [sic] is inserted where the rendering of Arabic words seems to us dubious or incomplete. In both cases, it is advisable for the reader to consult the source given in order to make his or her own assessment.

Three placenames are given with spellings which do not conform to the current cartographic versions. We have chosen to honour the spellings which appear in Yemeni sources; thus, al-Tuḥaytā, al-Fāzzah and Wādī Surdud appear instead of al-Tuḥaytah, al-Fazzah and Wādī Surdūd, all of which have found their way onto recent maps.

Arabic vocabulary words are set in italics; placenames and proper names appear in roman typeface, as do Arabic words when they are used as titles, such as Sharīf, Shaykh and Imām. Latin classifications of flora and fauna are rendered in large and small capitals, as for example THRESKIORNIS AETHIOPICUS. Furthermore, since the use of italics for Arabic words precluded the customary italicisation of scholarly terms such as et passim, sic and in situ, these have been left in roman typeface.

Due to the broad range of studies in this symposium, references and glossaries have been assembled by discipline and are presented with each chapter, despite the fact that this results in a certain amount of repetition across the book as a whole. It was felt that this arrangement would best facilitate use of the work by researchers with specialised objectives and limited time or access, as is often the case with library reading. The author of each paper has contributed his or her own bibliography, and the editor has furnished lists of further reading and further reference, as well as the glossaries.

Glossary entries are listed in English alphabetical order, and definitions give first the local meaning(s) of the word and then the standard modern Arabic (or classical Arabic) meaning if one exists and if it differs from the colloquial Tihāmah usage. The pronunciations that are indicated may not apply beyond the locale and the social settings where they were collected.

Finally, where an artist has inscribed a title or notes directly onto his work as it was done in the field, his designations of Arabic terms, placenames and proper names may not be rigorously accurate or consistent with one system of transliteration. The titles as they are cited in this book have been altered as little as possible from the originals; nevertheless, academic considerations have led to the assignment of new or amended titles in certain cases. This has been done with the artist's permission, and with apologies to art historians who will in consequence be confronted with title variations.

Should this book act as a catalyst for further, sustained research on the Tihāmah, it will have fulfilled its primary purpose. The papers offered here are quite clearly in the nature of surveys. They are not meant to fill a void, but to set out a range of apposite questions. One of the stimulating aspects of Tihāmah studies, to my mind, is that the Yemenis themselves have documented relatively little about the coastal plain (with the obvious exception of Zabīd), and they welcome research which will bring them information. Presumptuous though it is to endeavour to instruct the Yemenis about their own country, this is an area where the foreign researcher can make a respectable contribution. There is, moreover, an excellent opportunity for scholars of African Red Sea and Indian Ocean subjects to apply their knowledge to this Arabian flank. More could be done to interrelate the areas of knowledge which exist and to treat the Red Sea and Indian Ocean basin as a whole, culturally as well as geographically.

Ultimately, this book has another, more resounding objective, and that is to call attention to the pressing need for conservation of the Tihāmah's heritage, in particular the architectures, the crafts, the performing arts, and most important of all, the rare and endangered flora and fauna. If this volume is read and appreciated by men and women in positions of influence within Yemen, let it serve to speak out against the present neglect or destruction of the Red Sea houses of al-Luḥayyah, the traditional structures of Zabīd and Wādī Mawr, the indigo dyeing and weaving industries, the music of the Red Sea lyres, the gazelle, the Arabian bustard, the dugong. But foremost on the agenda for conservation should be the valley forest communities of Jabals Milḥān, Raymah, Bura' and Ḥarāz, whose exceptional plant and animal species are described by Keith Brockie, Torben Larsen and John Wood in this volume. As of 1982, the Yemen Arab Republic was not a signatory to the International Union for Conservation of Nature and Natural Resources based in Geneva, and this would seem to be the first crucial step toward active participation and training in international efforts at conservation. Effective programmes to preserve these fragile ecosystems cannot be embarked upon, however, without the support of local *shaykhs* and tribespeople on whom fall the burden of responsible action. Individuals whose work takes them into the areas of the Tihāmah near these valley forest communities can make a positive contribution by persuading local leaders of the value of farsightedness and cooperation. Without it, a natural treasure will be lost forever.

I would like to conclude by quoting from Henry Cassels Kay's own introduction to his *Yaman Its Early Mediæval History* (London, 1892), for he has said with charm and right-mindedness much of what I feel about the work of this book, in an expanded context:

> It is only by the labours of competent travellers, who may make the topography and the archaeological remains of the country an object of study, that any material advance in our geographical knowledge of Yaman will be achieved. I shall be well satisfied if the few notes I have collected in the pages of this volume prove of some little assistance to the explorer, and above all if I have succeeded in showing that a not unimportant and an interesting work offers itself to anyone able and willing to undertake it.[17]

Where he further quotes from the historian, Abū 'Abd Allah al-Ḥusayn ibn 'Abd al-Raḥmān al-Ahdal al-Ḥusaynī, "Let him who finds errors in my work correct them. From God cometh the aid that ensureth success",[18] Kay also echoes my hope that those with emendations to and elaborations on this material will be generous enough to offer them, and that in no way should the weight of our labours be taken as a fortress of pride. We have assembled what we know and offer it with the awareness that it is very little indeed.

I am sure all the contributors to this book join with me in wishing that enjoyment as well as enrichment will come from these pages, and that the Tihāmah and its people will above all be the ones to benefit.

Francine Stone
Shillingford, April 1984

17. Kay, op. cit., p. xxii.
18. Ibid., p. xix (from *Tuḥfat al-Zaman fī A'yān Ahl il-Yaman*).

Plate 0.2 **Village Views II** near Bājil Nankivell *505×380mm pencil drawing*

GEOLOGY

1.1: AN INTRODUCTION TO THE GEOLOGY OF THE TIHĀMAH

Ibrahim El-Domi

The Tihāmah Plain is a semi-arid, coastal plain, 25-45 Km. wide, which extends the length of North Yemen between the mountain highlands in the east and the Red Sea in the west. The estimated total area of the Tihāmah Plain is $16000km^2$.

The Tihāmah is a graben. It is the contact between the Red Sea and the mountainous basement that is marked by a major fault trending northwest-southeast.[1] At the time of the subsidence of the graben, the intensity of denudation increased. Large quantities of sediments derived from rivers were deposited in the Tihāmah region. The western part of the Tihāmah was the site of interplay between marine and terrigenous activities.[2] The subsurface of the Plain on the eastern side was formed from conglomerate and other ferrigenous deposits, and the western side from sand, silt, shale and limestone. By the end of the Pleistocene, fluviatile conditions prevailed throughout the Tihāmah region. The thick overburden testifies to this environment.

The configuration of the basement and the maximum thickness of the alluvium are poorly understood because of the limited extent and scope of existing data, which were gathered during the implementation of specific projects. The results of geophysical exploration indicates however that the maximum thickness of the alluvium in the coastal belt of the Tihāmah Plain may be on the order of 500-700m.

Approximately 100 wells have been drilled during implementation of various agricultural development projects. Most of these wells were completed to predetermined depths within the Tihāmah aquifier. Only a few wells, drilled in the upper part of the Tihāmah Plain, encountered bedrock at a depth ranging from 100 to 150m.

Stratigraphically, the Tihāmah alluvium can be divided into two lithologic entities: (i) the Older or Subrecent alluvium and (ii) the Younger or Recent alluvium. The Older alluvium was deposited during the early Holocene by primitive drainage system/systems. The sediments were derived from mountain stream catchments and were laid down in structural physiographic depressions in the Tihāmah region. It is composed of beds and lenses of gravel, sand, silt and clay. The sediments were subjected to post-depositional changes, i.e. compaction and cementation. The size assortment is generally poor, although sand beds and lenses in the lower half of the Tihāmah have better assortment. Presently, Older alluvium outcrops are located at higher elevations in the upper reaches of the Plain and are subject to erosion. In the lower reaches of the Tihāmah, the Older alluvium lies below Younger alluvium at a depth ranging from 100 to over 200m.

The Younger alluvium, consisting of unconsolidated gravel, sand, silt and clay, was laid down by the present drainage system. These sediments have been derived from outcrops of Older alluvium and the rocky mountain highlands. The size assortment is poor, except sand formations which have better assortment. In general, it has not been affected by post-depositional forces, i.e. compaction and cementation. The thickness of Younger alluvium ranges from a few metres in the upper reaches to 100-200m in the lower reaches of the Tihāmah Plain.

The Younger alluvium between the Ta'izz-Hodeida highway and the Red Sea is partly covered with stabilised and mobile sand dunes, which have produced undulating topography, and have reduced accessibility to coastal parts of the Plain. Mobile sand dunes are steadily advancing toward the east, threatening existing agricultural fields. (See Plate 1.1)

THE DRAINAGE PATTERN

The mean annual rainfall in the upper catchment (mountain highlands) of the Tihāmah ranges between 400mm and 1500mm, while in the lowland (the Tihāmah Plain itself) it is between 50mm and 300mm. Most of the rainfall comes in summer as widespread, relatively intense storms. The following seven major seasonal rivers (*wādīs*) drain the mountain catchment into the Tihāmah Plain:

Wādī Mawr	$9262km^2$	(North)
Wādī Surdud	$2506km^2$	
Wādī Sihām	$5137km^2$	
Wādī Rima'	$2887km^2$	
Wādī Zabīd	$4910km^2$	
Wādī Rasyān	$2081km^2$	
Wādī Ghayl	$1537km^2$	(South)
Total	$29295km^2$	

1. The Red Sea originated in faulting in the Eocene strata filling with water from the Tethys Sea. Later the connection with the Tethys Sea was lost and the connection with the Indian Ocean was established, probably in the latter half of the Pliocene. See N.B. Marshall, "Recent Biological Investigations in the Red Sea," *Endeavor,* Vol. II, 1952, pp. 137-142. [Ed.]
2. The isolated elevations on the west, such as the outcrops of al-Luḥayyah, are Tertiary to Quaternary clay, gypsum and rocksalt. Jabals al-Milḥ and Qumah are likewise rock salt dating from intensive evaporations of the Red Sea in Miocene times. We have been able to find out little else concerning the history or composition of the other isolated hills which dot the Tihāmah plain. H. Escher mentions that Jabal Mukhtārah is Jurassic chalk and sand-stone, and that Jabal Habial, southeast of al-Mu'araṣ, is a small basalt hill (*Wirtschafts und sozialgeographische Untersuchungen in der Wādī Mawr Region,* Wiesbaden, 1976, p. 28). (See Plates 1.1,II.) [Ed.]

The run-off generated in the upper catchment is utilised in the lowland (the Tihāmah Plain) for irrigation purposes. Only the exceptional floods reach the Red Sea.

FURTHER READING

Geukens, F., "Geology of the Arabian Peninsula: Yemen," (Professional Paper), *United States Geological Survey*, Washington, D.C., No. 560-B, 1966.

ILLUSTRATION

Plate 1.1 Brockie, 265 × 380mm, watercolour-pencil drawing.

Plate 1.1 **Near al-Munīrah, sand blowing off dunes, 2nd February 1982,** Jabal Qumah in the distance

1.2: LANDFORMS, SOILS AND CLIMATE OF WĀDĪ ZABĪD IN THE TIHĀMAH

Terence R. Forbes

GEOMORPHOLOGY

The area is underlain by a detrital cone of volcanic materials derived from the adjoining mountains to the east. At Wādī Zabīd this detrital material overlies volcanic basement rock. The plain was downthrown by faults to the west parallel with the deep tectonic graben of the Red Sea. This depression contains sediments approximately 200 to 1000m thick composed mainly of gravel, boulders and sand.

Wādī Zabīd and the surrounding area are characterized by a smooth, flat plain, sloping gently towards the Red Sea (see Figures 1.1 and 1.2). Microrelief is variable and areas of barchan and longitudinal dunes occur *(khabt* or *barr)*. Also the micro-relief of large areas of *wādīs* has been altered by human activities. Farmers have used spate irrigation *(saqy* or *rayy)* for centuries and constructed elaborate mosaic patterns of bunds *(zubur)*. Some adjacent fields show 2 to 3m difference in elevation. Repeated, controlled deposition of sediments by spate irrigation has caused these elevation changes.

CLIMATE

In Wādī Zabīd and all of Yemen the existing soil moisture regime (Soil Taxonomy, 1975) is an important limiting factor to any agricultural use of the soils. The soil moisture regime for Wādī Zabīd has been estimated with the scant climatic data available using the Franklin Newhall computer algorithum (Tavernier and Van Wambeke, 1976).

The soil climate of Wādī Zābīd and surrounding Tihāmah is aridic. At Zabīd, the mean annual rainfall is approximately 70 to 100mm. Sixty to eighty per cent of this precipitation falls in July and August.

VEGETATION

John Wood in the Flora chapter summarises the natural herbaceous vegetation typical of the *wādī*. Cultivated crops make up much of the present vegetation however, and these include sorghum *(dhurah)*, pennisetum *(dukhn)*, maize *(rūmī)*, cowpeas, tobacco *(tutun)*, *cotton (quṭn)*, sesame *(simsim)*, vegetables such as tomatoes, onions, okra and radishes, fruits such as limes and melons (for instance musk melon, CUCUMIS MELO, *shammām*), and especially date palms. (See Flora glossary, p. 17)

SOILS

Environmentally controlled processes and soil parent material formation

Two natural processes in the Wādī Zabīd area and probably all of the Tihāmah which result in the accumulation of soil parent material are aeolian deposition and desert sedimentation, or a combination of these two. Natural soil-forming processes which affect soil formation in the Tihāmah are the intermittent, low level of soil leaching and the low level or organic matter accumulation.

Aeolian deposition of soil parent materials

Large and widespread deposits of calcareous loess are observed throughout the mountains and on the Tihāmah. Recent and ancient dunes are a predominant feature of the Tihāmah coastal area also. Aeolian transport and deposition of soil parent materials is still an important factor of soil genesis in Yemen.

On the Tihāmah, sand, as well as finer materials, is transported by the wind. Dunes grow inland, driven by prevailing winds[1] from the Red Sea. (See Plate 1.1) Barchan and longitudinal dunes are frequently observed in the dry areas between *wādīs*. Soil profile development is slow in these areas of shifting sand and loess. Textures of soil near the border of dune fields and *wādīs* are coarse. Textures become finer towards the interior of the *wādī* (see Figures 1.2 and 1.3).

Sand and silt dunes are presently encroaching on many cultivated areas in the *wādīs* on the Tihāmah (see Figure 1.4). This sediment encroachment has no doubt been important in the past also. Much arable land is lost each year by this encroachment, which forces local farmers to create more farmland in stabilized areas.

Desert (alluvial) sedimentation

Sedimentation by water is important both along *wādīs* and on intermountain plains.

Sedimentary processes are particularly active along *wādīs*. Sedimentation accounts for the layering and thin-bedding of many *wādī* soils. This is observed at all the *wādīs* on the Tihāmah.

In a transect across Wādī Zabīd (see Figure 1.3) several levels of natural alluvial terraces, each with distinct textural compositions, are observed. The older, more extensive terraces contain less sorted, coarser materials (gravel and small boulders) while younger, less extensive terraces are typically better sorted and finer in texture.

In an east-west transect along the Wādī Zabīd from the volcanic mountains to the Red Sea, another sequence of sediments is observed (see Figure 1.2). This sequence of soil parent materials appears typical for the Tihāmah as a whole. In general, materials become finer eastward from the mountains until a zone of recent sedimentary marine deposits is reached near the Red Sea.

Soil-forming processes – environmentally controlled; intermittent and low levels of soil leaching

The Tihāmah region and its associated *wādīs* have an aridic soil moisture regime. As a result of the low level of leaching, soil mineralogy is characterized by a young

1. The prevailing winds of the Tihāmah are NNW May to September and SSE October to April. The northerly premonsoon wind is called al-Quway' (sp. ?) and the southerly (more specifically southwesterly) premonsoon wind, al-Zīyab. [Ed.]

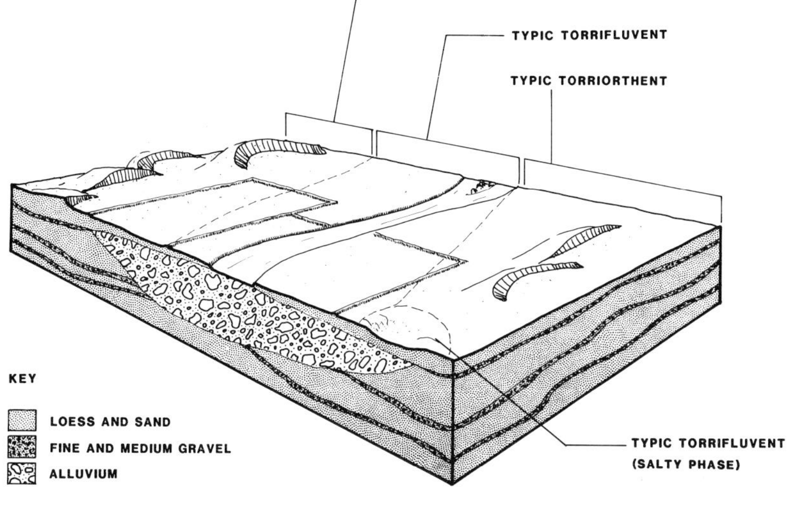

Figure 1.1 Landscape Relationships for the Tihāmah *Wādī* (TW) Mapping Unit

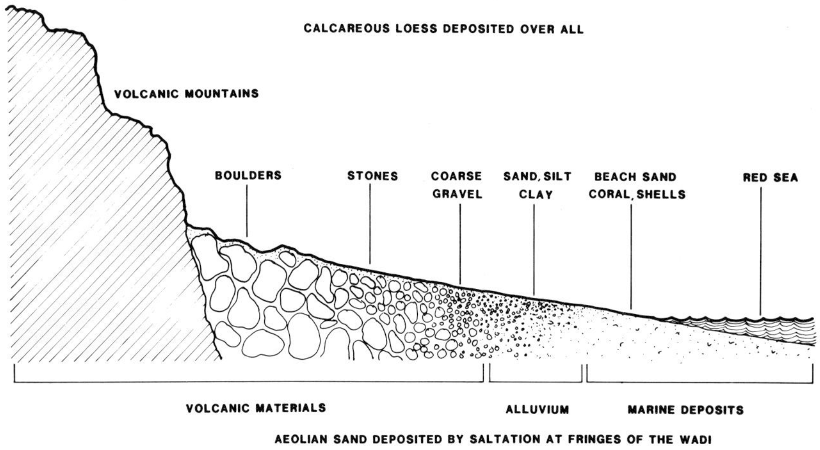

Figure 1.2 Parent Materials on an E-W Transect Along Wādī Zābīd

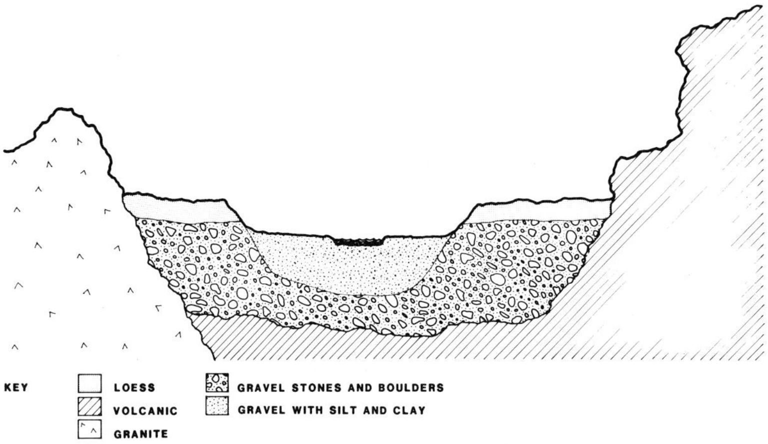

Figure 1.3 A N-S Transect Showing the Location of Major Alluvial Terraces Across Wādī Zābīd Near the Volcanic Foothills

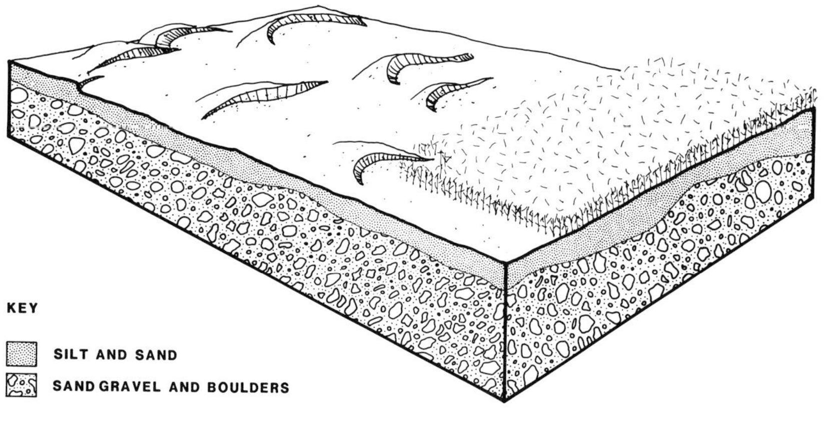

Figure 1.4 The Encroachment of Dune Fields on Cultivated *Wādī* Soils

weathering stage. The clay mineralogy is mixed, typically consisting of chlorite, micas, quartz, feldspar, vermiculite, montmorillonite, kaolinite, and some attapulgite.

Intermittent and low levels of leaching control the location of carbonates and carbonate morphology in the soil profile. All profiles examined in the field were at least slightly calcareous. Typically, some leaching of carbonates has occurred, so calcareous concretions were formed in B-horizons of soil soils.

Low levels of organic matter accumulation

In Yemen, as in most arid regions, there is little accumulation of organic matter in soil horizons. Only in areas of highest rainfall (as in the Ibb area) or at water collection positions in the landscape (lower-slope concave positions) does organic matter accumulate to any great extent in surface horizons.

Man-induced processes – parent material formation; accumulation of sediments by terracing and irrigation

It has been suggested that men have been constructing terraces in Yemen for at least 2000 years. In the mountainous areas, soil horizonation has been slowed or altered significantly by this human activity. Similarly, sedimentary processes have been controlled and modified by farmers building bunds, terraces and other barriers along *wādīs* on the Tihāmah.

The long periods of irrigation and water control have also modified the deposition of soil parent materials. Spate irrigation on the Tihāmah has increased the sedimentation on the lower, flatter areas. This sedimentation results in the formation of terraces often having differences in height of several metres.

Leaching of soil parent materials by irrigation

Irrigation of some form has been going on perhaps as long as the construction of terraces and bunds. Bunding and ridging makes the small amount of precipitation more effective by reducing runoff. Leaching of soil parent materials is increased to some degree and moisture is retained for cropping.

Increased accumulation of organic matter

Soils which have been intensively irrigated for cropping for long periods of time typically have higher amounts of organic matter in their surface horizons.

KINDS OF SOILS AND THEIR DISTRIBUTION

The association of soils as classified by the principles in Soil Taxonomy (USDA/SCS, 1975) along Wādī Zabīd typically consists of arid, brown soils or Typic Camborthids formed from loess deposits, salt-affected Typic Torrifluvents and Typic Calciorthids located principally in the western area near the Red Sea coast;[2] brown calcareous alluvial soils or Typic Torrifluvents with alternating silty and coarser layers; and brown soils (Typic Camborthids) affected by wind erosion with reworked aeolian surface layers (see Figure 1.1).

These soils are probably representative for all the major *wādīs* and intermediate coastal plains of the Tihāmah. The association accounts for approximately 20% of the entire land area of Yemen, but undoubtedly includes a higher proportion of the total arable land because of the dominance of rock outcrops in mountainous Yemen.

Within the association itself, based on detailed field work undertaken by Tesco-Viziterv-Vituki (1971) in the Wādī Zabīd area, approximately 30% are Typic Torrifluvents or calcareous alluvial soils, 69% are Typic Camborthids or wind-erosion affected soils and tropical arid brown soils, and 1% Typic Calciorthids.

BIBLIOGRAPHY

Soil Survey Staff, "Soil Taxonomy – A Basic System of Soil Classification for Making and Interpreting Soil Surveys," *Agriculture Handbook No. 436,* Soil Conservation Service, U.S. Department of Agriculture, U.S. Government Printing Office, Washington, D.C., 1975.

Tavernier, R., and A. Van Wembeke, *Détermination du régime hydrique des sols du Maghreb d'après Newhall Pédologie,* 26(2), 1976, pp. 168-178.

FURTHER READING

Land Resources Division, *Land Resource Bibliography II Yemen Arab Republic,* compiled by P.M. Reilly, Ministry of Overseas Development, Surrey, 1978.

ILLUSTRATIONS

Figures 1.1-1.4, provided by Terence R. Forbes, USAID/Cornell Soil Survey.

GLOSSARY

barr	the country, hinterland, "the bush"
dhurah	sorghum
khabt	desert, "the badlands"
quṭn	cotton
rayy	spate irrigation
rūmī	maize
sabkhah	crusted salt marsh
saqy	spate irrigation
shammām	musk melon, CUCUMIS MELO
simsim	sesame, SESAMUM INDICUM
tutun	tobacco
wādī	seasonal river bed
zubur	bund or baulk (var. of *zābūr*?)

2. For the coastal surface condition known as *sabkhah*, a crusted salt marsh, see Wood, p.14.

FLORA

2.1: THE VEGETATION OF THE TIHĀMAH

J. R. I. Wood

Although the Yemen Tihāmah is flat and scenically monotonous compared with the rest of Yemen, its vegetation is unexpectedly diverse. There are profound changes from west to east as the land rises from sea level to 500m and considerably differences from south to north, the vegetation at Bājil, for example, being quite different not only from that on the coast at Hodeida but also from that in the south around al-Mafraq.

South of the Wādī Sihām, the coast is almost bare of vegetation but further north there is a nearly continuous fringe of the White Mangrove, AVICENNIA MARINA *(shūrah)*. It is most abundant in the creeks and on the mud flats around al-Luḥayyah and Mīdī where it forms extensive areas of woodland 2-3m high. There is no obvious explanation for its scarcity further south.

Although the coast is not liable to tidal inundation, persistent on-shore winds carry salt spray at least one kilometre inland bringing about the development of a distinct habitat known as *sabkhah*. (See Plate I.) The coastal sands become saturated with spray and their surface is encrusted with salt. Few plants can tolerate these conditions and the dominant species, SUAEDA FRUTICOSA *(dālāk)*, a salt bush about 50cm high, is one of the few species present. With it often grows the grass AELUROPUS LAGOPOIDES and more rarely CRESSA CRETICA and the two sea lavenders LIMONIUM AXILLARE and L. CYLINDRIFOLIA.

Away from the coastal fringe, almost all the western half of the Tihāmah is covered in sand dunes of varying height. Apart from palm trees along the *wādīs* and around villages, this area is almost entirely treeless. (See Plates X,XI) Instead the dominant species are undershrubs. SUAEDA MONOICA *('asal)* and SALSOLA SPINESCENS *(harm)* often form communities near the sea in which they are almost the only species present. Further inland the dominant species are usually JATROPHA PELARGONIIFOLIA *('ubāb)* LEPTADENIA PYROTECHNICA *(markh)* or the spinescent grass, ODYSSEA MUCRONATA *(shawkām)*. Any of these five species may form dense communities with the plants only 1-2m apart or they may be much more widely spaced with large areas of open ground between them. Whichever species is dominant, however, the associated species are likely to include AERVA JAVANICA *(ra', ra'in)*, DIPTERYGIUM GLAUCUM *('alkah)*, HELIOTROPIUM PTEROCARPUM, the grass PANICUM TURGIDUM *(bukār)* and the legume TEPHROSIA PURPUREA *(sanāfī)*.

The vegetation in the eastern half of the Tihāmah is much less uniform, the area south of the Wādī Zabīd in particular having a vegetation quite different from that found further north. Here the sand dunes are replaced by gravel plain which is covered in ACACIA-COMMIPHORA bushland about 4m high. The bushland is often quite dense with the trees only some 2-4m apart but in other areas it is more open. The most common species are COMMIPHORA GILEADENSIS *(bisham)* and C. MYRRHA *(qafal)*, ACACIA EHRENBERGIANA *(salam)*, A. HAMULOSA *(kaṭāṭ)* and A. TORTILIS *(sumur)*. Other trees and shrubs occur but the most interesting are probably RHIGAZOM SOMALIENSE and SALTIA PAPPOSA. Climbers are quite common but the ground flora is surprisingly poor. Ephemeral species are very untypical and the common plants are coarse grasses like CYMBOPOGON SCHOENANTHUS, succulents like ALOE NIEBUHRIANA and EUPHORBIA TRIACULEATA and wiry undershrubs like CAMPYLANTHUS YEMENENSIS, INDIGOFERA SPINOSA and SCHWEINFURTHIA PEDICELLATA.

North of the Wādī Zabīd the sand dunes often extend into the eastern Tihāmah. Where this happens the dunes are surprisingly fertile. In prehistoric times they were probably covered in ACACIA EHRENBERGIANA woodland. Some vestiges of this survive, notably around al-Zaydīyah. In these relic woodlands, the ACACIA is often the only tree or shrub present and it forms a continuous, if rather thin, canopy. The ground flora is similarly monotonous consisting only of TEPHROSIA PURPUREA while the only other species of flowering plants are climbers like COCCULUS PENDULUS and CISSUS QUADRANGULARIS *(sila')*.

In most places, however, the woodland has been cleared and open dunes are found. In the dry season they are quite barren but at the onset of the rains they are planted with the Bulrush Millet *(dukhn)* which covers huge areas, notably around al-Manṣūrīyah, al-Quṭay' and al-Qanāwiṣ. (See Plate V.) If the rains are good a rich ground flora also develops. It includes hardy perennials like BLEPHARIS CILIARIS *(zughāf)*, CASSIA ITALICA *('ashraq)* and PANICUM TURGIDUM *(bukār)* as well as ephemeral species like ARISTIDA MUTABILIS, CROTALARIA MICROPHYLLA and INDIGOFERA ARGENTEA. At the end of the rains these species die down and the dunes revert to their usual barrenness.

There are no sands in the extreme east of the Tihāmah and they are replaced by extensive plains of alluvial silt washed down from the mountains. The silt plains are best developed between the Wādī Rima' and the Wādī Mawr. They are agriculturally rich and densely populated so natural vegetation is virtually non-existent. There is no doubt that they were afforested in prehistoric times and it is probable that the dominant tree was DOBERA GLABRA *(ḍubar)*. Today large areas of DOBERA parkland can be found in many places in the east of the Tihāmah. It was doubtless associated with species of ACACIA, particularly A. EHRENBERGIANA and A. OERFOTA *('urfūt)*. Few shrubs or herbs can survive under the trees but in open areas along tracks and in uncultivated areas a dense secondary scrub develops, dominated by ABUTILON PANNOSUM *(ra')* and INDIGOFERA OBLONGIFOLIA *(haṣar)*. In trodden places CORCHORUS DEPRESSUS *(waykah)*, DACTYLOCTENIUM SCINDICUM and OCIMUM FORSKOLEI *(habaqbaq)* may be frequent. Most plants found in this part of the Tihāmah, however, are weeds and the Sorghum fields bear a rich flora in the autumn which includes such plants as the annual shrub SESBANIA LEPTOCARPA, COMMELINA FORSKALAEI *(wa'lān)*, CYPERUS ROTUNDUS, DIGERA ARVENSIS *(dijir)*, HELIOTROPIUM LONGIFLORUM, SOLANUM COAGULANS and many others.

The alluvial plains are often broken by small gravel ridges which are colonised by ACACIA OERFOTA, ALOE VERA *(ṣabir)*, BLEPHARIS CILIARIS and LASIURUS SCINDICUS *(thamām)*. These merge into the foothills of the escarpment which rise out of the Tihāmah in the east. (See Plates IV,IX.) They are covered in an open bushland similar to that found all over the lower slopes of the escarpment. Although its detailed description is outside the scope of this paper, a brief sketch is necessary for a proper understanding of the Tihāmah vegetation. The trees are mostly about 3m high and consist mainly of ACACIA species, particularly A. EHRENBERGIANA and A. MELLIFERA *(ẓūbah)* and various species of COMMIPHORA. The beautiful Desert Rose, ADENIUM OBESUM *('adan)* is also abundant. Underneath the larger trees are a number of shrubs about 1 m high. Succulents are particularly well represented and include EUPHORBIA CACTUS *(killaḥ)* and E. INARTICULATA *(suyayb)* both of which prefer relatively flat ground. Other abundant species are ACALYPHA FRUTICOSA *(difrān)*, ANISOTES TRISULCUS *(mudh)* and GREWIA TENAX *khadar)*. Climbers are frequent and both CISSUS QUADRANGULARIS and C. ROTUNDIFOLIA *(halaṣ)* are abundant. The ground flora consists mainly of wiry perennials capable of withstanding drought and heavy grazing. The grass, CHRYSOPOGON PLUMULOSUS, the spiny INDIGOFERA SPINOSA and undershrubs like RUELLIA PATULA and SEDDERA VIRGATA are typical.

The influence of the *wādīs* on the Tihāmah vegetation is quite considerable. At their point of entry into the Tihāmah most of the larger *wādīs* have permanent flowing water but this is almost immediately diverted into irrigation channels and species like BACOPA MONNIERI, ECLIPTA ALBA and PHYLA NODIFLORA are only found at the eastern extremities of the Tihāmah where there is permanent water. Further west the *wādī* beds are quite dry. They are lined with Tamarisk trees, TAMARIX APHYLLA and T. ARABICA *(athl)* and the occasional SALVADORA PERSICA *(rāk)* bush. The sandy flood bed itself often supports an abundance of CALOTROPIS PROCERA *(qushār)* and CASSIA SENNA *(sanah)*.

It seems that for centuries the floods coming down from the mountains have petered out in the central Tihāmah since broad fans of fine silt have been laid down in this region at the points where the waters must have evaporated. Good examples can be seen west of Khalīfah (Wādī Sihām) and east of al-Ḥusaynīyah (Wādī Rima'). The silt deposits often support a dense scrub about 2m high dominated by SALVADORA PERSICA, CADABA ROTUNDIFOLIA *(qaḍab)* or CAPPARIS DECIDUA *(sidād)*. Climbing plants like CYPHOSTEMMA TERNATUM and CISSUS QUADRANGULARIS often find protection among these bushes but the ground flora is exceedingly sparse, the spaces between the bushes consisting of bare earth with the occasional JATROPHA GLAUCA, CASSIA SENNA or TRIANTHEMA TRIQUETRA.

Nearer the sea the ground water is close to the surface and the *wādī* lines can usually be recognised by the extensive plantations of the Date Palm, PHOENIX DACTYLIFERA. The natural vegetation, though, probably consisted of one of the Fan Palms, HYPHAENE spp. (see Plate 2.1) which also occur in local abundance. Where the *wādīs* enter the sea there are often freshwater lagoons and species tolerating mildy brackish water, like SCHOENOPLECTUS LITTORALIS or CYPERUS LAEVIGATUS, occur.

The vegetation which has been outlined in the previous paragraphs is of two main types. The plant communities of the western Tihāmah are typical of the Sahara-Sindian desert region which stretches from Senegal to N.W. India. Plants such as LEPTODENIA PYROTECHNICA, AERVA JAVANICA and PANICUM TURGIDUM, are found throughout this vast region while others, like BLEPHARIS CILIARIS, TAMARIX APHYLLA and DIPTERYGIUM GLAUCUM, are restricted to the eastern part. The eastern Tihāmah in contrast is Sudanian. The dominant ACACIA, COMMIPHORA and DOBERA species are all African in their distribution and similar plant communities are found throughout the Sudanian savannah regions. The Tihāmah is, not surprisingly, very poor in endemic species but a large and interesting group of species consists of those restricted to the Red Sea and Gulf of Aden regions. It includes ODYSSEA MUCRONATA, HELIOTROPIUM PTEROCARPUM, CROTALARIA MICROPHYLLA, SEDDERA VIRGATA and many others. The local abundance of such species is perhaps the prime interest of the Tihāmah vegetation.

2.2: VALLEY FOREST COMMUNITIES

J. R. I. Wood

The valleys penetrating the escarpment mountains from the Tihāmah have an interesting vegetation usually referred to under the name "Valley Forest". This is best developed where the escarpment is both steep and high particularly along the western slopes of J. Raymah, J. Bura', J. Milḥān and the Ḥarāz. The best example of valley forest is above Sūq al-Sabt al-Maḥrab on J. Bura' where there is continuous woodland for about a kilometre from 500-700m, but other outstanding examples can be found at similar altitudes above 'Alūjah in J. Raymah, in the Wādī Yūr, in the Wādī Ḥillah on J. Milḥān and elsewhere.

The botanical interest of these valleys lies partly in the fact that they are one of the few examples of a natural vegetation climax found in Yemen and partly in their role as a place of refuge for many African savannah species otherwise unknown in Asia. This is particularly the case with trees; ANTIARIS TOXICARIA, BAUHINIA TOMENTOSA, BRIDELIA SCLERONEURA, CELTIS TOKA, MIMUSOPS LAURIFOLIA and PILIOSTIGMA THONNINGII are outstanding examples, the MIMUSOPS being especially attractive and the BRIDELIA and ANTIARIS excessively rare, being limited to a few individuals. There are also a number of rare herbaceous plants including EUPHORBIA AGOWENSIS, E. PSEUDOHOLSTII, MUCUNA PRURIENS and the grass BRACHIARIA CHUSQUEOIDES. In contrast, the valley forests are poor in endemic species. Apart from underscribed species of ANEILEMA and PAVETTA, the endemic species present are plants like ABRUS BOTTAE, EUPHORBIA INARTICULATA, ORMOCARPUM YEMENENSE and PLECTRANTHUS ARABICUS which are widespread on the Yemen escarpment.

The survival of the valley forest communities till the present time is largely due to their isolation and to the very small population that live in the area. They are, however, extremely vulnerable and improved communications pose a particular threat since they enable the easy exploitation of the valleys for firewood.[1]

1. For further discussions of the valley forest communities, particularly those of Jabal Bura', see Brockie p.25 and Larsen p.27.

Plate 2.1 **Black Kite in Fan Palm** (*dawm*), HYPHENAE spp.

BIBLIOGRAPHY

These references are essentially ecological – not floristic – accounts and it is nearly everything that has been published relevant to the Tihāmah vegetation.

Deflers, A., *Voyage au Yemen,* Paris, 1889.
Hepper, F. Nigel, "Outline of the Vegetation of the Yemen Arab Republic," *Cairo University Herbarium,* Giza, Nos. 7 & 8, 1977, pp. 307-322.
Popov, G.A. and Zeller, W., "Ecological Survey Report on the 1962 survey in the Arabian Penninsula," *FAO* Rep. UNSF/DL/ES/6.
Vesey-Fitzgerald, D.F., "Vegetation of the Red Sea Coast South of Jedda, Saudi Arabia," *Journal of Ecology,* Vol. 43, July 1955, pp. 477-487.
——————, "Vegetation of the Red Sea Coast North of Jedda, Saudi Arabia," *Journal of Ecology,* Vol. 45, 1957. pp. 547-562.
Wissmann, H. von, "Arabien und seine kolonialen Ausstrahlungen," *Lebensraumfragen europäischer Völker,* ed. K.H. Dietzel et al., Vol. 2, 1941, pp. 379-387.
Wood, J.R.I., "An Outline of the Vegetation of the Yemen Arab Republic," *Cornell/USAID Soil Survey of North Yemen,* 1983.
——————, *A Handbook of the Yemen Flora,* Routledge & Kegan Paul, London, 1984 (in press).

FURTHER READING

Niebuhr, Carsten, *Flora Arabica,* Hasinae, 4 Vols., 1775.
——————, *Description de l'Arabie,* Amsterdam, 1774.
——————, *Travels in Arabia,* Edinburgh, 2 Vols., 1779.
Thesiger, W.F., "A Journey Through the Tihama, the 'Asir, and the Hijaz Mountains," *Geographical Journal,* Vol. 110, 1947, pp. 188-200.

ILLUSTRATION

Plate 2.1 Brockie, 250 × 205mm, pencil drawing (sketchbook).

GLOSSARY

'adan	Adenium obesum, Desert Rose
'alkah	Dipterygium glaucum, a herb
'asal	Suaeda monoica, an undershrub
'asraq	Cassia italica, a hardy perennial
athal	Tamarix arabica, a tree
bisham	Commiphora gileadensis, a shrub
bukār	Panicum turgidum, a hardy perennial
dālāk	Suaeda fruticosa, a salt bush
dawm	Hyphaene spp., Dom or Fan Palm
difrān	Acalypha fruticosa, a shrub
dijir	Digera arvensis, a herb
ḍubar	Dobera glabra, a tree
dukhn	Bulrush Millet, a cereal
habaqbaq	Ocimum forskolei, scrub
halaṣ	Cissus rotundifolia, a climber
harm	Salsola spinescens, an undershrub
haṣar	Indigofera scindicum, scrub
kaṭāṭ	Acacia hamulosa, a tree
khadar	Grewia tenax, a shrub
killaḥ	Euphorbia cactus, a succulent
markh	Leptadenia pyrotechnica, a shrub
mudh	Anisotes trisulcus, a shrub
qaḍab	Cadaba rotundifolia, scrub
qafal	Commiphora myrrha, a shrub
qushār	Calotropis procera, a shrub
ra'	Abutilon pannosum, scrub
ra', ra'in	Aerva javanica, a herb
rāk	Salvadora persica, a bush
ṣabir	Aloe vera, a succulent
salam	Acacia ehrenbergiana, a tree
sanāfī	Tephrosia purpurea, a legume
sanah	Cassia senna, a shrub
shawkām	Odyssea mucronata, a spinescent grass
shūrah	Avicennia marina, White Mangrove
sidād	Capparis decidua, scrub
sila'	Cissus quadrangularis, a flowering climber
sumur	Acacia tortilis, a tree
suyayb	Euphorbia inarticulata, a succulent
thamām	Lasirurus scindicus, a herb
'ubāb	Jatropha pelargoniifolia, a shrub
'urfūt	Acacia oerfota, a tree
wa'lān	Commelina forskalaei, a herb
waykh	Corchorus depressus, scrub
ẓūbah	Acacia mellifera, a tree
zughāf	Blepharis ciliaris, a hardy perennial

APPENDIX TO GLOSSARY

The following list of Tihāmah crops, provided by Ibrahim A.G. El-Domi, gives first the Latin name, then the Arabic name or names that are in use locally, and finally the classical or standard modern term in parentheses.

Field crops

Cotton	Gossypium hirsutum, *'uṭb (quṭn)*
Cowpea	Vigna unguiculata, *dujrah/dijrah (lūbiyā)*
Ground Nut	Arachis hypogaea, *ḥabb al-'azīz (fustuq al-arḍ, fūl sūdānī)*
Maize	Zea mays, *hind, rūmī (dhurah shāmī)*
Millet	Pennisetum typoides, *dukhn, dukhn maḥallī, dukhn Tihāmah (dukhn)*
Sorghum	Sorghum vulgare, *dhurah, qīra', ṣayfī, ḥamrā' (dhurah al-rafī'ah)*
Sesame	Sesamum indicum, *jalājil* [var. of *jiljilān*] *(simsim)*
Soya Bean	Glycine max, *fūl al-ṣūyā (fūl al-ṣōyā)*
Sunflower	Helianthus annuus, *'abād al-shams ('abād al-shams)*
Tobacco	Nicotiana tabacum, *tunbāk/tinbāk (tibgh)*

Vegetable and fruit crops

Banana	Musa sapientum, *mauz (mauz)*
Chilli	Capsicum frutescens, *bisbās, (filfil al-āḥmar)*
Citrus	Citrus spp., *līm (laymūn)*
Date Palm	Phoenix dactylifera, *tamr (nakhīl)*
Eggplant	Solanum tuberosum, *bādhinjān (bādhinjān)*
Onion	Allium cepa, *baṣal (baṣal)*
Pepper	Capsicum annuum, *baybār, (filfil al-ākhḍar)*
Tomato	Lycopersicum esculentum, *ṭamāṭ (ṭamāṭim)*
Sweet Melon	Cucumis melo, *baṭṭīkh (shammām)*
Water Melon	Citrullus vulgaris, *ḥabḥab (baṭṭīkh)*

FAUNA

3.1: WILDLIFE OF THE TIHĀMAH 1982
WITH EMPHASIS ON AVIFAUNA

Keith Brockie

ACKNOWLEDGEMENTS

I would very much like to thank the following people for their help and suggestions on various aspects of the expedition. Dr. E. N. Arnold (reptiles), Dr. David L. Harrison (mammals). Torben B. Larsen (butterflies), Michael C. Jennings and Richard F. Porter (birds), and John Wood (vegetation).

INTRODUCTION

This report details sightings of fauna observed and trapped during our fieldwork on the Tihāmah in January and February 1982. This was the height of the winter dry season, and furthermore it was, according to local reports, the third year of poor or failed rains.

Birds make up the main volume of the report. Most were observations with the aid of a telescope and binoculars. Some species, especially warblers, had to be trapped with the aid of mist nets for further identification.

Mammals were not much in evidence and were recorded whenever they were sighted. At each camp site I attempted to trap small rodents and bats on behalf of Dr. David L. Harrison for the Harrison Zoological Museum. I managed to trap some interesting rodents and bats despite the depredations of ants, and in one case a mongoose, which beat me to the traps some mornings. These are detailed in a report by Dr. Harrison.

An attempted collection of lizards proved a failure due to my inability to catch them and only a few were taken.[1] Various snakes were seen at night but these were given a wide berth due to the extremely venomous nature of most of them.[2]

A collection of butterflies and moths was made by Francine Stone and identified by Torben B. Larsen and E. P. Wiltshire, whose detailed species lists and comments follow.

SYSTEMATIC LIST OF TIHĀMAH BIRD OBSERVATIONS

The following lists document my observations made mostly on the Tihāmah region of the Yemen Arab Republic. The lists include 179 plus 2 unidentified species essentially of Palaearctic origin with Ethiopian influence and several endemic species. Five species were recorded breeding or nest building. These were Black Kite, Tawny Eagle, Verreaux's Eagle, Little Green Bee-eater and Ruppell's Weaver (for scientific names see List of Species Observed). Six are apparently first records for the Yemen and several are second recorded occurrences. A possible sub-species of the Arabian Babbler was observed. A lot of ground was covered in search of the Arabian Bustard for which various conservation bodies had voiced concern. Only one pair was located in an area of sparse cultivated grassland and tamarisk. The bustard is hunted by the Yemenis and is considered a delicacy. From discussions with some of the local *shaykhs* it was said to be present only occasionally and in small numbers.

I have followed the order and nomenclature used by Voous (1977). For convenience I have kept to the English names used by M.C. Jennings (1981). This is a selected and annotated list as it would have been impracticable to include all recorded observations. Where all recorded observations have been included the English name is followed by an asterisk*. Appendices I, II and III include observations of birds seen outside the Tihāmah region, elsewhere in the Yemen.

Very little has been documented on the avifauna of the Yemen which is very rich. I hope these observations will help a little to unravel some of the mysteries of status and numbers.

Plate 3.1 **Lizard AGAMA SINAITA**

1. In fact, 4 reptile specimens were delivered to the British Museum of Natural History. These were identified by Dr. Nicholas Arnold (in communication 22.3.83) as a Gecko PRISTURUS SLAVIPUNCTATUS, 2 Sinai Agama AGAMA SINAITA and one snake head PSAMMOPHIS SCHOKARI. [Ed.] (See Plates 3.1, XV)
2. A small (30cm), side-winding snake was observed in the sand and scrub near al-Khawbah, 1st Feb at night. This was likely to have been a Sand Viper CERASTES CERASTES or a Sand Boa ERYX JAYAKARY. Dr Nicholas Arnold and John Gasperetti kindly assisted with these conjectural identifications. Furthermore, Francine Stone observed two PSAMMOPHIS SCHOKARI at al-Sukhnah keeping company with a snake charmer in the *sūq*. These opisthoglyphs although poisonous were happy to be handled without striking. It was said that the tails could cure eye infections when rubbed across the eyeball. [Ed.]

Plate 3.2 **Pink-backed and White Pelicans** PELECANUS RUFESCENS **and** P. ONOCROTALUS

List of Species Observed

PODICEPS NIGRICOLLIS **Black-necked Grebe***
One in a brackish pool Nukhaylah 4th Feb.

SULA LEUCOGASTER **Brown Booby**
Small numbers offshore most coastal areas, maximum 4 Al-Fāzzah 19th Jan.
PHALACROCORAX sp? One far out to sea Hodeida 7th Jan.

PELECANUS ONOCROTALUS **White Pelican***
6 immatures Al-Luḥayyah 30 Jan; 1 immature Nukhaylah 4th Feb. (See Plate 3.2)

PELECANUS RUFESCENS **Pink-backed Pelican**
12 Nukhaylah 10th Jan; 19 on coast between Nukhaylah and Ghulayfiqah 11th Jan; 15 Ghulayfiqah 12th Jan; 3 Al-Marāziqah 13th Jan; at least 42 Al-Luḥayyah 30th Jan; 5 Al-Khawbah 1st Feb; 2 Ibn 'Abbās 2nd Feb. Adults and immatures, possible family parties observed. (See Plate 3.2)

BUBULCUS IBIS **Cattle Egret**
Common in all cultivated and *wādī* areas in association with man and livestock. Mainly flocks of 10 to 40; roost of 90 plus in a tree near Bājil 11th Feb.

EGRETTA GULARIS **Western Reef Heron**
Common most coastal areas visited. Maximum 24 Nukhaylah 10th Jan. Light and dark colour phases in roughly equal numbers.

EGRETTA GARZETTA **Little Egret**
2 Nukhaylah 4th Feb; 60 plus Wādī Surdud 15th Feb; 2 Wādī Zabīd 17th Jan.

ARDEA CINEREA **Grey Heron**
Small numbers most coastal and *wādī* areas with running water. Maximum 12 Al-Luḥayyah 30th Jan.

ARDEA PURPUREA **Purple Heron***
Adult and immature Al-Fāzzah (N) 19th Jan.

ARDEA GOLIATH **Goliath Heron***
One Al-Luḥayyah 30th Jan; 1 Al-Khawbah 1st Feb. Both near areas of mangrove.

SCOPUS UMBRETTA **Hammerkop**
Small numbers, usually singly in *wādīs* with running water and adjoining fields. Two old nests in trees Wādī Surdud.

THRESKIORNIS AETHIOPICUS **Sacred Ibis***
Adult pair Nukhaylah 10th Jan to 4th Feb; adult and immature Ghulayfiqah 11th Jan. Second recorded occurrence. (See Plate XII)

PLATALEA LEUCORODIA **Spoonbill**
21 Ghulayfiqah 11th Jan; 19 Al-Fāzzah (S) 19th Jan; 19 Mocha 21st Jan; 90 plus Al-Luḥayyah 30th Jan; 12 Nukhaylah 4th Feb.

PHOENICOPTERUS RUBER **Greater Flamingo**
Maximum 48 Al-Fāzzah 19th Jan; 3 Ghulayfiqah 11th Jan; 1 Al-Marāziqah 13th Jan; 3 Nukhaylah 4th Feb. (See Plate XIII)

TADORNA TADORNA **Shelduck***
2 females Nukhaylah 4th to 5th Feb. Second recorded occurrence.

ANAS PENELOPE **Wigeon**
16 Nukhaylah 10th Jan; 86 (N) and 500 (S) Al-Fāzzah 19th Jan.

ANAS STREPERA **Gadwall***
Pair Wādī Zabīd 17th Jan; 2 pairs Al-Fāzzah (S) 19th Jan. First recorded occurrence.

ANAS CRECCA **Teal**
18 (N) and 50 (S) Al-Fāzzah 19th Jan.

ANAS ACUTA **Pintail***
4 Al-Marāziqah 13th Jan; 3(N) and 45(S) Al-Fāzzah 19th Jan; 1 Nukhaylah 4th Feb.

ANAS CLYPEATA **Shoveler**
6 Wādī Zabīd 17th Jan; 8(N) and 100(S) Al-Fāzzah 19th Jan.

AYTHYA FULIGULA **Tufted Duck**★
Female Al-Fāzzah (S) 19th Jan.

MILVUS MIGRANS **Black Kite**
Very common around all human habitation; maximum 100 plus Bājil 13th Feb. Copulation and nest building observed from early Jan. (See Plate 3.3)

Plate 3.3 **Black Kite** MILVUS MIGRANS

NEOPHRON PERCNOPTERUS **Egyptian Vulture**
Locally common especially Wādī Mawr and Zabīd areas; maximum 10 soaring together Wādī Zabīd 17th Jan. (See Plate 3.4)

Plate 3.4 **Egyptian Vulture** NEOPHRON PERCNOPTERUS

GYPS FULVUS **Griffon Vulture**★
32 Wādī Zabīd 16th Jan; 3 Sūq al-Khamīs 28th Jan; 1 Jabal al-Jamā' 12th Feb.

CIRCAETUS GALLICUS **Short-toed Eagle**★
One Wādī Zabīd 20th Jan; 1 near Ḥays 21st Jan; 2 Al-Ḍaḥī 25th Jan; 1 Sūq al-Khamīs 28th Jan; 1 Jabal Bura' 6th Feb.

CIRCUS AERUGINOSUS **Marsh Harrier**★
Female Al-Fāzzah 19th Jan; female Al-Ḍaḥī 24th Jan; male and female Wādī Mawr 26th Jan; male and female Al-Luḥayyah 29th Jan.

CIRCUS CYANEUS **Hen Harrier**★
Female Zabīd 16th Jan; male Al-Manārah 25th Jan.

CIRCUS PYGARGUS **Montagu's Harrier**★
Male, 2 females Wādī Mawr 26th Jan; male and female near Al-Luḥayyah 29th Jan; 2 males Al Marāwi'ah 11th Feb; female Jabal al-Jamā' 12th Feb.

MELIERAX METABATES **Dark Chanting Goshawk**
Common in all habitats from coast to foothills. Especially prominent on roadside telegraph poles. (See Plate 3.5)

Plate 3.5 **Dark Chanting Goshawk** MELIERAX METABATES

MICRONISUS GABAR **Gabar Goshawk**★
Pair Al-Durayhimī *wādī* 9th to 10th Jan, much calling and display.

ACCIPITER NISUS **Sparrowhawk**★
Female Al-Manṣūrīyah 8th Jan; male Sūq al-Khamīs 28th Jan; pair Jabal Bura' 8th Feb.

BUTEO BUTEO **Buzzard**
Small numbers Bājil, Al-Durayhimī, Bayt al-Faqīh areas. Most eastern race B.B.VULPINUS, a few B.B.BUTEO including one freshly shot Bājil 5th Feb.

BUTEO RUFINUS **Long-legged Buzzard**★
Jabal al-Nārr 21st Jan; 1 near Al-Luḥayyah 29th Jan.

AQUILA RAPAX RAPTOR **Tawny Eagle**★
Pair, nest 2 fresh eggs Sūq al-Khamīs 28th Jan. Eyrie at 300 metres altitude, 10 metres up in a tree. Prey remains included Rock Hyrax, Helmeted Guineafowl, Domestic Chicken, Grasshopper. 3 old nests lying below the tree. Other records Tawny/Steppe Eagle A.R.NIPALENSIS; 2 adults plus 2 immatures Bayt al-Faqīh 8th Jan; 1 Wādī Zabīd 20th Jan; 1 Wādī Mawr bridge 25th Jan; 3 near Al-Luḥayyah 30th Jan.

AQUILA CHRYSAETOS **Golden Eagle**★
One immature near Ḥays 21st Jan on roadside telegraph pole.

AQUILA VERREAUXII **Verreaux's Eagle**★
Pair Jabal Bura' 8th Feb; Pair lining eyrie with fresh greenery Jabal al-Jamā' 10th to 13th Feb, cliff eyrie situated at 800 metres. Later visited by R.F. Porter and found to contain one chick.

HIERAAETUS PENNATUS **Booted Eagle**★
One pale phase Al-Durayhimī 9th Jan; 1 pale phase Wādī Surdud 15th Feb.

PANDION HALIAETUS **Osprey**
Common all along coastline, usually singly.

FALCO TINNUNCULUS **Kestrel**
Common in cultivated and semi desert areas.

FALCO PEREGRINUS **Peregrine Falcon**★
First year Al-Marāziqah 13th Jan; adult Al-Manārah 25th Jan; adult Wādī Mawr 26th Jan; adult female Nukhaylah 3rd to 4th Feb; adult Jabal Bura' 8th Feb. All apparently pale northern race.

ALECTORIS MELANOCEPHALA **Arabian Red-legged Partridge**★
Two pairs Jabal Bura' at 500 metres 7th Feb; pair Jabal al Jamā' 12th Feb.

AMMOPERDIX HEYI **Sand Partridge***
One Al-Manṣūrīyah 8th Jan; 5 near Hodeida 7th Jan.

Quail sp?* One near Hodeida 7th Jan.

NUMIDA MELEAGRIS **Helmeted Guineafowl**
Common in foothill areas of Sūq al-Khamīs, Jabal Bura' and Jabal al-Jamā' usually in flocks of 10 to 30. Roost of at least 50 in tree near Al-Sukhnah 5th Feb.

ARDEOTIS ARABS **Arabian Bustard***
Pair in cultivated land near Al-Luḥayyah 29th to 30th Jan. (See Plate 3.6)

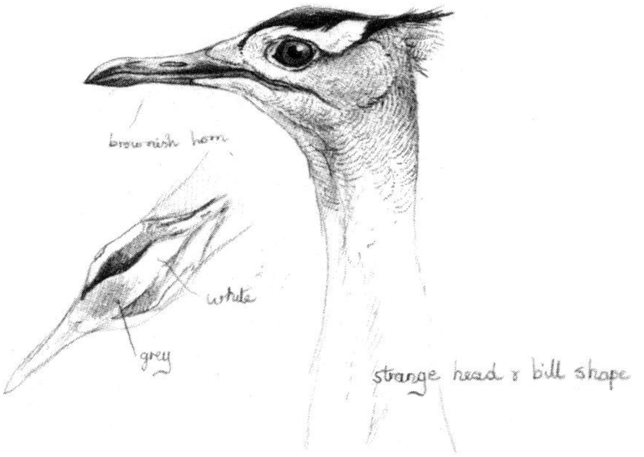

Plate 3.6 **Arabian Bustard ARDEOTIS ARABS**

HAEMATOPUS OSTRALEGUS **Oystercatcher***
16(N) and 10(S) Al-Fāzzah 19th Jan; 2 Mocha 21st Jan; 2 Al-Khawbah 1st Feb; 1 Ibn 'Abbās 2nd Feb; 3 Nukhaylah 4th Feb.

HIMANTOPUS HIMANTOPUS **Black-winged Stilt***
One Ghulayfiqah 12th Jan; 9 Wādī Mawr 26th Jan.

RECURVIROSTRA AVOSETTA **Avocet**
One Al-Marāziqah 14th Jan; 19(N) and 13(S) Al-Fāzzah 19th Jan; 15 Al-Luḥayyah 30th Jan; 8 Nukhaylah 4th Feb.

DROMAS ARDEOLA **Crab Plover***
One Ghulayfiqah 11th Jan; 38 Al-Luḥayyah 30th Jan; 32 Al-Khawbah 1st Feb; 2 Ibn 'Abbās 2nd Feb.

BURHINUS OEDICNEMUS **Stone Curlew***
One in stone desert with scattered acacia Wādī Sihām 11th Feb. BURHURUS sp: singles calling at night Al-Khawbah 1st Feb, Al-Sukhnah 5th Feb.

CHARADRIUS DUBIUS **Little Ringed Plover***
One Wādī Zabīd 16th Jan; 4 Nukhaylah 4th Feb; 1 Wādī Surdud 15th Feb.

CHARADRIUS HIATICULA **Ringed Plover**
Small numbers along coastline, maximum 32(S) Al-Fāzzah 19th Jan:

CHARADRIUS ALEXANDRINUS **Kentish Plover**
Common along coastline: 40 Al-Fāzzah (S) 19th Jan; 30 plus Al-Luḥayyah 30th Jan; 50 Al-Khawbah 1st Feb; 80 Nukhaylah 4th Feb.

CHARADRIUS MONGOLUS **Lesser Sand Plover**
Common along coastline: 50 plus Al-Khawbah 1st Feb; 120 Nukhaylah 4th Feb.

CHARADRIUS LESCHENAULTII **Greater Sand Plover**
Less common than C. MONGOLUS: maximum 50 Nukhaylah 10th Jan.

CHARADRIUS ASIATICUS **Caspian Plover***
11 Al-Suwayq 19th Jan.

PLUVIALIS DOMINICA **Lesser Golden Plover***
6 Al-Fāzzah (S) 19th Jan.

PLUVIALIS SQUATAROLA **Grey Plover**
Small numbers along coastline, maximum 10 Nukhaylah 4th Feb.

HOPLOPERTUS SPINOSUS **Spur-winged Plover***
2 holding territory Al-Marāziqah 13th Jan; 26 Al-Fāzzah (S) 19th Jan; 2 inland near Bājil 7th Jan.

CALIDRIS CANUTUS **Knot***
19 Nukhaylah 10th Jan. First recorded occurrence.

CALIDRIS ALBA **Sanderling**
Common along coastline, maximum 200 plus Al-Marāziqah 13th Jan.

CALIDRIS MINUTA **Little Stint**
Very common along coastline: 200 plus Nukhaylah 10th Jan; 200 Al-Fāzzah 19th Jan.

CALIDRIS TEMMINCKII **Temminck's Stint***
10 Nukhaylah 10th Jan; 2 Wādī Surdud 15th Jan; 3 Wādī Zabīd 16th Jan.

CALIDRIS FERRUGINEA **Curlew Sandpiper**
Common along coastline: at 200 Nukhaylah 4th Feb; 30 Al-Fāzzah (S) 19th Jan.

CALIDRIS ALPINA **Dunlin**
Small numbers: maximum 100 plus Al-Fāzzah (S) 19th Jan; 32 Nukhaylah 4th Feb.

LIMICOLA FALCINELLUS **Broad-billed Sandpiper***
2 Nukhaylah 4th Feb.

PHILOMACHUS PUGNAX **Ruff***
males, 2 females Al-Fāzzah (S) 19th Jan.

GALLINAGO GALLINAGO **Snipe***
3 Nukhaylah 4th Feb.

LIMOSA LIMOSA **Black-tailed Godwit***
2 Al-Fāzzah (S) 19th Jan.

LIMOSA LAPPONICA **Bar-tailed Godwit**
Common along coastline usually in flocks of up to 30. Maximum 140 Nukhaylah 4th Feb; 43 Al-Fāzzah 19th Jan.

NUMENIUS PHAEOPUS **Whimbrel**
Small numbers along coastline, maximum 16 Al-Luḥayyah 30th Jan.

NUMENIUS ARQUATA **Curlew**
Small numbers along coastline: 22 Al-Luḥayyah 30th Jan; 26 Al-Khawbah 1st Feb; 25 Nukhaylah 4th Feb.

TRINGA TOTANUS **Redshank**
Common along coastline and in *wādīs*, maximum 300 plus Nukhaylah 10th Jan.

TRINGA STAGNATILIS **Marsh Sandpiper***
15 Nukhaylah 10th Jan; 9(N) and 2(S) Al-Fāzzah 19th Jan.

TRINGA NEBULARIA **Greenshank**
Common along coastline and *wādīs*, maximum 46 Nukhaylah 10th Jan.

TRINGA OCHROPUS **Green Sandpiper***
2 Wādī Zabīd 17th Jan; 5 Wādī Surdud 15th Feb.

XENUS CINEREUS **Terek Sandpiper**
Common along coastline: 120 plus Nukhaylah 10th Jan; 50 plus Ghulayfiqah 11th Jan; 28 Al-Luḥayyah 30th Jan.

ACTITUS HYPOLEUCOS **Common Sandpiper**
Small numbers along coastline and inland *wādīs*. Maximum 5 Ghulayfiqah 11th Jan; 3 Wādī Zabīd 17th Jan.

ARENARIA INTERPRES **Turnstone**
Small numbers along coastline: 30 Al-Khawbah 1st Feb; 32 Nukhaylah 4th Feb.

LARUS HEMPRICHII **Sooty Gull**
Very common along coastline: 100 Hodeida 7th Jan; 500 plus feeding on dumped fish Al-Marāziqah 13th Jan; 60 Mocha 21st Jan; 100 Al-Khawbah 1st Feb.

LARUS LEUCOPHTHALMUS **White-eyed Gull***
Very few along coastline: 2 Hodeida 7th Jan; 7 Mocha 21st Jan; 2 Al-Luḥayyah 30th Jan; 1 Al-Khawbah 1st Feb; 1 Ibn 'Abbās 2nd Feb.

LARUS ICHTHYAETUS **Great Black-headed Gull***

3 Mocha 21st Jan; 1 Ibn ‘Abbās 2nd Feb.

Larus ridibundus **Black-headed Gull**
Locally common on coastline: 120 Hodeida 7th Jan; at 900 Mocha 21st Jan.

Larus genei **Slender-billed Gull***
1 Al-Fāzzah 19th Jan; 6 Mocha 21st Jan; 86 Al-Luḥayyah 30th Jan; 8 Al-Khawbah 1st Feb; 3 Nukhaylah 4th Feb.

Larus fuscus **Lesser Black-backed Gull**
Small numbers all along coastline: 30 Hodeida 7th Jan; 63 Al-Marāziqah 13th Jan; 16 Mocha 21st Jan; 20 Al-Khawbah 1st Feb.

Larus argentatus **Herring Gull**
Small numbers all along coastline: 40 Hodeida 7th Jan; 40 Al-Khawbah 1st Feb.

Gelochelidon nilotica **Gull-billed Tern***
32 Nukhaylah 10th Jan; 5 Ghulayfiqah 12th Jan; 1 Al-Marāziqah 13th Jan; 8 Al-Luḥayyah 30th Jan; 5 Al-Khawbah 1st Feb; 1 Ibn ‘Abbās 2nd Feb.

Sterna caspia **Caspian Tern**
2 Hodeida 7th Jan; 3 Ghulayfiqah 12th Jan (one ringed); 32 Al-Marāziqah 13th Jan; 15 Al-Luḥayyah 30th Jan; 10 Mocha 21st Jan; 2 Ibn ‘Abbās 2nd Feb.

Sterna bergii **Swift Tern**
Small numbers along coastline: 5 Hodeida 7 Jan; 250 plus Al-Marāziqah 13th Jan; 11 Al-Luḥayyah 30th Jan; 8 Mokha 21st Jan.

Sterna bengalensis **Lesser Crested Tern***
9 Mocha 21st Jan; 2 Al-Luḥayyah 30th Jan.

Sterna sandvicensis **Sandwich Tern***
66 Al-Marāziqah 13th Jan.

Sterna hirundo **Common Tern***
2 Mocha 21st Jan.

Sterna repressa **White-cheeked Tern***
150 Mocha 21st Jan.

Sterna saundersi **Saunder's Little Tern***
2 Nukhaylah 10th Jan; 5 Ghulayfiqah 12th Jan; 4 Al-Luḥayyah 30th Jan; 4 Al-Fāzzah 19th Jan.

Pterocles lichtensteinii **Lichtenstein's Sandgrouse***
Pair Jabal al-Nārr 21st Jan; 1 Sūq al-Khamīs 28th Jan. Male has more bare yellow skin around eye than depicted in Heinzel et al. 1976.

Pterocles exustus **Chestnut-bellied Sandgrouse**
Locally common all areas except foothills: 125 ten km west Hodeida 7th Jan; 80 Wādī Zabīd 20th Jan; 28 Mocha 21st Jan.

Columba livia **Rock Pigeon**
Common foothill areas: hundreds flying from foothills out into Wādī Mawr at dawn 26th Jan; 100 plus Jabal Bura‘ 9th Feb.

Streptopelia roseogrisea **African Collared Dove**
Small numbers palm and other vegetated areas: 10 plus Al-Marāziqah 13th Jan; 30 plus Jabal Bura‘ 9th Feb.

Streptopelia semitorquata **Red-eyed Dove***
26 Jabal Bura‘ 9th Feb; 1 Wādī Surdud 15th Feb: Both heavily wooded areas.

Streptopelia lugens **Dusky Turtle Dove***
4 Al-Durayhimī 9th Jan: 1 Ghulayfiqah 12th Jan; 1 Al-Marāziqah 13th Jan.

Streptopelia senegalensis **Palm Dove**
Common in all areas.

Oena capensis **Namaqua Dove**
Locally common in most areas, maximum 80 plus Al-Manārah 25th Jan.

Centropus superciliosus **White-browed Coucal***
3 Jabal Bura‘ 6th Feb; 1 Al-Sukhnah 5th Feb.

Caprimulgus nubicus **Nubian Nightjar***
2 calling (one dazzled and caught) Wādī Kuway 13th Jan; 3 calling Al-Khawbah 1st Feb; 4 calling Nukhaylah 4th Feb; 2 calling Jabal Bura‘ 6th Feb. (See Plate 3.7)

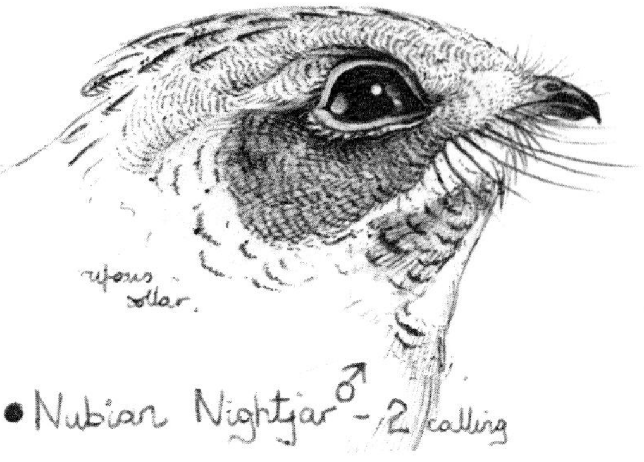

Plate 3.7 **Nubian Nightjar** CAPRIMULGUS NUBICUS

Apus melba **Alpine Swift***
2 Al-Zuhrah 29th Jan; 16 Jabal Bura‘ 6th Feb; 4 Jabal al-Jamā' 10th Feb.

Apus affinis **Little Swift***
Passage 80 plus north in 15 minutes Jabal Bura‘ 9th Feb.

Cypsiurus parvus **Palm Swift**
Common in parties 4 to 10 most palm groves from coast to foothills.

Merops orientalis **Little Green Bee-eater**
Common in all areas, usually in pairs. Nest scraping observed.

Coracias abyssinicus **Abyssinian Roller**
Common especially around habitation and roadside telegraph poles, usually in pairs. (See Plate 3.8)

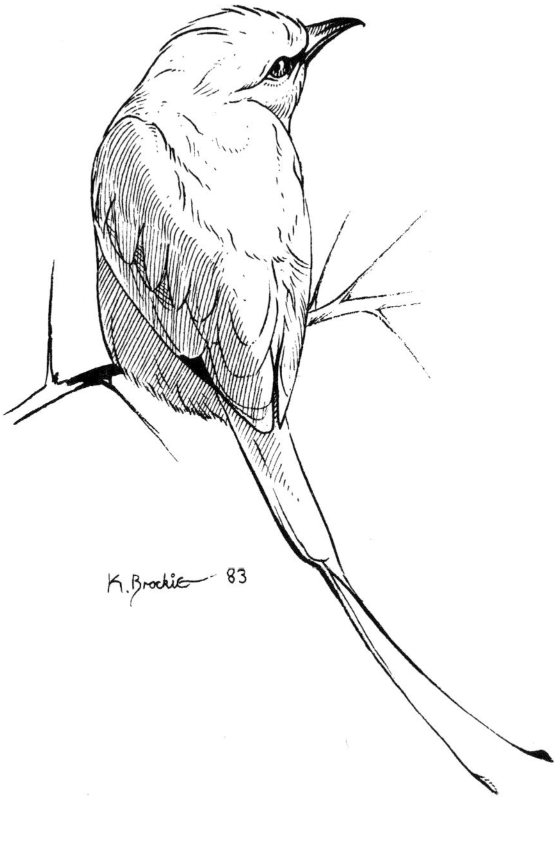

Plate 3.8 **Abyssinian Roller** CORACIAS ABYSSINICUS

TOCKUS NASUTUS **Grey Hornbill**
Small numbers wooded *wādīs* and wooded foothills; 16 Jabal Bura' 7th Feb.

MIRAFRA CANTILLANS **Singing Bush Lark**
Locally common in semi desert and cultivated areas, especially fallow-fields.

EREMOPTERIX NIGRICEPS **Black-crowned Finch Lark**
Common semi desert and cultivated areas.

ALAEMON ALAUDIPES **Hoopoe Lark**
Fairly common desert and semi desert areas usually singly or in pairs.

GALERIDA CRISTATA **Crested Lark**
Common most semi desert areas and more open cultivated ground.

RIPARIA RIPARIA **Sand Martin***
8 Al-Fāzzah (S) 19th Jan.

PTYONOPROGNE FULIGULA **African Rock Martin***
8 Jabal Bura' 8th Feb; 6 Jabal al-Jamā' 11th Feb.

PTYONOPROGNE RUPESTRIS **Crag Martin***
6 Wādī Surdud 15th Feb.

HIRUNDO RUSTICA **Swallow***
at 50 Al-Luḥayyah 30th Jan; 14 Al-Zuhrah 29th Jan; 3 Jabal Bura' 7th Feb.

HIRUNDO DAURICA **Red-rumped Swallow***
8 Jabal Bura' 7th Feb.

ANTHUS CAMPESTRIS **Tawny Pipit***
4 Bājil 7th Jan; 8 west of Hodeida 7th Jan; 1 Wādī Zabīd 17th Jan.

ANTHUS SIMILIS **Long-billed Pipit***
16 Al-Durayhimī *wādī* 10th Jan; 2 Al-Manārah 25th Jan; 2 Al-Luḥayyah 30th Jan; 1 Jabal Bura' 8th Feb; all feeding in fallow fields.

ANTHUS TRIVIALIS **Tree Pipit***
2 Wādī Zabīd 20th Jan.

MOTACILLA FLAVA **Yellow Wagtail**
Common small numbers all wet areas from coastal salt marsh to rivers.

MOTACILLA CINEREA **Grey Wagtail***
Male Jabal Bura' 8th Feb; Male, Female Wādī Surdud 15th Feb.

MOTACILLA ALBA **White Wagtail**
Common small numbers all areas except desert.

PYCNONOTUS XANTHOPYGOS **Black-capped Bulbul (Yellow-vented Bulbul)**
Very common all areas especially near human habitation and crops. 100 Al-Durayhimī 10th Jan feeding in sorghum and millet. (See Plate 3.9)

Plate 3.9 **Black-capped Bulbul PYCNONOTUS XANTHOPYGOS**

CERCOTRICHAS PODOBE **Black Bush Chat**
Fairly common bush country usually singly or in pairs.

IRANIA GUTTURALIS **White-throated Robin***
2 Jabal Bura' 7th Feb.

PHOENICURUS PHOENICURUS **Redstart***
Male Wādī Zabīd 18th Jan (nominate race)

CERCOMELA MELANURA **Blackstart**
Common foothills and stony desert areas.

SAXICOLA RUBETRA **Whinchat***
Male Wādī Sihām 11th Feb.

SAXICOLA TORQUATA **Stonechat***
4 Zabīd-Mocha 21st Jan; 1 Al-Ḍaḥī 25th Jan; 2 Al-Luḥayyah 30th Jan; 3 Wādī Sihām 11th Feb.

OENANTHE ISABELLINA **Isabelline Wheatear**
Small numbers most areas.

OENANTHE PLESCHANKA **Pied Wheatear***
Male Bayt al-Faqīh 8th Jan; male Al-Mazāriqah 15th Jan; pair Wādī Zabīd 17th Jan.

OENANTHE HISPANICA **Black-eared Wheatear***
Female (trapped) Wādī Zabīd 17th Jan.

OENANTHE DESERTI **Desert Wheatear***
Pair Nukhaylah 4th Feb.

MONTICOLA SAXATILIS **Rock Thrush***
Female Jabal al-Jamā' 12th Feb.

MONTICOLA SOLITARIUS **Blue Rock Thrush***
Female Sūq al-Khamīs 28th Jan; pair Jabal Bura' 7th Feb; male Jabal al Jamā' 11th Feb.

CISTICOLA JUNCIDIS **Fan-tailed Warbler**
Common in nearly all areas of sorghum and millet.

PRINIA GRACILIS **Graceful Warbler**
Common in nearly all areas of sorghum and millet, also in some areas of scrub vegetation. Song heard frequently.

SCOTOCERCA INQUIETA **Scrub Warbler**
Small numbers usually in dry scrub areas.

ACROCEPHALUS ARUNDINACEUS **Great Reed Warbler***
8 plus singing in mangroves Al-Luḥayyah 30th Jan. First authenticated occurrence.

HIPPOLAIS PALLIDA **Olivaceous Warbler***
2 Wādī Zabīd irrigation project compound 18th Jan.

SYLVIA CANTILLANS **Sub-alpine Warbler***
One (trapped) Al-Durayhimī 10th Jan. First recorded occurrence.

SYLVIA MYSTACEA **Ménétries' Warbler***
8 plus Al-Durayhimī *wādī* 10th Jan; female near Hodeida 7th Jan.

SYLVIA LEUCOMELAENA **Red Sea Warbler (Arabian Warbler)**
Fairly common in acacia covered foothills and Jabal areas.

SYLVIA CURRUCA **Lesser Whitethroat***
One Al-Durayhimī 9th Jan; 3 Wādī Zabīd 20th Jan; 2 Suq al-Khamīs 28th Jan.

SYLVIA COMMUNIS **Whitethroat***
Male near Zabīd 18th Jan.

PHYLLOSCOPUS FUSCUTUS **Dusky Warbler***
One Jabal al-Jamā' 13th Feb. Its harsh SYLVIA type call and uniform dark brown plumage ruled out other species.

TERPSIPHONE VIRIDIS **African Paradise Flycatcher***
8 Jabal Bura' 7th Feb.

TURDOIDES SQUAMICEPS **Arabian Babbler**
Fairly common in well vegetated areas, maximum 18 Jabal Bura' 7th Feb. All individuals were similar to the Arabian Babbler in size, shape and general plumage but had tatty greyish heads with whitish faces and supercilium giving a bald appearance. The bill and legs were pale yellow.

ANTHREPTES METALLICUS **Nile Valley Sunbird**
Very common all areas of acacia scrub, sorghum and millet fields.

NECTARINIA HABESSINICA **Shining Sunbird**
12 near Zabīd 18th Jan; 4 Sūq al-Khamīs 28th Jan; 200 plus Jabal Bura' 7th Feb; 4 Jabal al-Jamā'. (See Plate 3.10)

Plate 3.10 **Shining Sunbird NECTARINIA HEBESSINICA**

ZOSTEROPS ABYSSINICA **White-breasted White-eye**
50 plus above Sabt al-Maḥrab, Jabal Bura' 7th Feb.

LANIUS ISABELLINUS **Red-tailed Shrike**
Small numbers all areas. Apparent habitat preference between the two distinct forms, L.L.PHOENICUROIDES in the foothill areas and L.I.ISABELLINUS on the Tihāmah plain.

LANIUS MINOR **Lesser Grey Shrike***
1 Wādī Zabīd 20th Jan; 5 on roadside poles Zabīd to Mocha 21st Jan; 1 Jabal al Jamā' 11th Feb.

LANIUS EXCUBITOR **Great Grey Shrike**
Common most areas especially on roadside telegraph poles.

LANIUS NUBICUS **Masked Shrike***
1 Al-Ḍaḥī 24th Jan; 1 Jabal Bura' 7th Feb.

CORVUS SPLENDENS **Indian House Crow***
Pair Hodeida 7th Jan. Second recorded occurrence.

CORVUS RUFICOLLIS **Brown-necked Raven**
Common, usually in pairs from coast to foothills, max. 8 Zabīd 20th Jan.

CORVUS RHIPIDURUS **Fan-tailed Raven**
Small numbers around towns ie. Bājil, Zabīd. Flocks of up to 100 in foothill areas such as Jabal al-Jamā'.

ONYCHOGNATHUS TRISTRAMII **Tristram's Grackle***
35 Wādī Surdud 15th Feb, drinking by river.

STURNUS VULGARIS **Starling***
1 Zabīd 16th Jan. First recorded occurrence.

PASSER DOMESTICUS **House Sparrow**
Ubiquitous around most human habitation.

PASSER EUCHLORUS **Arabian Golden Sparrow**
Locally common near cultivation such as millet in flocks of up to 60.

PETRONIA DENTATA **Lesser Rock Sparrow***
Pair Zabīd irrigation project compound 17th Jan.

PLOCEUS GALBULA **Rüppell's Weaver**
Very common around all human habitation and crops especially sorghum and millet, also in acacia. Many nests in trees, also on telephone wires on the Ṣan'ā' to Bājil road. Nest building in early January.

ESTRILDA RUFIBARBA **Arabian Waxbill***
26 Wādī Surdud 15th Feb in reeds by stream (endemic to S.W. Arabia).

EUODICE CANTANS **African Silverbill**
Locally common around crop areas with trees, usually flocks 10-20.

EMBERIZA TAHAPISI **Cinnamon-breasted Rock Bunting***
7 Sūq al-Khamīs 28th Jan; 2 pairs Jabal Bura' 7th Feb; 16 Jabal al-Jamā' 11 Feb; pair Wādī Surdud 15th Feb.

MAMMAL OBSERVATIONS

The following list comprises mammals observed by the expedition members. The list excludes bats and rodents which I trapped for the Harrison Zoological Museum which are detailed separately. Most of the animals afforded only brief glimpses and were very wary due to human persecution.

PAPIO HAMADRYAS ARABICUS **Baboon**
50 plus Sabt al-Maḥrab, Jabal Bura' 6-9th Feb; 200 plus Jabal al-Jamā' 12-13th Feb. Both in troops with many small young in foothill areas. Feeding mostly on the flowers of acacia and ANISOTES TRISULCUS, very wary of humans, probably due to persecution.

MELLIVORA CAPENSIS **Honey Badger**
One road casualty near al-Ḥusaynīyah 25th Jan.

VULPES VULPES **Red Fox**
Individuals seen most areas visited from the coast to the foothills.

Mongoose sp?
Single seen al-Marāziqah 12th Jan, pelage uniform brown colour. Many tracks around and it was raiding my rodent traps before I could empty them.

HYAENA HYAENA **Striped Hyaena**
One seen in car headlights Wādī Mawr 27th Jan. A recently occupied den was shown to us by a local inhabitant on the summit of a hill near al-Sukhnah.

GAZELLA GAZELLA ARABICA **Arabian Gazelle**
Male in foothills near Sūq al-Khamīs 28th Jan.

PROCAVIA CAPENSIS JAYAKARI **Rock Hyrax**
Very common in foothill areas above 400m. (See Plate 3.11)

Plate 3.11 **Rock Hyrax PROCAVIA CAPENSIS JAYAKARI**

LEPUS CAPENSIS ARABICUS **Hare**
Small numbers mainly in the foothill areas.

HYSTRIX INDICA **Indian Crested Porcupine**
A quill was dropped in the middle of our camp site during the night of the 12th Feb.

Some **Felines** were glimpsed and heard at night but could not be identified due to the insufficient views obtained. A **Dugong** skull was collected on the shore at al-Khawbah (see Harrison, pp. 28-29) and whale remains (as well as Sea Turtle) were observed at al-Marāziqah beach.

HABITATS

The coastal areas were the most prolific for wildlife especially for birds. All along the sandy shores of the Red Sea conditions were good for gulls and terns, especially near fishing settlements where much waste fish was left after fishing trips. Military restrictions prevented access to what were probably some of the most rewarding coastal areas especially near Hodeida. The following sites were the richest in birdlife of the areas I visited.

Nukhaylah, map ref[3] KB 8416, sheet 1442 B4.

An expanse of tidal mud flat some 2km across with salt marsh bordered by sand and palm groves. Excellent for waders and waterfowl with good viewing points at high tide.

Al-Fāzzah (South), map ref KA 9557, sheet 1443 C3.

A large expanse of salt marsh studded with pools, much grazed by livestock. A good area for duck, flamingos and waders.

Al-Fāzzah (North), map ref KA 9363, sheet 1443 C3.

Large brackish pools running into the palm groves with some reed beds. Good for ducks and herons with small numbers of waders.

Ghulayfiqah, map ref KA 8596, sheet 1443 C1.

A large expanse of tidal sand flats with salt pans and a small area of salt marsh. Small numbers of pelicans, terns and waders.

Al-Luḥayyah, map ref (Series was not yet completed for this sector in 1982)

A large area of coastal reeds and mangrove backed by an extensive area of *sabkhah* on one side and the sea with tidal sand and mud on the other. Many offshore sand bars in the shallow water. An excellent area for pelicans, herons, spoonbills, gulls, terns and waders.

Inland the *wādī* systems were the best areas for birds, especially around the cultivated land. The fields of sorghum and millet were alive with warblers and other passerines. The fallow fields were well worth visiting for various larks and pipits. Further inland, the foothill and *jabal* areas such as Jabal al-Jamā' are well worth visiting with their stony hillsides and Acacia-Commiphora bushland. Here (Jabal al-Jamā') I found nesting Verreaux's Eagle as well as very large populations of Baboon and Rock Hyrax. Elsewhere on the Tihāmah, the alluvial plains with scattered Adenium Obesum and desert with Acacia bushland sustained a small but widely dispersed population of birds.

The most outstanding area beyond doubt was around Sūq al-Sabt (Sabt al-Maḥrab) in Jabal Bura'. This is the location of the only sizeable forest remnant in the Yemen Arab Republic and of outstanding botanical interest (see Wood, p. 15, Larsen, p. 27). Here I recorded 47 species of birds, despite these being the winter months, and large numbers of Baboon and Rock Hyrax. The Yemeni government should if possible take steps to conserve this area before it is exploited as other areas of natural forest have been. Whilst I was drawing in the valley here I observed chain saws being carried up above Sūq al-Sabt which does not bode well for the continuation of the forest.

CONCLUSION

Much work needs to be done in the Yemen especially in relation to proposing areas for conservation purposes. Areas like Jabal Bura' should be preserved; areas need to be set aside for the larger mammals such as the gazelle which appear to be overhunted. What is the status of the Arabian Bustard and other species? There are still many questions to be answered.

APPENDIX I

Observations in Ṣan'ā' 1st to 4th January.

Milvus migrans **Black Kite** – 40 plus
Streptopelia senegalensis **Palm Dove** – Very common
Motacilla flava sp. **Yellow Wagtail** – 1
Pycnonotus xanthopygos **Black-capped Bulbul** – common
Phoenicurus ochruros **Black Redstart** – 1 pair
Sylvia curruca **Lesser Whitethroat** – 1
Phylloscopus collybita **Chiffchaff** – 1
Zosterops abyssinica **White-breasted White-eye** – 4
Lanius exubitor **Great Grey Shrike** – 1
Corvus rhipidurus **Fan-tailed Raven** – 20 plus
Passer domesticus **House Sparrow** – Very common

APPENDIX II

Observations at Shibām and Kawkabān, 3rd January.

Milvus migrans **Black Kite** – 40 plus
Gyps fulvus **Griffon Vulture** – 3 adults
Falco tinnunculus **Kestrel** – 3
Falco biarmicus **Lanner Falcon** – 1 adult, sparring with kites for prey
Falco cherrug **Saker** – 2 adults
Streptopelia senegalensis **Palm Dove** – 10 plus
Motacilla cinerea **Grey Wagtail** – 1 Female
Pycnonotus xanthopygos **Black-capped Bulbul** – 6
Prunella fagani **Arabian Accentor** – 1 (endemic)
Phoenicurus ochruros **Black Redstart** – 2 pairs
Oenanthe lugens leugentoides **South Arabian (Mourning) Wheatear** – 1 pair
Scotocerca inquieta **Scrub Warbler** – 3
Nectarinia osea **Orange-tufted Sunbird** – 20
Zosterops abyssinica **White-breasted White-eye** – 2
Corvus ruficollis **Brown-necked Raven** – c. 25
Corvus rhipidurus **Fan-tailed Raven** – 50 plus
Onychognathus tristramii **Tristram's Grackle** – 80 plus
Serinus menachensis **Yemen Serin** – 6 (endemic)
Carduelis yemenensis **Yemen Linnet** – 14 (endemic)

APPENDIX III

Sūq al-Khamīs (Ṣan'ā' – Hodeida Road) 15th February

Gypaetus barbatus **Lammergeier** – 1 adult

---

3. These map references are keyed to the series: Y.A.R. 1:50,000 Edition: 1-D.O.S. 1980. See also the Survey Region Map on p. 3 for Mr. Brockie's survey areas. [Ed.]

BIBLIOGRAPHY

Brown, L., and D. Amadon, *Eagles, Hawks and Falcons of the World,* Country Life Books, 2 vols., 1968.

Etchécopar, R.D., and F. Hüe, *The Birds of North Africa,* London, 1967.

Heinzel, H., R. Fitter and J. Parslow, *The Birds of Britain and Europe, with North Africa and the Middle East,* London, 1972.

Jennings, M. C., "The Birds of Saudi Arabia: a Check-List," 1981.

___________, "A List of North Yemen Birds," 1981.

King, B., "April Bird Observations in Saudi Arabia. With Addendum 1, January 1977 Observations; Addendum 2 Arabian Bustard Expedition April 1977," *J. Saudi Arab. Nat. Hist. Soc.,* Vol. 21., 1978, pp. 3-24.

Mackworth-Praed, C. W., and C. H. B. Grant, *Birds of Eastern and North Eastern Africa,* London, 2 Vols., 1957-1960.

Meinertzhagen, R., *The Birds of Arabia,* Edinburgh – London, 1954.

Phillips, N. R., "Some observations on the Birds of the North Yemen in Autumn 1979," *Sandgrouse,* Vol. 4, 1982. pp. 37-59.

Porter, R. F., (Unpublished observations, April 1979)

Porter, R. F., and L. Cornwallis, "Spring Observations of the Birds of the North Yemen," *Sandgrouse,* Vol. 4, 1982, pp. 1-36.

Sclater, W. L., "The Birds of Yemen, south western Arabia," *Ibis,* Vol 10(5), 1917.

Thiollay, J. M. and L. Duhautois, "Notes sur les Oiseaux du Nord Yemen," *L'Oiseau,* Vol. 46(3), 1976, pp. 261-271.

Vous, Prof. K. H., *List of Recent Holarctic Bird Species,* 1977, 1982.

FURTHER READING

Niebuhr, Carsten, *Descriptiones Animalium,* Hasniae, 4 Vols., 1775.

___________, *Description de l'Arabie,* Amsterdam, 1774.

___________, *Travels in Arabia,* Edinburgh, 2 Vols., 1779.

ILLUSTRATIONS

Plates 3.1-3.11 provided by the author: *3.1* sketchbook detail, c.60 × 48mm, pencil; *3.2* sketchbook detail, c.140 × 210mm, pencil; *3.3* sketchbook detail, c.98 × 70mm, pencil; *3.4* sketchbook detail, c.140 × 167mm, pencil-watercolour; *3.5* sketchbook detail, c.93 × 120mm, pencil; *3.6* sketchbook detail, c.60 × 100mm, pencil-coloured pencils; *3.7* sketchbook detail, c.60 × 75mm, biro-coloured pencils; *3.8* 120 × 85mm, ink (based on sketchbook); *3.9* sketchbook detail, c.60 × 80mm, watercolour; *3.10* sketchbook detail, c.74 × 98mm, gouache-watercolour; *3.11* sketchbook detail, c.57 × 75mm, pencil.

3.2: ON A SMALL COLLECTION OF YEMEN TIHĀMAH BUTTERFLIES

Torben B. Larsen

During the course of a multi-disciplinary expedition to the Yemen Tihāmah in January and February 1982, Francine Stone et al. collected eighteen species of butterflies[1] as follows. Butterflies in no way formed a major objective of the expedition and the collecting activity is best described as incidental. Despite this fact, a number of interesting records were made in this poorly studied area.

LIST

PONTIA GLAUCONOME GLAUCONOME (Klug). Wādī Kuway. An eremic species, widely distributed in Arabia, but absent from the well watered parts of Yemen.

ANAPHAEIS AUROTA AUROTA (Fabricius). Wādī Surdud, Wādī Kuway. A migrant tropical species found in both India and Africa as well as throughout Arabia.

COLOTIS CALAIS AMATUS (Fabricius). Wādī Surdud, Wādī Nāqah. A common butterfly in the African Sahel, parts of Arabia and in India.

COLOTIS PHISADIA PHISADIA (Godart). Wādī Jāḥif, Al-Durayhimī. It is curious that this butterfly was caught in two localities distinct from those of the previous species, since they share SALVADORA PERSICA as larval food plant. The range of the species is as for C. CALAIS, but it extends to the Dead Sea area of Jordan.

COLOTIS DANAE EUPOMPE (Klug). Wādī Nāqah. One of the most widely distributed of the COLOTIS in Africa, India and Arabia. I have taken it on the Tihāmah two years ago.

COLOTIS DAIRA DAIRA (Klug). Wādī Sihām. This species is common in Africa. The Arabian subspecies was described from the Yemen or 'Asīr Tihāmah in 1832 and is endemic. Wādī Sihām is a typical locality for the species.

COLOTIS EVAGORE EVAGORE (Klug). Wādī Sihām, Al-'Ayn. The nominate subspecies is endemic to Arabia where it is limited to very dry localities in south-western Arabia. Other subspecies are found in the rest of Africa. The species is uncommon in Yemen; I have found it in the same locality as the expedition.

NEPHERONIA BUQUETI BUCHANANI Rothschild. Bayt al-Faqīh, Al-Manṣūrīyah. The first record I know of from the Tihāmah proper. A species widely distributed in Africa.

EUREMA HECABE SOLIFERA (Butler). Al-Manṣūrīyah, Al-Zuhrah. This brilliant yellow species is common throughout Africa, Asia and Australia, as well as southwestern Arabia. It is common on the wetter mountains of Yemen, but in the Tihāmah it is almost certainly linked to agriculture.

EUREMA BRIGITTA BRIGITTA (Stoll). Wādī Nāqah. This species is common in most of Africa and Asia, but it was not recorded from Arabia until a few years ago (Larsen, 1982). It seems surprisingly scarce. Talhouk collected a specimen near Jīzān, Robertson a specimen

1. 20 specimens from this collection have been donated to the National Entomological Collections, the National Museum of Natural History, Smithsonian Institution, ref. ENT-A-2185. [Ed.]

at Wādī Ḍahr and I have taken three specimens only at Wādī Dūr, Wādī 'Annah and in the middle of Ṣan'ā'. It is rather surprising that a female of the dry season should be present in the expedition material, the first female from Arabia.

SYNTARUCUS PIRITHOUS (Linné). Wādī Surdud, Wādī Nāqah. A widely distributed butterfly in Africa and southern Europe, known from Yemen, PDRY and Dhofar in Arabia. The specimens are unusually small, as they are often found in Cairo, but not as dark.

TARUCUS THEOPHRASTUS (Fabricius). Al-Durayhimī, Wādī Nāqah. An Afrotropical butterfly, well distributed in southwestern Arabia, but not extending elsewhere in Arabia or to India as is the case for two other members of the genus.

EUCHRYSOPS OSIRIS (Hopffer). Wādī Nāqah. An Afrotropical species, common in the 'Asīr, Yemen, PDRY and Dhofar.

FREYERIA TROCHYLUS (Freyer). Wādī Nāqah. A minute butterfly with a vast range covering all of Africa, Arabia, the Balkans, the Middle East and much of Asia. It feeds on heliotrope and indigo.

DANAUS CHRYSIPPUS (Linné). Al-Sukhnah, Al-Durayhimī, Al-Zuhrah, near Zabīd. The largest and most conspicuous of the Tihāmah butterflies. The four specimens represent the three distinct colour morphs known as DORIPPUS, ALCIPPUS and CHRYSIPPUS. The species has a vast Pantropical distribution with Mediterranean penetration. It is toxic and all three forms are mimicked by the following species (see Larsen and Larsen, 1980).

HYPOLIMNAS MISIPPUS (Linné). Zabīd (sight record). The distribution is almost as wide as that of its model. The female is a near perfect copy of the preceding species, including the three distinct colour morphs. The male is jet black with large, egg-shaped spots on the wings in white. They were seen circling flowering trees. (See Plate 3.12.)

JUNONIA HIERTA CEBRENE (Trimen). Wādī Nāqah. A widespread butterfly in Africa, southern Arabia and parts of Asia. Francine Stone commented on how frustrating it was to collect the species which sits provocatively on a rock and darts off again just before the net is within reach. This experience is echoed by most collectors!

YPTHIMA ASTEROPE (Klug). Wādī Nāqah. A species with the same distribution as the preceding species, fluttering weakly among grasses and rocks.

PELOPIDAS THRAX (Hübner). Al-Zuhrah. A widely distributed species in Africa and Asia.

DISCUSSION

The composition of the collection, formed by a collector with no previous experience, is interesting because it is very close to an a priori list of what might be expected from the Tihāmah during a season not particularly propitious for butterflies due to lack of rain. Only E. BRIGITTA is a real surprise.

Missing from the collection are two species which in Arabia are known only from the Tihāmah and do not penetrate the foot-hills nor to PDRY. They are CALOPIERIS EULIMENE (Klug) and COLOTIS EPHYIA (Klug) which confirms my impression that they are strictly localised in certain plant communities developed around CAPPARIS APHYLLA (Larsen, 1983).

I would like to thank Francine Stone for making this collection which provided a useful confirmation of my own limited knowledge of Tihāmah butterflies.

A RECOMMENDATION

During a trip to Yemen in May 1980 I was able to visit the forests around Sūq al-Sabt at the foot of Jabal Bura'. This habitat is almost unique in Arabia[2] and has till now avoided serious disturbance by man. Its designation as a nature reserve would be most desirable. During one day's collecting, I noted 36 different species, one of which (CHARAXES BERNSTORFFI Rydon) was new to science (Larsen, 1983).

BIBLIOGRAPHY

Larsen, T. B., "The Butterflies of Yemen," *Biol. Skr. Dan. Vidensk. Selsk.*, Vol. 23 (3), 1982, pp. 1-85.

———, *Butterflies of Saudi Arabia,* London, 1984.

Larsen, T. B. and K. Larsen, *Butterflies of Oman,* Edinburgh, 1980.

ILLUSTRATION

Plate 3.12 Kiki Larsen, 140 × 130mm, ink drawing.

Plate 3.12 Butterfly **HYPOLIMNAS MISIPPUS** feeding on **EUPHORBIA** blossoms

2. See Wood, p.15 and Brockie, p.25.

3.3: INSECTS OF THE YEMEN TIHĀMAH: LEPIDOPTERA (MOTHS)

E. P. Wiltshire

Fifteen specimens of MACRO-HETEROCERA and two of PYRALIDAE, taken by Francine Stone in January and February 1982 with the Tihāmah Expedition, have been submitted to me for determination.

Previous material from the Arabian Tihāmah, collected by Middle East Anti-Locust Units in 1944-8 was listed in my 1952 article. The present material has to some extent added to our exact knowledge of the moth fauna of this region, about which my articles of 1981 and 1982 provide further details.

LIST

Family GEOMETRIDAE

HEMIDROMODES SABULIFERA TRIFORMA (Wiltshire)
Wādī Nāqah, 1 ♂, 12.ii.; Al-Ḍaḥī, 1 ♀, 24.i.
BRACHYGLOSSINA probably sp.n.
Wādī Nāqah, 1 ♀ (Prep. 2216), 12.ii.
SCOPULA OCHROLEUCARIA (H.-S.)
Zabīd, 1 ♀ (Prep. 2217), 16.i.
PSEUDOSTERRHA PAULLULA (Swinhoe)
Wādī Nāqah, 1 ♀, 12.ii.

Family SPHINGIDAE

HIPPOTION CELERIO (L.)
Al-Zuhrah, 1 ex., 28.i.

Family LYMANTRIIDAE

EUPROCTIS FASCIATA SUSANNA (Staudinger)
Al-Luḥayyah, 1 ♂, 1.ii.
CASAMA INNOTATA (Walker)
Wādī Nāqah, 1 ♂, 12.ii.

Family NOCTUIDAE

SELEPA DOCILIS (Butler)
Wādī Nāqah, 1 ♀, 12.ii.
AUCHENISA CERURODES (Hampson)
Wādī Nāqah, 1 ♂, 12.ii. Previously known only from Somalia.
BEIHANIA ANARTOIDES (Warnecke)
Wādī Nāqah, 2 ex., 12.ii. A south-west Arabian endemic.
ACROBYLA KNEUCKERI (Rebel)
Al-Ḍaḥī, 1 ♂, 24.i; Al-Luḥayyah, 1 ♀, 1.ii.
ANOBA TRIANGULARIS (Warnecke)
Wādī Nāqah, 1 ex., a south-west Arabian endemic.
RHYNCHINA ALBISCRIPTA (Hampson)
Wādī Nāqah, 2 exs., 12.ii.

BIBLIOGRAPHY

Wiltshire, E. P., "Lepidoptera recently taken in Arabia," *Bull, Fouad Ent. Soc.*, Vol. 36, 1952, pp. 135-174.

———, "Insects of Saudi Arabia: Lepidoptera," *Fauna of Saudi Arabia*, Pro Entomologia, Bale, Vol. 2, 1981 ("1980"), pp. 179-240.

———, idem, Vol. 4, 1982, pp. 461-527.

3.4: SMALL MAMMAL COLLECTION

Dr. David L. Harrison

The following small mammals were collected by Keith Brockie during the Tihāmah Expedition, January-February 1982, and delivered to the Harrison Zoological Museum where they were identified and registered as follows:

LIST

Registration no.	Provenance	Identification
HZM 3.12048	Al-Khawbah	DUGONG DUGON skull
HZM 26.12054	Al-Durayhimī	NYCTICEIUS (SCOTEINUS) SCHLIEFFENI
HZM 48.12053	Al-Manārah	TAPHOZOUS PERFORATUS
HZM 143.12051-144.12052	Great Mosque, Zabīd	ASELLIA TRIDENS
HZM 9.12056	Mocha	PROCAVIA CAPENSIS JAYAKARI (mandibles from raptor pellets)
HZM 10.12057	Wādī Zabīd	GERBILLUS POECILOPS
HZM 3.12058	Al-Luḥayyah	GERBILLUS FAMULUS
HZM 3.12059	Nukhlayah	GERBILLUS FAMULUS
HZM 135.12060	Al-Khawbah	GERBILLUS NANUS MIMULUS
HZM 156.12061	Ghulayfiqah	ACOMYS DIMIDIATUS

DISCUSSION

Mr. Brockie found a most interesting selection. The little NYCTICEIUS Bat is, in fact, a first for North Yemen. It is actually an Ethiopian-African species which extends into south-west Arabia, where it is well known from South Yemen, but never before taken in North Yemen. All the Gerbils, as well, are rare and rather little-known species of which we have no previous material from the Yemen. See D.H. Harrison and P.J.J. Bates, "New geographical records of the Large Aden Gerbil (GERBILLUS POECILOPS, Yerbury and Thomas, 1895, Rodentia: Cricetidae) with observations on the osteology of the species," *Mammalia*, Paris, 48(2), 1984. G. POECILOPS is a primitive Gerbil, confined to south-western Arabia. It has a scaly, thick and untufted tail, quite unlike the long tufted tail of G. FAMULUS (see Figure 3.13), and it also differs from all the other Gerbils of the region in having relatively short feet. Lastly, the Dugong skull is, of course, a splendid contribution to any collection, as it is an aquatic mammal primarily of the Indian and Australian Oceans, the habits of which are still little-known.

ILLUSTRATION

Plate 3.13 Brockie, 140 × 190mm ink drawing (based on sketchbook)

GLOSSARY

This is a working list to aid the naturalist who is making field observations on the Tihāmah. The names given are all used on the Tihāmah, and some may be purely Tihāmah usage. These are marked "(Tih.)" or "(Tih.?)" where the word collected was unverifiable by secondary sources, or where it may well be used in other parts of the Yemen. [Ed.]

abū khaṭṭayn	snake, PSAMMOPHIS SCHOKARI
abū qardān	egret
'aqrab	scorpion, pronounced *'agrab*
a'raj	hyena, pronounced *awrag*
arnab	hare
babaghā'	parrot, any exotic bird such as flamingo
buṭan	whale
ḍab'	hyena
daqīl	dolphin (Tih.?)
dharr	ant(s)
farāshah	butterfly
farāshat al-layl	moth
ghazāl	gazelle
hamām	dove
ḥās	stinging gnat (Tih., Wādī Mawr)
jumbarī	shrimp, pronounced *gumbarī*
khārab	vulture
khufāsh	bat
laḥwum	Arabian bustard (the meat is considered delicious) (Tih.)
mujarib	pelican (Tih.?)
nash	ant (Tih., Wādī Mawr)
nasr	hawk or eagle, any bird of prey
nimr	leopard
qarsh	shark, pronounced *garsh*
qaṣub	baboon (Tih.?), pronounced *gaṣub*
qubqab	shrimp, pronounced *gubgab*
qunfudh	porcupine, pronounced *gunfudh*
ṣaqr	hawk
shuḥah	black kite
shukāri	snake, PSAMMOPHIS SCHOKARI The species name derives from Forsskal's work 1775 (Tih.?)
ṭayr al-baḥr	any wader bird
'uṣfūr	any small bird
wabr	rock hyrax (eaten for potency)
warrār	lizard (var. of *waral*?)
zukr	sea turtle (Tih.?)

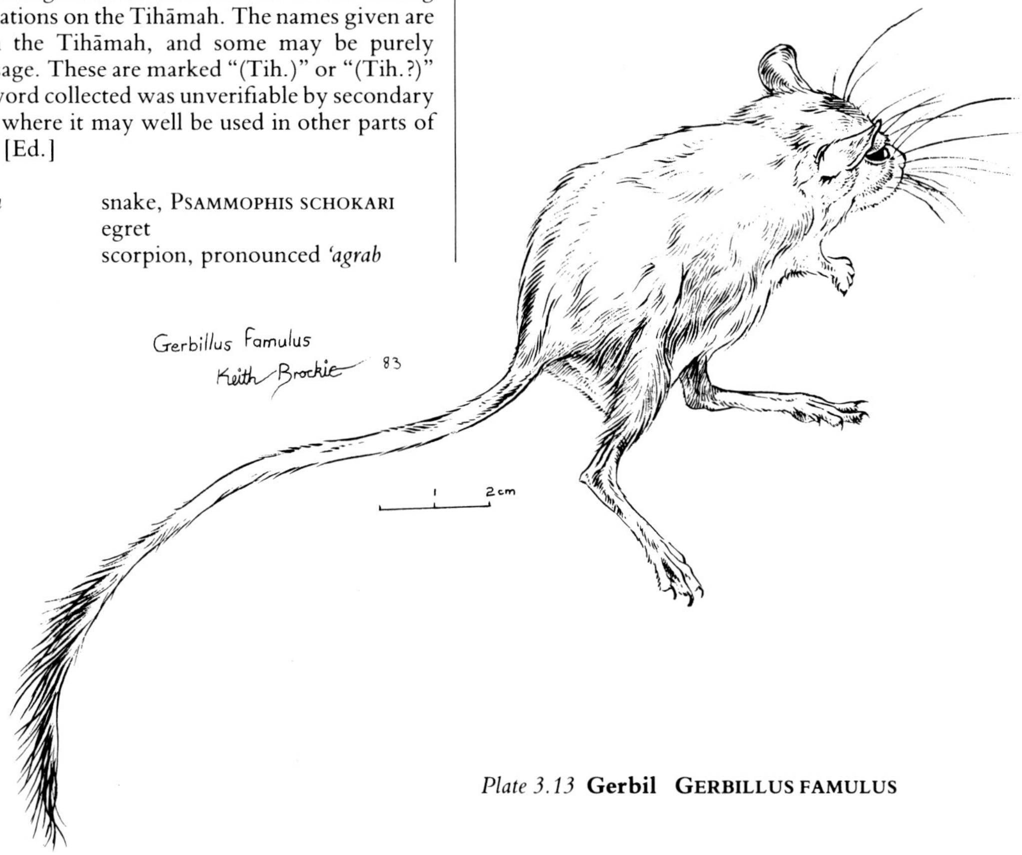

Plate 3.13 **Gerbil** **GERBILLUS FAMULUS**

HISTORY

4.1: DAWN IN THE TIHĀMAH: THE PRE-ISLAMIC PERIOD

Dr. Selma Al-Radi

In the southern part of the Arabian Peninsula, a thousand years and more before the rise of Islam, city states and kingdoms, Saba, Ma'in, Qataban, Ḥaḍramawt, Ḥimyar, rose and spread their influence.

It is well known that the wealth of these kingdoms of Arabia Felix was based on agriculture and trade. But the details are unknown: the size of the area under cultivation, the annual yield; the volume of goods exchanged and of the items traded. That incense and luxury goods, locally produced or imported from India and Africa, formed the pre-eminent part of this trade is an accepted fact. The bulk of the trade must have been agricultural produce, sorghum, wheat, salt, honey and other prosaic goods; however, this aspect has not been sufficiently studied, perhaps because it is not romantic enough.

The major trade routes were north-south, along the flat on the eastern side of the mountain range which forms the spine of Arabia, and through the centre of the highlands. The east-west route, over the mountains and down to the coastal plain of the Tihāmah is less well-known, since very little research has been done on the Tihāmah of pre-Islamic times. It is proven that the trade routes between Saba, the Anglicised Sheba, and Ḥabashat, now Ethiopia, were already established by the middle of the first millennium B.C.; the trade continues to this day.[1]

If one accepts the hypothesis that trade in ancient times followed the main courses of the *wādīs*, then there would have been way-stations, posts and villages where the traders and their animals could rest and shelter. There would also be ports to receive and discharge goods to sea. We can therefore expect to find sites along the major *wādīs* that offer ready access into the mountains, e.g. Wādīs Mawr, Surdud, Sihām and Zabīd. However, with the exceptions of al-Hāmid near Bājil,[2] an unnamed site near Zabīd[3] and a tentatively early site identified near Ghulayfiqah[4] (site sherded by the author 1983, where some plain and incised wares that look pre-Islamic and some Sassanian "hib" ware were found), no other pre-Islamic sites are yet known in the Tihāmah.[5]

Classical authors[6] writing between 300 B.C. and 300 A.D. make mention of places on the Arabian Red Sea which were linked up to the trade network between the Mediterranean and the Indian Ocean. *The Periplus of the Erythraean Sea*, a maritime document by an unknown author, gives a most detailed picture of the ports which served the Red Sea trade at the end of the first century A.D., or possibly a century later, the dating of *The Periplus* being problematic.

The Periplus describes a port called Musa, a reference which is assumed to correspond to an unidentified site in the Mawza'-Mocha area of the southern Tihāmah.[7] This entrepot was governed from afar by a vassal of the Ḥimyar kingdom seated in the highlands of Yemen, but it seems to have enjoyed a measure of autonomy by which it subscribed to the "international" trade regulations of the day. Spears, axes, small swords, awls and several kinds of glassware were manufactured in Musa. It was also responsible for the export of selected myrrh (stakte) and white marble were local products, we are told. Products mentioned by earlier writers – arabic perfume, Sambracene myrrh, incense and cinnamon – complete the picture of luxury goods which came from or passed through the Tihāmah in Classical times.

Apart from peaceful movements of people generated by trade, we know there were invasions. One was brief, circa A.D. 300; the second, circa A.D. 520, lasted for over fifty years during which the invading Ethiopian army occupied and caused a great deal of havoc in the highlands.[8] What was havoc in the highlands must have been disaster for the Tihāmah. Agriculture and attendant activities would have been interrupted, and the fruits of the harvest stolen by the invaders. The tantalising prize of this fertile plain with abundant ground water near shore as well as in the foothills must have drawn both the Ethiopians and the highlanders in pre-Islamic times, much as it was later conquered and raided in Islamic times and then taxed for all it was worth and more.[9]

Our present knowledge of the Tihāmah plain in pre-Islamic times is sketchy, to say the least; we hope this ignorance will fade as more information is gathered by research and fieldwork.

1. Inscriptions from al-Hāmid (Jamme, 1981) support this. See Al-Radi, p. 53 et infra.
2. See Al-Radi, p. 51.
3. E.J. Keall, 1983.
4. See Wilson, p. 35.
5. Although not strictly the Tihāmah, Farasān Island should be mentioned, where a collection of sites bearing pre-Islamic inscriptions have been surveyed but not published by B. Rihani and W. Facey for the Saudi Arabian Department of Antiquities 1978. We are grateful to W. Facey for bringing these sites to our attention. In addition, a pre-Islamic site in Wādī Rasyān was reported to the National Museum, Ṣan'ā', but it has not been officially confirmed. See also p.130, n.142 [Ed.]
6. Theophrastus 372-287 B.C., Eratosthenes 273-192 B.C., Strabo d. 25 A.D., Pliny d. 79 A.D., [Ed.]
7. The actual whereabouts of this site, although much conjectured, are not known. An inscription block (Ry598) measuring 80cm long × 24cm high with letters of the same height was sighted by Condé in 1959 (see *Le Muséon*, LXXII, 1960) and Dr. Gus Van Beek in 1964 in a well just outside of Mocha. We are grateful to Dr. Van Beek for letting us see his photographs and notes on this block. [Ed.]
8. See *The Cambridge History of Islam*, Vol. IA, pp. 14-15.
9. See Wilson, p. 35, Baldry, p. 46, et passim.

BIBLIOGRAPHY

The Cambridge History of Islam, Vol. IA, Cambridge, 1977.
Jamme, Albert, "Pre-Islamic Arabian Miscellanea," *Al-Hudhud: Festschrift Maria Höfner zum 80 Geburtstag,* ed. R.G. Steigner, Graz, 1981.
Keall, E.J., "The Dynamics of Zabid and its Hinterland: the survey of a town on the Tihamah plain of North Yemen," *World Archeology,* Vol. 14, No. 3, 1983.
________, "Zabid and its Hinterland: 1982 report," *Proceedings of the Seminar for Arabian Studies,* 13.
The Periplus of the Erythraean Sea, trans. and ed., G.W.B. Huntingford, Hakluyt Society, London, 1980.
____________________, trans., W.H. Schoff, New York, 1912.

FURTHER READING

Baldry, John, "Textiles in Yemen: Historical references to trade and commerce in textiles in Yemen from antiquity to modern times," *British Museum Occasional Paper No. 27,* 1982.
Al-Hāmdanī, al-Ḥasan ibn Aḥmad, *Ṣifat Jazīrat al-'Arab,* ed. D.H. Müller, Leiden, 1884-91.
Pirenne, Jacqueline, *Le Royaume Sud-Arabe de Qataban et sa Datation,* Louvain, 1961.
Trimingham, J.S., *Islam in Ethiopia,* Oxford, 1952.

4.2: THE TIHĀMAH FROM THE BEGINNING OF THE ISLAMIC PERIOD TO 1800

R.T.O. Wilson

During the Islamic period the Tihāmah has enjoyed both order and prosperity and suffered disorder, neglect and poverty. The decline of the Abbasid caliphate at the centre of the Islamic empire led in Yemen to the emergence of a succession of local dynasties, some in the Tihāmah itself, and others, concerned to maintain its prosperity. For a period of several centuries this coastal strip flourished with such abundance that it is difficult to imagine how it might have become the dry, patchily cultivated region that it is today. But these dynasties – the Ziyādids and the Najāḥids of Zabīd, succeeded by the Rasūlids and the Ṭāhirids – were followed by the arrival of the Mamluks and shortly thereafter the Ottomans. The Tihāmah dwindled: its towns fell prey to tribal attack, or to misrule by the agents and governors appointed by the Ottomans or the Yemeni Imāms. Only recently has its recovery begun.

THE EARLY ISLAMIC PERIOD: 622-819 A.D.

The tribes of the Tihāmah appear to have adopted Islam at an early date, along with the rest of Yemen, shortly after the *hijrah* or emigration of the Prophet Muḥammad from Mecca to Medina in 622. Until the early second century of the *hijrah* we learn little of the Tihāmah and cannot say with certainty how effectively it was governed during the periods of the Orthodox Caliphs (632-661), the Umayyads (661-750) and the early Abbasids (750-). We do know, however, that an attempt by the tribal group of 'Akk (which occupied the central Tihāmah, from Wādī Rima' to Wādī Mawr) to secede on the death of the Prophet was put down promptly by a general of Abu Bakr, first of the Orthodox Caliphs.

THE ZIYĀDIDS: 819-1011 A.D.

As centralised Abbasid rule began to decline towards the end of the second century after the *hijrah* there was a second revolt by the tribes of the Tihāmah, and then a third, this time by the 'Akk and their neighbours to the south, the Ashā'ir. This rising, in about 819, led the Abbasid Caliph al-Ma'mūn to appoint to the Tihāmah one Muḥammad ibn 'Abdullāh ibn Ziyād as governor. It is he who is said to have laid out and constructed the town of Zabīd beginning in 820, and he was the first of a dynasty which ruled the Tihāmah for two centuries. Before long Ibn Ziyād seems to have been given – or taken over – the responsibility for the governorship of the whole of Yemen on behalf of the Abbasids. In practice, he made himself independent of them, keeping only the reading of the *khuṭbah* (sermon) in the name of the Abbasids in order to legitimise his authority. It is claimed that he ruled the whole of Yemen, but, while it is possible that the *khuṭbah* was read out in the name of the Abbasids and the Ziyādids in Ṣan'ā', Ṣa'dah, Najrān and Bayḥān as the texts aver, it is unlikely that he actually exercised any effective rule beyond the Tihāmah and its immediate hinterland.

Most of the territory claimed by the Ziyādids fell out of their hands under Ibn Ziyād's immediate successors. During the time of the ineffectual Abu'l-Jaysh, the Ismā'īlī propagandist 'Alī ibn al-Faḍl attacked and plundered Zabīd; and it was during the same unhappy reign that in 903 Sulaymān ibn Ṭaraf, lord of the 'Asīr Tihāmah, asserted his independence from the Ziyādids. His district, which continued to bear his name after his death, was never effectively reincorporated into Yemen or the Yemeni Tihāmah. The Ziyādid dynasty was left in an even more precarious position when Abu'l-Jaysh died in 1001 leaving only an infant son to succeed him.

The reins of the Ziyādid dominion were taken over by a *wazīr* (minister), al-Ḥusayn ibn Salāmah, a Nubian slave. He made war on the areas which had fallen from Ziyādid control, and succeeded in recovering a good part. A wise and active regent, he obtained the confidence of his people and undertook a large number of construction works. He laid out the towns of al-Kadrā'[1] (on Wādī Sihām) and al-Mu'qar; and along the major routes, from Ḥaḍramawt to Mecca, he had wells dug, milestones set up and mosques constructed at each staging point ('Umārah, writing in the mid twelfth century).

1. See Al-Radi, p. 53.

THE NAJĀḤIDS: 1012-1160 A.D.

After the death of Ibn Salāmah in 1011 the Ziyādid house found itself once again with an infant successor, and power fell into the hands of Najāḥ, an Ethiopian slave[2] of the Ziyādids, in 1021, after a power struggle with his brother. Najāḥ was confirmed in his position by the Abbasid Caliph and ruled for some forty years until he was poisoned in 1060 at al-Kadrā' by the Ismā'īlī Ṣulayḥids who had taken control of much of the highlands. The Tihāmah itself became a province of the Ṣulayḥids for some years, governed by As'ad ibn Shihāb, brother-in-law of the Ṣulayḥid ruler. From the Tihāmah, it is said, he was able to send to Ṣan'ā' each year the sum of one million dinars. A similar sum is said by 'Umārah to have been raised by the Ziyādids in 977, presumably from agriculture, palms and local trade, since this sum excluded the taxes on precious woods, musk, camphor etc. brought by ship from India, or tax imposed on the ruler of the Red Sea island of Dahlak.

In 1080 Sa'īd al-Ahwal, a son of Najāḥ, attacked and killed the Ṣulayḥid ruler, 'Alī ibn Muḥammad, at al-Mahjam in the northern Tihāmah as he was on his way to make the pilgrimage to Mecca. Sa'īd put to death as many of the Ṣulayḥid family as he was able, and 'Alī's wife, Asmā', was taken as a captive to Zabīd. This renewal of Najāḥid control lasted only a short time. The Ṣulayḥid successor and son of Asmā', al-Mukarram, organised an expedition against Zabīd to release his mother. The Ṣulayḥids were successful and al-Ahwal fled to the coast on fast horses. From there he set sail in a boat which he had ready and waiting to the island of Dahlak.

Control of the Tihāmah passed regularly between the Ṣulayḥids and al-Ahwal for some time, the Ṣulayḥids taxing the Tihāmah in the cool winter, the Najāḥids in the summer. Al-Ahwal was eventually killed in a trap set up by the Ṣulayḥids in 1088, and the Ṣulayḥids once again took control of the coastal region. Al-Ahwal's brother Jayyāsh fled to India. After a short time he returned to Zabīd disguised as an Indian, and was able to muster a force to drive out the Ṣulayḥids once again. He ruled in Zabīd from 1090 until 1104. Some time later, after the deaths of Jayyāsh and his successor, a succession dispute broke out within the Najāḥid house which marked the beginning of the decline of their dynasty. Only nominal power remained with the family, and real control was taken over by a succession of Ethiopian slaves[3] who acted as ministers, the last and most notable of whom was Surūr al-Fātikī.[4]

Al-Fātikī was murdered in 1156 at the instigation of one 'Alī ibn Mahdī al-Ḥimyarī who had built up a following in one of the mountain districts overlooking the Tihāmah. Shortly afterwards, Zabīd fell to Ibn Mahdī, and he and his son 'Abd al-Nabī ruled the Yemeni Tihāmah for fifteen years. Their power extended also over a very considerable part of highland Yemen, including the town of Ta'izz. In the northern Tihāmah 'Abd al-Nabī was able in 1165 to rout the Banū Sulaymān who ruled that area from Ḥaraḍ.

THE AYYŪBIDS: 1173-1229 A.D.

Not many years later the Ayyūbids, who ruled in Egypt from 1169 to 1250, arrived to make Yemen a province of their empire. They rapidly gained control of the whole of Yemen, and governors were appointed to the main towns. They were energetic builders, and in their time Zabīd was rewalled, and schools and mosques were constructed. They were firm and competent administrators, although their attempt to appropriate all land to the *dīwān* (administration) and then rent it out to those who wished to farm it was a complete failure. Finally, however, the orderly administration of the province fell prey to conflict within the Ayyūbid house and competition between governors in Yemen. They entrusted control of the Yemen to al-Manṣūr 'Umar ibn 'Alī ibn Rasūl, whose family was to rule for more than two centuries, from 1229-1454.

THE RASŪLIDS: 1229-1454 A.D.

The Rasūlid dynasty was not a native Yemeni one, although their actual origins are obscure. They may have been Arabs who had become assimilated to a Turkoman tribe; alternatively they were of pure Turkoman stock, with a genealogy fabricated to show Arab ancestry. They succeeded in gaining control of most of Yemen, from Ḥaḍramawt to Mecca, and recovered its independence from Egypt. They built up a strong administrative network, capturing, constructing and repairing forts to this end. Their capital was Ta'izz, but the Tihāmah was an important part of their realm. The number of mosques and schools which they built and maintained with allocations of *waqf* (religious endowment) funds was impressive. Not all of these were in already established settlements. A village grew up around the mosque of al-Nūrī, situated between Zabīd and Ḥays, established by the first of the Rasulid line. His successor al-Muẓaffar (1250-1295) is said to have been the most prolific builder of the Rasūlid dynasty.

In the Tihāmah the Rasulids extended firm control to the north from the town of al-Mahjam, where al-Muẓaffar constructed the great mosque whose minaret remains to the present day.[5] (See Plate 4.1.) Taxation was regulated and, in the Tihāmah, a detailed count of palm trees was made by al-Muẓaffar's successor, al-Ashraf, in order to prevent excessive imposition, a tradition continued by later Rasūlids.

The rule of the fifth Rasūlid sultan, al-Mujāhid, was contested by relatives and by *mamlūk* (slave) troops of his predecessors, obliging him to carry out a number of campaigns to put down opposition. By about 1330 he had consolidated his power; but in 1343 a son of his who held the fief of the northern Tihāmah port of al-Luḥayyah rebelled and took the northern capital of the Tihāmah, al-Mahjam. Once again the rebellion had to be put down. The son was captured and died soon afterwards in prison (Ibn al-Dayba', writing in the early sixteenth century).

At the time of al-Mujāhid's death in 1363 the Rasūlid dominion was crumbling at its fringes. Al-Muẓaffar, another son of al-Mujāhid, rebelled in the

2. 'Umārah states that the kings of the Najaḥid dynasty belonged to an Abyssinian tribe named Jazali. Kay, *Yaman Its Early Medieval History,* p. 96. [Ed.]
3. 'Umārah says that Mufliḥ (*wazīr* to Fātik son of Manṣūr son of Fātik son of Jayyāsh) belonged to an Abyssinian tribe known by the name of Saḥrat. Kay, ibid., p. 104. [Ed.]
4. Of the Abyssinian tribe of Amḥarah, again according to 'Umārah. Kay, ibid., p. 117. [Ed.]
5. Detailed architectural drawings of the minaret were made in 1982 under the direction of Dr. Ed Keall, Royal Ontario Museum. [Ed.]

Plate 4.1 **Minaret, al-Manārah**, the ruins of al-Muẓaffar Mosque, al-Mahjam, near the present-day village of al-Manārah

south shortly before the latter's death, while a military commander, Muḥammad ibn Mīkā'īl, had taken control of al-Mahjam and all of the northern Tihāmah to as far north as Ḥaraḍ. This revolt was put down by a force sent by al-Mujāhid's successor, al-Afḍal, in a great battle at al-Qaḥmah in 1364. A second rebellion in the Tihāmah, once again initiated by Ibn Mīkā'īl (who had the support of certain of the highland Zaydīs) took place six years later. This spread to Zabīd, but once again Rasūlid forces were able to reimpose their authority in the Tihāmah, after a battle at Wādī Surdud in 1371 in which Ibn Mīkā'īl was defeated.

Despite the assistance given to Ibn Mīkā'īl by some of the Zaydī *ashrāf* (sherifs), Zaydī interests in the Tihāmah were limited (if not non-existent) with the exception of two campaigns. The first was during the time of al-Afḍal and was carried out by the Imām Ṣalāḥ al-Dīn ibn 'Alī in 1375, but his short, three-day siege of Zabīd was abandoned. His son 'Alī led a month-long siege of Zabīd during the time of al-Ashraf (1377-1400).

It would seem that the Tihāmah had suffered some neglect, for al-Ashraf undertook the repair and reconstruction of a number of mosques and schools in Zabīd. The interest shown by al-Ashraf in the Tihāmah was maintained by al-Nāṣir who followed him (1400-1424) and enlarged the area of Rasūlid authority once again, extending it in the Tihāmah as far north as Ḥaly, energetically putting down localised revolts, including two – in Zabīd and then Ta'izz – led by his brother Ḥusayn. Al-Nāṣir's reign also saw the beginning of a long series of risings among the various tribes of the Tihāmah, notable among them the Ma'āzibah and the Ashā'ir, and later the Qurashīyūn and the Zaydīyah, a *sunnī* (a branch of Islam) tribe associated with the area around what is now the town of al-Zaydīyah. Al-Nāṣir's immediate successors were short lived and ineffectual, and al-Ṭāhir (some texts read al-Ẓāhir), although he reigned for about ten years (from 1428 to 1439), faced constant tribal uprisings in the Tihāmah. In one of these the Qurashīyūn destroyed the town of Fashāl, near the present-day Bayt al-Faqīh.

THE ṬĀHIRIDS: 1454-1526 A.D.

The Rasūlid state did not long survive al-Ṭahir, and a continuation of tribal disorder together with a series of clashes between rival members of the Rasūlid house paved the way for the emergence of the Ṭāhirids (1454-1526). The home territory of the Ṭāhirids was in Laḥj and in the south-eastern part of what is now the Yemen Arab Republic. Although they were able to consolidate their rule over most of the former Rasūlid realm, and indeed extended it some distance to the east, to Ẓafār on the Indian Ocean, the Tihāmah was far from quiet. Ibn al-Dayba' tells of constant battles with the Arab tribes of the Tihāmah and of battles between those tribes. All the same, the Ṭāhirids appear to have been able to assert effective if intermittent authority in the northern Tihāmah and to collect tax there as from the tribal territories of the Zaydīyah and the Wā'iẓāt.

The reign of al-Ẓāfir 'Āmir (1489-1517), the fourth Ṭāhirid sultan, witnessed the arrival of a completely new element in the power balance of the region – the Portuguese. Having discovered the sea routes to the east around the southern tip of Africa, the Portuguese sought to take control of the trade routes to the far east and divert them from the Red Sea and the lands along its coasts. The last rulers of Mamluk Egypt (1250-1517) attempted with the aid of the Ottoman Turks to make the Red Sea secure. The Ṭāhirids withheld their assistance from the Mamluks, who attacked Zabīd with the support and encouragement of both the Zaydī Imāms of the highlands and the Sulaymānī ruler of the northern Tihāmah. The Mamluks had a rapid success as the Yemenis fled before the Mamluk firearms, the first to be used in Yemen.

THE MAMLUKS, OTTOMANS AND LOCAL RULE: 1517 A.D.–

The Mamluks took control of Zabīd and the coast; but soon, in 1517, news arrived that Egypt had fallen to the Ottomans. The Mamluks stranded in Yemen concentrated themselves in Zabīd and offered their allegiance to the Ottomans. It was another twenty years, however, before the Ottomans themselves arrived to take control of Yemen.

Not much is learned of the Tihāmah from the Yemeni histories for the next century and a half. The Ottomans succeeded in gaining control of the greater part of Yemen but were stopped and almost completely driven out by al-Muṭahhar, son of the Imām Sharaf al-Dīn. A renewed campaign by the Ottomans once again gave them mastery of the country, but they were driven back a second time, this time by the Imām al-Qāsim and his successors who finally expelled the Ottomans from Zabīd, their last foothold in Yemen, in 1635.

Yemen was left in the hands of the Zaydī *imāms* who appointed governors to look after the main centres and ports of the Tihāmah. The Zaydī imamate rapidly collapsed into disorder as the Qāsimī house was faced by revolt outside and dissension within the family. The Tihāmah was well into its decline by the time that the Danish expedition which produced the first detailed European description of Yemen reached the country in 1762. An important part of the expedition's report, written by Carsten Niebuhr, the only one to return to Denmark, concerns the Tihāmah. They travelled the length of the Yemeni Tihāmah from al-Luḥayyah to al-Mukhā' (Mocha) and were able to describe every aspect of Tihāmah life. It was evident to the members of the expedition, both from what they observed and from what they heard that the heyday of the Tihāmah had passed.

LIFE IN THE TIHĀMAH

It is unlikely that life in the Tihāmah, even in its most prosperous times, was very much different from what it was when the Danish expedition arrived, or even a few years ago. Settlements and cultivation, watering places and hence market sites were concentrated (as now) on the *wādī* courses between the mountains and the sea. Although the *wādīs* do not flow continuously the year round, fresh water is often not far below the surface, allowing cultivation in some places to within a few feet of the sea. However, it is clear that at its peak agriculture in the Tihāmah was more efficient and more extensive[6] than in recent times. Several authors comment on the variety of fruits and crops grown along the Tihāmah *wādīs*. Ibn al-Dayba' lists many, including grapes, pomegranates, figs, coconuts, palms, bananas, citrus fruits and jasmine. Ibn al-Mujāwir, writing in the mid thirteenth century, commented on the bananas and pomegranates of al-Qaḥmah and on the cultivation of Fashāl where, he says, there were about 800 villages, whose people cultivated millet and sorghum using only rainfall irrigation. In Ḥays and no doubt elsewhere there were oil presses. They are mentioned by 'Umārah and later writers, but it is not stated which plant the oil was obtained from. Today sesame is the principal oil crop.[7]

The cultivation of date palms was of especial importance, and Ibn al-Mujāwir describes the feasting and celebration associated with the harvest. People would come to Zabīd from the mountains, and from as far afield as Ḥaraḍ and Aden and stay there, according to Ibn al-Mujāwir, for two or three months of drinking and celebrating.

The population of the Tihāmah consisted of the townsfolk and the *'Arab,* the tribes who were said to have recurrently raided, robbed and fired the larger settlements of the Tihāmah.[8] The town populations were a mix which reflected the close links of the Tihāmah with East Africa, its trading connections with India, and the practice of most of the dynasties which controlled the Tihāmah of importing slave troops either from Africa or from the north. *Wazīrs,* or ministers, of the Ziyādid and Najāḥid periods included Ethiopians of various tribes; Ḥusayn ibn Salāmah, the Ziyādid *wazīr* was a Nubian. Turkish Oghuz *mamlūk* soldiers are mentioned, as well as Armenians. And, by the time that the Danish expedition reached Yemen, the trading towns – chiefly Bayt al-Faqīh and al-Mukhā' – must have had a distinctly cosmopolitan air, with communities of foreign merchants attracted from the Ḥijāz, Egypt, Syria, Turkey, Morocco, Ethiopia, Persia, India and Europe. The *'Arab* who lived outside the towns were in all probability not very much different from the present inhabitants of village Tihāmah, a mix of Arab and African[9] of long standing.

The most important town of the Tihāmah was Zabīd its capital, a cultural focus and centre of learning famous throughout the Arab world of the Middle Ages. A count made during the reign of the Rasūlid monarch al-Ashraf in 1391 showed about 230 mosques and schools in the town. Niebuhr and his companions some three and a half centuries later were impressed by the number of mosques and domes which, when they arrived, had been painted white for *Ramaḍān* (the month of fasting). Zabīd's special role allowed it to survive the long "dark age" of the Tihāmah more successfully than any other place. In general, the Tihāmah settlements had little intrinsic permanence, consisting of African-style huts constructed of palm and other vegetable matter;[10] and even Zabīd itself had few permanent dwellings. The lasting structures, some built of burnt brick,[11] were the mosques, schools and public buildings, and these were liable to alarmingly rapid decay, to judge from the frequent accounts of reconstruction and restoration. The narrowly clustered huts were at constant risk of fire and other natural hazards such as earth tremors,[12] and Zabīd suffered many horrifying conflagrations; so much

6. For the encroachment of sand on arable land, both past and present, see El-Domi, p. 10 and Forbes, p. 11
7. See Stone, p. 131.
8. *'Arab* here is most probably a social rather than a racial term indicating the mobile raiders as opposed to the townsfolk.
9. These African elements derive, in large part, from importations of slaves across the Red Sea. The tribes of origin are uncertain (often given as Danakil). G. Percival-Kaye, writing as recently as 1955, reported that slaves were then being obtained "from Shanakallas on the western border of Abyssinia. The Galla tribes... in the Ogaden desert supply considerable quantities. Aussa too... of the Inner Danakila, along with Warsangli and the Outer Dankila." He also mentions Guaratchi, presumably Gurагé, and Dinka and Bari-speaking Sudanese being brought across the straits of the Bab al-Mandeb for trade to Arabia. Percival-Kaye, "The Red Sea Slave Trade," *The Anti-Slavery Reporter,* Vol. 10, series VI (1955), pp. 49-52. [Ed.]
10. See Ehrlich, p. 64 et infra.
11. Specific mention being made of those at al-Kadrā' (Ibn al-Mujāwir).
12. The Expedition made note of daily tremors in Zabīd between from January 11 to January 18 (with the exception of 17 January) 1982. [Ed.]

so that the Ṭāhirid ruler al-Mujāhid imposed a ban on the use of inflammable materials for construction in 1468. This ban lasted only three years, however.

The lack of permanence helps partly to explain why a number of major settlements, once famous and prosperous, came to be replaced by others. Of note were towns such as al-Mahjam on Wādī Surdud, al-Kadrā' on Wādī Sihām, and al-Qaḥmah, perhaps not far from the present-day al-Manṣūrīyah;[13] and important villages such as Fashāl, slightly north of Bayt al-Faqīh which although founded in the mid-thirteenth century[14] was not developed until later. Of such towns we learn little in the histories beyond finding reference to battles in or around them, or incidental mention where people passed through on their way elsewhere. Sometimes they are recorded as being given in fief to ministers or sons of rulers. Apart from Zabīd, only al-Mahjam is mentioned in the histories with any great frequency, because it was in essence a northern capital for the Tihāmah, a twin of Zabīd. It probably enjoyed its highest point during the period of the Rasūlids, who also used it as a base for governing the mountain districts bordering the northern Tihāmah; but its only monument of note seems to have been the mosque of al-Muẓaffar, described as having 360 columns *(sāriyah)* and decorated with the entire text of the *Qur'ān* on the walls and columns. However, it was already in ruins by the mid-seventeenth century (Ibn al-Ḥusayn, writing in the mid-seventeenth century). Many of the settlements mentioned above never recovered from the uprisings of the Tihāmah tribes in the mid-fifteenth century.

While the history of the towns other than Zabīd is obscure, the history of the tribes outside those towns is even more so. Al-Hamdānī, the Yemeni scholar writing in the early tenth century described the tribal structure of the Tihāmah. The principal tribes were the Ashā'ir in the region of Zabīd and southwards, with 'Akk to the north of them in the district between Wādī Rima' and Wādī Mawr; and north of them lived the Ḥakam. With the passing of time different tribe names came to the fore. A section of the 'Akk, the Ma'āzibah, emerged as one of the main tribes of *'Arab* whose depredations caused such disruption to the Tihāmah from the late Rasūlid period; but by the time of the second Ottoman occupation in the nineteenth century it was the tribe known as the Zarānīq – supposedly named after a branch of the Ma'āzibah – which played a leading part in tribal resistance. Other important tribal names are those of the Wā'iẓāt, in the northern part of the Yemeni Tihāmah; al-Zaydīyah, concentrated around the present-day town of that name, between al-Ḥudaydah (Hodeida) and al-Zuhrah; and the Qurashīyūn, close to Zabīd. These tribes were confederations of smaller tribes, as they are today. They were settled cultivators for the most part, but were able, especially from the end of the Rasūlid period, to mobilise with horses and cause widespread disorder in the Tihāmah. Whether there were ever true *badw* (bedouin) in any numbers between the settled areas associated with the *wādīs* is uncertain. Ibn al-Mujāwir notes that the inhabitants of one village were said to have once been tent dwellers, but he does not indicate whether this was common or not.[15]

It is probable that the tribes did not benefit greatly or directly from the order imposed upon them from the Tihāmah towns and that they submitted to taxation unwillingly under force or threat of force. The series of rebellions which took place as the Rasūlid grip began to weaken may have been a reaction to the relatively efficient and sometimes harsh impositions of Rasūlid rule and a manifestation of the tribal resistance to centralised authority.

TRADE

Commerce was an important part of life in the Tihāmah. Trade routes passed up and down it – one close to the sea, and the other inland, linking the main towns. These towns as well as regular markets not attached to major settlements attracted trade from the mountains fringing the Tihāmah. The scale of such internal commerce is hinted at by the northern Tihāmah market of al-Jurayb. This market, stated al-Hamdānī in the tenth century, attracted an estimated 10,000 people each market day.

The ports linked the Tihāmah with neighbouring Red Sea countries, and to a degree with countries as remote as India and China (although most Yemeni trade with these remote lands was probably through Aden). Contacts with Ethiopia and the East African coast were especially close. Zabīd appears to have had a succession of ports, although the information about these is confusing and sometimes contradictory. Ghulāfiqah (var. Ghulayfiqah)[16] was the port most generally associated with Zabīd, although it is almost thirty kilometres north of the closest point on the coastline to Zabīd. Perhaps because it was so far away,[17] a site nearer Zabīd was sought, and the port of al-Ahwāb was developed at the closest point of the shoreline. Ibn al-Mujāwir attributes its founding to a Persian on his way to perform the pilgrimage in 1138. It was provided with markets, a mosque and shops. Teak *(sāj)* wood was brought for the mosque from India, but Ibn Mahdī destroyed the mosque in 1160 to carry the wood away for reuse in Zabīd. The site was probably not ideal for a port, and Ibn al-Mujāwir notes the request of a man from Zayla' to have his taxes set aside for ten years so that he could construct a breakwater of rocks and earth. Al-Ahwāb came later on to be known as al-Buq'ah. A new anchorage was constructed at the orders of the Rasūlid al-Nāṣir in 1419 at al-Fāzzah,[18] slightly to the north of al-Buq'ah.

---

13. See Al-Radi, p. 54.
14. See Muḥammad al-Akwa' al-Ḥiwālī, *Al-Yaman al-khaḍrā' mahd al-ḥaḍārah,* Cairo, 1971, p. 89.
15. For a discussion of present-day, migrant harvesters *(makhāḍirah),* see Mitchell-Escher-Mundy, "A Baseline Socio-Economic Survey of the Wadi Mawr Region," pp. 196-201. The Expedition observed these people living under reed-mat tents on the fringes of Wādī Mawr, and again one family moving southward near al-Munīrah, their belongings loaded on a camel. Prof. R.B. Serjeant discusses the *makhāḍirah* and their possible mention in a Rasūlid fiscal survey (1411-12) in *Studies in Arabian History and Civilisation,* London, 1981, IX, pp.234-5. [Ed.]
16. The site of Ghulayfiqah, yielding shards from the 9-10th centuries, was located by the Expedition, January 1982, and subsequently surveyed by Dr. Ed Keall (*Proceedings of the Seminar for Arabian Studies,* 1983). See also Al-Radi, p. 30 for possible pre-Islamic remains at Ghulayfiqah. Prof. S.D. Goitein has very kindly drawn our attention to four passages from the Cairo Geniza texts which mention Zabīd and its port, Ghulayfiqah, in the thirties and the forties of the twelfth century. These are to be found in the Taylor-Schechter Collection, University Library, Cambridge, England, and are: TS 20.130, 11. 42-47 (1133); TS 12,235, verso, 1. 1; TS 8.19, 11. 1-5; and MS University Library Cambridge Or 1080J 171, top of the page, 11. 6-9. [Ed.]
17. The process of silting-up was also apparently a factor in its disuse, and indeed this has been a common reason for the relocation of several Tihāmah ports. [Ed.]
18. See Keall, op.cit. [Ed.]

The northern Tihāmah was served by al-Luḥayyah, apparently founded by Aḥmad ibn 'Alī al-Zayla'ī in 1402.[19] There may also have been an older, but minor, port at al-Ḥirdah opposite al-Mahjam. Little is known of it, however. Al-Mukhā', associated in particular with the coffee trade to Europe, was the chief port of the southern Tihāmah, and it also served Ta'izz. The main port of the present day, al-Ḥudaydah, was developed relatively late, perhaps from the beginning of the seventeenth century.

A great number and variety of commodities were traded through these ports, some produced or for use in Yemen, others in transit westwards and eastwards. Fruit, cloth, dyes, spices, glass, pottery and china changed hands there; one early fifteenth century document provides a detailed customs classification containing hundreds of items. Even though the Tihāmah had passed its golden age when Europeans first reached the waters of the Red Sea, a considerable trade still passed through al-Mukhā'. The Dutchman Pieter van den Broecke described a caravan which arrived there in 1616 consisting of 1,000 camels loaded with goods from Hungary, Venice and different Muslim countries. The British and Dutch set up factories at al-Mukhā' in the seventeenth century, and with the development of the coffee trade – which made the name of Mocha familiar in Europe – traders visited also Bayt al-Faqīh, where good coffee was also to be bought. Zabīd seems to have had only a minor role in the trade of the seventeenth and eighteenth centuries.

After the departure of the Ottomans in 1635 the Tihāmah came loosely under the rule of the Zaydīs of the highlands. Although trade continued, Europeans began more and more to have difficulties with arbitrary and either greedy or bankrupt governors. Faced with such problems, it was hardly surprising that al-Mukhā' rapidly lost out when the British took over Aden in 1839 and seized with it a great part of the Tihāmah trade.

BIBLIOGRAPHY

Cahen C. and Serjeant R.B., "A fiscal survey of the mediaeval Yemen," *Arabica,* 4, i, Leiden, 1957.

Chelhod, J., "Introduction à l'histoire sociale et urbaine de Zabīd," *Arabica,* 25, i, Leiden, 1978.

Al-Ḥadramī, A., "Tihāmah fi'l-tārīkh," *Al-Iklīl,* 1, ii, Ṣan'ā', 1980.

Al-Ḥadramī, A., *Jāmi'at al-Ashā'ir, Zabīd,* Ṣan'ā', 1974.

Al-Hamdānī, al-Ḥasan, *Ṣifat Jazīrat al-'Arab,* ed. M. al-Akwa', al-Riyāḍ, 1974.

Ibn al-Dayba', 'Abd al-Raḥmān, *Bughyat al-mustafīd fī tārīkh madīnat Zabīd,* ed. A. al-Ḥibshī, Ṣan'ā', 1979.

Ibn al-Mujāwir, Jamāl al-Dīn Yūsuf, *Tārīkh al-mustabṣir,* ed. O. Löfgren, Leiden, 1951-54 (repr. Ṣan'ā', n.d.).

Lewcock, R. and Serjeant, R.B. (eds.) *Ṣan'ā', an Arabian Islamic city,* London, 1983.

Niebuhr, C., *Voyage en Arabie & en d'autres pays circonvoisins,* Amsterdam and Utrecht, 1776, 2 Vols.

Playfair, R.L., *A history of Arabia Felix or Yemen,* Bombay, 1859 (repr. St. Leonards, Amsterdam, 1970).

Serjeant, R.B., *The Portuguese off the South Arabian coast,* Beirut, 1974.

Stookey, R.W., *Yemen,* Boulder, 1978.

Yaḥyā ibn al-Ḥusayn, *Ghāyat al-amānī fī akhbār al-quṭr al-Yamānī,* ed. S.A. 'Āshūr, Cairo, 1968, 2 parts.

Al-Yamanī, 'Umārah ibn 'Alī, *Tārīkh al-Yaman,* ed. M. al-Akwa', Yemen (?), 1979.

Al-Yāmī, Muḥammad ibn Ḥātim, *Al-Simṭ al-ghālī,* ed. G.R. Smith, *The Ayyubids and the early Rasulids in the Yemen,* London, 1974-78.

FURTHER READING

Baldry, J., "Textiles in Yemen: Historical references to trade and commerce in textiles in Yemen from antiquity to modern times," *British Museum Occasional Paper No 27,* 1982.

Barbosa, Duarte, *A Description of the Coasts of East Africa and Malabar in the Beginning of the 16th Century,* trans. Hon. Henry E.J. Stanley, London, 1866.

Al-Khazrajī, 'Alī ibn al-Ḥasan, *The Pearl Strings; a history of the Resúliyy dynasty of Yemen,* trans. J.W. Redhouse, Leiden-London, 1906-18.

Pires, Tomé, *The Suma Oriental of Tomé Pires,* trans. Armando Cortesao, Lichtenstein, 1967.

Roque, Jean de la, *A Voyage to Arabia Foelix, 1708-1710,* London, 1732.

Schuman, L.O., *Political History of the Yemen at the Beginning of the 16th Century – Abu Makhrama's account of the years 906-927 H. (1500-1521 AD) with annotations,* Gröningen, 1962.

Tritton, A.S., *The Rise of the Imams of Sanaa,* Oxford-Madras, 1925.

Varthema, Ludovico de, *Travels,* ed. G.P. Badger, Hakluyt Series, London, 1863.

ILLUSTRATION

Plate 4.1 Nankivell, 685 × 505mm, pencil drawing.

---

19. He is buried in the Great Mosque of the city. His offspring are understood to have founded the towns of Ibn 'Abbās and al-Ṣalīf to the south of al-Luḥayyah. [Ed.]

I

II

III

IV

V

VI

VII

VIII

IX

I **Al-Marāziqah** Bream *180×280mm watercolour*
II **East of Mocha** Bream *130×205mm watercolour*
III **Al-Sukhnah Rocks** Bream *280×380mm watercolour-gouache*
IV **Above Sūq al-Khamīs** Bream *130×205mm watercolour*
V **Near Bājil** Bream *190×255mm watercolour*
VI **Al-Khawbah at Dusk** Bream *130×280mm watercolour*
VII **Al-Sukhnah Rocks** Bream *130×280mm watercolour*
VIII **Al-Sukhnah Looking Southeast** Bream *140×395mm watercolour*
IX **Wādī Surdud** Bream *150×205mm watercolour*

X **Al-Durayhimī** Bream *180×280mm watercolour*

XI **Al-Jāḥ** Bream *180×280mm watercolour courtesy of Private Collection*

XII **Pair of Sacred Ibis feeding in salt marsh at Nukhaylah, 3rd & 4th February 1982**
Brockie *280×380mm watercolour-gouache courtesy of Rothmans of Pall Mall (Overseas) Ltd*

XIII **Greater Flamingoes feeding, Ghulayfika (Ghulayfiqah), 12th January 1982**
Brockie *205×280mm pencil-coloured pencils courtesy of Denzil Baring*

XIV **Egyptian Vulture** Brockie *255×205mm (sketchbook)*
pencil-watercolour

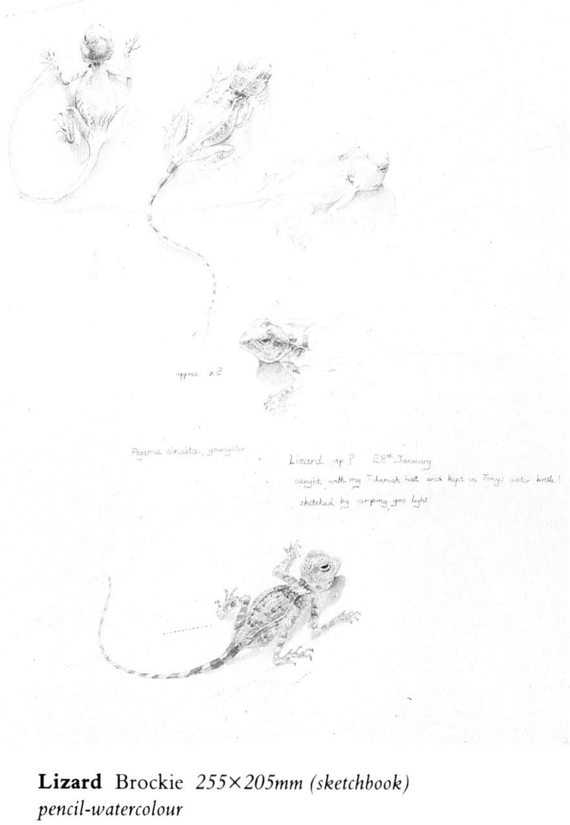

XV **Lizard** Brockie *255×205mm (sketchbook)*
pencil-watercolour

XVI **Hodeida Old *Baladīyah*** Bream *205×305mm watercolour courtesy of Private Collection*

XVII **Hodeida Doorway** Bream *205×130mm watercolour-gouache courtesy of Michael Weinstein*

XVIII **Hodeida Bāb Mishrif** Bream *150×255mm gouache courtesy of Private Collection*

XIX

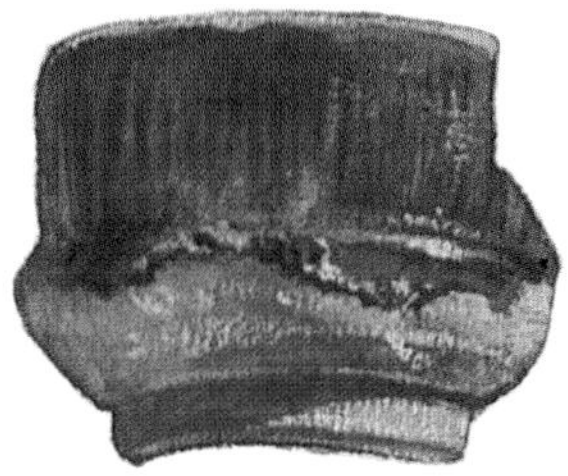

XXIII

XX

XXIV

XXV

XXI

XXII

XXVI

XIX **Sherd, "old Manṣūrīyah"** Bream *150×205mm watercolour* "Ḥays ancien" ware cup, 16th to 18th century A.D.

XX **Alabaster, al-Hāmid** Brockie *100×150mm watercolour* Fragment of alabaster or limestone with panels of incised lines, probably Pre-Islamic

XXI **Sherds, al-Ja'āmīyah** Bream *205×150mm watercolour* Variants on the turquoise under glaze ware (?), Rasūlid

XXII **Sherd, al-Ja'āmīyah** Bream *200×150mm watercolour courtesy of Dr and Mrs John Swanson* Late Ḥays ware, 16th-17th century A.D.

XXIII **Sherd, "old Manṣūrīyah"** Bream *150×205mm watercolour courtesy of Private Collection* Fragment of turquoise under glaze ware bowl, Rasūlid

XXIV **Sherd, al-Ja'amīyah** Bream *100×205mm watercolour* Fragment of Tihāmah "blue and white" ware, Rasūlid

XXV **From al-Kadrā', medieval Islamic site** Brockie *380×280mm watercolour courtesy of Private Collection* Upper: Fragment of steatite lamp, Islamic, date uncertain. Middle: Fragment of steatite cooking pot, same. Lower: Fragment of stone (banded limestone?) bowl, same

XXVI **Sherd, al-Kadrā'** Nankivell *330×410mm coloured pencils courtesy of Private Collection* Sgraffito ware plate, Seljuk, 11th-13th century A.D.

XXVII **Interior Courtyard, Fort at al-Muʻtariḍ**
Bream *380×255mm watercolour*
courtesy of Anthony Ramsay

XXVIII **Fort and Mosque, al-Muʻtariḍ, Wādī Mawr**
Nankivell *approx. 435×760mm coloured pencils courtesy of Tent Gallery*
The Fort of al-Muʻtarid was built 150 years ago by Sharīf ʻAlī Maḥmūd al-Barāq.
The Mosque adjoining it bears the name Jāmiʻ al-Sharīf Maḥmūd.

XXIX

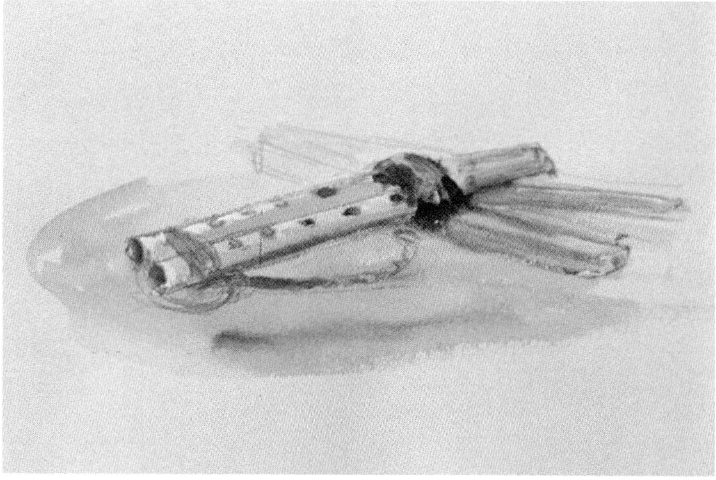

XXXI

XXX

XXXII

XXIX **Drum (*Tablah*)** Bream *255×205mm watercolour courtesy of Rothmans of Pall Mall (Overseas) Ltd*

XXX **Drum (*Marfa'*)** Bream *255×205mm watercolour courtesy of Rothmans of Pall Mall (Overseas) Ltd*

XXXI **Reed Pipes (*Mizmār*)** Bream *205×255mm watercolour courtesy of Rothmans of Pall Mall (Overseas) Ltd*

XXXII **Al-Turaybī playing *ṭumbarah*, Zabīd, 20th January, 1982** Brockie *380×280mm Conté pencil courtesy of Private Collection*

XXXIII

XXXIII **Fishing raft by the Red Sea, al-Marāziqah, 14th January 1982** Brockie *265×370mm watercolour courtesy of George and Jill Kassis*

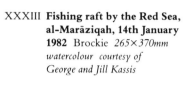

XXXIV

XXXIV **Bayt al-Faqīh, 22nd January 1982** Brockie *380×280mm watercolour courtesy of Rothmans of Pall Mall (Overseas) Ltd*

4.3: THE HISTORY OF THE TIHAMAH FROM 1800 TO THE PRESENT

John Baldry

INTRODUCTION

During the past two hundred years the Yemeni Tihāmah has been subjected to numerous invasions by both land and sea. Occasionally opposition to the invaders was organized from the highlands by the Zaydī *imāms,* but this was the exception rather than the rule, for it was only rarely that the *imāms's* authority extended much beyond the immediate vicinity of their own capitals. Moreover, the *shaykhs* of the Tihāmah usually had little desire to acknowledge the suzerainty of the *imāms,* for when an *imām* succeeded in subduing the Tihāmah his rule often proved as burdensome as that of the foreign invaders.

Thus defending the Tihāmah was usually the task of the local *shaykhs*. Although many of these *shaykhs* came from distinguished families that had for generations provided tribal leaders, their authority did not often extend beyond their own tribal boundaries and only rarely did tribes unite to oppose an invading force. Indeed, it was not unknown for a tribe to ally itself with the invaders as a means of crushing the power of a neighbouring tribe.

The lack of tribal cooperation in the event of external threat, the absence of the *imāms's* control over the Tihāmah together with the flatness of the coastal plain enabled a determined force to occupy the Tihāmah with relative ease.

The repercussions of foreign occupations of the Tihāmah were serious. Communications between the Tihāmah and the independent highlanders were hindered which not only impeded trade but also tended to accentuate the differences between the tribes of the highlands and those of the lowland Tihāmah. Later this strengthened the determination of the coastal tribes not to accept the authority of the Zaydī *imāms* whenever the Tihāmah regained its independence. The occupying forces also increased dissension among the Tihāmah tribes themselves. The antagonisms felt by the Tihāmah tribes for the highlanders, a feeling which had been encouraged by the Turks, had become so bitter by the 20th century that it took Imām Yaḥyā ten years from the Turkish evacuation at the end of the first World War to bring some of the Tihāmah tribes under his control.

The almost constant warfare which prevailed in the Tihāmah coupled with tribal reluctance to accept the central authority of the *imāms* meant a continuation in the decline of most Tihāmah towns, a process which had begun before the first Turkish occupation of the 16th century. Conversely, the town of al-Ḥudaydah (Hodeida) became increasingly important as successive rulers made it their administrative and military headquarters. This also contributed to the decline of the ports of al-Mukhā' (Mocha) and al-Luḥayyah as major commercial centres. After Aden was declared a free port by the British, the Turks concentrated almost all of Turkish Yemen's foreign trade at al-Ḥudaydah in an attempt to make the town a rival to Aden as the principal port for the importation of goods into Yemen. At the same time foreign merchants were welcomed, not only for the increased trade their presence brought, but also as a means of preventing the local Arabs from acquiring wealth and influence.

Plate 4.2 **Al-Shādhilī Mosque, Mocha**

THE ZAYDĪ IMĀMS LOSE THE TIHĀMAH

Following the expulsion of the Turks from Yemen in 1636 the authority of the Zaydī *imāms* stretched from the Ḥaḍramawt to 'Asīr but within less than a century many areas had seceded from the central government. It was from Abū 'Arīsh near Jīzān in present-day Saudi Arabia that Sharīf Aḥmad seized control of the Tihāmah from the Imām around 1730. Sixty years later the authority of the *ashrāf* of Abū 'Arīsh extended from al-Qunfidhah in the north to Bayt al-Faqīh in the south. But their successes were short lived, and the sovereignty of the Tihāmah was to be continuously contested for over a century.

In 1805/06 sovereignty over the Tihāmah was won by the Wahhābīs when Abū Mismār, the Sharīf of Abū 'Arīsh, reluctantly gave his allegiance to Sa'ūd ibn 'Abd al-'Azīz's commander Abū Nuqṭah. When in 1809 Abū Mismār renounced his loyalty to the Sa'ūds, a Wahhābī force marched southwards from Jīzān looting and burning al-Luḥayyah and al-Ḥudaydah. As a result of this expedition there remains scarcely a building in the Yemeni Tihāmah north of al-Ḥudaydah which pre-dates 1809.[1]

Having regained control of the Tihāmah, the Sa'ūds reinstated Abū Mismār as governor of the Tihāmah. By this time the forces of the Egyptian viceroy Muḥammad 'Alī were meeting with considerable success against the Wahhābīs. In these circumstances the Sharīf of Abū 'Arīsh thus voluntarily offered his allegiance to the Viceroy thereby placing the Tihāmah indirectly under Egyptian sovereignty.

Further changes in the sovereignty of the Yemeni coast occurred in 1832 when the newly appointed Ottoman governor of the Ḥijāz, Türkçe Bilmez, took it upon himself to seize the Yemen on behalf of Turkey and occupied the Tihāmah as far south as al-Mukhā'. By 1837 an Egyptian force which had followed Türkçe Bilmez to the Yemen had not only regained al-Ḥudaydah, Zabīd and al-Mukhā' but had pushed on southwards to the Shaykh Sa'īd peninsula. When the force then moved south-eastwards towards Aden, the British fearing for the safety of their newly acquired possession, secured the cooperation of several European powers who jointly pressured Muḥammad 'Alī to evacuate his forces from Arabia in 1839. As Egyptian troops were leaving Yemen, Ḥusayn, the Sharīf of Abū 'Arīsh, assembled a 20,000 strong force thereby obliging Muḥammad 'Alī to cede the Tihāmah to him rather than to the Imām of Ṣan'ā'.

THE THIRD TURKISH OCCUPATION

Control of the Yemeni Tihāmah did not remain long with the *ashrāf* of Abū 'Arīsh, but the transfer of sovereignty to Turkey occurred without bloodshed. When in 1842 British merchants trading in Yemen were charged 9% customs dues, a sum considerably higher than that demanded of other nationalities, Britain protested to Constantinople. By sending a commission to Zabīd to investigate the causes of British complaints against Sharīf Ḥusayn, the Porte acknowledged its responsibility for affairs in the Yemeni Tihāmah. The commission concluded its inquiries by recognizing the Sharīf as governor of the Tihāmah when he acknowledged his dependence upon the Porte.

In the next few years the Zaydī *imāms* made several attempts to seize the Tihāmah, and for a short time in 1848 Bājil, al-Hudaydah, Zabīd, Bayt al-Faqīh and al-Mukhā' fell under the Imām's control. These assaults by the *imāms* against the Sharīf appear to have been partially responsible for the Turkish decision to reoccupy the Yemeni Tihāmah for the first time since 1636. Accordingly a Turkish force landed at al-Ḥudaydah in April 1849. Tawfīq Pasha became governor of the northern Tihāmah with his headquarters in al-Ḥudaydah while 'Abdullāh 'Awn, a member of the ruling, *sharīf* family of Mecca, was made responsible for the government of the southern Tihāmah. Sharīf Ḥusayn then received a pension and retired to Abū 'Arīsh.

Both the civilian administration and the military authorities rapidly acquired a reputation for corruption, neglect and cruelty. These factors and the tribes's fierce attachment to their independence was the cause of constant rebellion, but it was not until Imām Yaḥyā came to power in 1904 that opposition to the Turkish occupation took the form of a national movement rather than isolated tribal uprisings.

Opposition to the Turkish occupation came also from 'Asīr when a large force besieged al-Ḥudaydah in 1856, only desisting when 3,000 of their number died from cholera. A second 'Asīrī assault against al-Ḥudaydah occurred in 1870.

Corruption and misrule had soon become so widespread that as early as 1879 the British consul in Jiddah was predicting that the tribes would rise up and massacre the Turks. The pashas, he observed, arrived in Arabia "in poor [financial] circumstances but they generally retire rich." When from 1899 numerous tribes refused to pay taxes and attacks on garrisons and other military installations increased throughout Yemen, so Turkish repression intensified. These were not the sole causes of dissatisfaction and in 1901 in a letter to the *muftī* of Ḥamāh, Imām Muḥammad alleged that

> The [Turkish] officials were not giving Allah His due, nor respecting His Laws, nor those of the Prophets of Allah, but they have rather set up unto themselves a religion that was offensive to the sight of Allah and antagonistic to His Law...

Despite the dispatch of an Ottoman commission to Yemen to examine complaints, no improvements in the lot of the people were made and isolated revolts continued throughout both the Tihāmah and the highlands. The retaliatory military campaigns against the dissident tribes were, according to the British vice-consul in al-Ḥudaydah, "characterised by cruelty and excesses... and by assaults on women that aroused the Arabs." For its part the Turkish administration in Yemen had to contend with the seeming indifference to its fate of the central government in Constantinople: insufficient funds were remitted to Yemen with the result that transport to move troops rapidly to trouble spots was inadequate. It became commonplace for troops to go

1. Notable exceptions being mostly mosque and tomb sites, i.e. Jāmi' al-Kabīr, al-Ḍaḥī (7th century A.H.); Ibn 'Abbās mosque and tomb (317 A.H., with Kufic inscriptions not in situ); Bayt 'Aṭā' tomb (7th century A.H., subsequently rebuilt); the minaret of al-Muẓaffar mosque, Mahjam (circa 577 A.H. given locally as the construction date, see A. Saint-Hilaire, *Je Reviens du Yemen,* p. 96.) and a Turkish mosque at Dayr Ḥarīsh east of al-Ḍaḥī (presumably from the first Turkish occupation, although this was not verified). [Ed.]

several years without pay and to be posted to the highlands with inadequate food and clothing for the cold winters.[2]

IMĀM YAḤYĀ'S UPRISING OF 1904-1907

Following the drought of 1904 the British vice-consul in al-Ḥudaydah reported on the "sad spectacles ... of swarms of hungry and starving men, women and children." In the same year Imām Yaḥyā came to power and immediately took advantage of the disaffection occasioned by the Turks' continuing corruption and misrule as well as their failure to alleviate the effects of the drought. He organized a rebellion which lasted until 1907 and which spread to all parts of Yemen under Ottoman rule. So successful was the insurrection that almost all Turkish garrisons, including that defending the capital, had surrendered by April 1905. Two months later almost 43,000 reinforcements had reached Yemen for the reconquest of the country, but it was not until September that Turkish forces advancing from the coast recaptured Ṣan'ā'.

Imām Yaḥyā explained to Edward VII of Britain the reason for the revolt:

> ...agriculture, trade and industry have been ruined and suffering has been universal and widespread. And so at length the people have of necessity appealed to us and besought us to espouse their cause. They came to us willing to die in search of relief from the oppression and distress and ignominy...

Travellers and consular officials confirmed that the Imām was in no way exaggerating the situation then prevailing throughout the country.

With the recapture of Ṣan'ā', support for the Imām decreased, nonetheless Turkish garrisons in both the Tihāmah and highlands continued to be harassed until 1907 when the Imām accepted a three-month truce while the Turks undertook to implement a number of reforms. This policy was continued the following year when the Young Turks appointed Ḥasan Taḥsin as Commander in Chief in Yemen with instructions to replace corrupt officials, to reorganize the police, to end malpractice in tax collection and to increase the number of schools. In the Turkish capital plans for the administrative reform of Yemen were advanced: these, had they been implemented, would have given the government of the northern Zaydī highlands to Imām Yaḥyā, with the Turks retaining responsibility for the remainder of the country. *Sharī'ah* law was to be administered throughout the country except in the Tihāmah where it was considered impractical for the needs of international commerce.

THE UPRISING OF SAYYID MUḤAMMAD AL-IDRĪSĪ

While the Turks were hesitantly moving towards an accommodation with Imām Yaḥyā, a new threat to Turkish sovereignty appeared in the Tihāmah. This came from Sayyid Muḥammad al-Idrīsī (henceforth referred to as the Idrīsī) whose great grandfather had settled in Ṣabyā in 1833 at the invitation of the population. Gradually the renown of the family spread beyond Ṣabyā as the family was called on to settle disputes and feuds. In 1909 Sayyid Muḥammad's prestige had so increased that the tribes between al-Zaydīyah and Ḥajjah protested to him, and not to Imām Yaḥyā, that a prominent pro-Turkish *shaykh,* Bawni Pasha, was levying illegal taxes on the Tihāmah tribes. The Idrīsī responded by proclaiming Bawni Pasha's dismissal which encouraged the tribesmen not only to raze the Pasha's headquarters but also to seize al-Qanāwiṣ, al-Zaydīyah and al-Luḥayyah. It took the Turks three months to restore their authority in the region.

Meanwhile the failure of the Turks to implement the reforms promised to Imām Yaḥyā led the Imām and the Idrīsī to prepare for a joint offensive against the Turks. The uprising began in September 1910 when tribesmen loyal to Imām Yaḥyā began harassing the Turks in Dhamār, Ta'izz, Yarīm, Ānis and Ḥajjah. At the same time the Idrīsī contacted the Zarānīq[3] and tribal leaders in Waṣāb and Zabīd while simultaneously attacking Turkish garrisons in the 'Asīrī highlands and cutting communications between Abhā and the coast.

THE SIEGE OF ṢAN'Ā', 1911

Cooperation between the Imām and Sayyid Muḥammad was of short duration and at the beginning of 1911 the Imām's military operations against Ṣan'ā', Yarīm, al-Ḥujaylah, 'Ubāl, 'Amrān, Kawkabān and Radā' were made entirely independently of the Idrīsī. In face of this new insurrection a 22,500-strong Turkish force advanced from al-Ḥudaydah for the relief of Ṣan'ā' but only succeeded in breaking the siege of the capital on 4 April 1911. In the next few months the Turks also regained other garrison towns seized by the Imām's supporters. Negotiations were then held between the Imām and the Turks which ended in the conclusion of the Treaty of Da''ān which accorded the Imām a certain autonomy in the Zaydī highlands. Both sides observed the terms of the treaty until the Turks evacuated Yemen in 1919.

The conclusion of the Turkish-Yemeni agreement enabled the Turks to move their forces from the highlands for a campaign against the Idrīsī in the northern

2. Yemen is mentioned, woefully, in Turkish folk songs of the period. [Ed.]
3. The Zarānīq (see Wilson, p. 35) are a remarkable and at times infamous tribe whose background and customs deserve special study. (For unique elements of Zarānīq costume, see Stone, p. 115.) Today they describe their own tribal territory, perhaps a little exaggeratedly, as extending from near Bājil south through al-Ḥusaynīyah to Bayt al-Faqīh and west to the coast at al-Ta'if, Ghulayfiqah, and al-Jāḥ. Zarānīq Shaykh 'Abduh Ḥusayn al-Fashiq resides in al-Ḥusaynīyah; Shaykh Muḥammad Yaḥyā Qawqar (sp.?) near Bājil. They border on the lands of the Qurayshī tribe to the south. [Ed.]

Figure 4.1 Al-Luḥayyah from the sea

Yemeni Tihāmah and in the 'Asīrī highlands. However, when a large Turkish force disembarked at Jīzān in readiness for the projected advance against the Idrīsī in Ṣabyā and his forces besieging Abhā over a thousand Turkish soldiers were killed, thus obliging the Turks to postpone their campaign against the Idrīsī.

Upon the outbreak of the Turkish-Italian War in 1911 the Italians bombarded all Turkish-Yemeni ports including al-Ḥudaydah, al-Luḥayyah, al-Mukhā' and Shaykh Sa'īd, but it was not until the following year that the Italians cooperated with the Idrīsī against the Turks. In March two Italian warships timed their bombardment of Mīdī to coincide with the Idrīsī's attack by land, thus enabling Sayyid Muḥammad to occupy the town. The next month Idrīsī forces failed to capture al-Luḥayyah when the Italians shelled the town from the sea, but the Idrīsī had nonetheless laid his claim to the Yemeni Tihāmah. He had better success in June 1912 when he seized the Farasān Islands while the Italians blockaded them.

When peace was concluded between Turkey and Italy in October 1912, the former repelled Idrīsī partisans from much of the Yemeni Tihāmah, but the Idrīsī's campaign continued in the highlands of 'Asīr whence the Turks were obliged to withdraw large numbers of their troops in view of the war which was looming in the Balkans.

In the full knowledge that they could not defeat the Idrīsī militarily the Turks in discussions in March 1913 offered Sayyid Muḥammad limited autonomy in and around Abū 'Arīsh and total control over Ḥabl, Mīdī, Jīzān and Birk. The talks were discontinued when the Sayyid, believing that the Turkish presence in Arabia was in any case limited, demanded independence for 'Asīr, the retention of Mīdī, Jīzān and the Farasān Islands, the right to grant concessions to foreigners for the construction of mines and railways and the right to establish relations with foreign powers. The Turks retaliated by blockading the Idrīsī-controlled coast, thus depriving him of Italian assistance. They were therefore able to reoccupy Mīdī and Jīzān while Imām Yaḥyā in collaboration with the Turks captured twenty villages from the Idrīsī.

THE ANGLO-IDRISI ALLIANCE

By 1914 the Turks were facing a predicament: they required the Idrīsī's support in the World War, the outbreak of which appeared imminent. This could only be acquired by granting him some kind of autonomy which would alienate Imām Yaḥyā who would see recognition by the Turks of the Idrīsī's territorial claims to both the Yemeni Tihāmah and 'Asīr as a very inimical act. This dilemma was solved for them when an Idrīsī delegation reached Aden in September 1914. The British Resident there was authorised to open negotiations in the course of which he offered the Idrīsī not only British "protection and friendship" but also arms and ammunition in return for the Idrīsī's undertaking to wage war on the Turks. These preliminary contacts culminated in the Anglo-Idrīsī Treaty of April 1915.

By the terms of this agreement the Idrīsī received a monthly subsidy, arms ammunition and food supplies as well as protection of his seaboard from all attack. British officers were subsequently seconded to Idrīsī territory to assist Sayyid Muḥammad's military campaigns against the Turks, and small numbers of Idrīsī tribesmen received military training in Aden. Certain of the Idrīsī ports were exempted from the British blockade of the east coast of the Red Sea. Later British warships and seaplanes bombarded Turkish positions as far south as al-Luḥayyah and al-Zuhrah whilst Idrīsī tribesmen launched simultaneous attacks by land.

In the meantime Britain had been unsuccessfully seeking to conclude an agreement with Imām Yaḥyā by which he would renounce the Treaty of Da''ān and join the Allies in their war against Turkey. Imām Yaḥyā while always cordially receiving British overtures declined to fight his co-religionists. Moreover, after British warships had bombarded Turkish positions at every port, however small, along the Yemeni coast, Imām Yaḥyā suspected that Britain intended to occupy the Yemeni coast. He was also convinced that by concluding an agreement with Britain he would facilitate an eventual British occupation of the Tihāmah. When it had become apparent that the Imām was not prepared to join the Allies, the Idrīsī's subsidy was increased to enable him to acquire the active participation in the war of those highland tribes opposed to Imām Yaḥyā's alliance with Turkey. However the effectiveness of these Zaydī tribes who joined the Idrīsī was limited due to their reluctance to fight for long periods far from their own territories.

THE IDRĪSĪ OCCUPATION OF THE TIHĀMAH

The situation at the end of 1918 was complicated by the rival claims and counter claims to the sovereignty of the Tihāmah. With the Armistice the Turks were required to evacuate the Arabian peninsula and their departure left a power vacuum. In Yemen a fierce struggle for the sovereignty of the Tihāmah again brought Imām Yaḥyā and the Idrīsī into conflict. By early 1919 Idrīsī forces had occupied the northern Tihāmah as far south as al-Zaydīyah. Al-Ḥudaydah had been occupied by British forces in December 1918 to facilitate and supervise the evacuation of Turkish forces from Yemen and 'Asīr. The tribes to the east and south of al-Ḥudaydah, especially the Zarānīq, 'Absīyah and Quḥrah, preferred to retain their independence from the Imām, Idrīsī and Britain, but when forces of the Imām advanced towards the Tihāmah these tribes reluctantly called upon the Idrīsī to protect them from Imām Yaḥyā, thus enabling the Idrīsī to extend his influence almost to Zabīd. When in January 1921 the British evacuated al-Ḥudaydah they permitted the Idrīsī to occupy the town, the Imām's claim to sovereignty not being entertained due to his occupation of parts of the Aden Protectorate.

Meanwhile the Idrīsī and Imām's forces continued to oppose each other in the foothills of the Tihāmah for possession of the coast, but it was not until 1925 that the matter was settled when the Imām, armed by Italy, was able to seize al-Ḥudaydah whence in a rapid campaign he advanced northwards, expelling the Idrīsī administration to a point just north of Mīdī. Imām Yaḥyā then concentrated on his territorial claim to 'Asīr which brought him into conflict with 'Abd al-'Azīz ibn Sa'ūd whose protection the Idrīsī had sought in face of the Imām's gradual encroachments into that region. Moreover Ibn Sa'ūd had undertaken to regain all the Idrīsī's former territory in the Tihāmah up to, but excluding, al-Ḥudaydah.

AL-ḤUDAYDAH AFTER 1914

As a result of British bombardments of al-Ḥudaydah during the World War, most of the population had fled into the interior. Thus, from an estimated 40,000 inhabitants in 1914 there were less than 2,000 civilians in the town when it was seized by the British at the end of 1918. When the British permitted the local merchants a share in the administration of the town's affairs confidence was slowly restored and the population returned. Idrīsī rule brought almost all trade in the town to an end as forced loans, high customs duties and other excessive taxation were imposed to pay for the continuing war against Imām Yaḥyā. The situation worsened when the country between Ṣabyā and al-Ḥudaydah was briefly ravaged by civil war as rival members of the Idrīsī family fought for control of the Idrīsī imamate.

With the installation of Imām Yaḥyā's administration in the town in 1925 attempts were made to alleviate the conditions of the merchants and taxes were either abolished or reduced. But Imām Yaḥyā's coffers were drained by the expense of maintaining a military presence in the Aden Protectorate and in 'Asīr in support of his territorial claims to those territories. Considerable expenditure was also caused by measures he took for the defence of the Tihāmah, for he rightly suspected that Mussolini would seize a propitious moment to occupy the Tihāmah and turn the Red Sea into an Italian lake. An additional run on the Treasury came from garrisoning Shaykh Sa'īd to counter possible French moves to implement their claim to that locality first made in 1868.

SINCE 1934

The failure of negotiations to resolve the conflicting claims to the sovereignty of 'Asīr and to settle the frontier between his own country and that of Ibn Sa'ūd brought Yemen and Saudi Arabia into conflict in 1934 when once again the Yemeni Tihāmah was the scene of hostilities. Despite the fortifications Imām Yaḥyā had constructed in the Tihāmah,[4] a Saudi force under Amīr (later King) Fayṣal ibn 'Abd al-'Azīz rapidly advanced along the coast and occupied al-Ḥudaydah in May 1934 as many of the leading *shaykhs* deserted the Imām. The Saudi administration lasted six weeks during which time most government departments were re-established under Saudi control. The Saudis only withdrew when Imām Yaḥyā recalled his forces from the 'Asīr highlands and surrendered members of the Idrīsī family who had participated in Imām Yaḥyā's campaign against Ibn Sa'ūd following the Saudi absorption of Idrīsī country into Saudi Arabia.

During the inter-regnum between the evacuation of the Yemeni administration and the arrival of the Saudi occupying force in al-Ḥudaydah, the town was occupied by British and Italian troops, the former to safeguard British subjects and property in the town. The Italians hoped that from al-Ḥudaydah they would be in a position to come to the assistance of Imām Yaḥyā if and when he chose to attempt to expel the Saudi force from Yemen.

4. Rural forts built by the Imām which were specifically noted during fieldwork were: the *ḥuṣns* at al-Ḥusaynīyah and al-Jāḥ, and the *ḥukūmah* at al-Ḍaḥī. (See Plate 6.6.) [Ed.]

It was not until the death of Imām Yaḥyā in 1948 that Yemen was opened to a limited foreign presence when roads were constructed, al-Ḥudaydah port modernized and agricultural projects inaugurated. But it was only after the Yemeni civil war in 1970 that the development of the Tihāmah began in earnest.

Since 1800 the Tihāmah has been subjected to almost constant warfare and foreign occupation. Most of the régimes left some mark on the region, but the period has been principally characterized by destruction rather than construction. It was only after Imām Yaḥyā's occupation of the littoral that the Tihāmah was restored to the mainstream of Yemen.

Plate 4.3 **Hodeida Street Scene**

BIBLIOGRAPHY

Books

Baldry, John, *Britain and the Idrisi Imamate of Asir and Yemen,* (in press).

————, "Textiles in Yemen: Historical references to trade and commerce in textiles in Yemen from antiquity to modern times," *British Museum Occasional Paper No. 27,* London, 1982.

Articles

Baldry, John, "Anglo-Italian Rivalry in Yemen and Asir, 1900-1934," *Die Welt des Islams,* Vol. XVII, pp. 155-193.

————, "The Arrest of the British Vice Consul in al-Hudaydah and the subsequent protection of British interests in Yemen, 1914-1918," *Journal of Islamic Studies,* New Delhi, (in press).

__________, "The British Military Administration of al-Hudaydah, Yemen, December 1918 to January 1921," *Zeitschrift der Deutschen Morgenländischen Gesellschaft,* Weisbaden, (in press); this article has already been published in Arabic in *Al-Yaman al-Jadid,* Ṣan'ā', n.d.

__________, "British Naval Operations against Turkish Yemen," *Arabica,* Leiden, Tome XXV, Fasc. 2, pp. 148-197.

__________, "The Commercial Activity of al-Hudaydah, Yemen in 1897," *American Journal of Arabic Studies,* Salt Lake City, (in press).

__________, "The French Claim to Shaykh Said (Yemen) and its International Repercussions, 1868-1939," *Zeitschrift der Deutschen Morgenländischen Gesellschaft,* Weisbaden, Band 133, Heft 1, 1983, pp. 93-133.

__________, "Al-Hudaydah and the Powers during the Saudi-Yemeni War of 1934," *Arabian Studies VI,* Cambridge, pp. 7-34.

__________, "A Hundred Years of Yemeni History," *L'Arabie du Sud: Histoire et Civilisation,* ed. J. Chelhod, Editions G.-P. Maisonneuve et Larose, Paris, Chapter 10, Vol. 1, (in press).

__________, "Imam Yahya and the Yemeni Uprising of 1904-1907," *Abr Nahrain,* Leiden, Vol. XVIII, pp. 33-73.

__________, "Imam Yahya and the Yemeni Uprising of 1911," *Annalli dell'Instituto Orientale de Napoli,* Naples, Vol. 42, 1982, pp. 426-459.

__________, "The Powers and Mineral Concessions in the Idrisi Imamate of Asir, 1910-1929," *Arabian Studies II,* Cambridge, pp. 76-107.

__________, "The Struggle for the Red Sea: Mussolini's Policy in Yemen, 1934-1943," *Asian and African Studies,* Bratislava, Vol. XVI, pp. 53-89.

__________, "The Turkish-Italian War in the Yemen, 1911-1912," *Arabian Studies III,* Cambridge, pp. 51-65.

__________, "Al-Yaman and the Turkish Occupation, 1849-1914," *Arabica,* Leiden, Tome XXII, Fasc. 2, pp. 156-196.

FURTHER READING

Baldry, John, "The Detention in Bajil of the Jacob Mission to the Imam of Yemen in 1919," *Journal of Islamic Studies,* New Delhi, (in press).

__________, "The Early History of the Yemeni Port of al-Hudaydah," *Arabian Studies VII,* Cambridge, (in press, 1983).

__________, "Foreign Interventions and Occupations of Kamaran Island," *Arabian Studies IV,* Cambridge, pp. 89-112.

__________, "The Ottoman Quarantine Station on Kamaran Island, 1882-1914," *Studies in History of Medicine,* New Delhi, Vol. 11, March-June 1978, pp. 3-138.

__________, "Railway Projects in Yemen, 1905-1921," *The Arab Gulf,* Basrah (Iraq), Vol. 14, No. 1, 1982, pp. 33-39.

__________, "Soviet Relations with Saudi Arabia and the Yemen, 1917-1938," *Middle Eastern Studies,* London, (in press).

__________, "The Yamani Island of Kamaran during the Napoleonic Wars," *Middle Eastern Studies,* London, Vol. 16, No. 3, October 1980, pp. 246-266.

Bury, G. Wyman, *Arabia Infelix,* London, 1915.

Hunter, F.M., *An Account of the British Settlement of Aden in Arabia,* reprinted London, 1968.

Manzoni, Renzo, *El Yemen,* Rome, 1884.

Rihani, Ameen, *Around the Coasts of Arabia,* London, 1930.

Stripling, G.W.F., "The Ottoman Turks and the Arabs," *Illinois Studies in the Social Sciences,* Vol. XXVI, No. 4, 1942.

Valentina, Viscount George, *Voyages and Travels to India, Ceylon, the Red Sea in 1802...* 1806, London, 1809.

FURTHER REFERENCE

The *faqīh* of Ibn 'Abbās, Muḥammad Aḥmad Suwayd.
The *faqīh* of al-Ḍaḥī, 'Umar Ya'anī.

ILLUSTRATIONS

Plate 4.2 Bream, 380 × 505mm, gouache (study for oil); *Plate 4.3* Bream, 280 × 125mm, gouache; *Figure 4.1* Ehrlich.

GLOSSARY

'Arab	a mobile raider as opposed to a townsman (in this context, see Wilson, p. 34, n. 8)
ashrāf	(sing. *sharīf*) those able to trace their descent to the Prophet Muḥammad. In the context of the Zaydīs (the sect which from the tenth century ruled northern highland Yemen more or less continuously until the Revolution of 1962 A.D.), relatives or descendants of one of the *Imāms*
badw	bedouin, i.e. tent dwelling nomadic pastoralists
dīwān	administration
faqīh	local historian, learned person
hijrah	emigration of the Prophet Muḥammad from Mecca to Medina in 622 A.D.
ḥukūmah	(place of) government
ḥuṣn	fort
imām	spiritual and temporal leader of the Zaydīs, a title denoting the same
khuṭbah	sermon
makhāḍirah	migrant harvester(s)
mamlūk	a slave, or slave soldier
muftī	a person with the authority to deliver formal legal opinions
Ramaḍān	the fasting month of the Muslim year, the ninth month of the lunar calendar
sāj	teak
sāriyah	column of stone or baked bricks
Sharī'ah	the law of Islam
sharīf	(pl. *ashrāf*) a title denoting a person able to trace his descent to the Prophet Muḥammad
sunnī	belonging to what is known as the "orthodox" branch of Islam, and distinct from the *shī'ah* branch of Islam. The northern highlands of Yemen (and at times the whole of Yemen) were ruled by the Zaydīs, a sect of the *shī'ah*. The remainder of Yemen – the Tihāmah and the south – was *sunnī*, as today
wādī	seasonal river
waqf	religious endowment
wazīr	minister

ARCHAEOLOGY

5.1: ARCHAEOLOGICAL SURVEY REPORT

Dr. Selma Al-Radi

For ten days, from February 4 to 14, 1982, I accompanied the Tihāmah Expedition (leader: Anderson Bakewell, members: Antony Bream, Keith Brockie, Steven Ehrlich, John Nankivell and Francine Stone) with the intention of locating and surveying as many ancient sites as possible within the region lying between Bājil and Bayt al-Faqīh. A list of sites had been given to us by John Baldry (ex British Council in Hodeida who was supposed to join the expedition but could not at the last moment); this list formed the basis of the survey which started and ended in Bājil. Other information was collected from the archives of the National Museum, Ṣan'ā' and from the local authorities who were most helpful; special mention must be made of Shaykh Muḥammad 'Alī al-Muzarīyah of Bājil who went out of his way to help us.

The sites will be listed according to their regions;[1] all the pottery and other fragments collected during this survey have been deposited at the National Museum in Ṣan'ā'.

BĀJIL AREA

Walī Shamsī or Dayr al-Khadāmah

4km WSW of Bājil, the site is located in the vicinity of the tomb of Walī Shamsī Ahdal, the nearest village being Dayr al-Khadāmah. The annual *ziyārah* to the *walī* coincided with our visit, i.e. the first Thursday/Friday of Rabī' al-Thānī or 4/5 February 1982. The *ziyārah* is particularly interesting because the rituals appear to be basically pagan thinly covered with Muslim overtones.[2] The legend attached to the *ziyārah* is as follows: in times past the village was plagued by an ogre or monster who lived in the hill adjoining the village and yearly demanded one virgin as a sacrifice for the safety of the rest of the inhabitants. One year, Shamsī Ahdal came by (the Ahdals are a famous Tihāmah family [3] and can count many leaders, learned men and the founder of the Kilwa Dynasty on the East African Coast during the 13th century, among their members); on seeing the situation in the village he offered his services in exchange for recognition of his authority. The villagers accepted, he went up the hill and using the girl as bait he lured the ogre out of his cave and cut off his head so that it rolled off "like a watermelon". The villagers were duly grateful, and when he died he was buried there and the yearly *ziyārah* was established in honour of his person. Every year during those two days hundreds of people converge and congregate in the area and the festivities continue without a break.

The site extends over an area of 400×500m around the tomb of the *walī* and most of the area is covered by the local cemetery. No architectural remains are evident on the surface of the mound, but there is at least one metre of blown sand over it. However, the pottery spread is extensive and a representative collection was made. The pottery is mostly Early Islamic in date, i.e. Umayyad/Abbasid period, with the characteristic "red-brown zig-zag" ware in the majority. Some later plain incised wares and glazed wares of the Rasūlid period, especially some "turquoise under-glaze painted" wares, would however indicate that the site continued to be in use at least into the 13th or 14th century.

Al-'Ayn

17km ENE of Bājil, 1.5km east of al-Hāmidah (Lat. 15°03′ Long. 43°28′). Poor modern village, equally poor ancient site, no trace of any architectural remains apparent on the surface but there is some depth of occupation. The maximum area of the ancient settlement is about 200×150m. The pottery is Islamic, post-14th century from the available evidence, mainly "Ḥays ancien" yellow/green glazed cups and some Rasūlid "scratched design" wares. According to a local man, Salīm, there is a large site called Ḥuṣn due north of al-'Ayn, about three hours walk away, with the remains of houses, cisterns and inscriptions (he is illiterate and therefore cannot say what kind of writing is represented on the inscriptions).

Bāb al-Nāqah

11km from Bājil on the main Ṣan'ā' road, small track to the right. Two hours walk up to the mountain top are the remains of a castle, houses, cisterns etc., said to have been built by Sayf ibn dhī Yazan (a semi-mythical king referred to in many texts e.g., the *Sīrah* of Ibn Isḥāq, he was the second last Ḥimyaritic king and got rid of the Ethiopians, c.572 A.D.) The structures can just be seen from the valley below.

Al-Ḥāmid or Dayr al-Turāb

19km SSE of Bājil and situated on the first terrace above Wādī Sihām (260m above sea level), on the southwest slope of Jabal al-Ḍāmir and opposite the western flank of

1. Each archaeological site mentioned in this paper, with the exception of al-'Ayn, appears on the Survey Region Map on p. 3 and is marked by a symbol designating it as an archaeological site. [Ed.]
2. See Stone, p. 123.
3. Including a branch to which belong the past and present *manāṣib* (pl. of *manṣab*, Sufi master, see Stone p. 118) of al-Marāwi'ah. Also a well known branch in Zabīd where the jurist, Sayyid Yaḥyā ibn 'Umar al-Ahdal, founded a religious college (*rab'*). [Ed.]

Figures 5.1-5.6 **INSCRIPTIONS FROM AL-HĀMID, DAYR AL-TURĀB***

Temple Inscription

Fig. 5.1 One long line of script carved into the side panel of a building block previously positioned in the north wall of the temple (on the outside), now in Muḥammad al-Shamīrī's house in Bājil. Broken in two. Limestone.
L: 2.12m, W: 0.39m, H: 0.14m, Letters: 6-8cms
Dh'bn bn Ybḥhmw bn Gdnm hqny dht Ḥmym ẓbym wkl wldhw b'm Shfq d...
Dha'aban son of Yabḥaham of the family of Gadan and all his sons presented to Dhat Ḥimyam (sun goddess) a gazelle (?statue) in the name of 'Am Shafaq...

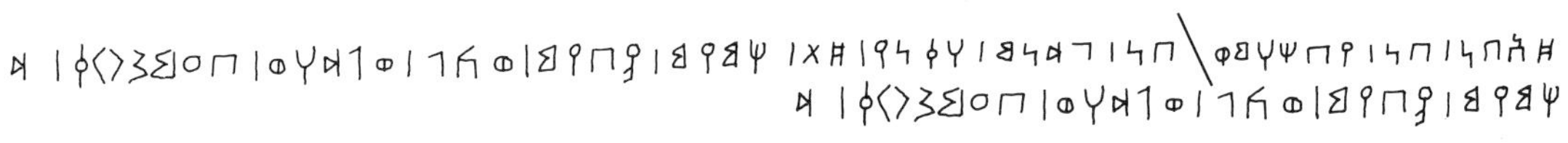

JA 2896

Small Inscriptions
(All in Muḥammad al-Shamīrī's house in Bājil.)

Fig. 5.2 Three line inscription, boustrophedon script. Sandstone.
L: 39.5cm, W: 19.5cm, Letters: 4cm
Mtf'm bn Hblm hqny 'lmqh kl wldhw.
Matf'am son of Hablam and his sons presented (this?) to Almaqah.

JA 2895

Fig. 5.3 Two line inscription, boustrophedon script (one letter reversed). Sandstone.
L: 45cm, W: 20cm, Letters: 5.5cm
'ibq bn Ftḥm hqny 'lmqh kl wldhw.
'Albaq son of Fatḥ and all his sons presented (this?) to Almaqah.

JA 2893

Fig. 5.4 Two line inscription, boustrophedon script. Sandstone, incomplete.
L: 32.5cm, W: 16cm, Letters: 5cm
...**lmqh sb' bḥtm hq**...
...**presented to Almaqah seven statuettes**...

JA 2894

Fig. 5.5 Two line inscription, boustrophedon script. Sandstone, incomplete.
L: 36.5cm, W: 24.5cm, Letters: 7cm.
...**m hqny 'lmqah bḥtn wk**...
...**m and (all His sons) presented to Almaqah (a) small statue**...

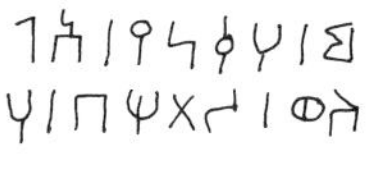

JA 2892

Fig 5.6 Two line inscription, boustrophedon script. Sandstone, incomplete, eroded.
L: 33.6cm, W: 19cm, Letters: 5cm
...**('lm)qh sb' bḥtm...qlb (?)**...
...**seven stelae to Almaqah**...

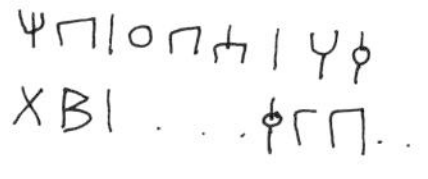

(previously unpublished)

Miscellanea

Column base, stepped ridges and shallow, square depression at the top. Limestone. In Muḥammad al-Shamīrī's house in Bājil.
L: 35cm, H: 29cm, W: 32cm

Two large spouts buried in the site itself.
Sandstone one in two pieces. L: 102cm; H: 20cm; Max. W: 41cm
Limestone. L: 68cm; H: 15cm; Max. W: 20cm
Both these spouts were found inside the temple. They are both incomplete.

* Fr. Albert Jamme has published five of the al-Hāmid inscriptions as JA 2892-2896. See A. Jamme, "Pre-Islamic Arabian Miscellanea," *Al-Hudhud: Festschrift Maria Höfner zum 80 Geburtstag*, ed. R.G. Steigner, Graz, 1981, pp. 95-97 and tracings on p. 111. [Ed.]

Jabal Bura' (Long. 43°25′E, Lat. 14°55′N). The land is owned by Muḥammad 'Abd al-Raḥmān al-Shamīrī, who lives in Bājil. The site extends over an area roughly 500×600m and numerous remains of square and rectangular houses can be seen on the surface plus an enormous amount of fallen stones. The debris is extensive. One rectangular building, measuring 11.4×9m, has been previously identified as a temple on the basis of the inscriptions found therein by Aḥmad Nājī Sari and Father Albert Jamme in 1976. The only blocks with marginally drafted, pecked masonry were found in association with the temple, and around it; the other houses were constructed from rough-cut stones and boulders. Pottery was collected from the site; it consisted mainly of burnished reddish-brown, plain or incised wares belonging to the pre-Islamic period. Only one piece of worked alabaster was found although the surface of the site was littered with unworked alabaster fragments. (See Plate XX.) On our return to Bājil we searched out Muḥammad al-Shamīrī and recorded and photographed the inscriptions that he had removed to his house there. He had five small inscriptions, carved in sandstone, written in a poor almost illiterate fashion, and in boustrophedon. There was also one column or statue base with three shallow steps made from limestone and almost square in shape. The big temple inscription had been reburied in the temple itself but Muḥammad al-Shamīrī wanted to remove it and bring it to Bājil for safe-keeping because a local *shaykh* in Wādī Sihām had been taking stones from the site. We therefore returned to the site the following day and excavated the inscription. It was of limestone, broken in two pieces and over two metres long. It had one line of inscription on its narrow side panel; the carving was better than that on the other smaller inscriptions. There were also two large spouts or possibly offering tables, one of sandstone and one of limestone. Both were reburied on the site after being photographed and measured. The inscription however, was taken to Bājil where it will stay with the other objects (see p. 52) till such time as a museum can be constructed for the Tihāmah region. Muḥammad al-Shamīrī says that there are a lot of graffiti on the slopes of Jabal al-Ḍāmir. He has taken great pains to preserve the site and has given strict instructions to the local farmers about showing the place to any passing tourists; it would be wonderful if more landowners felt the same way. He should be complimented and encouraged for his good work.

The site in al-Hāmid is a very important one. It is the only certain pre-Islamic site in the Tihāmah with inscriptions, and should therefore get more official protection especially if the tribes from across Wādī Sihām have started to show an interest in the stones that litter the surface of the site. It would not be very difficult to map and draw most of the houses, they are preserved to a minimum height of one metre in most places and appear to have simple internal divisions. This ancient village would have acted as one of the stations or staging posts on the Wādī Sihām trade route from the highlands to Ethiopia. These routes existed along most of the major *wādīs* coming down from the mountains, like Wādīs Surdud, Mawr and Zabīd, with two Tihāmah stations per route, one at the foothills, the other at the port on the coast. They should all be relatively easy to locate. Prof. Yūsuf 'Abdullāh of Ṣan'ā' University would date these sites generally to the first half of the first millennium A.D., i.e. 1-600 A.D. when the Ethiopian connection was at its highest.

The six inscriptions from the site (see Figures 5.1-5.6) indicate a B.C. rather than an A.D. date. They are not monotheistic, dedications are to both the sun and moon gods, and they are archaising if not archaic in appearance. All the five small inscriptions are written in boustrophedon, Sabaean script. The writing is of very poor quality and therefore difficult to date on palaeographic grounds. A date towards the end of the first millennium B.C. would seem to fit the bill (personal communication from Prof. Yūsuf M. 'Abdullāh).

AL-MARĀWI'AH AREA

Al-Kadrā'

12km SE of Marāwi'ah and on the banks of Wādī Jāḥif which feeds into Wādī Sihām. It has three small modern villages surrounding it, al-Rudumah which has surface pottery of the Rasūlid period scattered on its surface, al-Quz'ah and al-Ḥajwar. It is a huge site that covers an area roughly three by three kilometres, with a four to five-metre high deposit of human habitation in the central area and shallower remains towards the outer edges of the site. Bricks, cut stones, *quḍāḍ* (cement plaster), burnt areas and ash layers can be seen in the sections of the deep gullies on the north-west side of the mound. The site is very rich in surface finds. These include a majority of Rasūlid wares, glazed – mainly "turquoise under-glaze painted" in all its variations, incised and plain wares (see Plate 5.1) including those with "scratched designs" both with and without slips. Some porcelain (including some white that may be as early as the 9th century), some celedon wares, some 13th-century sgraffito ware, (see Plate XXVI) one sherd of 9th century Samarran splash ware and one of imitation porcelain of either Iraqi or Fatimid manufacture (9-12th century), was also found. Enormous quantities of worked steatite fragments (see Plate XXV) in the form of bowls, cooking pots and lamps were strewn on the mound; a sample collection was made. No "Ḥays ancien" pottery was found on this site. The ancient name of this site was the same as today and it is mentioned in a number of Islamic books including Ibn Ḥātim's *Kitāb al-Simṭ*.[4]

The information of these chronicles does not contradict in any way the dating evidence provided by the pottery. Therefore, a date around 1000 for the founding of the city would be accurate; there does not seem to be much evidence that the site continued in use much after the 14th century.

Al-Kadrā' was one of the main stops on the road from the south to Najrān and the north. In 1357 both Fashāl[5] and al-Kadrā' were sacked and razed to the ground; they both never really recovered.[6]

4. See G.R. Smith, *The Ayyubids and Early Rasulids in the Yemen*, London, Vol. 2, 1978, pp. 57-58. The town was attacked in the year 538 H/1143-4 by 'Alī ibn Mahdī and his army but they were defeated by the local Najāḥid *qā'id* (commander) named Isḥāq. It is also listed in Abū 'Abdullāh Yāqūt al-Ḥamawī's *Mu'jam al-buldān* (Beirut, n.d., Vol. IV, p. 441) as a city in Yemen in Wādī Sihām founded by al-Ḥusayn ibn Salāmah around 400 H/1030, and in al-Hamdānī's *Ṣifat Jazīrat al-'Arab*, ed. Muḥammad al-Akwa', al-Riyaḍ, 1974, p. 74, "a city inhabited by 'Akk, a section of the al-Azd tribe." See also Wilson, p. 31 et passim.
5. See Wilson, p. 33 et passim.
6. See R.W. Stookey, *Yemen*, Boulder, 1978, p. 123.

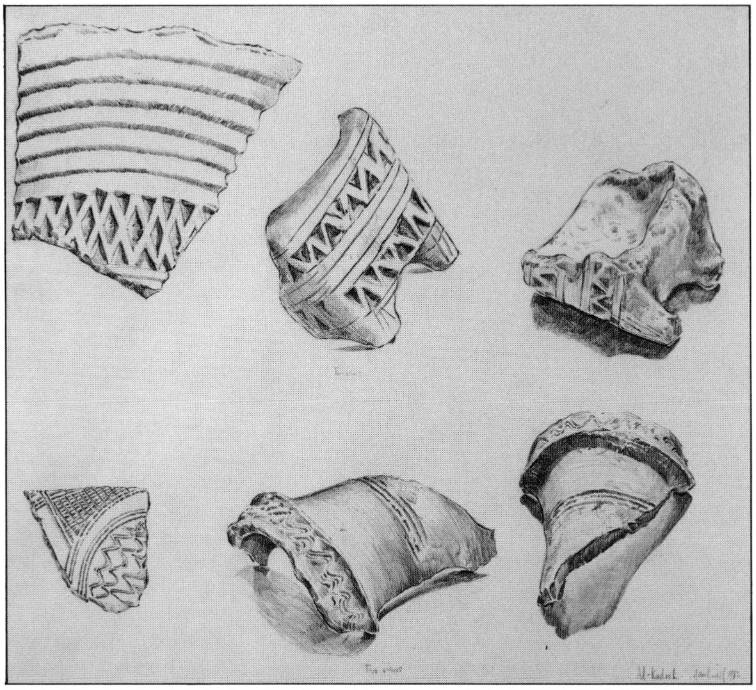

Plate 5.1 **Sherds, al-Kadrā'**, Rasūlid plain and incised wares
Upper: pot sherd, incense brazier (two views) Lower: pot sherd, neck of jar (two views)

AL-MANṢŪRĪYAH AREA

Wādī Raṭib[7]

Wādī Raṭib is due east of al-Manṣūrīyah and 10km out on the road to al-Jabī, a side road leading off the main al-Manṣūrīyah to al-Sukhnah road. There are numerous castles and sites on the hills on either side of this *wādī*, all appear to be late Islamic. Ḥuṣn Bakr Sharaf on hill to the right of the road which also leads to **Masjid Bulaybilah** a small mosque belonging to a village of the same name. A date, 1013 H., is inscribed in the *quḍāḍ* of the cistern, therefore making the mosque 16th-century at least, in origin. Further up the road is another *ḥuṣn* or castle called **Kabbat al-Shāwush** which has a potters' village at the foot of it. The potter's wheel has obviously not been invented here for the potter was turning around the pot.[8]

"Old Manṣūrīyah"

3km to the east of present-day al-Manṣūrīyah, in an arc between the main road to al-Sukhnah and the old road to al-Jabī is a cluster of three sites. The nearest village on the road to al-Sukhnah is that of Dayr Sajj and on the road to al-Jabī that of al-Maybilīyah. The whole area is called Bilād al-Manāṣirah after a section of the Zarānīq[9] tribe that lives in the region.

Site No. 3 is situated on the main al-Manṣūrīyah to al-Sukhnah road, in fact the road cuts the eastern ridge on which the city was built. Sites Nos. 1 and 2 are satellite villages and are situated close to the old road to al-Jabī. Site No. 3 extends over two ridges the westernmost of which has quantities of "turquoise under glaze, painted" wares, Tihāmah "Blue and White", "Ḥays ancien" and the usual plain and scratched wares, all characteristic of the Rasūlid period, i.e. from the 13th to the 15th century. (See Plates XIX,XXIII.) A section in the southern part of this ridge has a large scatter of slag on it: perhaps there was some sort of industrial smelting work being carried out there. The northeast ridge of the city had a larger variety of plain and incised wares that are pre-Rasūlid in date evident on the surface, the presence of some characteristic Rasūlid glazed wares indicated that it too continued into that period. The area covered by the two ridges extends to over two kilometres. No architectural remains are visible on the

7. This appears on the Survey Region Map on p. 3 as Wādī Ribāṭ, as per the Y.A.R. 1:50,000 Edition: 1-D.O.S. 1980. [Ed.]
8. See Stone, p. 112.
9. See Wilson, p. 35, Baldry, p. 47 et passim.
10. There is ample proof to identify the site named as "Old Manṣūrīyah" as the ancient town of al-Qaḥmah. J.W. Redhouse describes it thus:

> The city of Qaḥma, once of importance, now almost non-existent, was at lat. 14°38′ N., long. 43°24′ E. It is shown on the maps as "Káhhme", about five miles north from Beytu'l Faqíh. In the Merásid it is said to have been the chief town of the Vale of Dhuwál, at a distance from Zebíd of a day's journey and a half, with the town of Feshál lying between the two. It was a royal fief.

(Al-Khazrajī, *The Pearl Strings; a History of the Resúliyy Dynasty of Yemen*, trans. J.W. Redhouse, Leiden, 1907, Vol. III, p. 90, n.541.) Of Dhuwāl, he says, "Dhu'ál is the name of the vale, on the stream of which the town of Qaḥma was then situated, in about lat. 14°38′ N., long. 43°27′ E." (Ibid., Vol. III, p.75, n. 437.) The *wādī* near al-Manṣūrīyah is still referred to as Dhuwāl, and although the site has no watercourse near it today, there is a remnant *wādī* bed between the two mounds (now fields), and another on the south side. (On the Y.A.R. 1:50,000 Edition: 1-D.O.S. 1980, Sheet 1443 A4, the site would stand at lat. 14°41′ N., long. 43°20′ E. [Ed.]) See Wilson, p. 33 et passim.

site, the sand drifts are between 2-3m thick on most parts of the tell end only the deepest sections in the gullies show traces of occupational levels. Fragments of glass, worked steatite bowls and lamps, an array of stone tools (grinding slabs, mortars, pestles) and a few beads were collected from all the three sites. Sites Nos. 1 and 2 had a smaller percentage of glazed wares on the surface and what there was consisted mostly of "Ḥays ancien"; plain cooking wares were the most common wares found. Site No. 2 has a cemetery with built tombs on it. The three sites together form an important complex and should be studied further.[10]

BAYT AL-FAQĪH AREA

Al-Ja'āmīyah, or **Maḥall al-Ja'āmīyah** 4km SSE of Bayt al-Faqīh, it is a modern village situated on an ancient mound. Locals say that it antedates Bayt al-Faqīh by about 200 years but we found no evidence for that from the pottery on the surface which consisted of the usual Rasūlid mixture of wares, "turquoise under glaze", Tihāmah "Blue and White" and "Ḥays ancien". (See Plates XXI-II, XXIV.) A *madrasah* and mosque, probably dating back to the Rasūlid period, was still in use and had been redecorated in 1303 H., i.e. at the turn of the century, by Muḥammad Pasha, the Ottoman governor of the region. An inscription next to the *miḥrāb* honours the occasion. The site itself is quite large and covers an area of 500 by about 600 metres if not more, with a high depth of accumulated deposit in the centre.

Bayt al-Faqīh

We checked two mosques within the confines of the city itself. **Masjid al-Mashra',** in the southwest section, is a 700 year old mosque with nine domes over the prayer hall. It had been completely buried under the sands and was only recently dug up and redone in concrete and yellow acrylic paint. A porch has been added. The attached *madrasah* has very beautiful wall paintings on the inside and outside, done in black and red paint with geometric designs; there is also some stucco decoration. There is the tomb of a *walī* in the courtyard outside the *madrasah*. **Masjid al-Mās**, situated in the southern end of the city, has been redone in concrete.

Shaykh 'Umar al-'Ajīl, just southeast of the city, on a hill, is a small mosque in which Shaykh 'Umar ibn Ibrāhīm ibn 'Alī ibn 'Umar al-'Ajīl[11] was buried. The mosque sits on an ancient site, a small village of the Rasūlid period to judge by the sherds picked up from the surface. One coin, still indecipherable, was also found on the site.

Masjid Al-Akza', 2km due east of Bayt al-Faqīh, in the plain, are the remains of a ruined mosque, roofless and buried in the sand and surrounded by an ancient cemetery. All the tombs have built ridges around them, the remains of straw mats and broken pots with traces of burnt charcoal and probably incense in them. Some have baskets that would have no doubt contained offerings, and some have string and rope tied around the stones. The tomb situated inside the mosque belongs to Walī al-Akza'. The locals informed us that the women put these offerings on the tombs (none of which are modern) as a pledge or votive offering. There are no traces of any buildings in the immediate vicinity of the cemetery. There were also no pottery fragments, glass or other detritus of human occupation; it had therefore never been a habitation site.

DISCUSSION

Although pre-Islamic cities seem to have been of limited number in the Tihāmah, there is sufficient evidence that they did exist along the major *wādī* routes towards the coast and along the coastline itself. They were, however, entrepots and way stations with a small permanent population rather than large cities or villages. Al-Hāmid or Dayr al-Turāb is a good example of one such station along the route of Wādī Sihām. The interesting change seems to occur in the Tihāmah in the early Islamic period, especially from the 10th century through to the Early Rasūlid period, when a boom period occurred in the Yemen, and especially in the Tihāmah. As the Abbasid caliphate declined, the trade routes shifted from the Arabian Gulf back to the Red Sea. Trade in the Yemen prospered as did the agriculture. Taxes were severe but presumably flexible enough to permit the accretion of wealth for both the people and their rulers. The Tihāmah was "an intensively cultivated, populous region which sustained the strong Ziyād and Najāḥ states for three centuries and netted 'Alī al-Ṣulayḥī an annual million dinars in revenue".[12] Misrule by the Rasūlids and their agents and overtaxation forced the people eventually to abandon their lands. By the middle of the 14th century, the rot had set in firmly and the decline of the Tihāmah region remained a fact until the last few years.

ILLUSTRATION

Plate 5.1 Nankivell, 360 × 420mm, pencil drawing, courtesy of Private Collection; *Figures 5.1-5.6* Provided by the author.

GLOSSARY

ḥuṣn	castle, fort, citadel
madrasah	school
manṣab	sufi master
miḥrāb	prayer niche
qā'id	commander
quḍāḍ[13]	cement plaster (var. of *qaḍāḍ*)
rab'	religious college (often no more than the residence of an eminent teacher with several students living-in)
shaykh	headman of a tribe
sīrah	biography (of the Prophet, understood)
wādī	seasonal river bed
walī	saint
ziyārah	saint's day festival, visitation to a saint's tomb

---

11. Presumably a member of the family of the founding father of Bayt al-Faqīh, given by al-Khazrajī in Redhouse's translation as 'Ebú'l 'Abbás Aḥmed b.Músá b. 'Aliyy b. 'Umer b. 'Ujeyl, 1212-1291. (Ibid., Vol. I, p. 221.) [Ed.]
12. See R.W. Stookey, op.cit. p. 121.
13. For a description of *qaḍāḍ*, see R. Lewcock, "The Houses of Ṣan'ā'", *Ṣan'ā' an Arabian Islamic City*, eds. R.B. Serjeant and R. Lewcock, London, 1983, pp. 479-480. The remarkable durability of *qaḍāḍ* is explained by R. Lewcock (in communication) as being due to the fact that it is hard enough to be waterproof, but not hard enough to crack in the sun. Its structure is non-crystalline. [Ed.]

ARCHITECTURE

INTRODUCTION

Three major and two minor styles of traditional architecture grace the Tihāmah plain. These can be categorised by construction material as coral masonry buildings on the coast, brick and plaster structures inland, and thatch houses. The minor categories include palm-tree structures of the date groves, and mixtures of river stone, plaster and thatch found in the foothills.

The issue of foreign influence on Tihāmah architecture is a complex one and little studied. Many important buildings constructed during the medieval period under the non-Yemeni Ayyūbids, Rasūlids, Mamluks and Ottomans[1] are documented in chronicles and inscriptions. It is in more recent times, since the decline of Tihāmah culture, that less attention has been paid to its architectural history. The Ottomans, while undoubtedly influential in fashioning the "Red Sea" structures of Hodeida and al-Luḥayyah, were by no means the only clients of Tihāmah builders in the last two centuries. Indeed, the term "Turkish" is much overused to describe and explain the structures standing today from this period. Certainly other dynamics were at work. Followers of the Idrīsī[2] were responsible for a number of buildings on the northern Tihāmah, notably at Ibn 'Abbās. Highland Yemeni styles found expression in the forts and *ḥukūmahs* erected by the Imām in the early 1930s, such as at al-Ḍaḥī and al-Ḥusaynīyah, as well as giving rise to certain hybrid house styles in Zabīd and Bājil. And in Wādī Mawr, the agents of the great landowning families, such as al-Hayj[3] and al-Barāq,[4] built large fortified residences. These *ḥuṣns,* with their ornate brickwork and multi-storied keeps, may have been erected during the Ottoman occupation, but they represent a distinct and indigenous architecture. The two other main influences, Indian and African, also need closer appraisal; Indian workmanship is generally associated with certain details of woodcarving on the "Red Sea" buildings, and it may be a factor in aspects of Zabīdī ornamentation. But specific documentation is still lacking. Furthermore, the array of thatch hut architecture, commonly thought of as African in origin, probably evolved independently, its affinities with African types arising from the nature of the vegetable matter found across the subtropical sahel belt into the Tihāmah.

Of all the Tihāmah architectures, it is possible that the domestic architecture of Zabīd and environs is unique.[5] Nevertheless, an extensive study of the Zabīd style houses has yet to be produced. The salient features and the development of substyles need to be identified, and only when this is done can the foreign influences be assessed.[6] Zeal in tracing these influences, however, should not obscure the fact that Zabīd's domestic architecture stands as a remarkable, sophisticated achievement in its own right.

In fact, the entire question of foreign influence on Tihāmah architecture may ultimately prove intractable, since the many strands woven from centuries of trade, migration and occupation in the Red Sea and Indian Ocean basin are knottily intertwined.[7]

The following papers and drawings by John Nankivell and Steven D. Ehrlich serve to describe the range of architectures that exist on the Tihāmah. Neither contribution constitutes a formal or a comprehensive study. Neither lays claim to scholarly authority. Since relatively little has been published on Tihāmah architecture, the picture provided in these surveys is meant as a point of departure for further study. The major issues which are not addressed by them include various construction techniques (two thatch house construction techniques were documented), patterns of use, foreign and historical influences, and regional boundaries of architectural styles and substyles. These matters await extended research of the kind not possible in a short field trip. [Ed.]

1. See Wilson, pp. 32-34. See Plate 4.1.
2. See Baldry, p. 47.
3. See H. Escher, *Wirtschafts und sozialgeographische Untersuchungen in der Wadi Mawr Region (Arabische Republik Jemen),* p. 43; also see M. Mundy, *A Baseline Socio-Economic Survey of the Wādī Mawr Region,* pp. 170-172.
4. This family, with connections in the 'Asīr, John Baldry states (in communication), was also responsible for the construction of the present Bāb Mishrif in Hodeida, in the first quarter of the nineteenth century. See Plates XVIII and XXVII, XXVIII.
5. Thus argues J. Chelhod in his article, "Introduction à l'Histoire Sociale et Urbaine de Zabīd," *Arabica,* Vol. 25, 1978, pp. 48-88. However, houses exist on Farasān Island so similar to those of Zabīd as to challenge Zabīd's claim. Nevertheless, this particular house style on Farasān is referred to locally as "Yemeni", thereby allowing the conjecture that it was imported from Zabīd or its environs. The Editor is most grateful to W. Facey for calling attention to the Farasān example which he has photographed in detail.
6. Similarities with certain elements of West Indian house decoration and plan are noteworthy.
7. As Antonin Besse commented when asked his opinion about the workmanship on a carved door in al-Luḥayyah, it was more than likely "it came off the back of a camel."

6.1: TIHĀMAH ARCHITECTURE – AN ARCHITECTURAL ARTIST'S VIEW

John Nankivell

Mr. Nankivell brings to this discussion and to his drawings a trained architectural eye with more than ten years experience in the architectures of India, Sri Lanka and Indonesia. As it was his first visit to the Yemen, his point of reference remains further east, and this is reflected in his terminology. Arabic words have been added where appropriate. However, one should refer to Mr. Ehrlich's drawings for the majority of architectural terms collected on the Tihāmah. Mr. Ehrlich and Mr. Nankivell worked closely in the field, and Mr. Nankivell's paper is meant to complement that of Mr. Ehrlich in so far as it deals with "Red Sea" houses and inland fortresses, the Wādī Mawr hut interior and the Zabīd house in considerable detail. Mr. Nankivell's narrative and visual descriptions provide the lay reader with an introduction to the most impressive Tihāmah architecture. A broader-based and more technical approach is offered by Mr. Ehrlich in the subsequent paper. [Ed.]

This is a brief examination of the variety of the architecture in the Tihāmah coastal area of the Yemen Arab Republic, starting with the village reed hut – circular or oblong, the village fortress – of indeterminate date and mixed style, the prosperous Red Sea towns – with high stone or rubble buildings of stucco and wood, and the inland towns – with mud-brick and stucco buildings.

The reed villages of the Tihāmah are a remarkable feature of the flat coastal plain. The first impression is always the distant silhouette of the two basic shapes – the pointed or rounded hut, and the conical shape of the large sorghum stalks. These two forms rival each other in the image of the village, and combined with walls, thicket fences, occasional tall mud brick forts and domes and minarets of modest mosques and the occasional oasis of luxuriant trees, form memorable visual groups.

The houses vary considerably in form and shape rather than in actual construction. The northern Wādī Mawr region favours the circular ground plan and pointed shape, while further south the houses are somewhat smaller and built as an oblong rising to a ridge. (See Figures 6.40-6.42.)

The basic sequence of building in Wādī Mawr begins in a raised and patterned mud floor about eight inches higher than the surrounding ground. A round wall of platted wood, thatched and woven on the outside holds a tall thatched roof which is held firmly in shape by beautifully made, generously thick ropes knotted both at the peak and at a horizontal line just below the roof base on the drum of the walls. Usually there are two wooden doors with decorated ventilation panels above them. (See Plate 6.1 and Figure 6.45.)

The enclosure may possess a more simple storage/kitchen hut with a similar dwelling huts for other family members. Within this outer protected space of wood/mud walls and thorn fences, the life of the home is centered around large wooden beds in shady spots, animals stand tied and feeding, and the women of the household prepare meals and maintain the clothes and effects of the family. (See Figure 6.44.)

Internally the village hut at its best can be a dramatic revelation of scale and decoration. The interior is completely mud-smoothed throughout in a pleasing pale sandy tone, the large floor is hand decorated with fan-like patterns in the wet mud as it is laid down. In several places, notably near the doors, mud shelves and plinths for utensils and work have been built. Much of the wall area has been decorated with paint, which culminates in a concentration of pattern in the top third of the pointed ceiling.

The decoration, which is painted by a specially appointed local woman who is paid some 100 YRs per day for at least a twelve day period consists of descending bands of intricate coloured designs interdispersed with heavenly bodies, Islamic texts, floral displays, common implements and the symbols of a disturbed and changing society – tanks, aeroplanes, cars and lorries, ships, soldiers and guns.

Between this revolving glorious patterning and above the clear wall space occupied by the double rows of Tihāmah beds and couches, ornamental chests, cabinets and stacked tin trunks of possessions is the main surface of the inside walls of the hut. This large area is occupied by horizontal rows of wooden pegs set into the walls and usually surrounded by little buds of coloured petals or patterning. Even by themselves these simply carved wooden pegs would be attractive, but they are only the framework for a wealth – visually and materially – of objects hanging from them. Numberless chinese plates richly decorated in porcelain and enamel (cherished, these are passed down from mother to daughter at marriage), pots, pans, pictures of the family, the President, movie stars, and Islamic texts, mirrors, baskets, buckets, mugs, tea glasses and trays. The overall effect combined with the cushioned beds, the glittering locks and hinges on the chests and a polished multimetal hooka with its rainbow coloured smoking tube is one of overwhelming colour, splendour and complexity. (See Plate 6.2 and Figure 6.46.)

If anything, the oblong larger houses to the south of Wādī Mawr are even more elaborate, with plinths, ledges, cupboards and shelves fashioned and painted like frosted gingerbread on the daub-covered interior. (See Figure 6.42.)

The contrast between the quiet soft tones of the rush exterior of these houses and their intense and complex interiors is the chief feature that remains – together with the regal hospitality of the people – in one's memory.

There appears to be no really definitive pattern to the design of the village mosque or fortress. As in most countries, the scale and grandeur seem to depend on the prosperity, position and significance of the locality. The basic village mosque plan is a single dome or a simply oriented arcade of three domed spaces linked internally by two arches, walled on three sides and accompanied by a small minaret. (See Plates 6.3, 6.4 and Figures 6.7-6.20.) The larger mosques merely increase their arcades to six or nine domes. There are considerable variations on this basic idea. A tomb of a local holy man may dominate the adjoining mosque (as at Ibn 'Abbās or Bayt 'Aṭā', see Figures 6.25-6.29), the enclosure walls may be higher and grander than usual, or the minaret be distinctive by its size and form. As with the huts and sorghum stacks in the flat Tihāmah plain, the silhouette plays an important part in the signature of the structure; as a medieval cathedral spire would beckon to the faithful, so the shimmering white dome on the edge of the horizon or the white pillar of the minaret above the pointed line of houses guides the hot traveller towards water, prayer and repose.

The fortress, since the Revolution, has obviously lost a good deal of its importance. Formerly the barracks and/or living accommodation for the local Governor/

'āmir/shaykh, and therefore almost always a dominant building, most now seem to have been abandoned except for the occasional storeroom or high *mafraj*. As architecture they can be rich in local mud brick decoration as at al-Rāfi'ī or al-Ḍaḥī (see Plates 6.5, 6.6) or plain and unprepossessing even in their decay as at Nukhlayah. (See Plate 6.7 and Figure 6.35.)

The coastal towns and ports are a complete contrast to the villages. Built on a grand scale, they like so many colonial settlements show the influences of the builders' attempt (doomed to failure in the Yemen?) to make themselves feel at home. The only limit to the quality of these settlements appears in the lack of substantial building materials, which indeed have proved the fatal flaw in their survival, for these towns have suffered not only from the disintegration of the Ottoman Empire and from the withdrawal of the colonial and merchant populations, but the very fabric they left behind has, like scenery, collapsed only moments after the principal actors have left the stage. (See Plates 6.8-6.10.)

This lack of proper building materials is critical. The stone used appears merely to have been red lava coral, fragile and heavily veined, and pure coral sometimes cut but more often just as lumps, its uneveness being filled in with deeper stucco. Wood was used extensively throughout the construction and seems generally to have been of good quality (some imported from the East Indies and Africa), except for the lack of really massive beam timber (most of it was rounded smallish tree trunks) and for its irresistible attractiveness to termites. All was finally covered in a coating of semi-stucco.

In, for example, the British colonial buildings of South East India when stucco was used upon brick, rubble or wood, the builders took great care to make it of the finest quality. Its final skin, from ground-down sea shells was polished to a glittering rock hard white, making Madras in its day one of the most elegant cities in the East. This encased and protected the buildings from decay and, if this was maintained undamaged, they survived. When the materials were poor or neglected and the surface broke, the climate soon ripped them to pieces.

It is fascinating to note design flaws which in the past centuries seem to have dictated the survival of entire architectural civilisations. Putting apart earthquake and similar natural and man-made catastrophes, much of the Mogul architecture of north central India does not survive purely because of the weakness of a bracket, holding the umbrella-like slabs on the top of every facade. A break and the little roof falls. The delicate facade with all its tiles, its stucco and its patterns dissolves; at the next monsoon, it is undermined and eventually all is lost.

There seems to be little formal pattern in the arrangement and design of the port houses, examples of which are known as Red Sea architecture. They have a basic unity and structural layout but vary considerably from house to house. (See Plates 6.8-6.12 and Plate XVII.)

In al-Luḥayyah, most begin with richly decorated doorways, wood-carved and surrounded by stucco patterns (see Plate 6.9), above may be some external balconies and windows that are latticed and multi-arched. The internal ground floor courtyard is often surrounded by storerooms, perhaps for the household and/or its business. The living floor was often the first floor above the stores, held up by tall stuccoed coral columns. Here the main life of the house evolved – bathrooms, workrooms, open-walled salas and corridors, reception rooms, sleeping rooms, verandas and smoking rooms. Decoration was lavish with wood and plasterwork and painting gently lit by stained glass and latticed windows.

Each settlement as always possesses several mosques which again can be modest or grand. Similar materials used in their construction have doomed them to the same fate as the secular architecture, although a major attempt has been made in al-Luḥayyah to restore the huge arcades of al-Zayla'ī mosque.

Zabīd is an extensive, complex town (considerably larger in earlier days)[8] on the interior flat agricultural lands some twenty miles west of the rising foothills of the Yemeni mountains. It presents itself today as largely decaying from its prosperous past. Its mosques, which number at least eighty-six[9] and even its great fort are visibly neglected. Its centre is not the irregular square before the fortress and *ḥukūmah*, but rather the wandering area of the *sūq* (see Figure 6.34) which however sordid – and it is indeed that – is still the main artery, soon however to be overtaken by the new automobile-based settlement astride the nearby main road.

The chief visual glory of Zabīd must obviously be its mosques. Yet a very close second must come its houses. These don't appear to rival the mosques at first sight because of the very nature of their planning. It could be said that the larger a Zabīd house, the more intricate does its architectural arrangement become. Some houses occupy an entire block of the town and while the simpler ones merely have one basic living pavilion with perhaps a side building for domestic work, it is often difficult to isolate where one residence begins and the other stops.

The larger the house is, the more it attempts to hide its splendour behind high walls. Thus the entire city is characterised by these tall dark, mud brick, battered walls, sometimes surmounted by a cornice, frieze or finials in the Mogul inspired motif of a bud or flame (see Figure 6.64) which line the deep and winding alleys. Some of the very large houses which choose to go up as well as spread their size, display some of their material grandeur on the decoration of the facades of the upper rooms while reserving the best decoration for internal eyes. However they often are unable to refrain from an outward display of wealth in patterned brick and stucco moulding.

The entrance to the Zabīd house tries to be as tortuous as possible, presumably to protect the privacy of the women of the household. Doorways already hidden back in the walls often lead into corridors and small rooms which then double back on themselves through a series of doors. Here it is interesting to note that for example in the Wāqidī house, the main doorway *(bawwābah)* was hidden and protected, but one small entrance – which was obvious – led straight into the men's afternoon, ground floor smoking room. (See Figure 6.58.)

Not all the grand houses however forbear to grandify their main doors. A definite style exists throughout the city of high Mogul-style arches filled with complex geometric and floral plasterwork above the lintel, beneath which two tall oblong main wooden doors stand, richly carved.

The large house will have several pavilions, each a separate structure, facing onto a courtyard, perhaps above or opposite a similar room. Usually again, one pavilion appears to be the principal reception room

8. See E. Keall, "Zabīd and its Hinterland: 1982 Report," *Proceedings of the Seminar for Arabian Studies*, Vol. 13, 1983.
9. This was a preliminary count taken by members of the Royal Ontario Museum team led by Dr. Ed Keall, Zabīd 1982. [Ed.]

(liwān) of the house while others are reserved for the women and children or the men of the establishment. While family men may be allowed anywhere, outsiders are definitely restricted in access to the rest of the house.

The pavilion facade is always symmetrical, a small flight of steps walled with blank balustrading leads to the main carved central door. Each side of which the same number of internally shuttered windows, two to eight in all, extend. The centre structural lines are vertical, but the side walls often have a considerable batter on them. All areas of the large facade are divided into sections of deeply incised design work, as complex and varied as possible, and again as in the street doorway, using geometric and floral based designs for the chief motifs. (See Plate 6.13.)

Internally the floor of the pavilion is raised about two feet off the ground level; this does not stop the rising damp, the curse and in the final analysis one of the principal factors of decay in the town (the second factor being termites). The high room is wood beamed with plaster infilling (in humbler parts of the house the infilling is just in small base wood branches), each beam can be painted in designs and flowers. The walls are deeply decorated with friezes of plasterwork, niches and inset with beautifully carved wooden cupboards often holding old manuscripts, the prize possession of the leading families. Whatever the scale of the room, its proportions are always well balanced. Furnishing is mainly the high Tihāmah couches, covered in rich houses with persian carpets and many silk and patterned cushions. Beneath, or beside these, are trunks, some old and decorated, some in new metal, holding clothes and other valuables. Decoration on the walls can vary from passe-partouted Islamic coloured texts, clocks, machine guns, lethal looking knives, and shelves can hold the latest vulgar bazaar vase or the electronic paraphernalia now the chief glory of modern Yemen (after the petrol station), indeed the whole peninsula.

The focal point of many pavilions is no doubt the long rows of hookas, an ostentatious display of wealth since one hooka alone can cost 1000 YRs. In the case of the Wāqidī house, these were placed on a long plain wooden table in the centre of the room, rather like the gilded candlesticks on a Catholic altar. (See Plate 6.14.)

The great Zabīd houses possess large rooms high up where the men of the family and friends spend the hot afternoons in the cool breezes smoking and chewing langourously. These rooms are among the more finely decorated ones and similar to the *liwān* room in most features. Stained glass in the windows and cushions on the floor rather than on high beds are some of the main differences between the high and low saloons.

Zabīd undoubtedly is better known for its wealth of mosques, from the small and simple to the grand and daring ones. The Great Mosque covers an extremely large area, basically an enclosed oblong with the minaret in the centre of one of the long-sided wall, interestingly enough of similar design to the Mahjam minaret at al-Manārah. (See Plate 4.1)

Inside the Great Mosque, the many arched aisles, outer walls and domes were once heavily decorated in plaster designs, roundels, friezes of flower motifs and Koranic inscriptions. The aisles are all grouped around a large open courtyard containing a well. Because of its horizontal scale, the Great Mosque is not impressive at first sight.

The several large mosques of later date and non-Yemeni influence are indeed the most impressive of the town at first glance. The fort mosque, al-Iskandarīyah, with its slender minaret, and huge dome on a simple octagonal base and traces of exquisite decoration is said to be Ottoman but may well have been built earlier.[10] Across the main road to the east in a former, now vanished, area of the city, a large many-domed mosque, al-Muṣṭafā Pasha, somewhat resembles that vast and beautiful corpse of the Hagia Sophia in Istanbul.

Although the mosques of Zabīd appear in perilous decay, they seem to be more solidly constructed than the doomed domestic architecture of the town and could still be saved, given the will of the authorities. Certainly Zabīd as an historic settlement[11] deserves to be conserved as much as possible. Even now it is a fascinating city. However modern architecture will soon transform much of the traditional character of this unique town into a suburb of 20th century developed squalor. Yet for just a few years more Zabīd exists and looks from a distance at least as romantic and picturesque as it has done for the last ten centuries.

10. See Keall, op. cit.
11. See Wilson, pp. 34-35.

6.2: TIHĀMAH PORTFOLIO – A SELECTION OF DRAWINGS AND COMMENTARY BY THE ARTIST

John Nankivell

Plate 6.1 Nankivell *405×505mm pencil drawing courtesy of Private Collection*

Wādī Mawr Hut Exterior, al-Muʻtariḍ. The owner of this traditional village hut, Muḥammad ʻAlī Sulaymān, rests blissfully on his Tihāmah couch listening to his new radio. Behind him one of the two tall double doors leads into the cool interior. Externally the low platted wall of the hut supports a vast rising roof of branches and thatch, the whole held in place by a magnificent array of woven ropes.

Plate 6.2 Nankivell *1015×760mm pencil drawing courtesy of Victoria & Albert Museum*

Wādī Mawr Hut Interior, al-Mu'tariḍ. While the hut exterior is both elegant in silhouette and admirable in construction, nothing prepares one for the extraordinary interior. Circular and mud-plastered to the apex, the top third of the dome is hand painted by a professional artist (a woman) in a whirl of coloured patterns and figures. Beneath this, rows of wooden pegs act as hooks for a multicoloured galaxy of painted enamel dishes, bowls, mirrors, trays, etc. Anything that is needed is fetched down with a long pole. At floor level a circle of cushioned Tihāmah beds completes the amazing ensemble. Our host lies on his back in the centre, chewing his afternoon *qāt* and conversing in shouts with the ladies outside in the harem courtyard.

Plate 6.3 Nankivell *560×505mm pencil drawing*

Two Studies of a Small Mosque, al-Durayhimī. This single domed mosque is set in a pretty, low walled compound on the northern edge of the oasis of al-Durayhimī, and from its ridge it overlooks the rather fine village and has considerable views to the north. A raised gazebo, the minaret, occupies a corner of the courtyard wall. Internally the mosque is simple, but satisfying and very peaceful.

Plate 6.4 Nankivell *505×685mm pencil drawing*

Mosque Interior, al-Durayhimī. This splendid mosque of 'Abdullāh ibn 'Alī in the village of al-Durayhimī is as elegant internally as it is externally. Triple domed and linked by two fine arches, it is both majestic in scale and sophisticated in its detailed plaster work around the *miḥrāb*. It was however hot, dusty, dirty and unpleasant to draw in.

Plate 6.5 Nankivell *405×505mm pencil drawing courtesy of Private Collection*

Mud Fort at al-Rāfiʿī, Wādī Mawr. A large, semi-derelict mud brick fortress, carrying rich decoration, lies on the north-eastern side of this village deep in Wādī Mawr. The long structure of the fortress is divided into three sections, and crowned with a balustrade, Mogul-style giant flames and an ever-present dramatic host of pigeons. Complex and elegant panels and bands of patterned brick cover the facade. The central doorway has recently been beautifully painted in pale greens, blues, greys and white.

Plate 6.6 Nankivell *430×685mm pencil drawing courtesy of Mr. and Mrs. Anthony Richmond-Watson*

Mud Fort, al-Ḍaḥī. The large mud brick fort *(ḥuṣn)* of an extensive inland village, surrounded by rubble and rubbish and with the addition of a petrol station on one side, it is overgrown with scrub on the inside. The main range with many bastions and windows is still used, mostly as a goal and barracks, but the rest of the fortress is beginning to crumble. Externally the tall battered towers are still impressive with their brick bands and white-edged windows. The fort was built in 1934 of bricks which were robbed out of the ruins of al-Mahjam. A great stir was caused by my substitution of a Yemeni national flag for the huge new radio and television aerial on the main roof – something I refused to record.

Plate 6.7 Nankivell *430×570mm pencil drawing*

Lone Fort at Nukhaylah. On a solitary eminence overlooking a lagoon stands this "toy" fort. It is a small building and extremely well preserved. Its upper room, with its many windows and exciting views in all directions, was so pleasant we decided to make it our camp. The surrounding coastal waters were a paradise for waders and seabirds.

Plate 6.8 Nankivell *455×660mm pencil drawing courtesy of Victoria & Albert Museum*

Seafront House with Birds, al-Luḥayyah. A large house typical of those still standing in the town. The coral-block structure is in its death throes, collapsing in all directions. Its bath house leans to the north at crazy angles, the centre is a mound of damp salty rubble, while the main facade totters to the south. Even the huge latticed balcony *(rawshan)* has become detached from the wall and threatens to pitch onto the soggy promenade.

Plate 6.9 Nankivell *430×505mm pencil drawing*

Old Doorway, al-Luḥayyah. Narrow alleys on the southern side of the town lead to a tepid sea fringed with mounds of 19th century shards. That this area once contained far more substantial houses is evident by the number of finely carved rotting doorways obscured by piles of refuse. This doorway has a delicacy almost surrealistic amid such squalor.

Plate 6.10 Nankivell *915×860mm pencil drawing*

Bayt Wadūd Interior, al-Luḥayyah. One of the largest houses left standing, barely, in the crumbling Turkish town of al-Luḥayyah. This was once the home of a wealthy pearl merchant. One half of the building, its eastern wing, has already collapsed into a mound of broken woodwork and rubble. The central block faces a western courtyard, its first floor raised above storerooms on unstable pillars. There are only two rooms on this floor – a fine, high-ceilinged bathroom and this long sitting room, its high wooden benches now deep in dust. Its only occupants now are some one hundred, noisy, smelly bats who live amid the flowers of the ceiling. Beautiful views of the city can be seen from the surrounding grand and screened balconies, and directly above lies a small smoking pavilion, the last retreat from the heat of the summer time.

Plate 6.11 Nankivell *505×380mm pencil drawing courtesy of John Julius Norwich*

House in the Turkish Quarter, Hodeida. Now an extensive modern port, the old quarter of Hodeida still contains many elegant and beautiful buildings such as this one. Not far from the *sūq*, its tall ground floor is obviously a busy store, while the upper floors are an extensive house. The doorway undoubtedly had richer plaster decoration than remains today.

Plate 6.12 Nankivell *680×505mm pencil drawing courtesy of George and Jill Kassis*

John Baldry's House, Hodeida. Deep in the old Turkish quarter of town, this corner house, now used as a goldsmith's shop, has an intricate plaster floral arch over the ground floor doorway. The main feature of the facade is its first floor wooden balcony *(rawshan)*, a marvellous eye-catcher in the narrow street, and echoed by others, some even more refined in nearby alleys. The house was constructed in 1809.

Plate 6.13 Nankivell *610×660mm pencil drawing*

Bayt Wāqidī Exterior, Zabīd. As with all the Zabīd pavilioned houses the facade though complex is completely symmetrical. This is one of at least three such structures within the tall blank mud brick walls of this large family home.

Plate 6.14 Nankivell *860×915mm pencil drawing*

Bayt Wāqidī Interior, Zabīd. Proportionally excellent, long and tall this room presents a rich example of the prosperity of the upper class of Zabīd. From its painted beamed ceiling, its plasterwork and tall carved Tihāmah couches to its array of flashy possessions, the scene presented is one of considerable comfort and luxury. An equally fine upper room in the same house complex carried a construction date on its lintel of 1364 A.H., that's to say some two generations old.

6.3 TIHĀMAH ARCHITECTURE – AN ARCHITECT'S SURVEY DRAWINGS

Steven D. Ehrlich

This set of architectural drawings by Steven D. Ehrlich constitutes a survey of the major vernacular forms on the North Yemen Tihāmah with the exception of "Red Sea" houses and inland fortresses, both of which are treated extensively by Mr. Nankivell.

The drawings are arranged in the following sequence: Religious structures, Public structures, Military structures, Domestic structures and constructions, and lastly Architectural details. Religious structures are subdivided into Mosques, Mosques and Schools, and Mosques and Tombs. The internal order of each category progresses from temporary to permanent materials, from basic to complex design.

The brief descriptions which precede the drawings have been compiled by Yamini Patel based on Mr. Ehrlich's work-books and other related field notes. The drawings themselves incorporate data concerning Arabic terms, history and use of the structures studied. These notes were gathered by various members of the Expedition in conjunction with Mr. Ehrlich. [Ed.]

RELIGIOUS STRUCTURES

Figures 6.1-6.2

The palm tree mosque located on the northern edge of al-Marāziqah is a basic structure constructed out of organic materials. It stands on the north side of a circular compound which is defined by a palm leaf wall with an entrance from the south. The mosque walls are made of palm trunks, a *miḥrāb* on the north wall. The roof is constructed out of palm leaf, the ridge being a palm trunk.

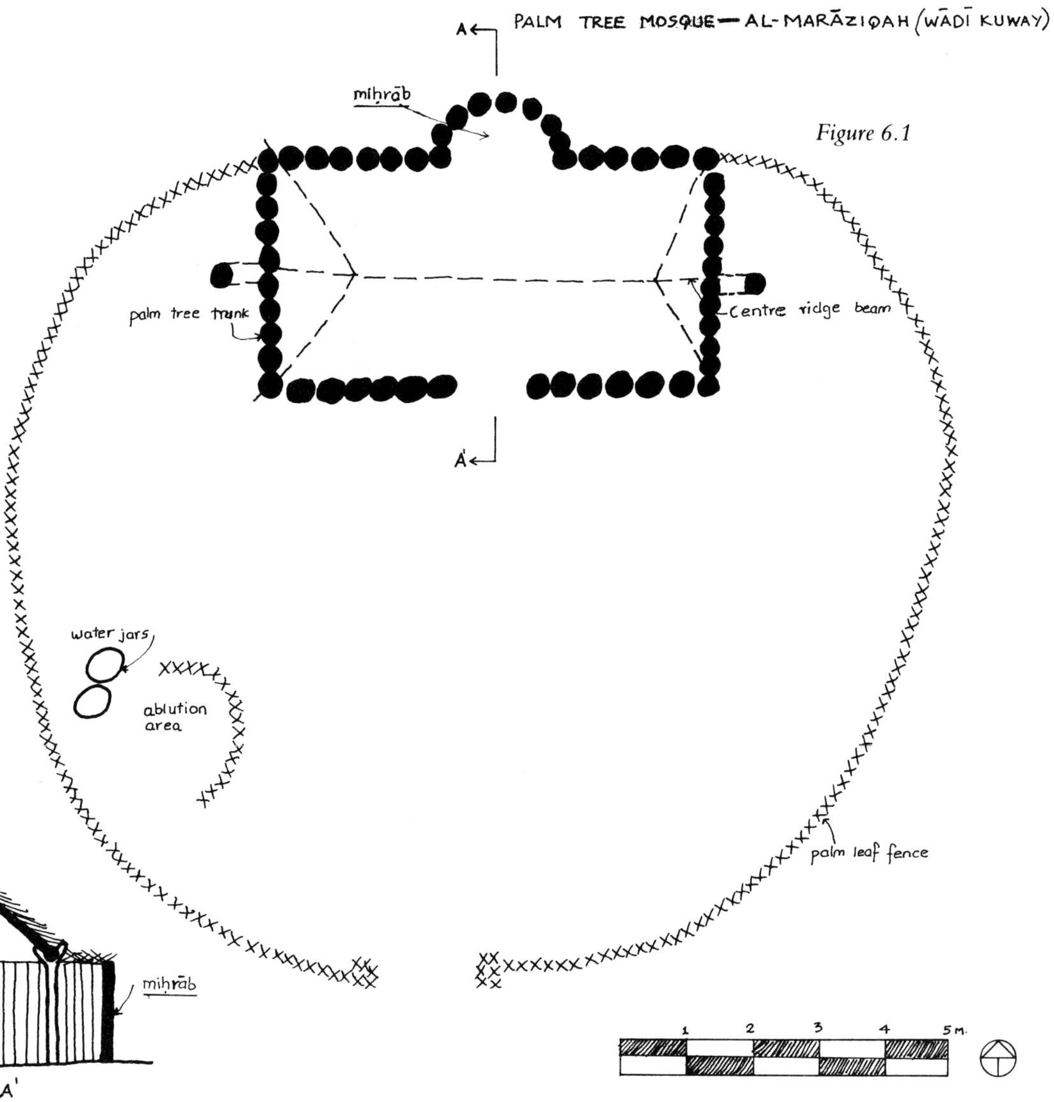

Figure 6.1

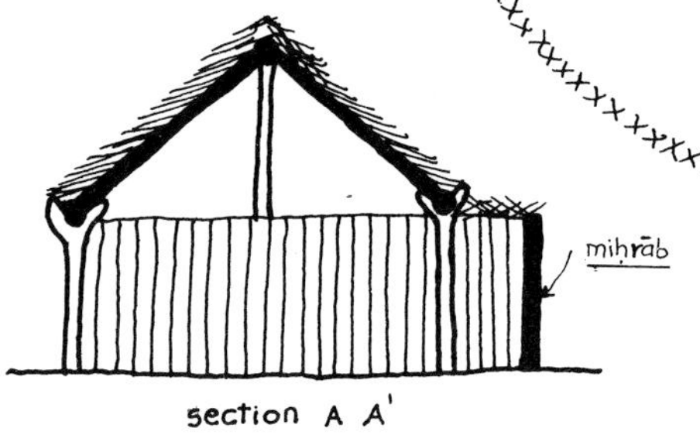

Figure 6.2

Figures 6.3-6.6

The river stone mosque at al-Ṣanīf consists of three spaces. It has a courtyard defined by river stone walls with a raised opening from the east, an ablution area with cistern in the north courtyard wall and a prayer hall on the west. The prayer hall has an arched doorway in the south wall with an arched *miḥrāb* on the north wall. The interior of the prayer hall is divided by arches, while the walls support a flat roof.

Figure 6.3

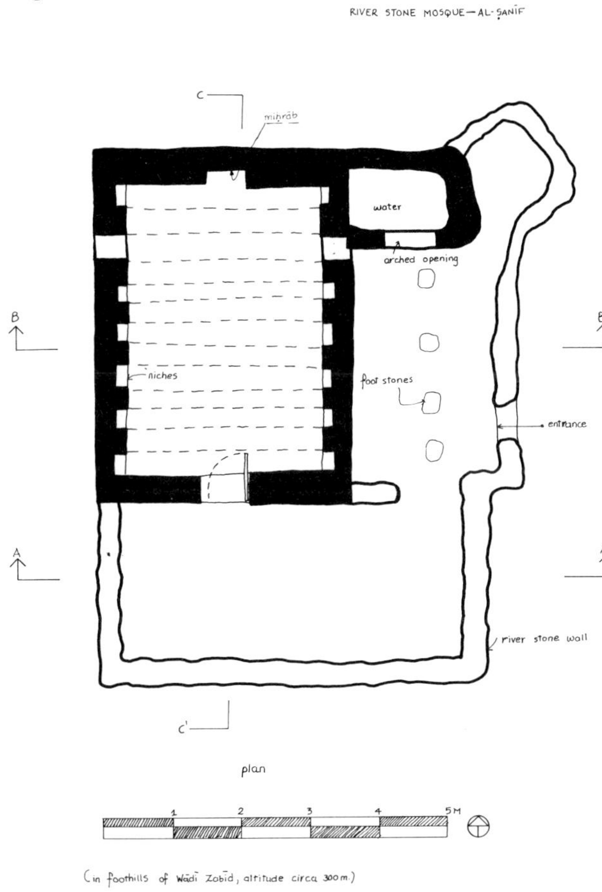

Figure 6.4

Figure 6.5

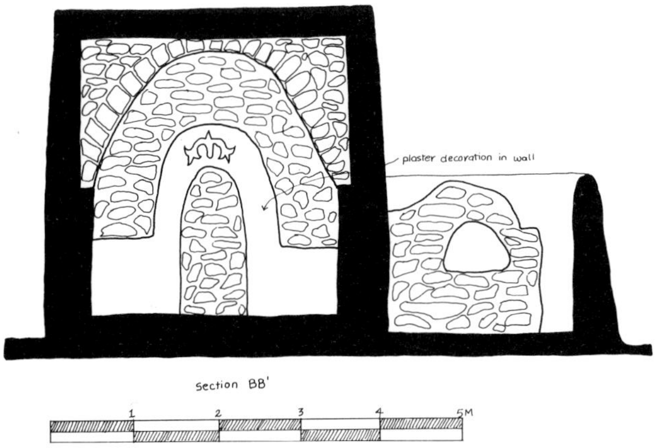

Figure 6.6

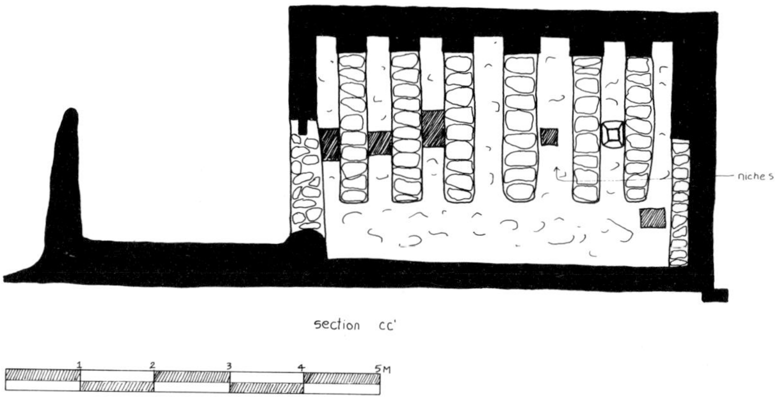

Figures 6.7-6.9

The single cupola mosque at al-Durayhimī is located on the western edge of the village. The mosque precinct consists of four spaces with a raised main entrance in its east wall. At the entrance, steps lead down into the ablution area. The minaret, free standing from the building, is structured into the south-west courtyard wall, with a series of steps leading up from the courtyard. The prayer hall located north of the precinct is square in plan with a single cupola. It has a raised opening in its south wall and an arched *miḥrāb* on its north wall. Externally the mosque has been plastered white with blue paint detail. (See Plate 6.3.)

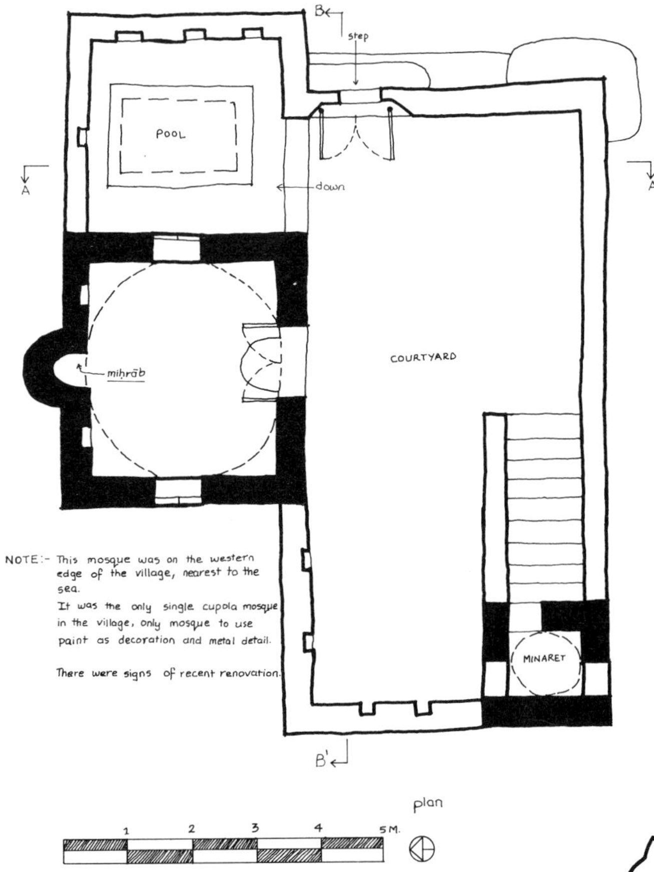

Figure 6.7

UNNAMED MOSQUE WITH ONE CUPOLA — AL-DURAYHIMĪ

Figure 6.8

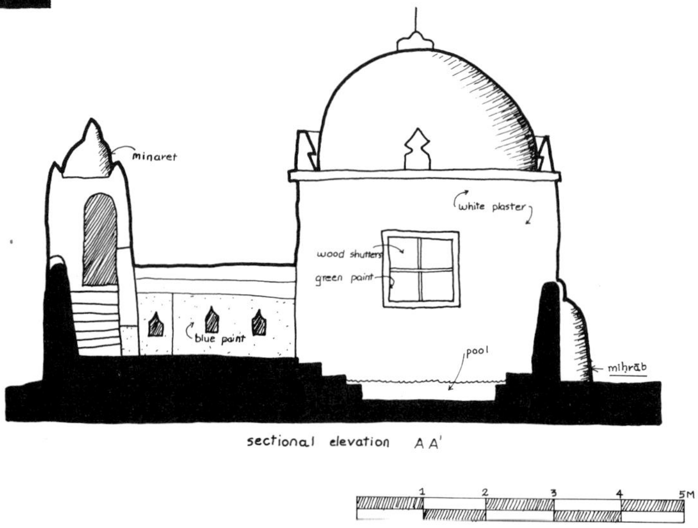

Figure 6.9

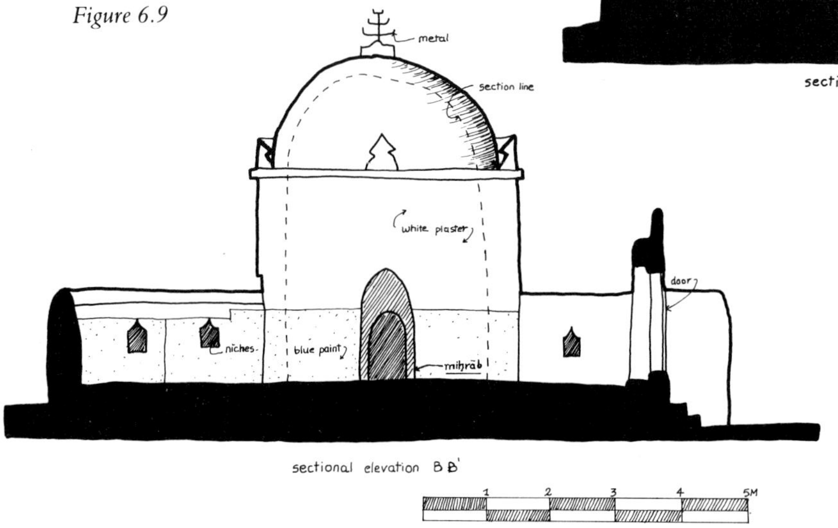

Figures 6.10-6.12

The triple cupola 'Abdullāh ibn 'Alī mosque at al-Durayhimī comprises a prayer hall, a minaret, an ablution pool, and a well which is structured into the south courtyard wall. The main doorway into the courtyard is through a raised level in the east wall, while a raised ablution pool is situated on the west. The prayer hall is a rectangular building with three cupolas, three entrances in its south wall and a *miḥrāb* on the north wall. Internally, the prayer hall is divided into three spaces by arches with smooth plaster on the domes and corbelled brick on the walls. A *minbar* consisting of recessed steps is structured into the north wall of the centre chamber, to the right of the prayer niche. A doorway through the north face of the prayer hall leads into the minaret. (See Plate 6.4.)

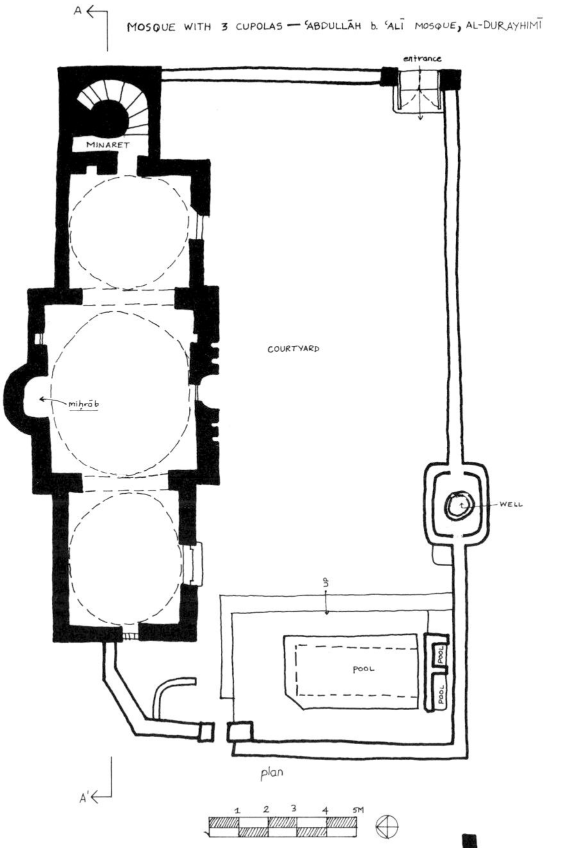

Figure 6.10

Figure 6.11

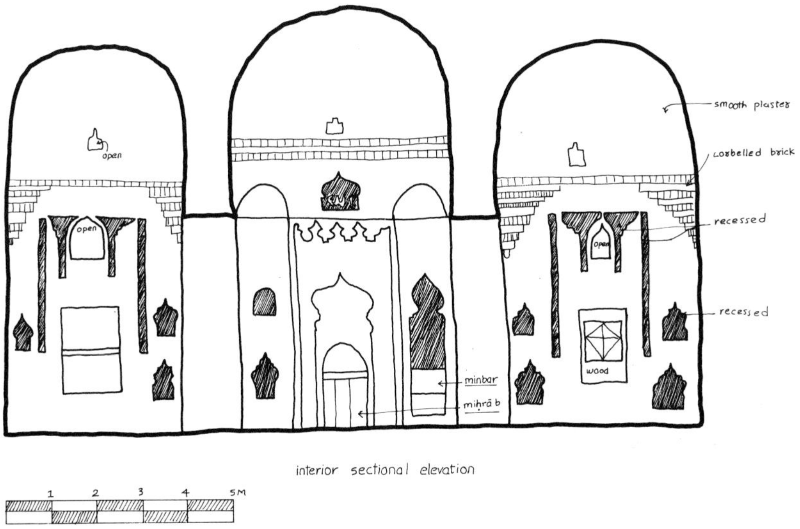

Figure 6.12

Figures 6.13-6.14

The al-Mās mosque at Zabīd has a school (*madrasah*) and a flat-roofed prayer hall facing each other on either side of a courtyard. The prayer hall is rectangular in plan and has two entrances in the south wall. The *madrasah* is also rectangular in plan with openings on the north and south sides. The main entry point into the courtyard is on the west, through a raised level, with the ablution pool located on the south of the complex. The cisterns are located behind the *madrasah* while the minaret is structured into the wall of the entrance.

Figure 6.13

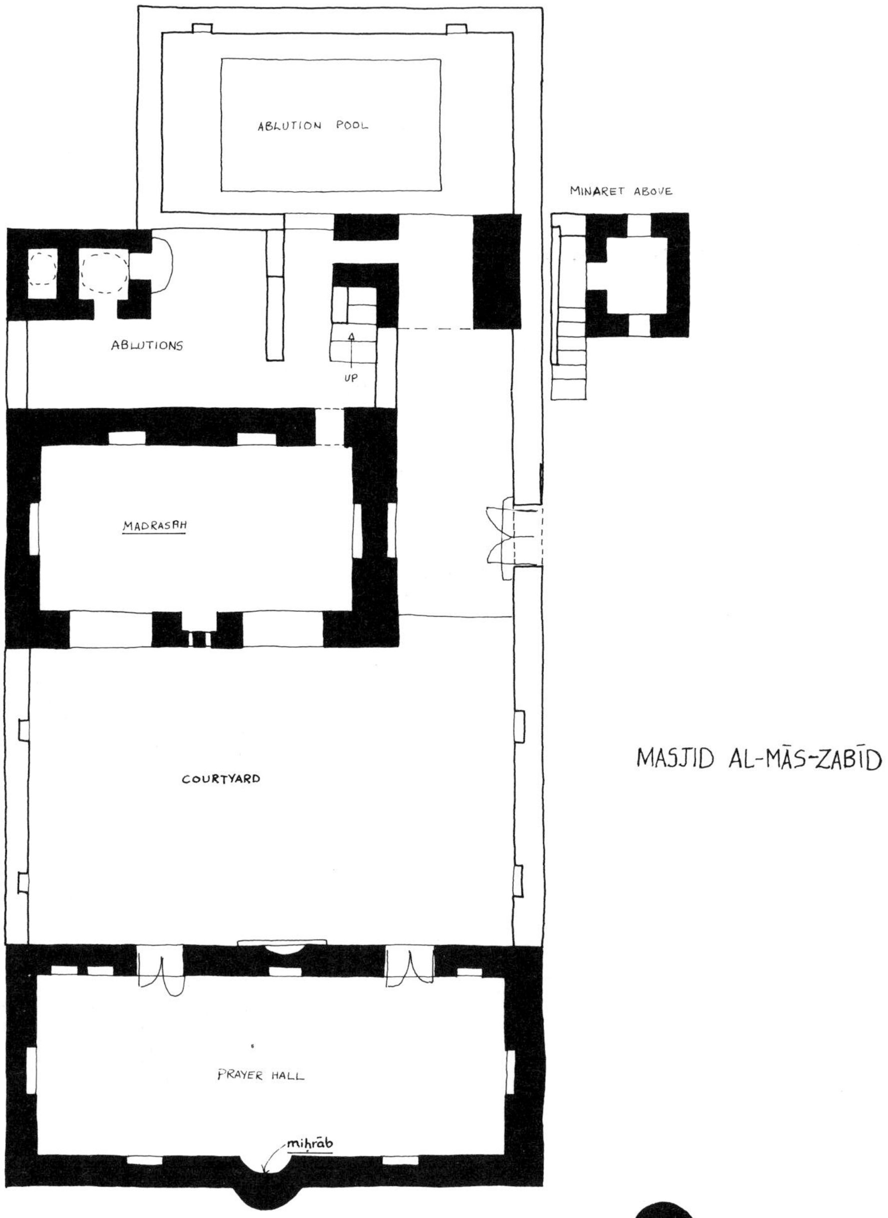

Figure 6.14

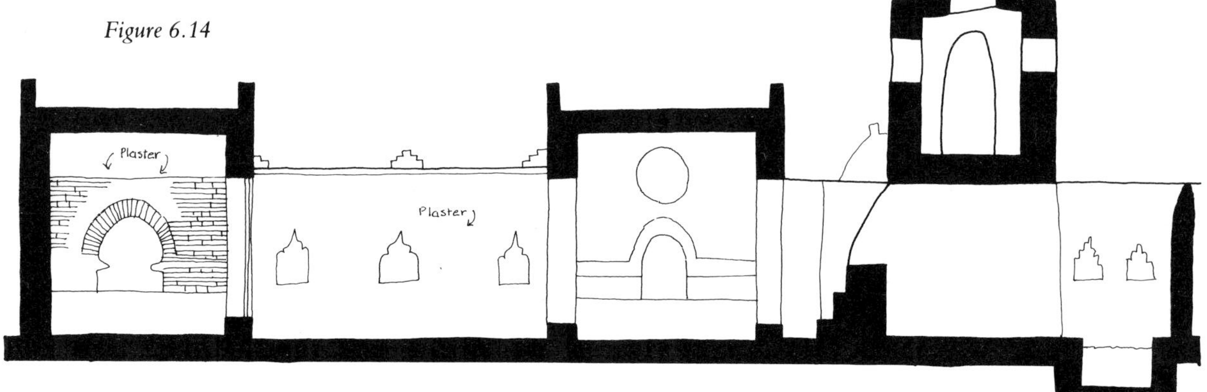

Figures 6.15-6.17

Al-Dayba‘ mosque with double cupola and school in Zabīd is complex in nature with a series of small courtyards divided by low walls. The main entrance is in the west wall. A narrow passageway leads down the centre of the precinct to an ablution area, with the minaret superimposed on the *madrasah* near the entrance. The *madrasah* and prayer hall face each other across the divided courtyard. The prayer hall is rectangular in plan with entrances in its south wall. Internally, the double domed hall is divided into two chambers by an archway, and the *miḥrāb* is structured into this arch. The *madrasah* is flat-roofed. The mosque is built of brick and plaster.

Figure 6.15

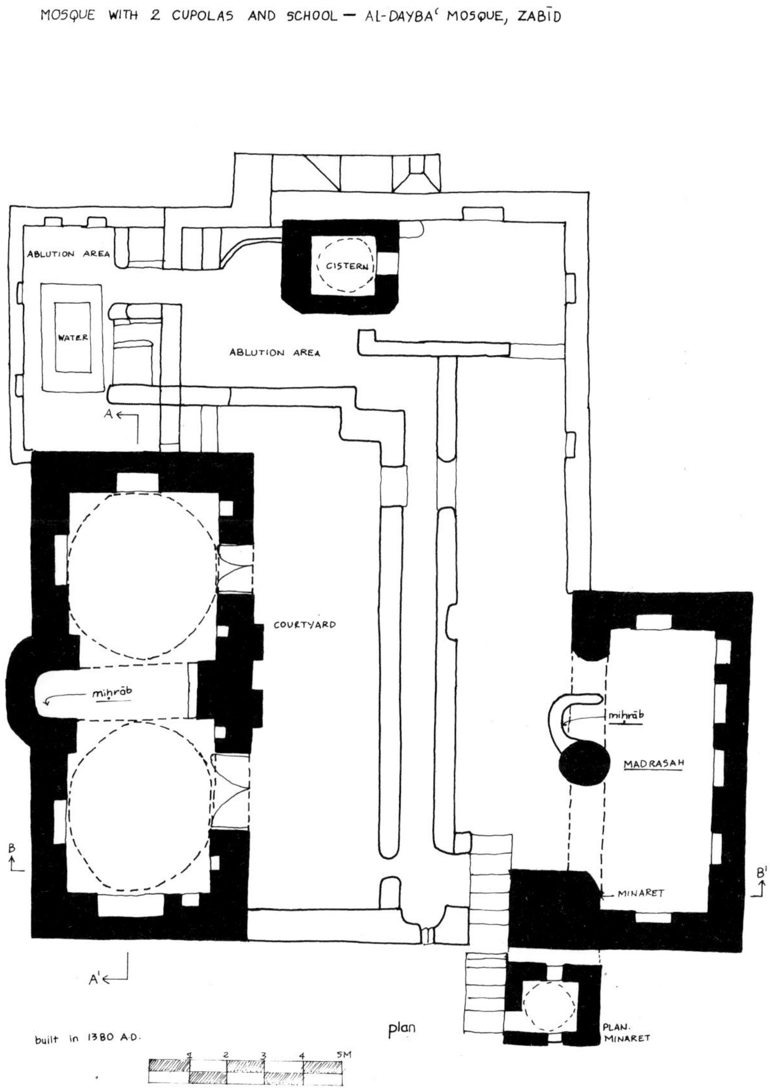

Figure 6.16

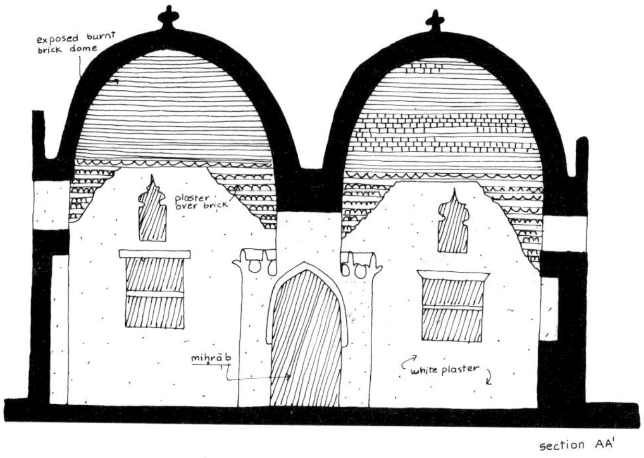

Figure 6.17

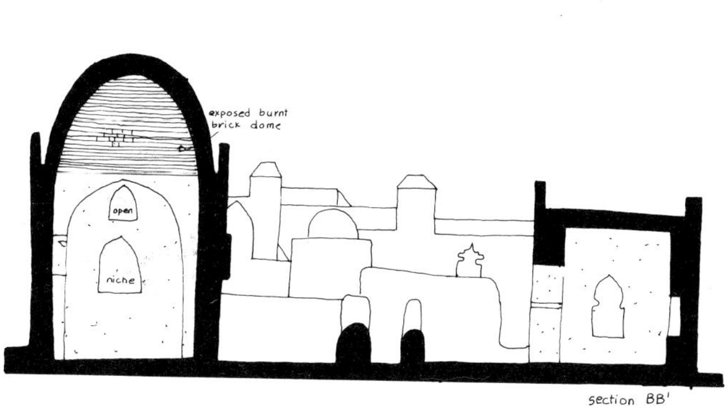

Figures 6.18-6.20

Al-Dūwaydār mosque in Zabīd with triple cupola and school is also complex in nature. From the street entrance in the west wall, a narrow passage leads behind the *madrasah* and up a level to an ablution area with cisterns and a disused pool. The minaret is superimposed over this passageway and structured onto the *madrasah* near the street entrance. The *madrasah* and the prayer hall are oriented facing each other, separated by a main courtyard. The prayer hall is rectangular in plan with three cupolas. Internally the mosque is divided into three spaces by arches with a *miḥrāb* on the north wall, defined by a low raised arch. The *madrasah* is rectangular in plan, covered with a flat roof. Next to the *madrasah* a series of steps leads up into the minaret. This mosque is elaborately decorated with plaster and brickwork.

Figure 6.18

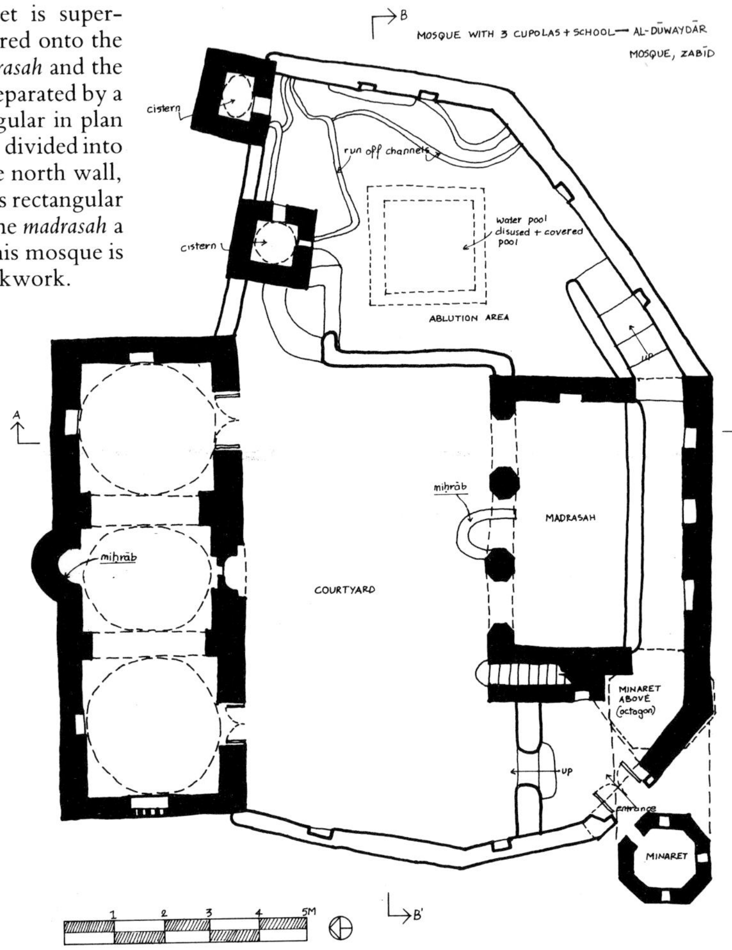

Figure 6.19

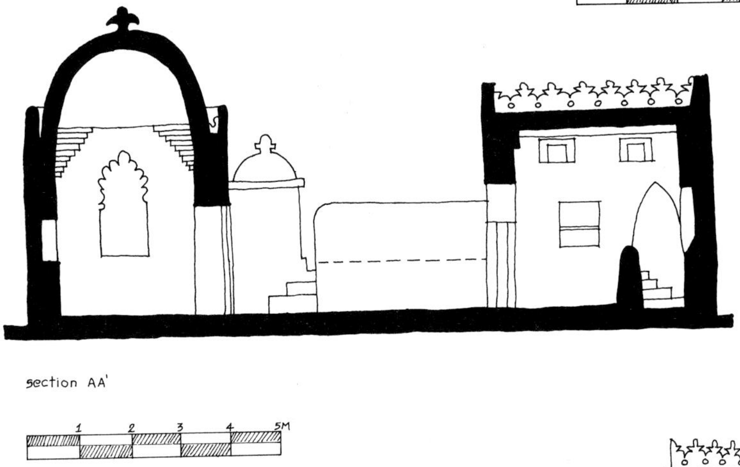

Figure 6.20

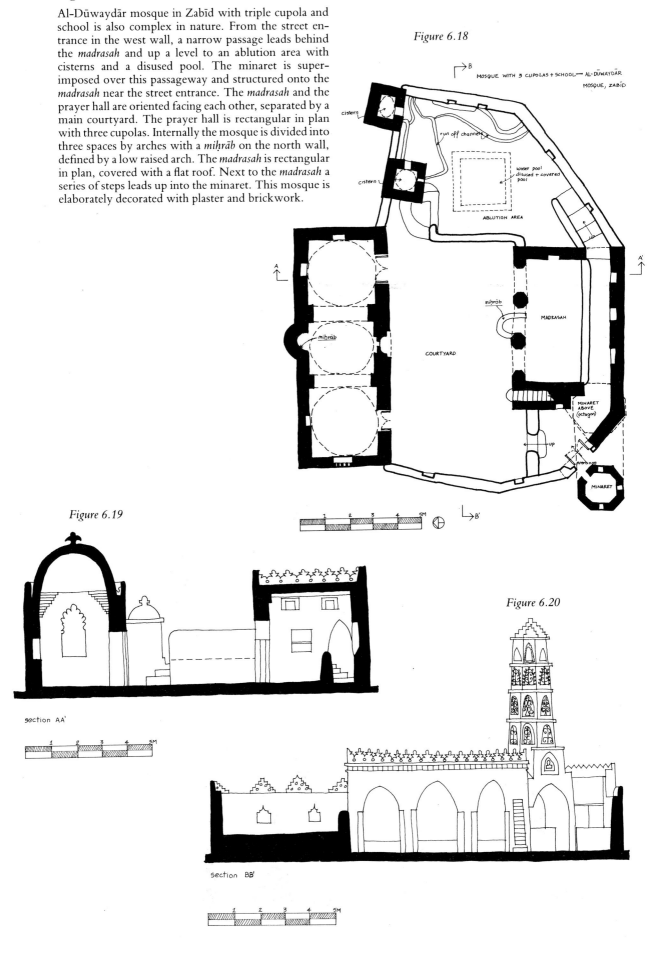

Figures 6.21-6.24

The saint's tomb at al-Raws, standing on its own to the east of the village, has a grave centrally placed in a walled courtyard which is entered through the east wall. The *miḥrāb* is structured into the north courtyard wall. The tomb grave is a low raised platform with head and foot stones.

SAINT'S TOMB (QABR LI'L-WALĪ) — AL-RAWS

Figure 6.21

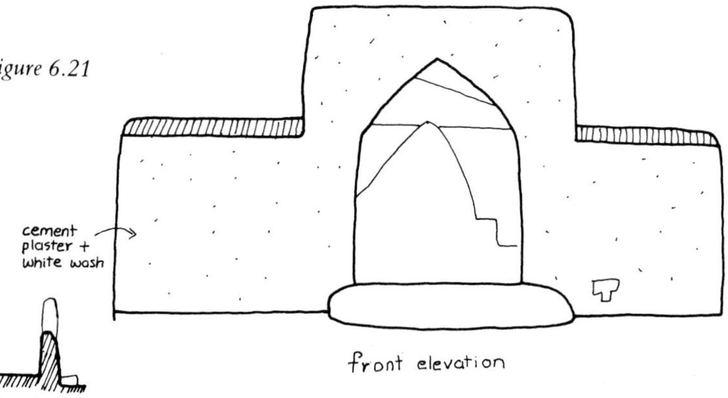

Figure 6.22

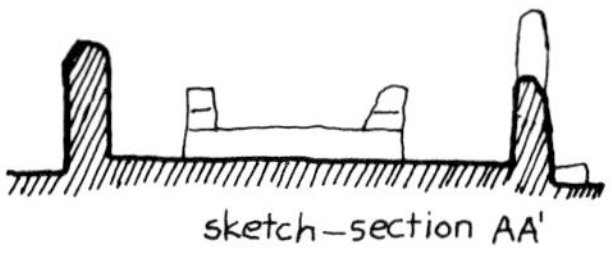

Figure 6.23

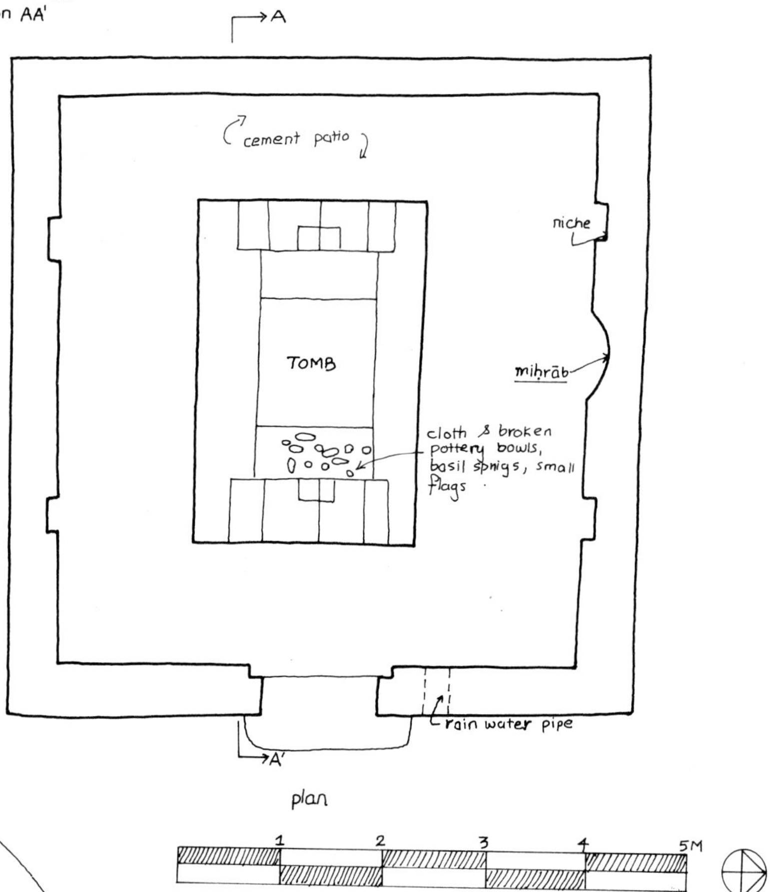

Figure 6.24

Figure 6.25

The mosque and tomb of Ibn 'Abbās is located on the waterfront on the north-eastern edge of the village. The rectangular prayer hall is covered by six domes. The tomb adjoining the prayer hall has a single dome, and the minaret is also surmounted by a small cupola. The entrance is by a wide staircase leading up from ground level on the east.

Figure 6.25

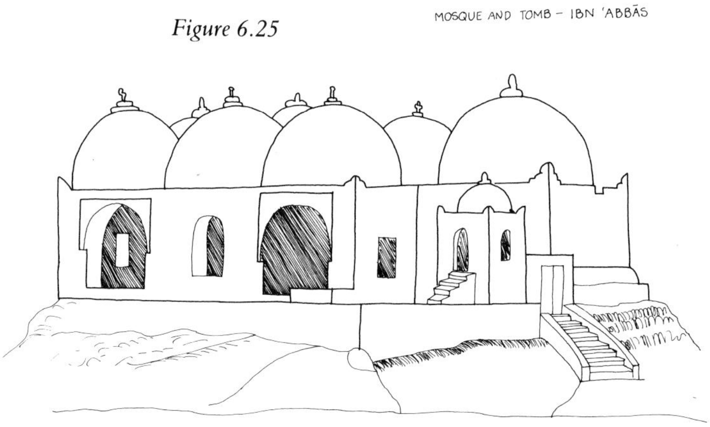

Figures 6.26-6.29

The mosque and tomb at Bayt 'Aṭā' is located on the north-eastern edge of the village. The main entrance is through a raised level in the west wall with the ablution area north of the entrance. The tomb, square in plan, is set back from the main courtyard plan, with an entrance in its west wall and covered by a single cupola. The prayer hall is square in plan, surmounted by nine domes and decorated with white plaster. The minaret is free standing, structured into the south east corner of the courtyard wall.

Figure 6.26

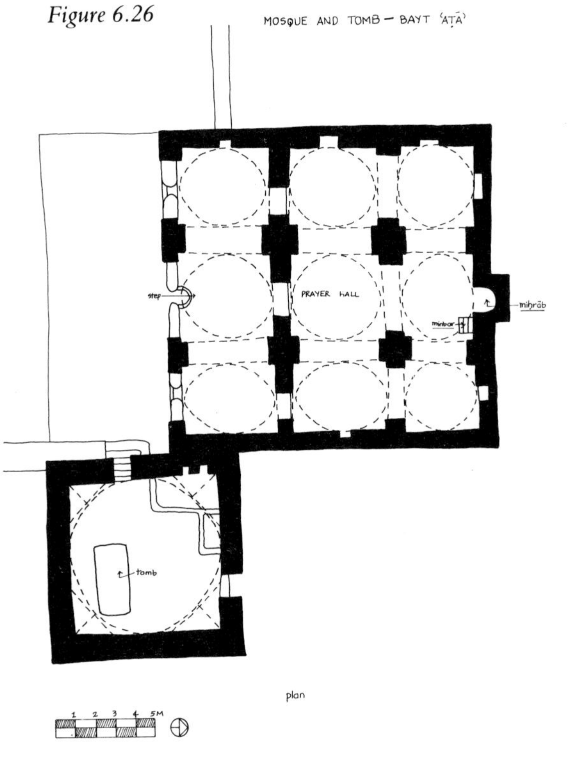

Figure 6.27

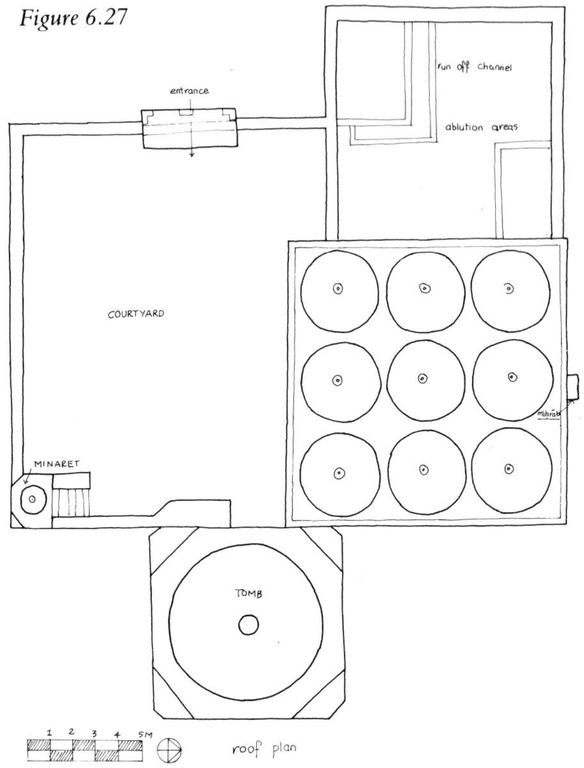

Figure 6.28

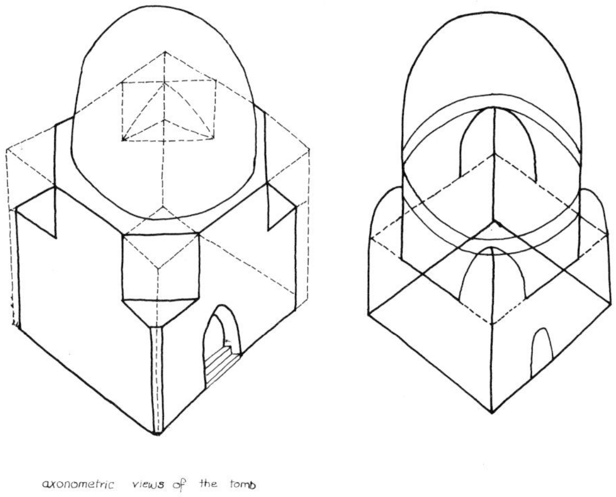

Figure 6.29

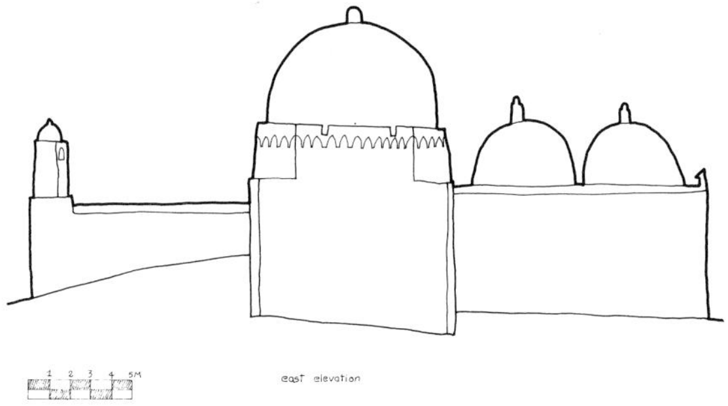

PUBLIC STRUCTURES

Figure 6.30

The coffee-house (*maqhā*) at al-Jāḥ is located in the *sūq* which stands on the southern edge of the village. The coffee-house-cum-inn is a semi-permanent, irregular shaped structure of organic materials. The main shape is defined by circular palm trunks and bamboo-like canes. It is largely open to the east, facing onto the *sūq*. The main walls are made of palm trunks implanted in the ground. The gable roof is supported by rafters and palm trunks.

Figure 6.30

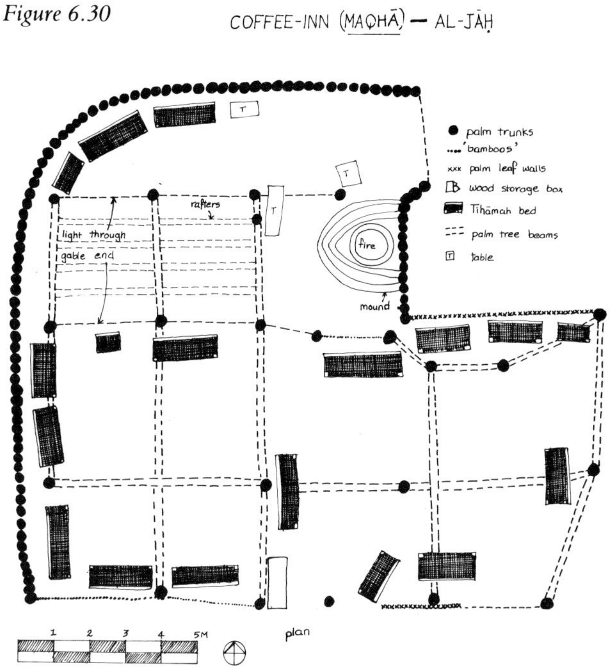

Figures 6.31-6.32

The palm tree "village hall" located in the centre of al-Marāziqah is constructed of semi-permanent materials. It is rectangular in plan, with a gable roof. The major structural members are palm trunks which stand at intervals while the infilling is reed lattice work. It is surrounded by a compound wall made of reeds and grasses.

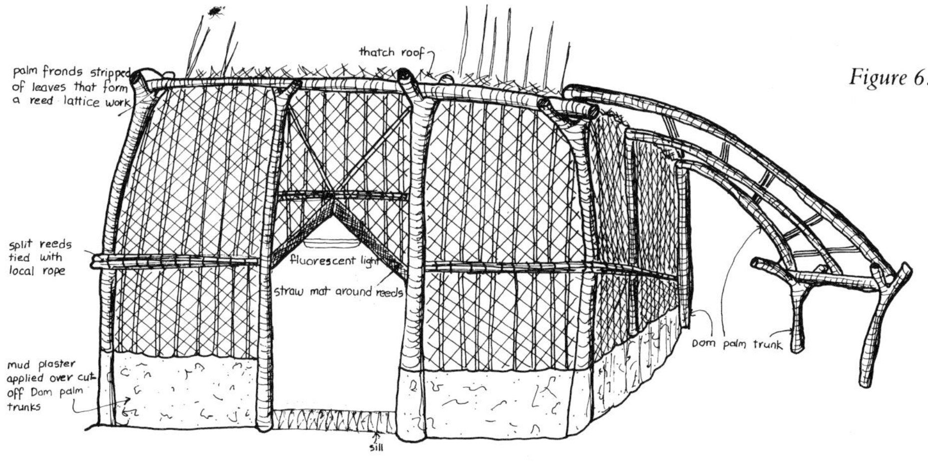

Figure 6.31

Figure 6.32

Figure 6.33

The *funduq* at al-Ṣanīf is a single storey structure, rectangular in plan, and constructed out of river stone.

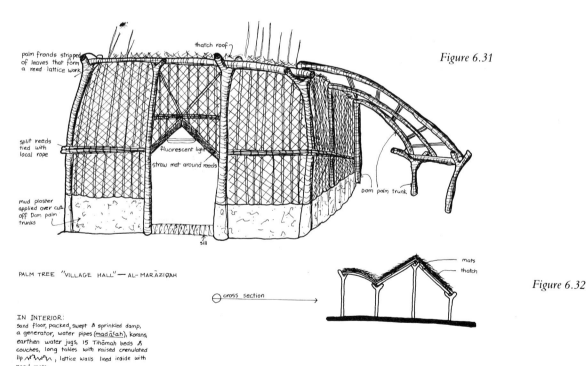

Figure 6.33

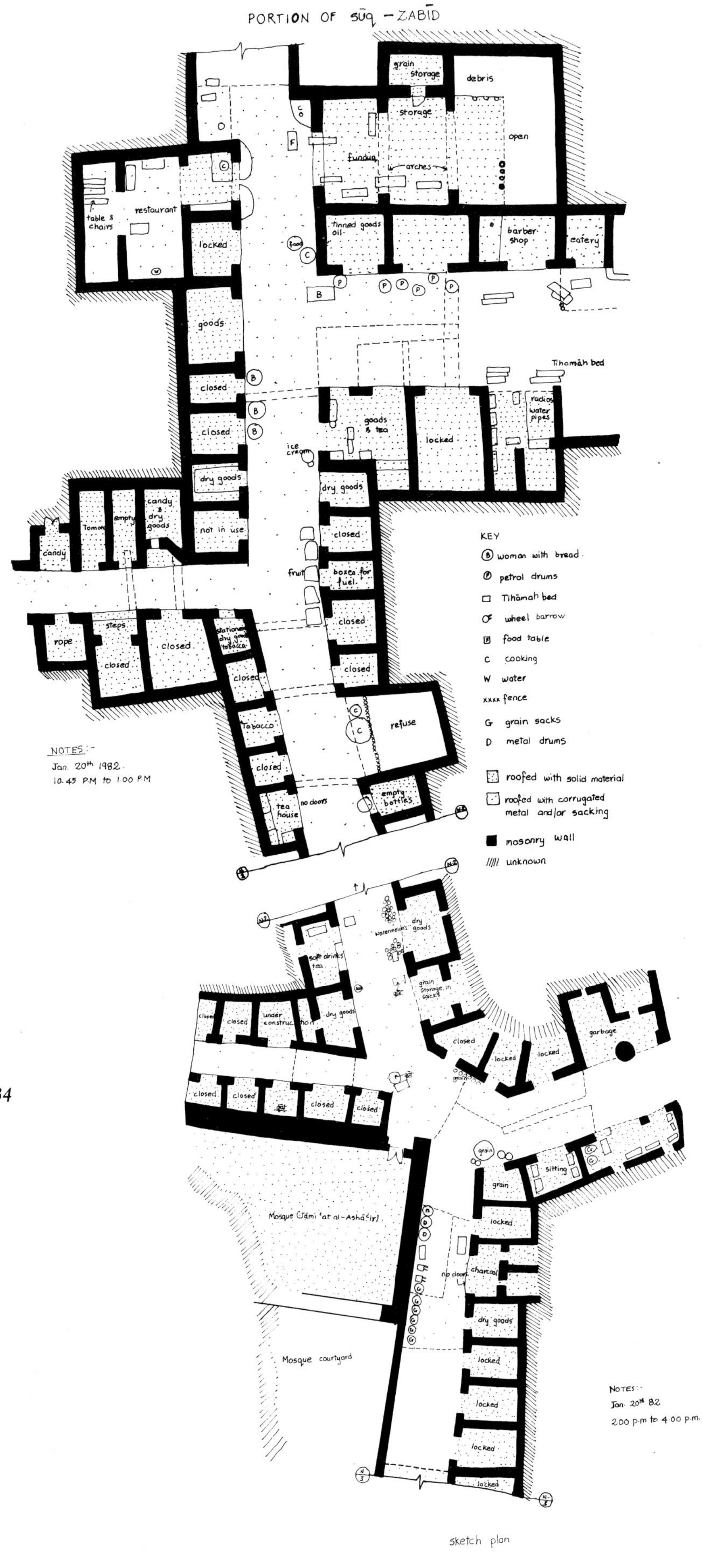
PORTION OF SŪQ – ZABĪD
grain storage
debris
storage
open
funduq
arches
restaurant
table & chairs
locked
tinned goods oil
barber shop
eatery
goods
closed
closed
goods & tea
locked
radios water pipes
Tihāmah bed
ice cream
dry goods
candy & dry goods
empty
not in use
candy
dry goods
closed
fruit
boxes for fuel
rope
steps
closed
closed
stationery dry goods tobacco
closed
closed
closed
tobacco
refuse
closed
empty bottles
tea house
no doors
NOTES:-
Jan. 20th 1982.
10.45 P.M to 1.00 P.M
KEY
woman with bread
petrol drums
Tihāmah bed
wheel barrow
food table
C cooking
W water
xxxx fence
G grain sacks
D metal drums
roofed with solid material
roofed with corrugated metal and/or sacking
masonry wall
unknown
soft drinks tea
watermelons
dry goods
grain storage in sacks
closed
closed
under construction
dry goods
closed
locked
locked
garbage
closed
closed
closed
closed
grain
sitting
grain
Mosque (Jāmi 'at al-Ashā'ir)
locked
no doors
charcoal
dry goods
Mosque courtyard
locked
locked
locked
locked
NOTES:-
Jan. 20th 82
2.00 p.m to 4.00 p.m.
sketch plan

Figure 6.34

Figure 6.34

The portion of the Zabīd *sūq* studied here is part of the *sūq* complex occupying a mound site in the centre of the town. It is organic in nature and laid out in a maze of narrow streets. The shops are generally rectangular in plan with some of them extending out onto the alleyways. The main structure is masonry and roofed with corrugated metal, while some of the shops are roofed with permanent material of mud and timber. In this *sūq*, the alleys are semi-roofed, making the *sūq* an integral unit. The commerce in this portion includes shops for rope, candy, food, dry goods, etc., with hawkers selling their wares in the passageways as well, and Tihāmah couches put around to form communal spaces. Coffeehouses, eating houses and *funduqs* are scattered amongst the shops.

MILITARY STRUCTURES

Figure 6.35

The coastal fort at Nukhaylah consists of a walled enclosure, rectangular in plan, with two towers structured in the north-east and south-west corners of the walls and a two-storied guard house structured into the south-eastern corner. A series of steps leads up to the parapet which runs along the eastern wall. The south-western tower has a stairway from ground level, and both towers have gun parapets on their rooves. The construction material is stone packing and mud-brick covered in plaster. The entrance to the enclosure is found in the east wall. (See Plate 6.7.)

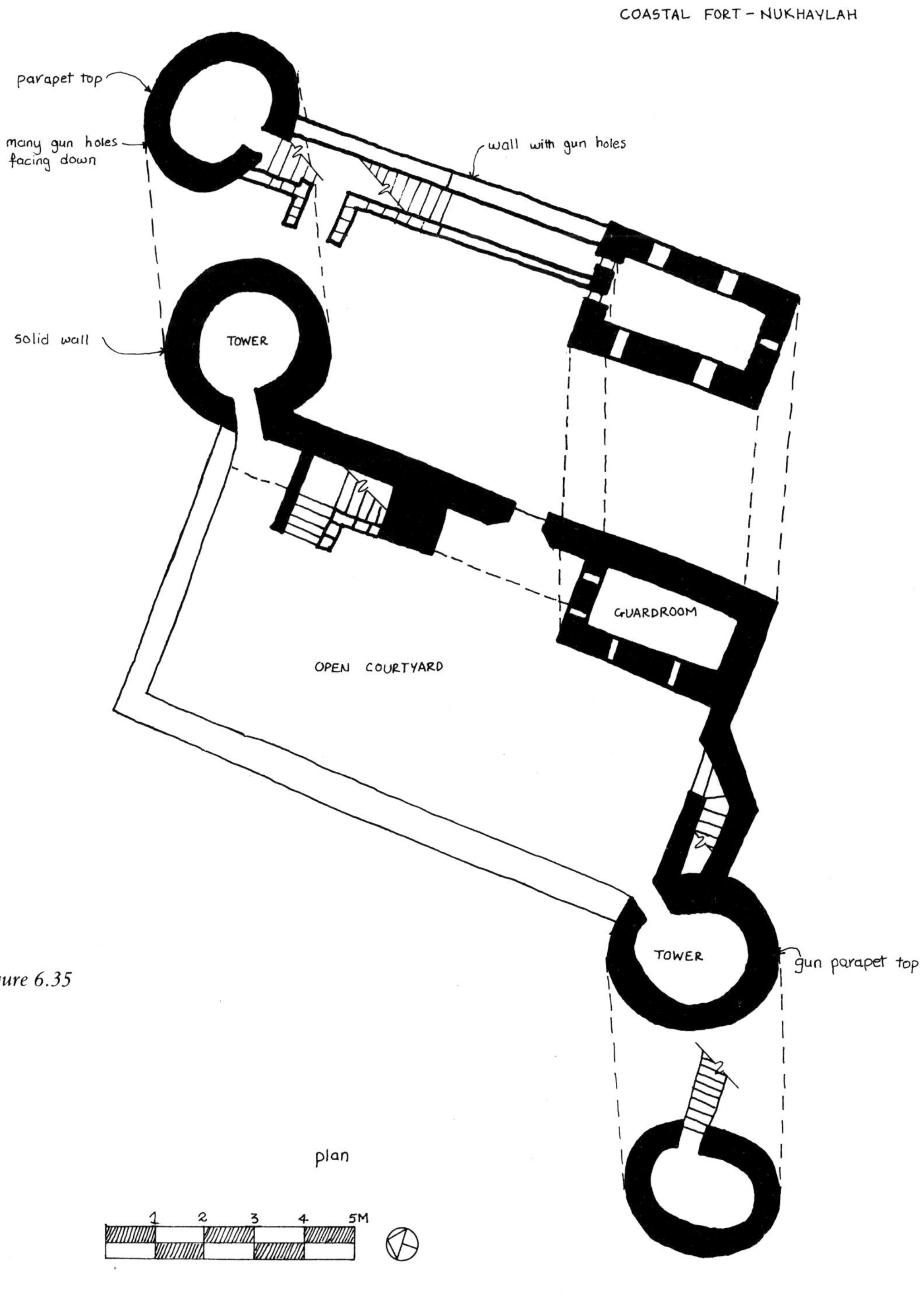

Figure 6.35

DOMESTIC STRUCTURES

Figures 6.36-6.39

The compound of a Zarānīq family located on the northern edge of Ghulayfiqah is roughly circular in shape, consisting of six structures and compound wall. The kitchen, reception hut, and shelter for goats are situated in the outer compound. The kitchen is circular in plan, while the rest of the structures are rectangular in plan, all constructed out of palm trunks. There are two entrances to the outer compound, from the north and the west. The inner compound with a single entrance consists of a hut for women and children and an open-air reception. The dwelling for women is rectangular in plan with a gable roof and constructed from palm trunks and woven palm leaves. Behind the huts to the south is an area for ablution and for storage of fodder and fuel, as well as a kitchen garden.

Figure 6.36

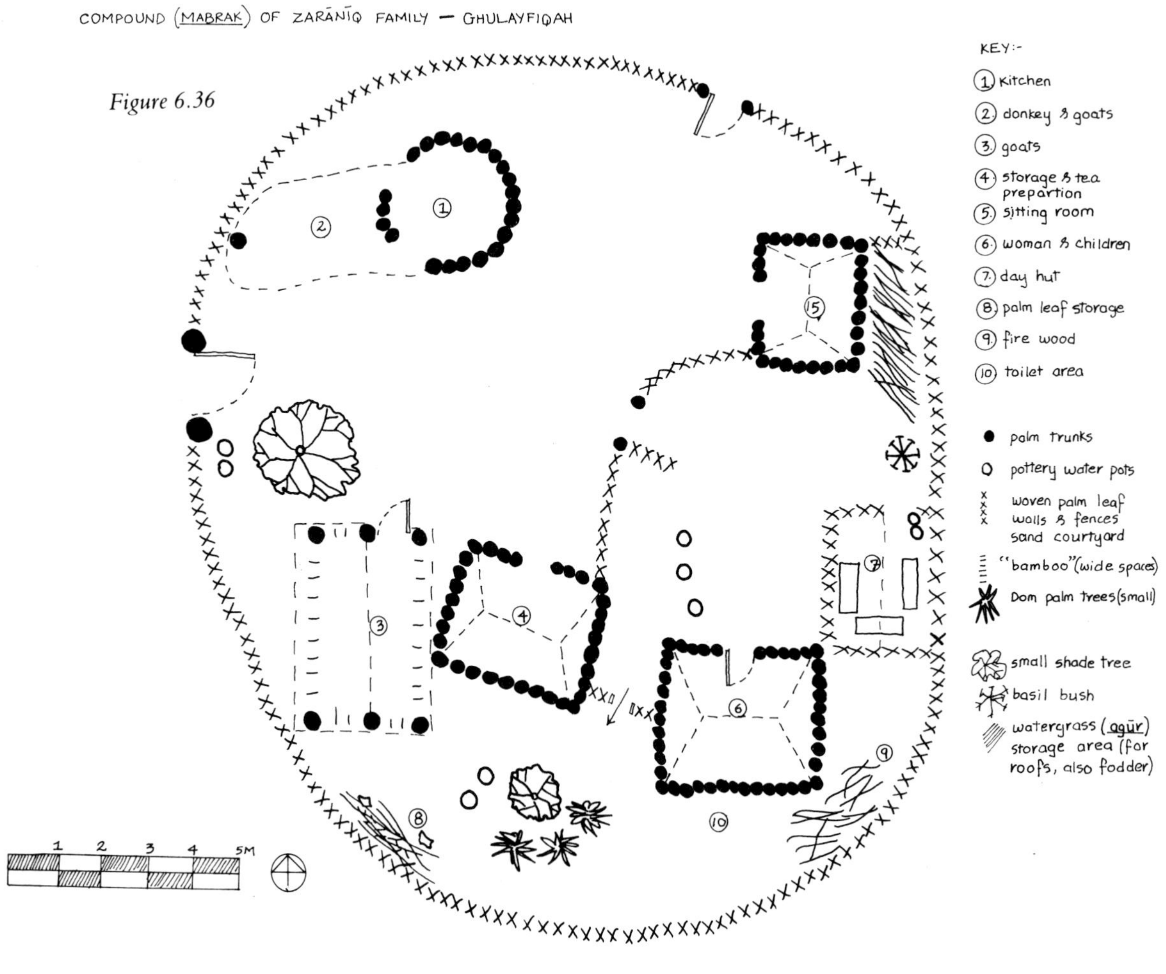

Figure 6.37

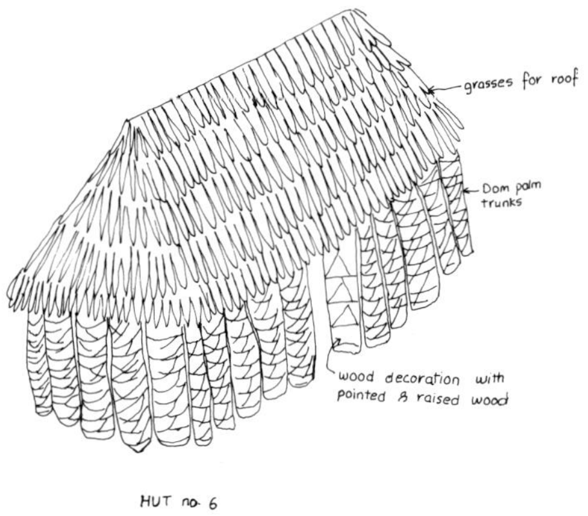

Figure 6.38

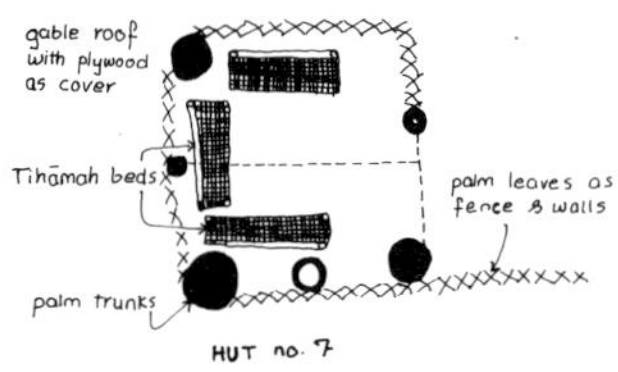

Figure 6.39

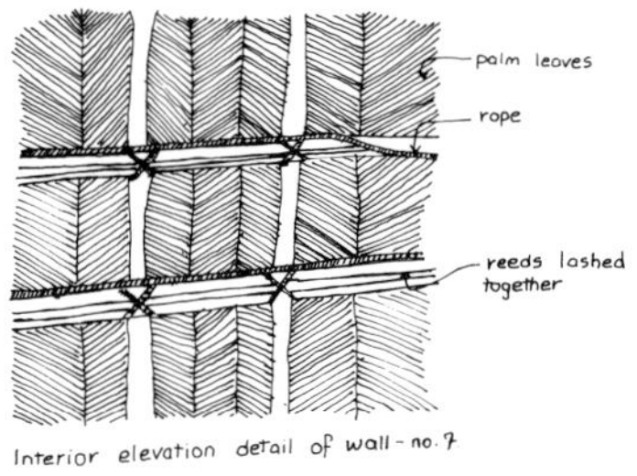

Figures 6.40-6.41

The house at al-Bāridah is situated in the centre of the village. It is rectangular in plan with a saddle roof. It has a raised entry on the east wall and air vents in the opposite and the southern walls. The major construction member is palm timber which forms a framework to support the bundles of thatch. The roof is internally supported by a centrally located wooden post and a ridge beam. The purlins and rafters support the weight of the thatch which is held down with criss-crossed ropes. The interior is highly decorated with sculpted loam shelves and painted figures.

Figure 6.40

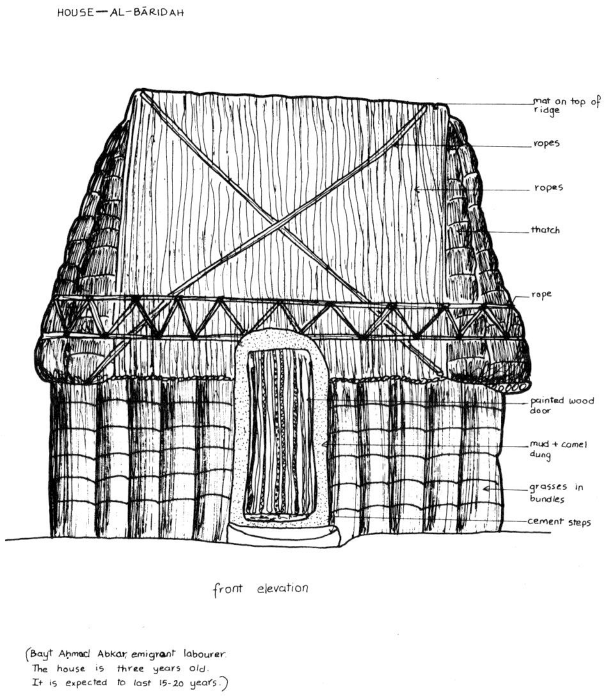

Figure 6.41

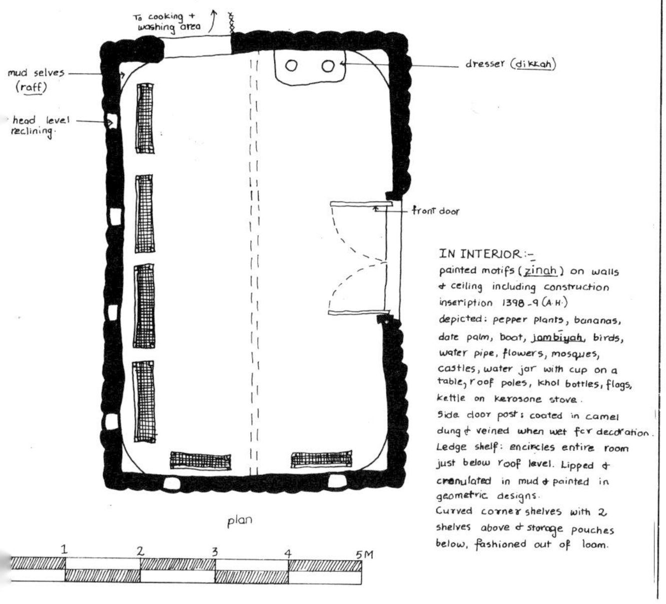

Figures 6.42-6.43

The house at al-Luḥayyah is located on the northern edge of the town. Compared to the house in al-Bāridah, it has a more elaborate ridge decoration and an intricate system of woven thatching on the walls. The interior however is unadorned.

Figure 6.42

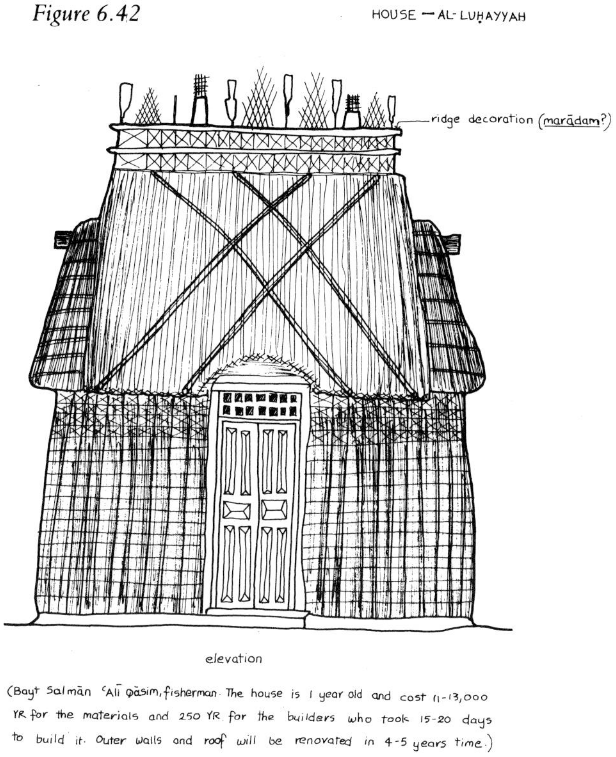

Figure 6.43

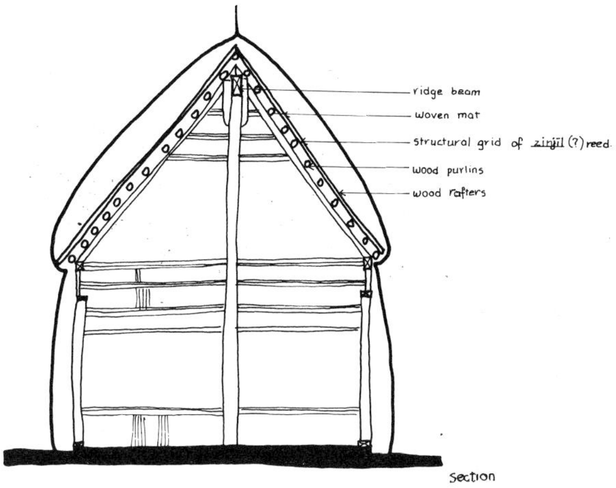

Figures 6.44-6.46

The family compound at al-Muʻtariḍ, located in the centre of the village, is semi-circular in shape and defined by a mounded wall. The entrance is a wide gap in the north, and the interior of the compound is readily visible from the street. The compound area is shared by an extended family and therefore divided into four sections for the head of family, his brother and his two sons, with a communal area in the centre. Except for the women's hut, which is rectangular, the rest of the buildings are circular in plan with rounded walls and pointed roofs. The main dwellings, constructed out of organic materials, are grouped in a semi-circle around the centre of the compound. The secondary structures are placed in a circular manner at the periphery of the compound. Each dwelling has an area for bathing and cooking. Spaces on the very edge of the compound are used for storage, kitchen gardening and for animal sheltering. The head of the family's dwelling, the largest in the compound, is circular in plan, the sides having bundles of thatch and the roof which is conical is hung from a centrepole. The interior is elaborately decorated with painted motifs. (See Plates 6.1-6.2.)

Figure 6.44

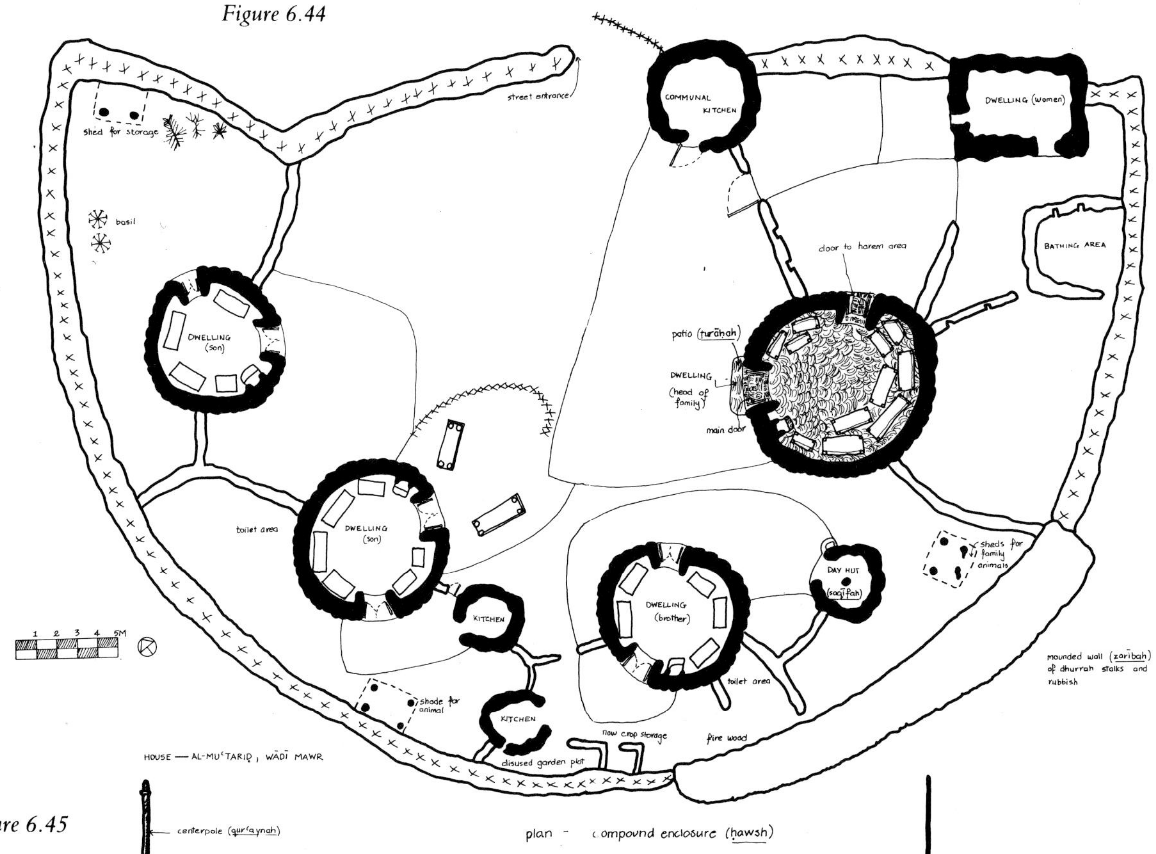

Figure 6.45

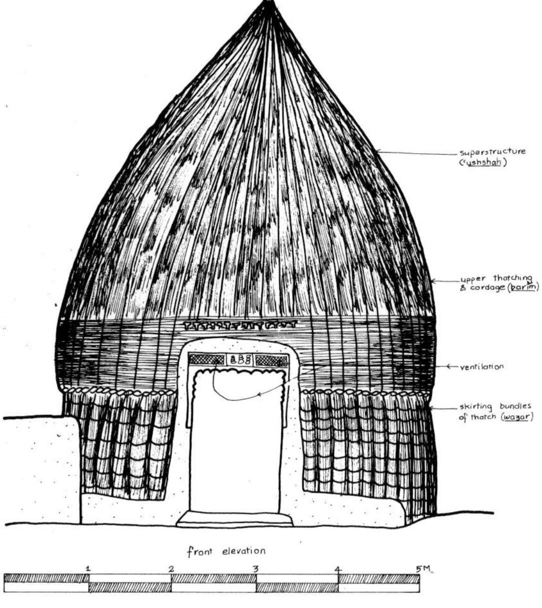

(Bayt Muḥ. ʻAli Sulaymān, farmer. The structure is 14 years old)

Figure 6.46

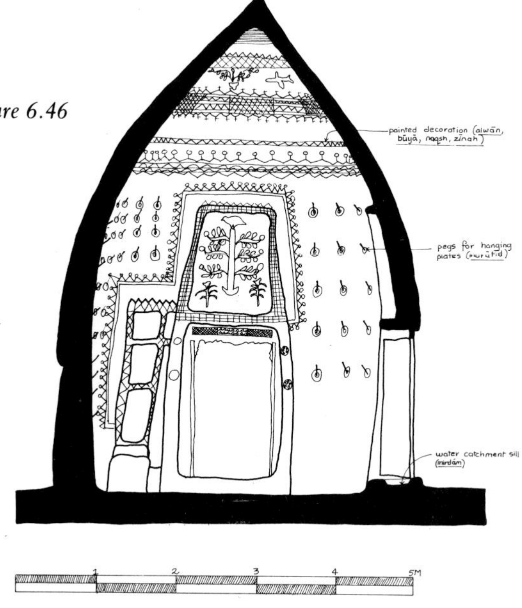

Figures 6.47-6.55

A round, mud-and-thatch house in al-Mu'tariḍ is shown under construction.

Figure 6.47

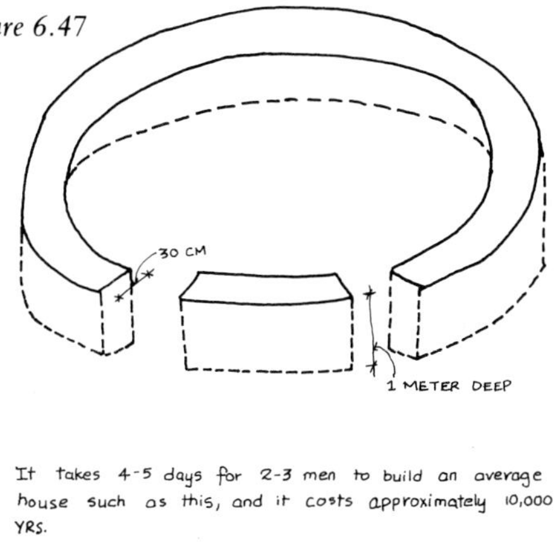
30 CM
1 METER DEEP
It takes 4-5 days for 2-3 men to build an average house such as this, and it costs approximately 10,000 YRS.

Figure 6.48

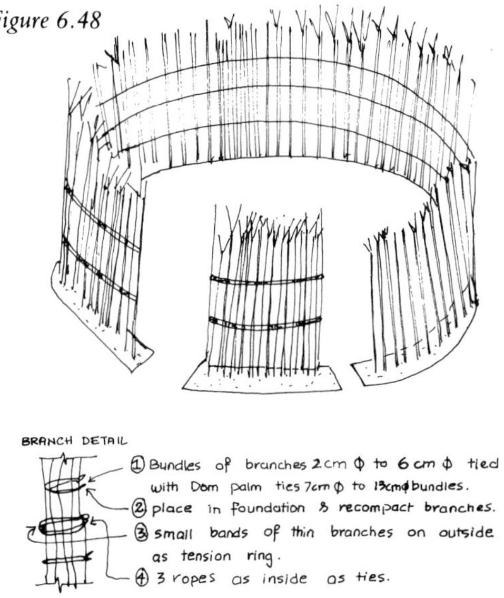
BRANCH DETAIL
① Bundles of branches 2cm ϕ to 6 cm ϕ tied with Dom palm ties 7cm ϕ to 15cm ϕ bundles.
② place in foundation & recompact branches.
③ small bands of thin branches on outside as tension ring.
④ 3 ropes as inside as ties.

Figure 6.49

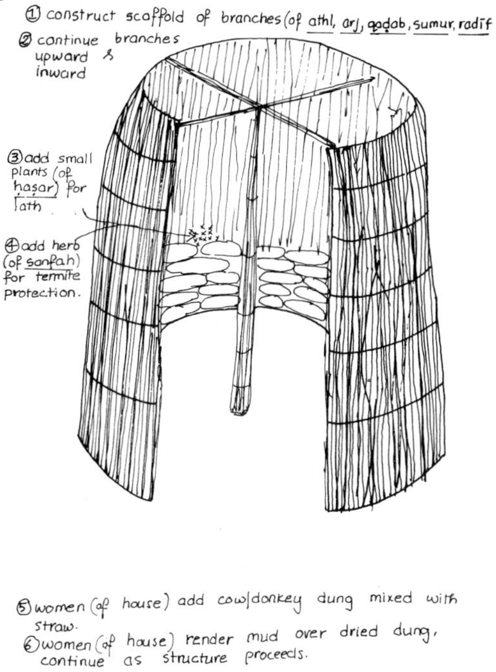
① construct scaffold of branches (of athl, arj, qaḍab, sumur, radīf
② continue branches upward & inward
③ add small plants (of ḥasar) for lath
④ add herb (of sanfah) for termite protection.
⑤ women (of house) add cow/donkey dung mixed with straw.
⑥ women (of house) render mud over dried dung, continue as structure proceeds.

Figure 6.50

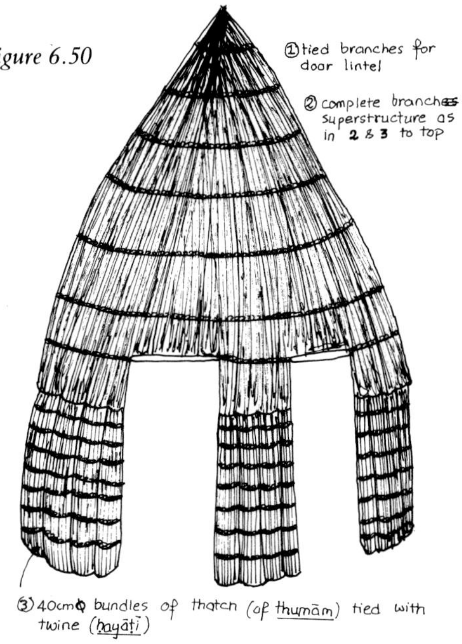
① tied branches for door lintel
② complete branches superstructure as in 2 & 3 to top
③ 40cm ϕ bundles of thatch (of thumām) tied with twine (ḥayāṭī)

Figure 6.51

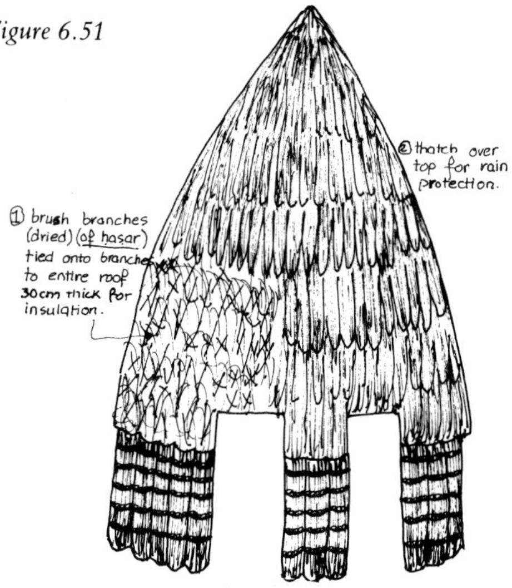
② thatch over top for rain protection.
① brush branches (dried) (of ḥasar) tied onto branches to entire roof 30cm thick for insulation.

Figure 6.52

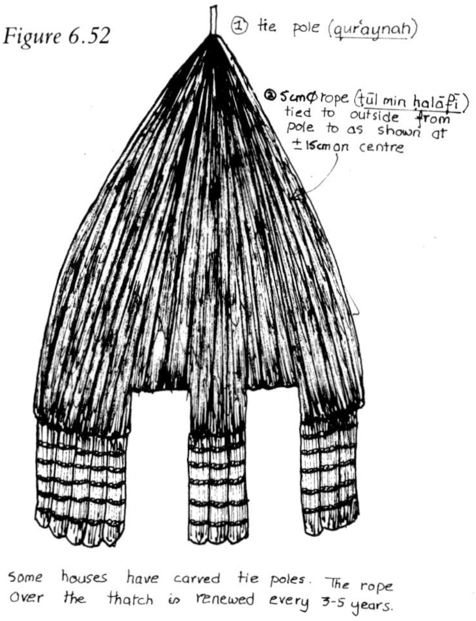
① tie pole (qur'aynah)
② 5cm ϕ rope (ṭūl min halāfī) tied to outside from pole to as shown at ± 15cm on centre
Some houses have carved tie poles. The rope over the thatch is renewed every 3-5 years.

Figure 6.53

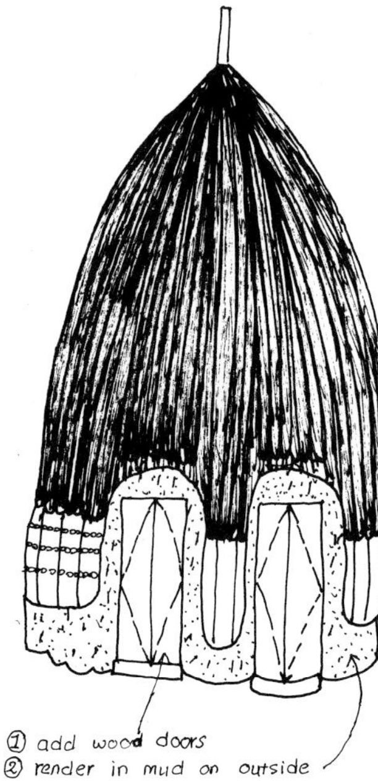
① add wood doors
② render in mud on outside

Figure 6.54

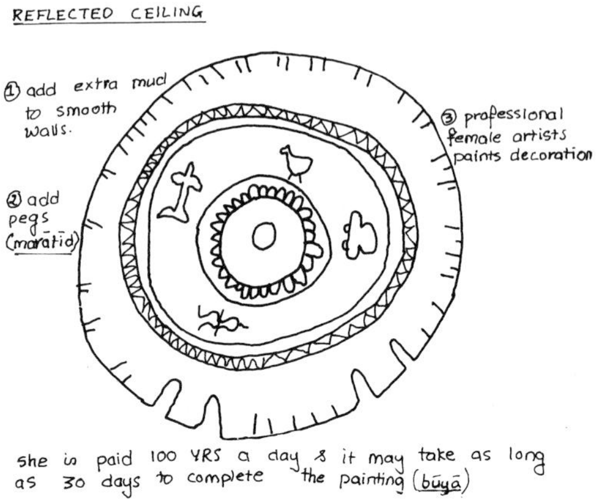
REFLECTED CEILING
① add extra mud to smooth walls.
② add pegs (maratid)
③ professional female artists paints decoration
she is paid 100 YRS a day & it may take as long as 30 days to complete the painting (būyā)

Figure 6.55

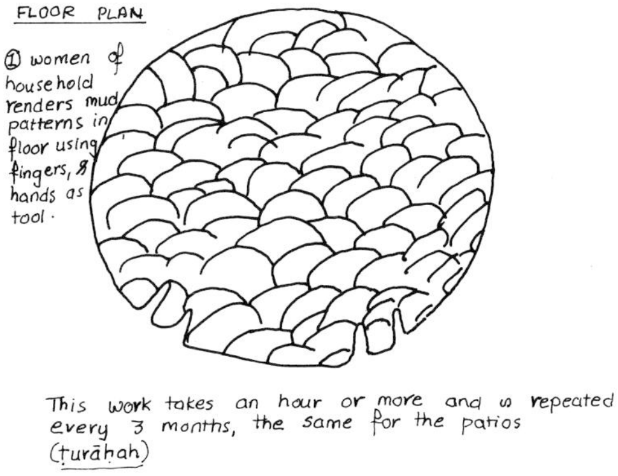
FLOOR PLAN
① women of household renders mud patterns in floor using fingers, & hands as tool.
This work takes an hour or more and is repeated every 3 months, the same for the patios (turāhah)

Figure 6.56

A house in al-Durayhimī is shown under construction. It is rectangular in plan with mud brick walls covered in plaster and surmounted by a saddle roof with timber members and thatching.

Figure 6.56

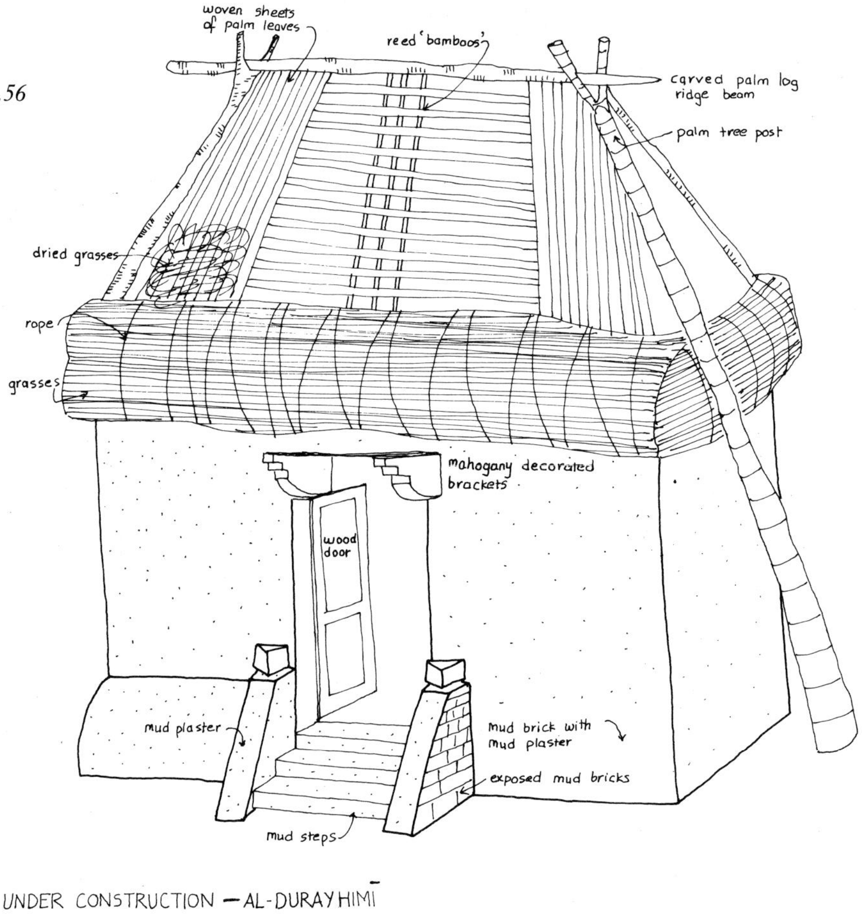
woven sheets of palm leaves
reed 'bamboos'
carved palm log ridge beam
palm tree post
dried grasses
rope
grasses
mahogany decorated brackets
wood door
mud plaster
mud brick with mud plaster
exposed mud bricks
mud steps
HOUSE UNDER CONSTRUCTION — AL-DURAYHIMĪ

Figures 6.57-6.58

The Wāqidī house complex of Zabīd is situated in the western sector of the town and is constructed out of mud brick and plaster. The portion of the complex studied here consists of nine enclosures and a courtyard. The principal elements are a men's reception room and a woman's salon across a courtyard from each other. The main entrance from the street is through a door in the north wall. All the spaces are rectangular in plan, with niches and a staircase structured into the internal walls. The main rooms are furnished with Tihāmah couches and tables. A sitting/sleeping room is located on the first floor overlooking the courtyard. The exterior and the interior of the men's reception room are elaborately decorated with brick and plaster details. The compound continues on two sides of the portion studied, comprising a vast complex of the extended Wāqidī family. (See Plates 6.13-6.14)

Figure 6.57

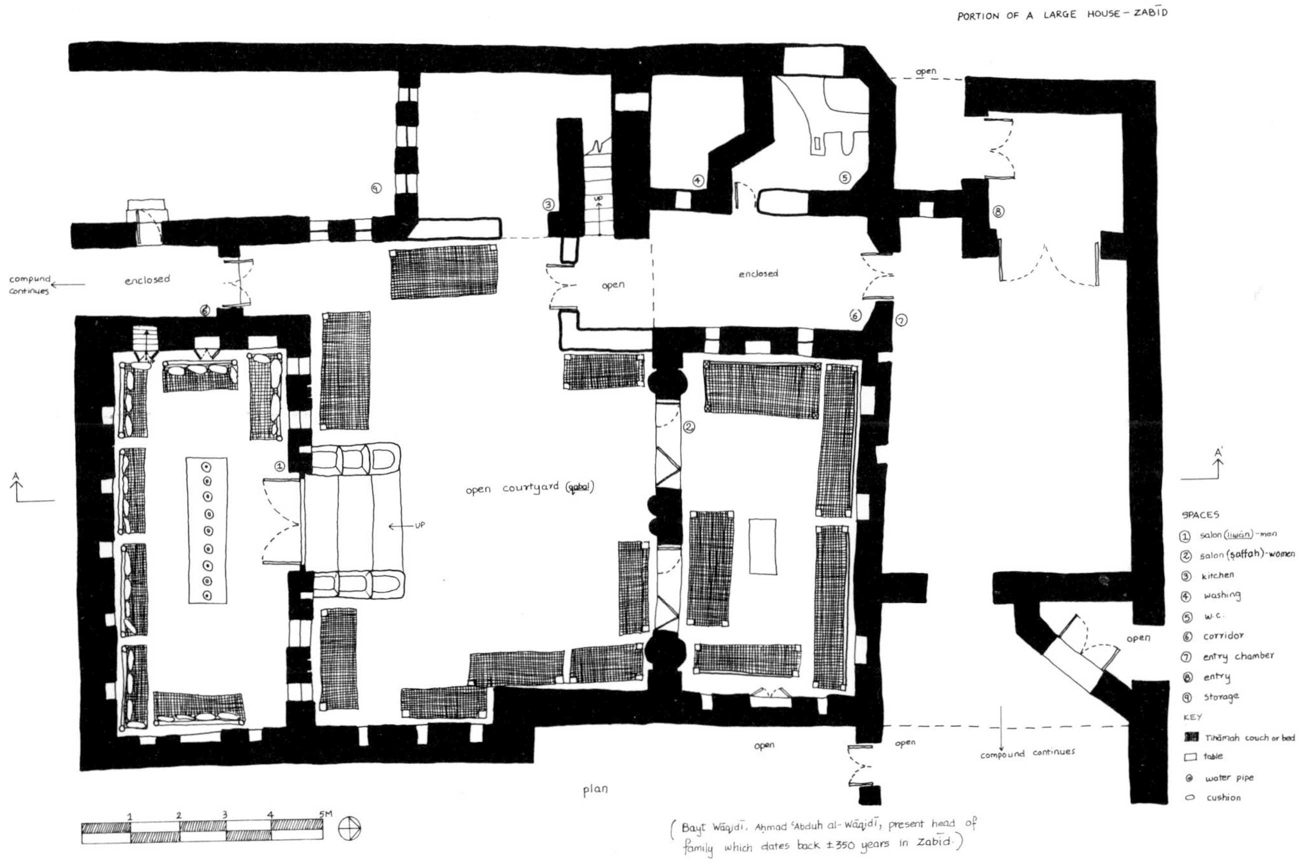

Figure 6.58

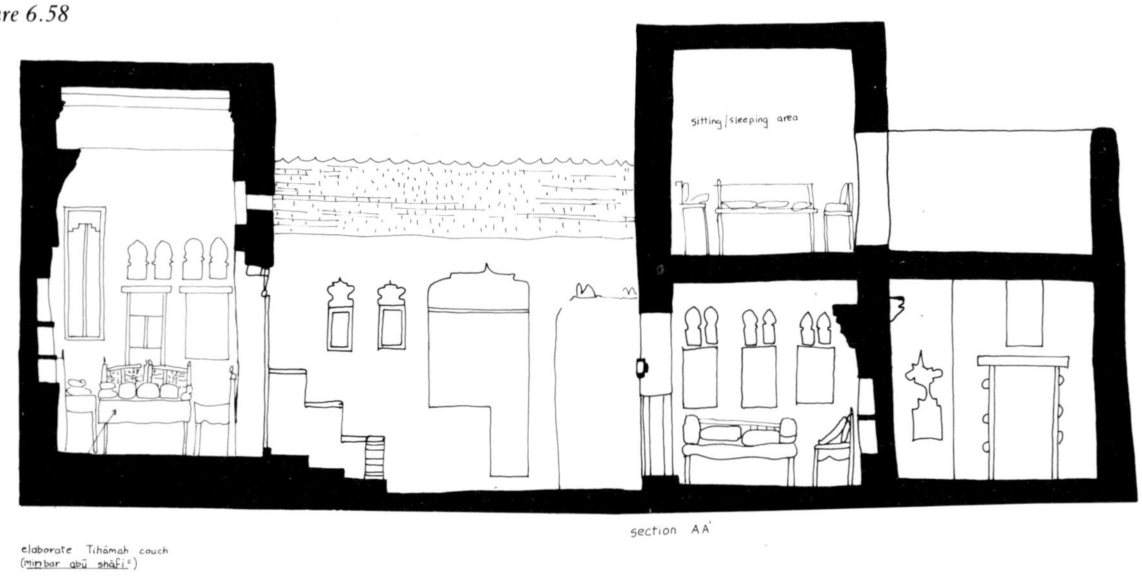

ARCHITECTURAL DETAILS

Figures 6.59-6.60

An interior vent from a house in al-Bāridah has a central air space with branches on either side acting as structural members. On the external face the branches are covered with a layer of thatch, while reed and slats are structured on the inside face at right angles to the horizontal branch members. The mud of the interior elevation is further decorated with paint and lime.

Figure 6.59

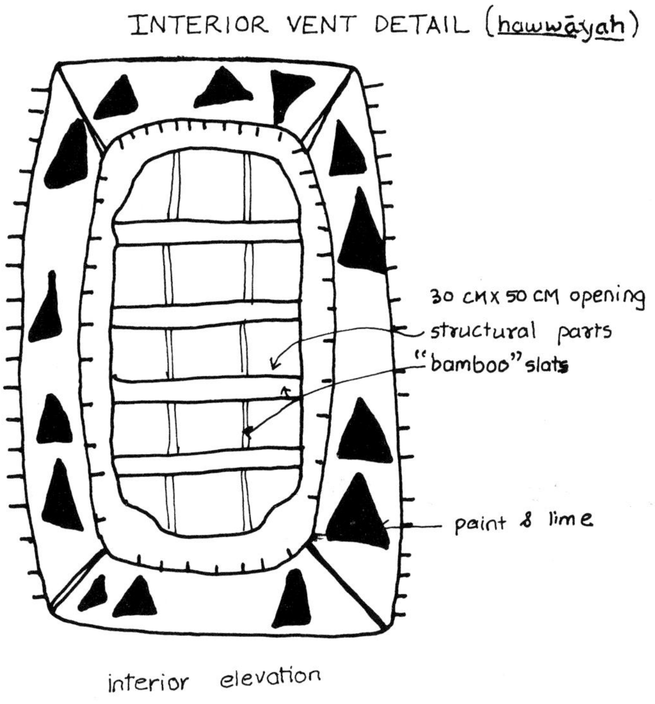

Figure 6.60

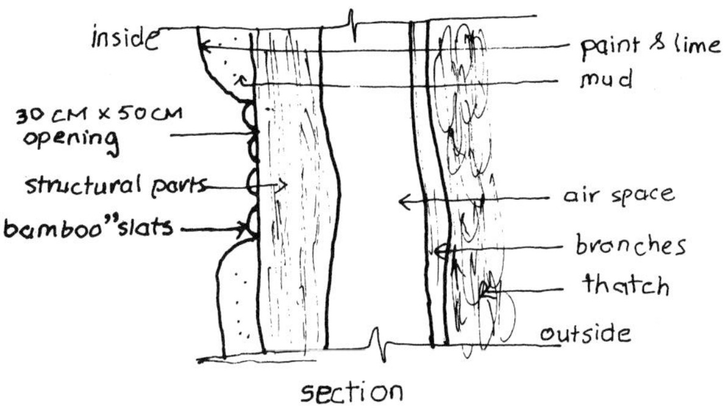

Figure 6.61

An internal door in al-Shādhilī mosque, Mocha, is made of carved wood with ornamental portion in plaster above. (See Plate 4.2.)

Figure 6.61

Figure 6.62

A window from a house in al-Tuḥaytā has a wooden shutter set in elaborately recessed mud-brick courses. Additional detail is rendered in plaster. Above the principal window is a small, secondary opening, also shuttered with wood.

Figure 6.62

Figure 6.63

An interior wall niche from a house in Zabīd is decorated with bud, leaf and flame motifs rendered in plaster. Two wooden shelves are set into the recess. (See Plate 6.14.)

Figure 6.63

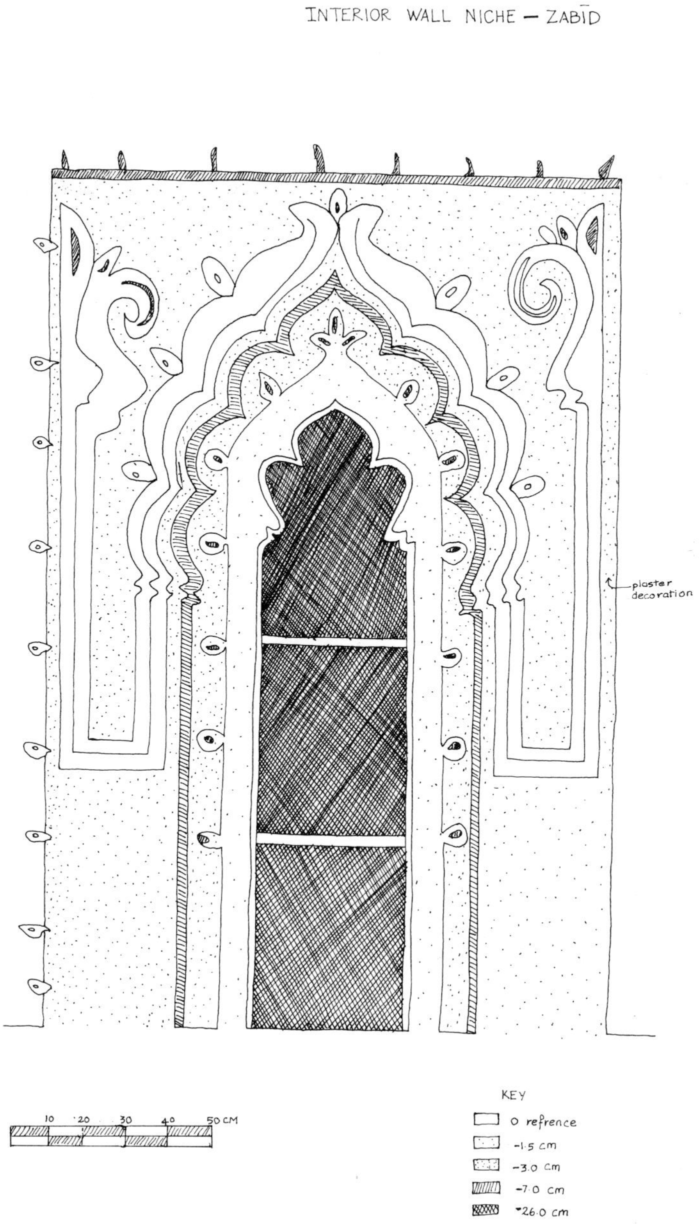

Figures 6.64-6.68

The principal furniture elements of the Tihāmah consist of wooden frame, hemp-strung beds, couches and chairs.

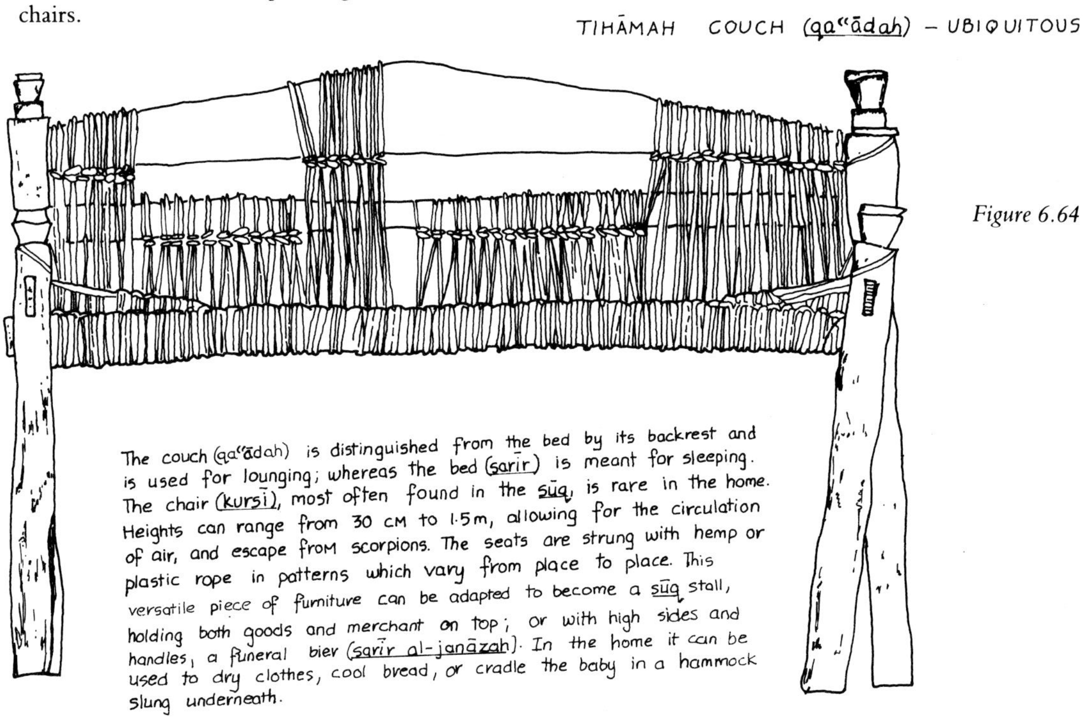
TIHĀMAH COUCH (qa‘‘ādah) – UBIQUITOUS
The couch (qa‘‘ādah) is distinguished from the bed by its backrest and is used for lounging; whereas the bed (sarīr) is meant for sleeping. The chair (kursī), most often found in the sūq, is rare in the home. Heights can range from 30 cm to 1·5m, allowing for the circulation of air, and escape from scorpions. The seats are strung with hemp or plastic rope in patterns which vary from place to place. This versatile piece of furniture can be adapted to become a sūq stall, holding both goods and merchant on top; or with high sides and handles, a funeral biev (sarīr al-janāzah). In the home it can be used to dry clothes, cool bread, or cradle the baby in a hammock slung underneath.

Figure 6.64

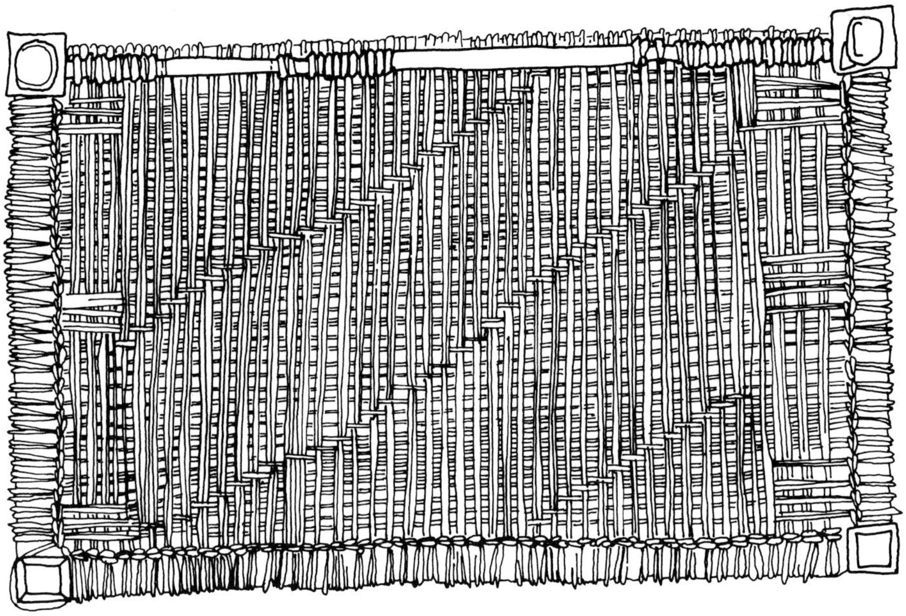

Figure 6.65

Figure 6.66

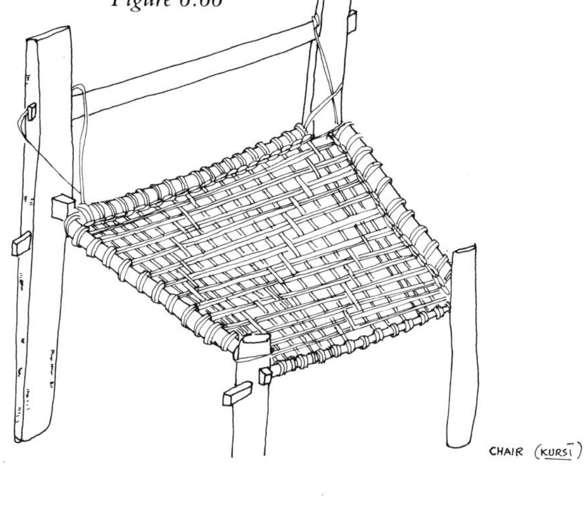
CHAIR (KURSĪ)

Figure 6.67

blue
R
W
B
WH
KEY
WH - white paint
R - red paint
B - blue paint
G - green paint
Y - yellow paint
WO - wood Mahogany
DETAIL OF DECORATED BACKREST

Figure 6.68

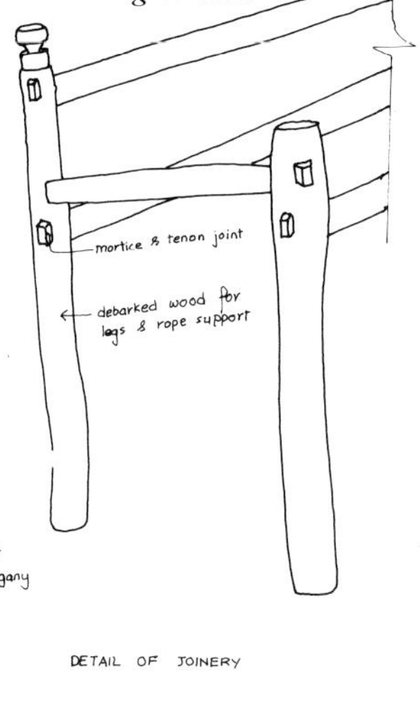
mortice & tenon joint
debarked wood for legs & rope support
DETAIL OF JOINERY

6.4: REFLECTIONS ON THE VERNACULAR ARCHITECTURE OF THE NORTH YEMEN TIHĀMAH

Steven D. Ehrlich

Within this long, narrow, flat, desert-like strip of land between the Red Sea and the mountains of Yemen, one finds an extraordinary richness of vernacular architecture. There are three principal activity types, each with their subsequent architectural solutions:

1. Living – the dwelling compound
2. Prayer – the mosque
3. Commerce – the *sūq*, tea house, *funduq* and petrol station

One is struck by the architectural variety in Tihāmah, ranging from the elegant mud brick compounds of Zabīd to the conical mud, wood and thatch huts of Wādī Mawr; the palm tree houses and mosques in al-Jāḥ to the stone construction in the foothills, and the "Red Sea style" in the ports of al-Luḥayyah, Mocha and Hodeida.

The variety of architectural styles can be a function of many factors including available constructions materials, climate variations (i.e., coastal, *wādī*, foothills, desert, etc.), historical influences, and personal preference.

Rather than look at the Tihāmah from the perspective of either building type categories or regional categories, I have chosen to study architectural phenomena (elements, recurring themes, order and organisation) in 12 main topics:

Courtyards
Symmetry
Interlocking space
Proportion
Wall thickness
Changes in level
Natural light
Veiled space
Statement of entry
Form and texture
Furniture and use
New directions

These categories form mini-chapters and shall encompass all the architecture I have studied on the Tihāmah. Concurrent with the text will be small explanatory diagrams and reference notes to my drawings as well as to the work of other members of the Tihāmah Expedition.

COURTYARDS

One of the principal organising features of Tihāmah architecture is that of the courtyard. The courtyard in a domestic compound becomes the heart of the house. It is the main distributory area by which most rooms are inter-connected. It is often the space through which light enters each room.

The intense Tihāmah climate dictates an interplay of indoor and outdoor living, depending on the time of day. (See Wall Thickness section.)

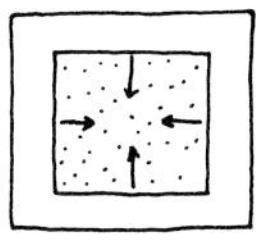
CIRCULATION

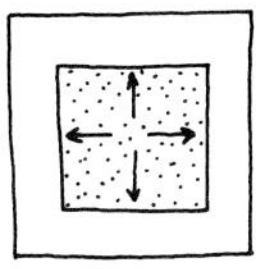
LIGHT

The existence of the courtyard allows the essential outdoor space to be private and integral with the house.

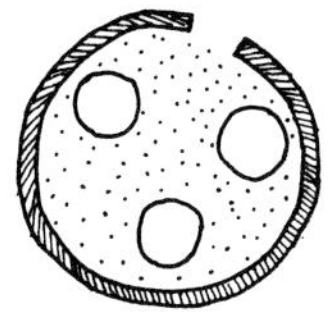
PRIVACY

The courtyard creates its own micro-climate. Protected from winds, capable of being cooled with water and planting, it offers the first level of protection in the severe climate of the Yemen Tihāmah.

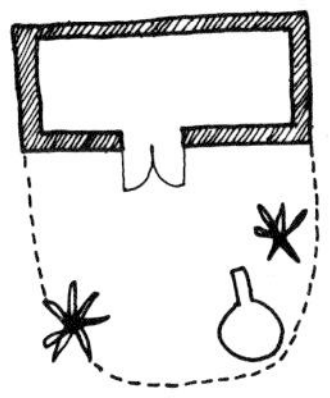
WATER & PLANTING

The use of the courtyard reaches its finest architectural expression in the mosque architecture of the Tihāmah. Here, several courtyards may interlock with each other. (See Interlocking Space section.) Their purity of light and form, and the manner in which the enclosed space relates to the courtyards, are statements in simplicity and beauty.

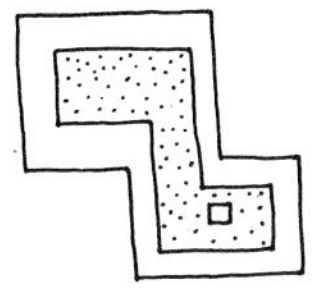

SYMMETRY

Symmetry with its inherent formalism is a recurring theme in Tihāmah architecture – both secular and religious. Symmetry provides a certain peacefulness and serenity. In the smaller mosques of the Tihāmah, one typically finds three domes. The *miḥrāb* would always be in the centre, pointing northwards to Mecca. The *miḥrāb* of a two-domed mosque, however, is also located symmetrically, inserted into a thickened arch. (See Figure 6.16.) Even a single cupola will have its doors, windows and *miḥrāb* symmetrically arranged. (See Figure 6.7.) A mosque of palm trees for walls in al-Marāziqah is also symmetrical in plan, despite the heavy texture and crudeness of materials. (See Figure 6.1.)

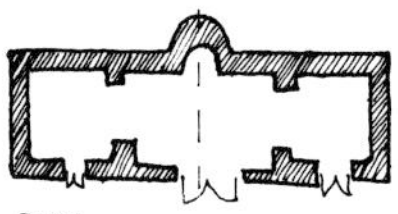

PLAN

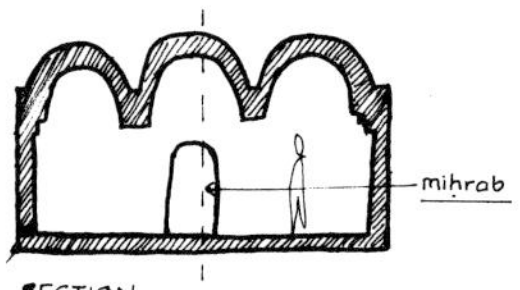

SECTION

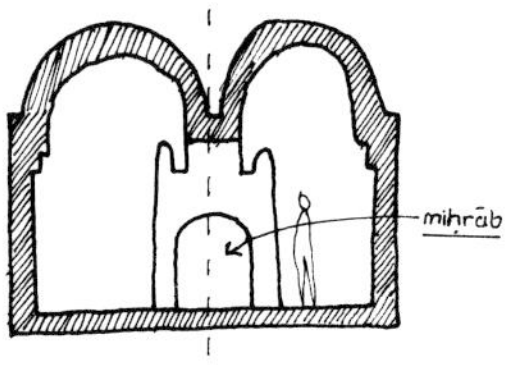

SECTION

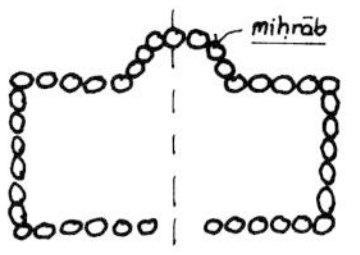

PLAN

Domestic architecture also exhibits a symmetrical plan and cross-section. This could evolve as much from structural expression, such as the circular huts of Wādī Mawr (see Plates 6.1-6.2 and Figures 6.44-6.46) or the gable end of the rectangular houses in al-Luḥayyah (see Figure 6.43) or al-Bāridah (see Figures 6.40-6.42) or Ghulayfiqah (see Figures 6.37-6.38) as from the desire for symmetry itself.

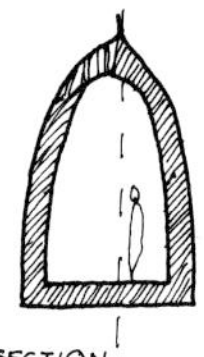

SECTION

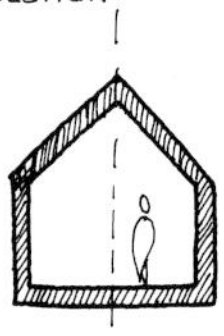

SECTION

Decorations and details also use symmetry as their main organising element. Often, architectural elements such as wall niches, which in themselves are symmetrical, will be composed in symmetrical series; when, however, a series is arranged asymmetrically (see Figure 6.12), the effect can be high-spirited.

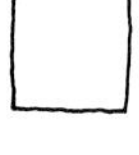

WALL NICHE

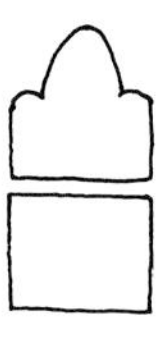

WALL NICHE

Technical factors in part dictate the need for symmetry, and enhance it as well. Due to the organic nature of the construction materials – mud, brick, grasses, reeds and palms – the symmetrical organisation has a fluidity to it, an imprecision that somehow suits the symmetry. To the Tihāmah builder, symmetry is not the only doctrine, but the natural one. Furthermore, these symmetrical, enclosed structures are usually within a far more amorphous and usually non-symmetrical context of the compound walls – be it the mosques of Zabīd or al-Durayhimī or the walled compounds of domestic architecture.

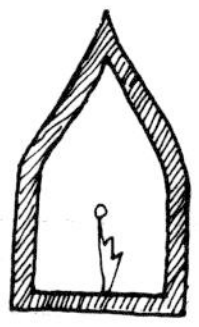

SECTION

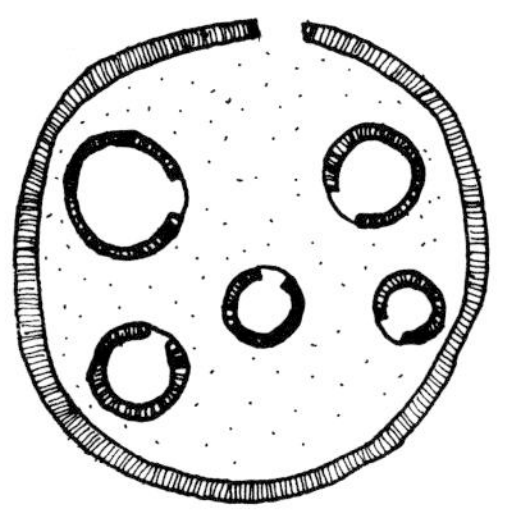

PLAN – WĀDĪ MAWR COMPOUND

The juxtapositions of architectural elements onto a symmetrical theme can often create an added energy such as is the case with the minaret of the ʻAbdullāh Ibn ʻAlī mosque in al-Durayhimī (see Figure 6.11) and al-Dūwaydār mosque in Zabīd (see Figure 6.20).

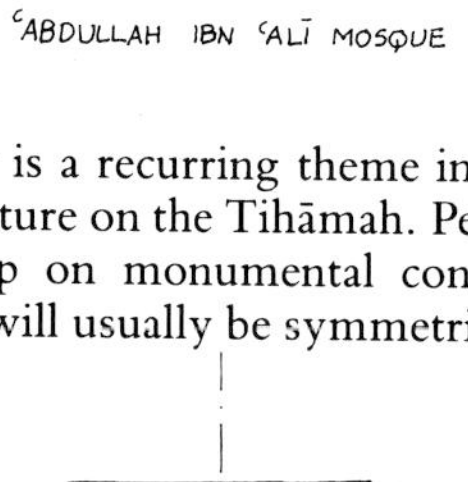

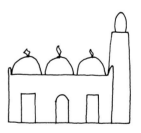

ʻABDULLAH IBN ʻALĪ MOSQUE

Symmetry is a recurring theme in the new Petrol Station architecture on the Tihāmah. Petrol pumps will often be set up on monumental concrete pedestals. Series of these will usually be symmetrically arranged.

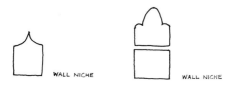

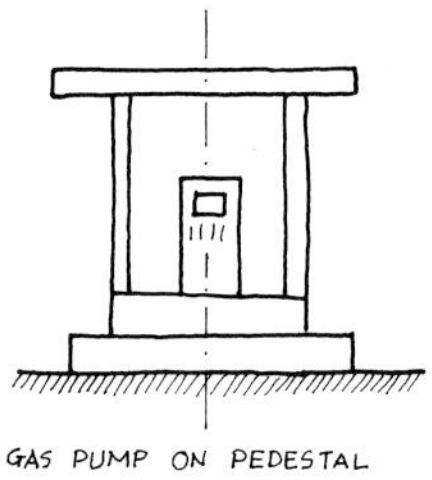

GAS PUMP ON PEDESTAL

INTERLOCKING SPACE

The principal rooms of domestic compounds tend to be enclosed structures whose main source of light as well as access is through the doors which open onto the compound's courtyard. (See Figure 6.58.) The inside space is strongly connected to the outside space; however, they are distinctly different. During the day, the outside space is hot (except where there is a coastal breeze). Inside it is dark, cool, has fewer flies. In essence, there is a strong sense of interconnected elements, rather than a fusion of inside and outside.

PLAN

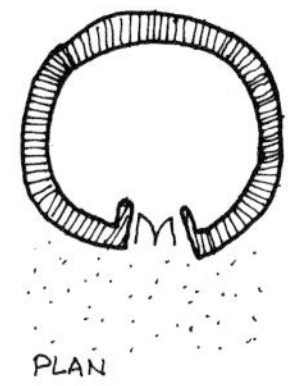

PLAN

This same observation holds true for a great deal of the smaller mosques that were studied with the notable exception of those in Zabīd, where many of the mosques had a roofed area for the Qur'ān school (*madrasah*), neither indoors nor out of doors, quite open and interconnected to the courtyard. (See Figures 6.13-6.20.)

It should be noted that these spaces would be found opposite enclosed areas that had doors and a distinct feeling of being a separate (interior space) entity.

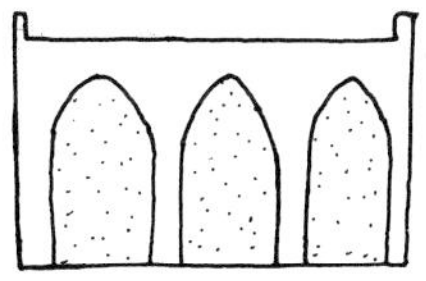

ELEVATION

How the various exterior courtyards of the smaller mosques spatially interlock is of significant architectural merit. In these mosques, there are two courtyard types: the principal courtyard onto which open the prayer halls, and the ablutions courtyard with its water source and pools.

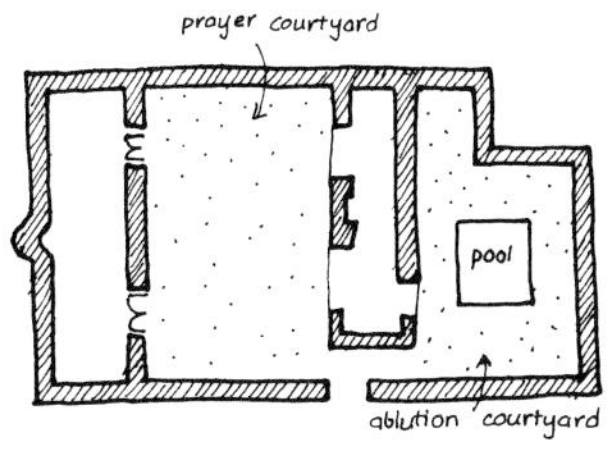

PLAN

The builders of these mosques had a fine sense of proportion and appreciation for level changes (two topics to be discussed later). To best explain some of these observations, we can walk through my favourite mosque in Zabīd, 500 year-old al-Dūwaydār mosque. (See Figure 6.18.)

One enters through a well-expressed gate into a small entry courtyard. The ablutions courtyard is the first destination, and one goes through a deep arch under the vertical element of the minaret and passes into the shelter of the Qur'ān school. Because this roofed space is open and interconnected with the prayer hall courtyard, one has an exciting experience of spatial kinetics whilst en route to the ablutions courtyard which cannot be seen, due to a bend in the wall, but the stairs and wall of which are bathed in sun. This courtyard is 1 metre above the rest of the mosque precinct, and one feels the sense of freshness that the water of the ablution pools and vista into the rest of the mosque afford. Now, descending a new set of stairs, one is in the prayer hall courtyard and can go into the enclosed mosque or the roofed Qur'ān school area or remain in the prayer hall courtyard. Upon exiting, one sees the minaret in its full decorated glory; in one's vision too is the passage through which one began the experience and the entry courtyard and street door.

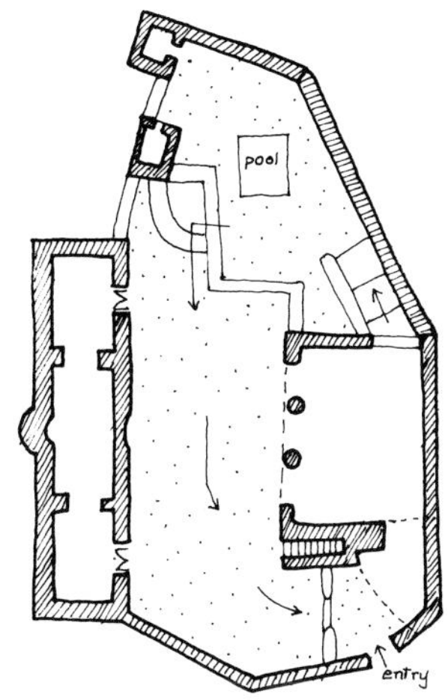

PLAN

This small Zabīdī mosque is a beautiful architectural experience and best typifies the richness of interlocking space. (See also Figures 6.10, 6.13, 6.15.)

PROPORTION

The overwhelming theme in statements of proportion on the Tihāmah is verticality. The reasons for this could be several, and I speculate:

1. To contrast with the flatness of the Tihāmah, man has built vertically. It gives a village a silhouette that becomes an identifiable landmark.
2. To allow heat to rise far above the floor where man is as cool as possible.
3. To produce the sense of space and the majesty ascribed to vertical volume.

There are many examples of domestic, religious and commercial architecture that exemplify this sense of vertical proportion. Some are the houses of Wādī Mawr (see Figures 6.45-6.46), al-Luḥayyah (see Plates 6.8, 6.10) and Zabīd (see Figure 6.59). The *sūq* and the mosques of Zabīd are also good examples. As a general rule, the Wādī Mawr huts are as tall as their interior diameter. In al-Luḥayyah and al-Bāridah, huts are taller at the ridge than the width of the rooms.

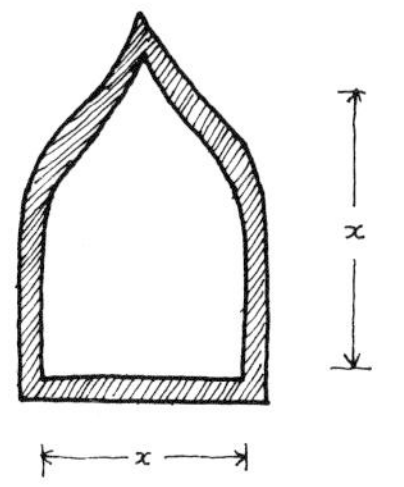

WĀDĪ MAWR MOSQUE

Domed mosques seem to exhibit the approximate proportion of the full height being 1.75× larger than the width of the room.

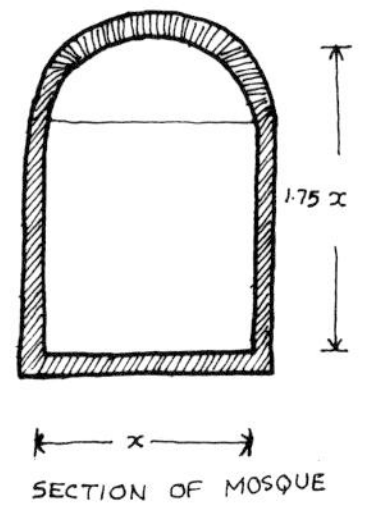

Another observation of typical proportions is that residential rooms tend to be long and narrow (round huts being an exception, of course). This seems to derive from structural necessity and economy. Narrow rooms have far shorter spans, and the span matches the lengths of available timber, which is a scarce material in any event. This long narrowness has had a great impact on furniture and life style. (See the Furniture section.)

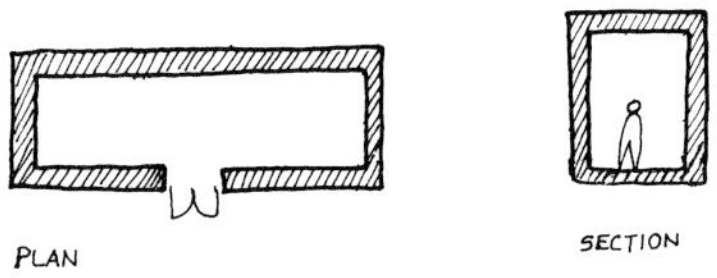

The use of the square (cube) and circle (dome) is frequent. These are shapes and volumes of mathematical proportions that have been used for centuries. They are pure, the essence of simplicity. Mosques typically display these proportions in plan as well as in section. (See Figures 6.7-6.9, 6.25-6.29.) Wall niches and plaster relief decorations also employ the square and the circle or multiples of these proportions. (See Plates 6.4, 6.10.)

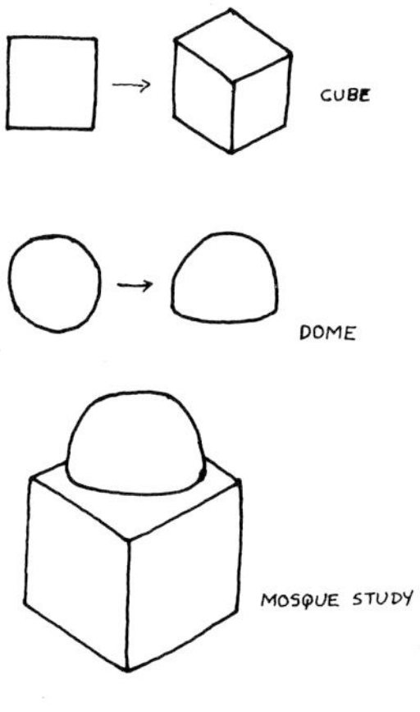

WALL THICKNESS

Builders on the Tihāmah construct thick walls and make rich use of them. Various common wall materials are:

1. Fired mud brick, such as those found in Zabīd and al-Durayhimī.

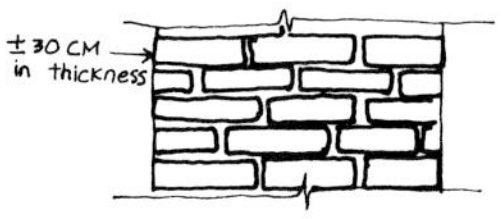

2. Palm logs found in Ghulayfiqah and al-Jāḥ.

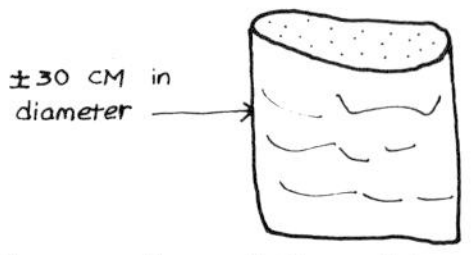

3. Branches and mud found in Wādī Mawr.

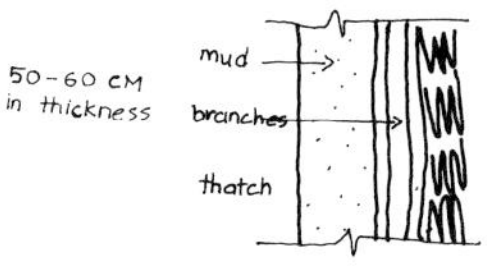

4. Thatch and reeds such as those found in al-Luḥayyah and al-Bāridah.

Thick walls have not only the inherent feature of structural strength, but also the comfort qualities of thermal mass. The thicker and more massive a material, the greater its thermal mass. Stone, mud, and brick are materials with excellent thermal mass attributes, which means they will retain heat or cold over a long time period. This works very well in hot, dry climates. For during the heat of the day, massive walls store the previous night's coolness, and therefore the room is cool (doors and windows would be closed and shuttered during this time of day). In the night, the room will be hot from absorbing the day's heat; however, the inhabitants will spend the evening and often sleep in the courtyard. 35cm of massive material will give approximately a twelve-hour lag time. This shows why a 20cm thick cement block wall (sometimes with a cavity) cannot offer the necessary comfort of thicker walled structures.

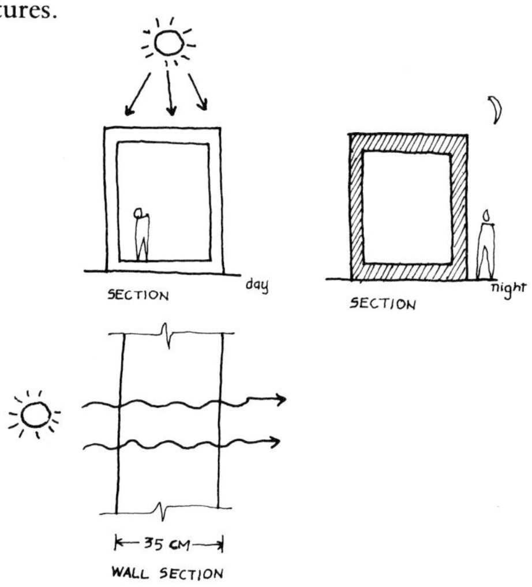

In the hot, humid areas, cross ventilation plays the key role in providing comfort. The decorated ventilating holes in al-Bāridah houses (see Figure 6.42) are the best examples of this phenomenon. They are located just above bed height for direct effect.

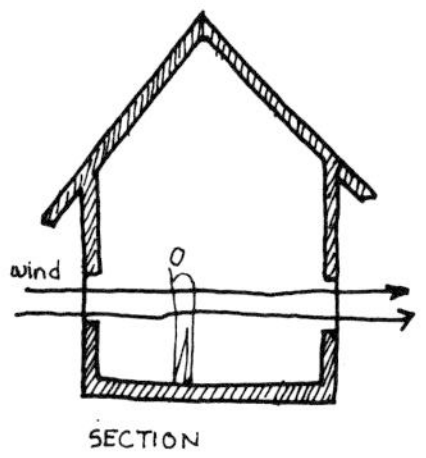

Tihāmah builders have a history of using thick walls for great artistic benefit. Interior niches and shelves are finely detailed and excellent places for putting household items. (See Plates 6.2, 6.14 and Figure 6.64.) Indentations and recesses in exterior walls constructed in brick (either exposed or plastered over) are a trademark of the Zabīd style of architecture. (See Plate 6.13 and Figure 6.63.)

CHANGES IN LEVEL

Changes in level have already been alluded to in the walk through al-Dūwaydār mosque in Zabīd (see Interlocking Space). A close study of the sections reveals a subtle yet effective use of level change. (See Figures 6.18-6.20.) Inspection of the South Elevation of the mosque with one cupola, al-Durayhimī (see Figures 6.7-6.9), reveals such a level change from the sandy, hot street to the cool cement-covered mosque courtyard. The Ibn 'Abbās mosque is set on a pedestal dating back 1,000 years. The entry stairs are an important element of the total composition. (See Figure 6.25.)

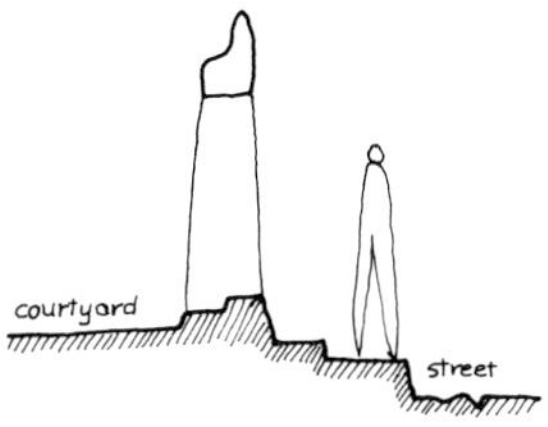

Level changes (in small increments) are a subtle way to differentiate changes in spatial feeling and mood. Two interlocking courtyards are further defined by a level change, or entry into an enclosed space is accentuated by a level change from the courtyard.

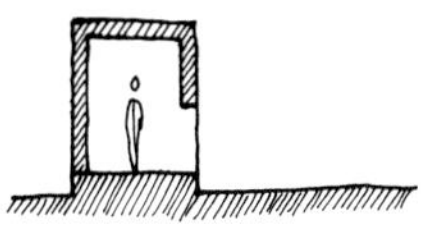

It should be pointed out that the series of steps used for these changes are often sculptural masses of great delight and architectural merit. (See Figure 6.19.)

The other principal level change phenomena are the stairs up to minarets in mosques. These elements rise to the stature of pure sculpture whilst performing the practical function of giving access to the minaret tower. (In fact, today most of the medium and large mosques have amplification systems, and let the electricity do the climbing.)

There are three generic types of mosque stairs:
1. The protruding stair as exemplified by 600 year-old al-Dayba' mosque in Zabīd. (See Figure 6.15.)
2. The interior stair as exemplified by al-Dūwaydār mosque in Zabīd. (See Figure 6.18.)

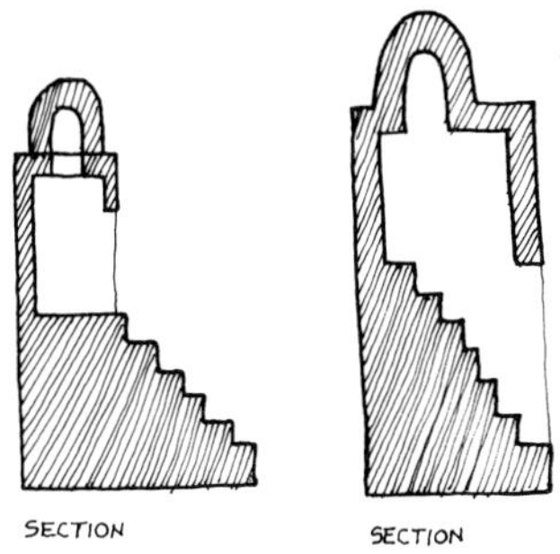

3. The spiral stair as exemplified by the ruined minaret of al-Muẓaffar mosque in al-Mahjam (modern village name, al-Manārah; see Plate 4.1.) and the minaret stair of al-Shādhilī mosque in Mocha.

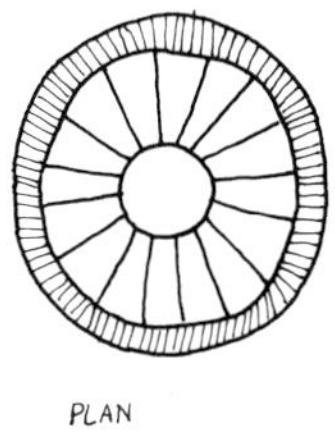

Often a combination of the first two types of stairs will take place. The first condition offers the most sculptural possibilities, and these elements act as visual foci inside the small mosque courtyards.

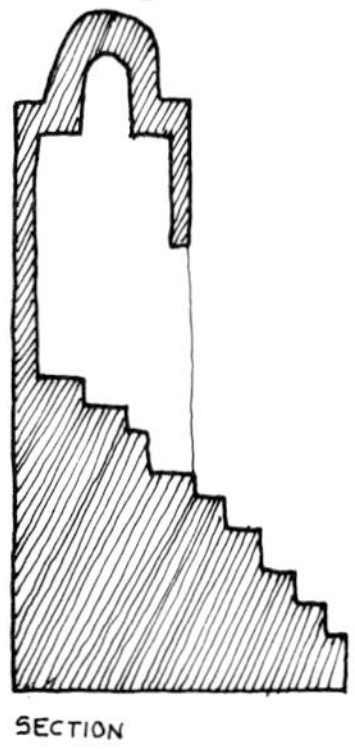

NATURAL LIGHT

In Tihāmah architecture, there are three observations that largely hold true regarding light:

1. The majority of the light comes through the door opening.
2. The rooms tend to have small or no windows (with the notable exception of Red Sea architecture).
3. Doors and shutters can be closed, and the rooms darkened at midday.

The reasons for this are cultural as well as climatic, and are perhaps best explained by the Dogon (of Mali) builder's response when asked by an anthropologist why he builds with no windows, "When I want light, I go outside," the Dogon replied.

The climatological reason for the small windows, thus is that the rooms remain cool during the heat of the day. The Tihāmah culture has established a slow-down or siesta period which lasts from about 1:00 pm to 4:00 pm. This lengthens in the summer.

A further explanation for narrow windows, especially for the burnt brick construction, is that a small window has a short span and therefore needs a modest sized lintel, and is more economical.

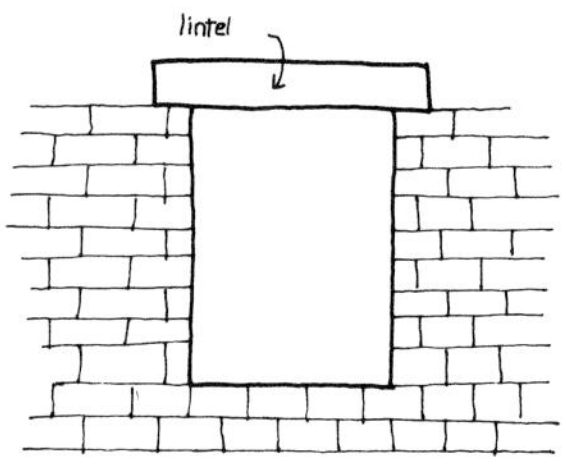

WINDOW DETAIL

The domed mosques I have studied not only have doors, but often have small openings in the domes. This lets in a soft ray of light. It also acts as an escape outlet for the hot air that rises.

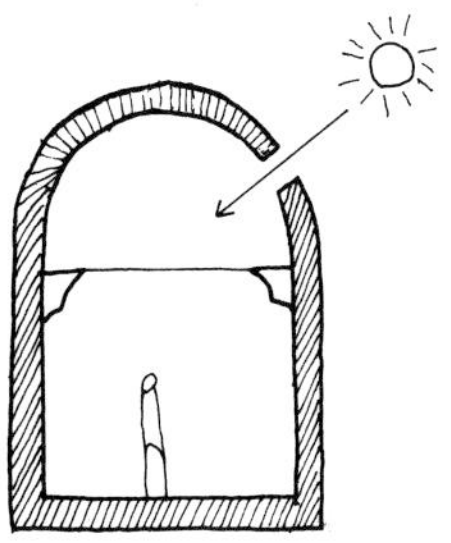

SECTION

In mosques one also finds "veiled windows", which are windows that have a grille or lattice over them. These baffles allow a soft light to penetrate and reduce the glare that one encounters at the midday prayer time.

WINDOW DETAIL

VEILED SPACE

The best way to describe veiled space is to look at a very exciting example of it in al-Luḥayyah in the ruined house of Shaykh 'Abduh Wadūd. (See Plate 6.10.) This is a superb example of Red Sea architecture, uninhabited since 1962. The second floor is devoted to the main *diwān*. What is interesting about this space is that it is surrounded by a veranda with floor to ceiling grille-work (*mashrabīyah*).

In essence, it is organised thus: the "inner sanctum" (*diwān*) has a veiled space around it. The extensive wood

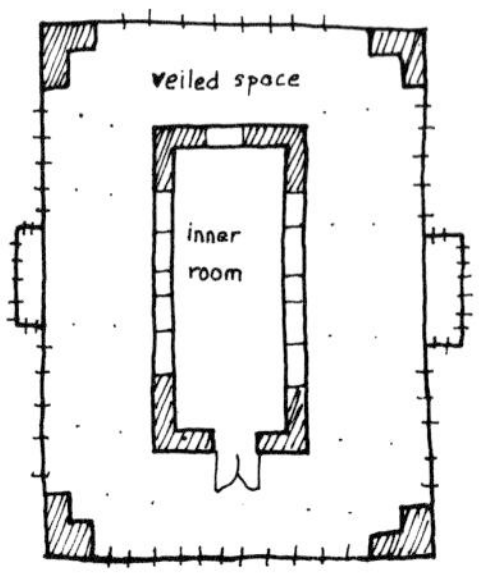

PLAN

lattice-work allows light and air onto the veranda, allowing cross-ventilation while reducing glare from the intense sunlight – the key to comfort in a hot, humid climate. This veiled space lends comfort to the *diwān* in the midday heat and makes an ideal space for morning and evening use.

Other forms of veiled space occur in the *sūqs*. In Zabīd, for example, the street space has corrugated metal roofing and hessian awnings over it. These sheets of iron and sacking however have spaces between them every so often, or they are placed at different heights. This allows a certain amount of baffled-light into the street and shops. The street then is a veiled space itself and a tributary light source for the shops.

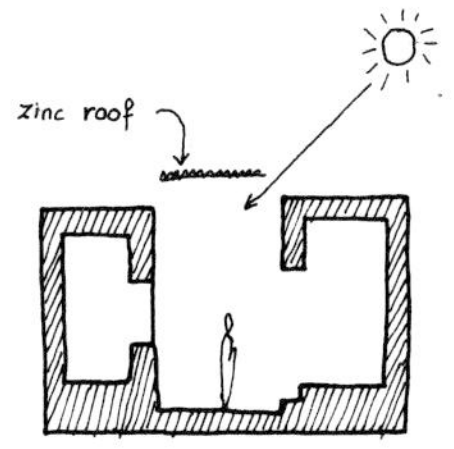

SECTION

STATEMENT OF ENTRY

The act of entering is architecturally celebrated in Tihāmah structures. There are two principal types of entry:

1. From outside into an open courtyard (from a public outside space into a private or religious courtyard).
2. From outside, or from an open courtyard, into an enclosed space.

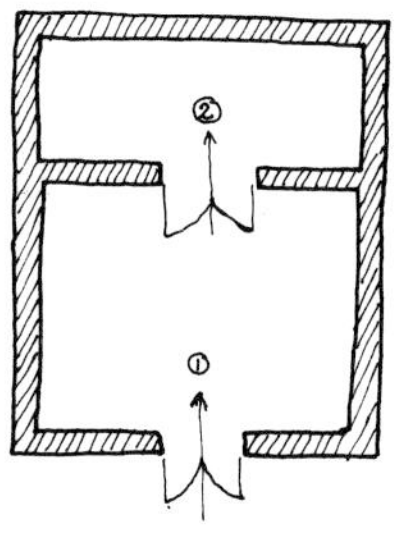

Most enclosed spaces will be entered through a courtyard (Entry type 2) which have been entered from outside (Entry type 1).

The courtyard entry door usually has a distinct architectural expression which is often an increase in wall height.

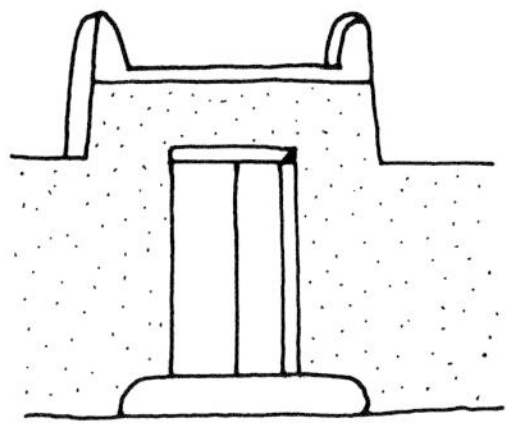

DOOR ELEVATION

This increase in wall height ceremoniously enhances the act of entering. This rise in height also visually marks the location of the door being approached from outside the buildings.

Doors entering into the enclosed rooms are also carefully detailed and expressed. In Wādī Mawr for example, the wooden bifolding doors are usually merely slats of wood. However, the deep recess created in mud allows the open doors "to disappear". (See Plate 6.2 and Figure 6.46.) The opening of the doorway is surrounded in mud. This is an architectural invitation to enter. In al-Luḥayyah, the typical door (to the reed house) has some simple wood detailing. (See Figure 6.43.)

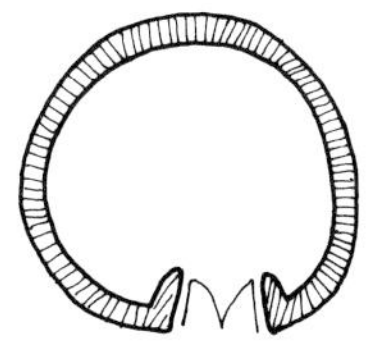

PLAN

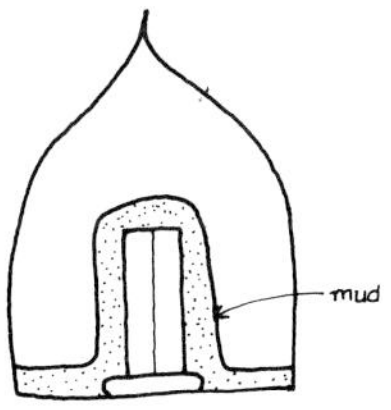

ELEVATION

In the Red Sea architecture of al-Luḥayyah, the door covering and decoration reach the highest degree of detail extant on the Tihāmah. (See Plate 6.9.)

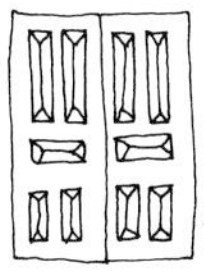

AL-LUḤAYYAH REED HUT DOOR

In al-Bāridah, a simply constructed door is colourfully painted in alternating stripes, as well as being further defined by a mud-coated surround. (See Figure 6.40.)

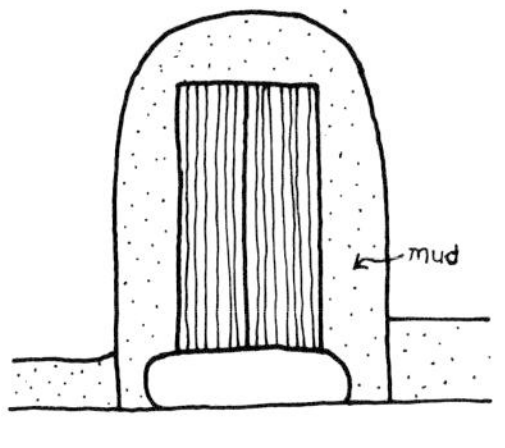

ELEVATION DETAIL

FORM AND TEXTURE

For this vast subject, five main regions shall be examined: 1. Zabīd, 2. Coastal, 3. Wādī Mawr, 4. Red Sea, and 5. Foothills.

Zabīd

The domestic architecture is not one of which the essence is expressed in mass (form), as the Westerner normally thinks of it, but rather it is an experience of time and negative space – open, uncovered spaces such as streets and courtyards. Similar architecture is found in Morocco and Tunisia and in the mud city of Kano in Nigeria. It is an architecture which grows from massive walls that enclose private worlds within each compound and are tied together with narrow streets.

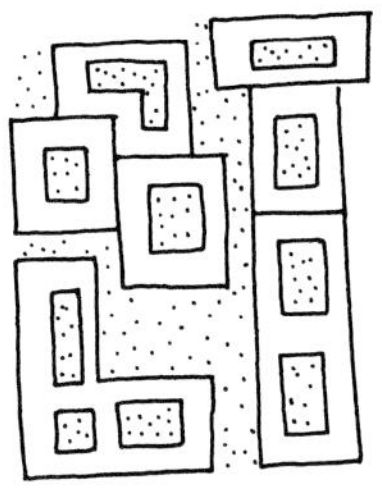

THEORETICAL PLAN

The texture of Zabīd architecture is varied, elaborate and often refined. There are two main types of facade decoration. One is created by the burnt brick itself and interconnected by creative use of recesses and shadows in geometric patterns. (See Figure 6.63.) The other is a bas-relief plaster-work. (See Plate 6.14 and Figure 6.64.) These decorations seem to be a unique artistic expression that is not found in North and West African architecture nor directly in Indian and Indonesian architecture (in my experience and that of John Nankivell). This Zabīdī expression seems to be a fusion of an African and an Islamic spirit.

EXPOSED BRICK

PLASTER DECORATION

Coastal

In al-Jāḥ, al-Marāziqah and Ghulayfiqah, one finds compounds where the huts are built of palm logs that rise above the palm leaf walls and are therefore formal expressions of mass, readily identifiable. (See Figures 6.36-6.39.) The texture of these villages is precisely that of the organic materials which come from the local environment. The palm log walls, the palm front roofs and siding echo the palm oasis. The above observations also apply to the indigenous houses of al-Luḥayyah. However, here the texture and decoration are more refined. Subtle details have been achieved with patterns of tied ropes, applied paint and ridge decorations (which now include upside-down bottles of Canada Dry).

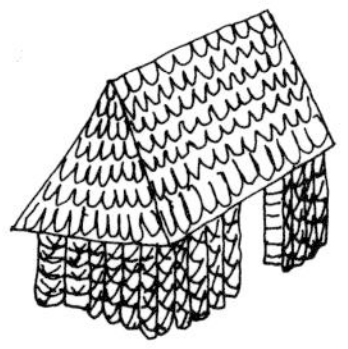

COASTAL HUT

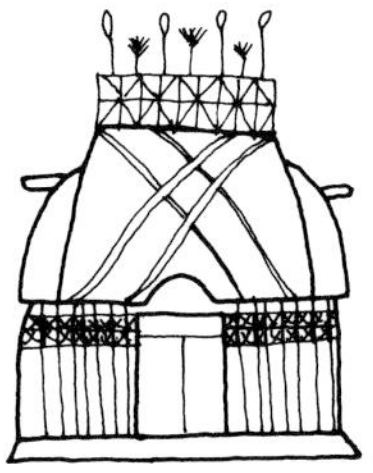

ELEVATION

Wādī Mawr

Wādī Mawr architecture is very similar in exterior form to the African hut found in many parts of West Africa. Its shape is most reminiscent of the Kanuri tribe's huts on the shores of Lake Chad. However, construction techniques are unlike anything I know in West Africa. (See Figures 6.47-6.56.)

In the interior of these huts, a coating of mud, smoothed over the face of the conical dome, is wonderfully painted and adorned with coloured plates. (See Plate 6.2 and Figure 6.46.)

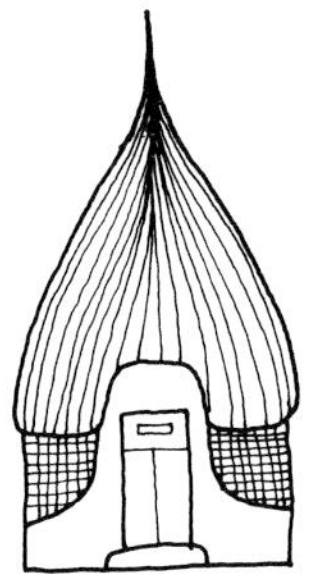

ELEVATION

Red Sea

This is a generic term for a Turko-Egyptian amalgam of styles found in the Red Sea ports of Jiddah, Suakin, al-Luḥayyah, Hodeida, Mocha and others. A rich architecture sprung from a wealthy merchant class and their understandably hedonistic lifestyle in this hot, humid climate. These houses (see Plates 6.8-6.10, XVII) with their fantastic hidden courtyards were often isolated masses, separately identifiable. Today they are decayed and largely ruined.

The texture of walls, built of coral and stone and enhanced by richly carved wooden window boxes (*rawshan*), create a powerful yet intricate architecture. Many of these walls would have been plastered, reducing the textural statement of the coral and stone, and thereby heightening the effect of the woodwork.

Foothills

In the foothills, one is struck by two significant architectural phenomena. Firstly, the sites are no longer flat, and secondly, the use of stone is now economically feasible.

In the foothill village of al-Ṣanīf in Wādī Zabīd, there is a tiny *funduq* (inn) built of varying sizes of smooth, riverbed stone. (See Figure 6.33.) The mosque in al-Ṣanīf (see Figures 6.3-6.6) is a work of art in stone. This small structure with its stone arches has the sense of power and scale of a building of much larger size.

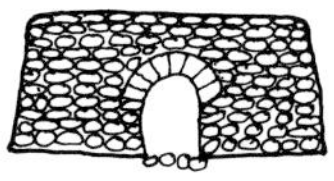

FUNDUQ ELEVATION

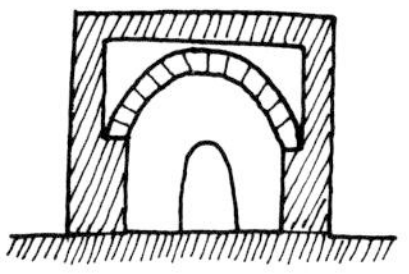

MOSQUE ELEVATION

Foothill architecture stands out as isolated building masses; texture varies with the elevation into the mountains. The higher the elevation, the greater amount of stone is used in construction and the less use of mud.

It should be noted that when one finally goes above an elevation of +600m, one is out of the Tihāmah. By that point, the architecture is built of stone and expresses a cubistic aesthetic.

FURNITURE AND USE

There is one piece of furniture in the Tihāmah – the Tihāmah bed/couch. (See Figures 6.65-6.69.) This is made of a wood frame with mortise and tenon joinery of debarked tree trunks 4cm to 8cm in diameter. The seemingly more popular beds/couches today are made of imported mahogany (*sīsum*) and painted bright colours. The actual seating or sleeping surface is a netting of woven ropes (hemp or nylon) acting in pure tension against the wooden framework. One can be seated or reclining on these beds/couches, although those intended for seating have backrests and sometimes armrests.

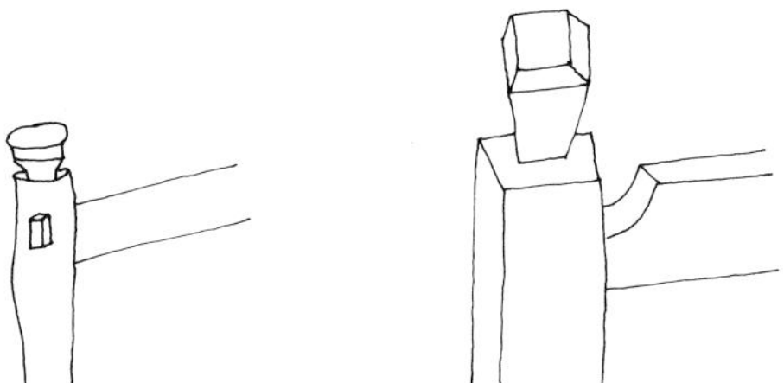

In a rectangular hut, the beds are arranged against the walls. Since the rooms are long and narrow (see Proportion), from 3 to 5m wide, this creates two U-shaped areas with a good human scale for interaction.

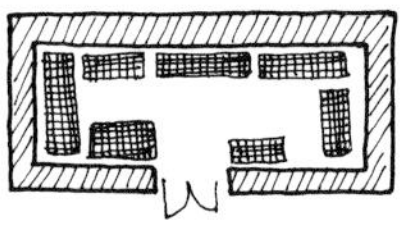

In the large round houses of Wādī Mawr, the beds/couches are arranged in tiers of two. (See Figure 6.44.) The walls in many instances become back supports. This places the bed directly against the walls and consumes a minimum of space (unlike the conventional couch placement in the West).

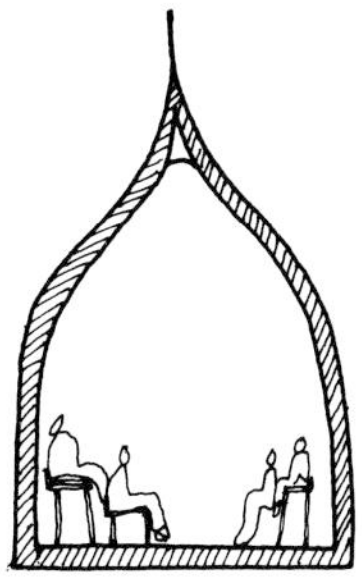

Another important aspect of this furniture is that it is portable. This allows their movement inside or outside as demanded by climate, time of day, and social activity.

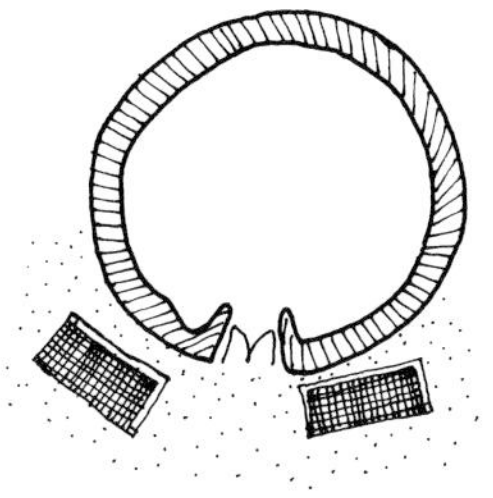

These beds/couches are also used in public architecture such as tea and coffee houses and *funduqs* and *sūqs*. (See Figures 6.30, 6.34.)

NEW DIRECTIONS

The future of architecture in the Tihāmah is quite bleak with few shining lights. Natural, cool and inexpensive materials are rapidly losing ground to cement block, corrugated iron, and aluminium sash windows. These materials tend to be imported (therefore an economic dependence) and are often used inappropriately (see Thick Walls). The use of these materials has usually led to the demise of the traditional grace and sense of proportion employed by the indigenous builders. One refreshing exception to this are some of the new cement block houses in al-Luḥayyah.

The image of a cement block house, with a makeshift corrugated iron roof decorated with discarded plastic bags caught on protruding edges, is a sad one that even the architectural optimist finds unredeeming.

There is, however, a beacon in the night, the harbinger of a new Yemeni architecture. That is the petrol station, glistening in the night with its coloured fluorescent lights, like television on the scale of the highway. The analogy seems more relevant when one sees a group of Yemenis at the petrol station sitting on their Tihāmah beds, staring out at the night through the geometric matrix of coloured lights, into the headbeams of vehicles passing by.

There is a raw, vital energy about these petrol stations. They come alive at night when their harlequin fluorescent lights glow to the mechanical drum beat of the generators.

The pump stations can be quite ceremonial with the petrol pump symmetrically located on a concrete pedestal. (See Symmetry.)

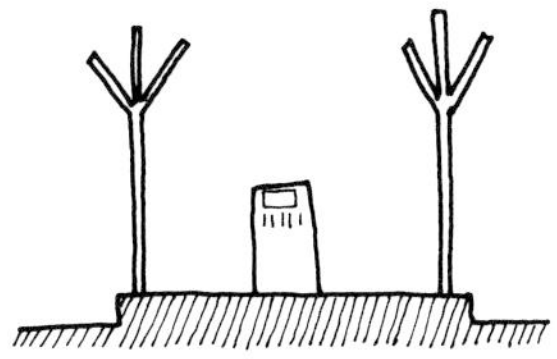

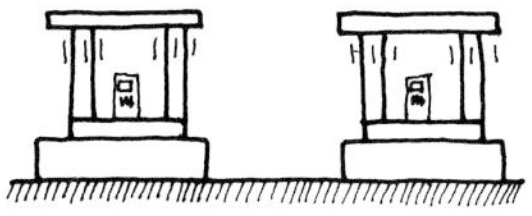

Unlike the Yemenia Airways building in Ṣan'ā', which is symbolic of a totally inappropriate imported architecture, the Yemeni petrol station has an indigenous quality. It is a building form that deals with new technology both in construction and purpose of structure. The builders have taken these elements and celebrated them. The best petrol stations are freshly painted and have a multitude of lights. This relatively new building form monumentalises the lorry, auto and motorcycle as if demigods.

One cannot be sentimental and tell the Yemenis that they "don't need" cement and zinc roofing, cars, or television. Technology has its all too mesmerising power. No Westerner has the right to say "don't need" to the Yemenis. However, it is now necessary for the new builders to appreciate their rich heritage of vernacular architecture, and apply its axioms within the context of new materials and requirements.

Petrol stations have made the leap, and as pop art in the night, they call for all Yemenis to pour their creative energy into the new technological challenge, with the hope that a new Yemeni architecture will not discard its history, and its genius, but incorporate it.

FURTHER READING

Bornstein, Annika, "Report on a visit to Yemen. Al-Zohrah – An agricultural village in the Tihāmah," *United Nations Development Program, Special Fund Project, Food and Nutrition Programme*, Yem/71/513, 1974.

Baldry, John, *Britain and the Idrisi Imamate of Asir and Yemen*, (in press). See also other relevant articles by J. Baldry listed on p. XX.

Chelhod, J., "Introduction à l'Histoire Sociale et Urbaine de Zabīd," *Arabica*, Vol. 25, 1978, pp. 48-89.

Costa, Paolo and E. Vicario, *Arabia Felix A Land of Builders*, New York, 1977.

Dubach, Werner, *Yemen Arab Republic, a study of traditional forms of habitation and types of settlement*, Zurich, 1977.

Escher, Hermann A., *Wirtschafts und sozialgeographische Untersuchungen in der Wādī Mawr Region (Arabische Republik Jemen)*, Wiesbaden, 1976.

Fayein, Claudie, "Al-Zohrah, Village de la Tihāma," *Objets et Mondes*, Vol. 13, part 3, 1973, pp. 161-172.

Greenlaw, Jean-Pierre, *The Coral Buildings of Suakin*, Stocksfield, London and Boston, 1976.

Harris, P.C., "The Arab Architecture of Zanzibar," *RIBA Journal*, 4 April 1925, pp. 341-345.

Keall, E.J., "Zabīd and its Hinterland: 1982 Report," *Proceedings of the Seminar for Arabian Studies*, Vol. 13, 1983.

King, Geoffrey, "Some observations on the architectures of south-west Saudi Arabia," *Architectural Association Quarterly*, London, Vol. VIII, 1976, pp. 20-99.

Lewcock, Ronald, "Architectural Connections Between Africa and Parts of the Indian Ocean Littoral," *AARP*, Vol. 9, 1976, pp. 341-345.

——————, "Three Medieval Mosques in the Yemen," *Oriental Art*, Vol. 20, London, 1974, pp. 1-12 (parts I & II).

Mathews, Derek H., "The Red Sea Style," *Kush*, Vol. 1, 1954, pp. 60-86.

——————, "Suakin Postscript," *Kush*, Vol. 3, 1955, pp. 99-111.

Niebuhr, Carsten, *Description de l'Arabie*, Paris, 1779.

——————, *Travels through Arabia*, Edinburgh, 1792.

——————, *Voyages en Arabie*, Amsterdam, 1774-1780.

Prochazka, Theodore, Jr., "Architectural Terminology of the Saudi Arabian South-West," *Arabian Studies*, London, Vol. IV, 1978, pp. 113-121.

——————, "Observations on the Architectural Terminology of the South-west of the Arabian Peninsula," *Arabian Studies*, London, Vol. VI, 1982, pp. 97-115.

Serjeant, R.B. and Ronald Lewcock, eds., *Ṣan'ā' an Arabian Islamic City*, London, 1982.

Steffen, Hans, *Final Report – on the Airphoto Interpretation Project of the Swiss Technical Co-operation Service, Berne carried out for the CPO, Ṣan'ā'. The Major Findings of the Population and Housing Census of February 1975 and the Results of Supplementary Demographic and Cartographic Surveys done in the districts of Turbah, Jabal 'Iyāl Yazīd, al-Luḥayyah and in the Mashriq of Yemen*, Zurich, 1977.

Varanda, Fernando, *Art of Building in Yemen*, London and Cambridge, Mass., 1982.

——————, "Colour in Contemporary Yemen Architecture," (unpublished).

ILLUSTRATIONS

Schematic sketches provided by the author.

GLOSSARY

alwān	painted decorations. Interior house decoration, Wādī Mawr and elsewhere. (pl. of *lawn*, colour)
agūr	spikey grass-like water-grass, identity unknown. Used in house construction, Ghulayfiqah. Unconfirmed. Possibly *'agūr*
'āmir	inhabitant, denoting a ruling house
athl[1]	TAMARIX ARABICA or T. APHYLLA, branches. Used in house scaffolding, Wādī Mawr. Pronounced *athil*
arj[2]	ZIZYPHUS SPINA-CHRISTI, also known as *'ilb* and *sidr*. Same use as *athl*
asās	foundations (of a house)
barīm	cordage. Used in house construction, Wādī Mawr
barūd	day hut
bawwābah[3]	portal, main street entrance to house, Zabīd
būyā	painted decoration. Interior house decoration, Wādī Mawr and elsewhere. Commonly used for oil paint in Yemen. From Turkish
dikkah	dresser for dishes, a platform. Interior house feature, Wādī Mawr and elsewhere. Pronounced *dekkah*
funduq	inn, wayside shelter
ḥalfah	DESMOSTACHYA BIPINNATA, a large coarse grass growing only in Wādīs Mawr and Ḥaraḍ. Pl., *ḥalāfī*, more common
ḥaṣar	INDIGIFERA OBLONGIFOLIA, common Tih. undershrub. Used for lathing and insulation in house construction, Wādī Mawr
ḥayātī	rope. Used in house construction, Wādī Mawr
hawwāyah'	vent. House feature in al-Bāridah
ḥukūmah	governor's palace
ḥuṣn	fort
ḥuzmah	bundle, sheaf, specifically a bundle of *thumām*
jambīyah	dagger
kūrsī	chair
ḥawsh	enclosure, courtyard. Pronounced *ḥūsh*
liwān[4]	large men's salon, Zabīd
mabrak	compound, Ghulayfiqah
madā'ah	waterpipe
madrasah	school, specifically a *Qur'ān* school adjoined to a mosque
mafraj	belvedere, highest sitting room
maqhā	coffee-house. Pronounced *magā*
marādam	roof ridge decorations in al-Luḥayyah. Possibly to deflect natural or supernatural harm. Unconfirmed. Probably associated with *mirdām* below
marātīd	pegs. Interior house feature in Wādī Mawr and elsewhere
minbar	pulpit

1. See also Flora Glossary, Chapter 2.
2. See also Music Glossary, Chapter 7, and Ethnography Glossary, Chapter 8.
3. See J. Chelhod, op. cit., p. 50.
4. Ibid.

minbar abū shāfi'[5]	an elaborate Tihāmah couch, Zabīd
miḥrāb	prayer niche, a recess in a mosque indicating the direction of prayer
mirdām	water catchment sill. Exterior house feature in Wādī Mawr. Pronounced *mardām*
naqsh	plaster decoration. Domestic and religious architecture in Zabīd; sculpted mud decoration. Interior house decoration in Wādī Mawr and elsewhere. Pronounced *nuksh*
masjid	mosque
qa''ādah[6]	couch, a hemp-strung angareeb with a back rest. Pronounced *ga'ādah*
qabr li'l-walī	saint's tomb. Pronounced *gubr li'l wellī*
qabal[7]	forecourt, Zabīd
qaḍab	CADABA ROTUNDIFOLIA. Used in house scaffolding, Wādī Mawr. Pronounced *gadab*
qaṣab	sorghum stalks. Used in *zarībah* construction, Wādī Mawr and elsewhere. Pronounced *guṣub*
qāt	CATHA EDULIS, a narcotic leaf. Pronounced *gāt*
qur'aynah	centrepole. Used in house construction in Wādī Mawr. Pronounced *guraynah*
qushāsh	painted motifs on interior of house, al-Bāridah. Unconfirmed
radīf	a wood, identity unknown. Used in house construction in Wādī Mawr. Unconfirmed
raff	shelf, ledge
rawshan	large, latticed window box. Typical of "Red Sea" houses. From Persian
ṣaffah[8]	women's salon, Zabīd
sanfah	TEPHROSIA PURPUSEA, a legume genus typical of and in the Yemen specific to the Tih., it is poisonous (in East Africa it is used to stupefy and catch fish). Used for termite protection in Wādī Mawr[9]. Also given as *sanāfī*
saqīfah	day hut, Wādī Mawr and elsewhere. Pronounced *sagīfah*
sarīr[10]	bed, hemp-strung "angareb" with no arms or backrest
sarīr al-janāzah	funeral bier
sumur	ACACIA TORTILIS, a flat-topped acacia seen on the Tih., also known as *ḥaraṣ*, also as *sumūr* in eastern Yemen. Used in house scaffolding in Wādī Mawr
sūq	marketplace. Pronounced *sūg* and *sawg*
thumām	LASIURUS SCINIDUS, thatching. Used in house construction in Wādī Mawr and elsewhere
ṭūl min ḥalāfī	ropes made of local grass, see *ḥalfah*. Used in house construction in Wādī Mawr. Pronounced *dul min halāfī*
ṭurāḥah	patio, Wādī Mawr
'ushshah	thatch hut or house, also refers to the superstructure of houses in Wādī Mawr. Pronounced *ushshah*
wazar	skirting, lower courses of bundled thatch on houses in Wādī Mawr
zarībah	mounded wall of animal stockade and compound, Wādī Mawr and elsewhere
zīnah	painted decoration. Interior house feature, Wādī Mawr and elsewhere. Pronounced *zaynah*
zinjīl	reed stalks, identity unknown.[11] Used in house construction in al-Luḥayyah.

5. Ibid., p. 51.
6. Ibid.
7. Ibid., p. 50.
8. Ibid.
9. See also V.I. Deriabin, "Harmfulness of the termite MICROTERMES PROBLEMATICUS Grasse in the conditions of the Yemen Arab Republic and measures of controlling it," *Uzbekskii Biologischeskii Zhurnal*, 19(4), 1975, pp. 45-47. See Wood, p. 14.
10. J. Chelhod, op. cit., p. 51.
11. See Stone, p. 125, n. 107.

MUSIC

7.1: MUSIC ON THE TIHĀMAH

Anderson Bakewell

INTRODUCTION

I undertook, during the course of the Expedition, a survey of Tihāmah music, primarily to further identify its place in the context of the Yemen and the Red Sea area. Special attention was paid to the instruments, the setting of the music and its performers, who were queried and recorded at private sessions and public festivals and ceremonies, both rural and urban. What emerged from the study was an interesting and lively musical tradition that will, I hope, be served by this and further efforts to document it.

The paper outlines different types of music to be heard on the Tihāmah, with particular reference to the practices of the professional itinerant musicians. A description of the instruments and brief profiles of selected musicians are appended to the text.

It is important to acknowledge here the invaluable assistance with recording equipment given by Ragnar Johnson, who also offered good, sound advice both before and after the survey. Lucy Duran of the British Library (National Sound Archive) and Jean Jenkins also made useful pre-expedition suggestions, and 'Abdullāh al-Rudaynī generously offered clarification of some regional aspects of Tihāmah music. In the field, Shaykh 'Alī al-Muzarīyah, Aḥmad Fatḥī, and 'Abd al-Raḥmān al-Ḥaḍramī were all indispensable.

THE MUSIC AND ITS SETTING

Music on the Tihāmah can be divided into several distinct categories depending on its content, setting, and the social status of the musician. Work songs that accompany routines such as cultivating, fishing, or drawing water from a well are sung by amateurs and, as such, are purely folk music. Whereas, what could be termed "popular art" music, that is to say colloquial poems (often in the *ḥumaynī* [1] tradition) sung with *'ūd* [2] and occasionally orchestral accompaniment, is normally performed by professionals. Essentially a synthesis of the poetic and folk traditions, it is an urban phenomenon, and Hodeida, Bayt al-Faqīh, and Zabīd have all produced artists *(fannān* or *'awwād)* of national repute.

There is a rich tradition of poetry on the Tihāmah and much of it, as in the Yemen highlands, is imbued with religious feeling. Of the poems recited at the major religious festivals *('īd, ziyārah, mawlid)* and meetings of religious brotherhoods *(ṭarīqah)*, many are of Tihāmah origin; composed by local poets and sung to a melody *(laḥn)* identifiable as Tihāmī.[3]

Secular, non-rhymed sung poetry *(muwwāl* or *ṭāriq)* is also commonly heard, often accompanied by an exceptionally liberated free-form vocalist. The services of professional poets are much in demand, and they are hired, sometimes with an accompanying flute *(shubbābah)*[4] for a *qāt* party or all-night celebration.

Quite distinct from these is the music of the professional itinerant musicians (*muṭabbil* or *muṭambil*) who perform at weddings, religious and agricultural festivals, circumcisions *(khitān)*, exorcism ceremonies *(zār)*; indeed at nearly all the important occasions of Tihāmah life. Generally referred to as *ṭibbāl*, this is highly rhythmic music that, as the Arabic name suggests, features a variety of drums. Rarely are fewer than two types of drums employed by ensembles that consist, typically, of 4 or 5 musicians. Great effect is achieved by setting off, for instance, the stick-beaten *marfa'* and *mishkal* against the hand-beaten *ṭablah*. Further contrast is created by the periodically muted *ṣaḥfah* and by the introduction of a melody instrument, usually a reed flute (*qaṣabah*) or reed pipes *(mizmār)*.[5]

This effective exploitation of the instruments' distinctive voices seems a characteristic feature of the *ṭibbāl* music, and makes it particularly well suited to the dance, which it accompanies at nearly all these public occasions. In fact, most rhythms in the *ṭibbāl* repertoire are named after the dances they accompany – commonly the *marīsī (maraysī?)*, *shanab* (a fast-tempo stick dance also done on horseback), *farasānī* (a regional wedding dance of the northern coastal tribes), *sharaḥ*, *khudāmī*, and *sharqī*.[6] The rhythms that correspond to these dances contain a high degree of syncopation. When performing them, each drummer in the ensemble concentrates on a specific pattern, continuing it relentlessly with some embellishment, until a rhythm change is announced by either the melody musician or the lead drummer (most often the *marfa'*).

The dances vary with the occasion and some are aligned with specific ceremonies. At the *ziyārah* of al-Shamsī Ahdal,[7] for instance, musicians are called

---

1. *Ḥumaynī*, or *malḥūn*, is one of the two genres of traditional Yemeni poetry. It differs from the more formal *ḥakamī* in that it does not strictly adhere to classical rules of versification and language. See Muḥammad 'Abduh Ghānim's *Shi'r al-Ghinā' al-Ṣan'ānī* (Beirut and Ṣan'ā', n.d.).
2. Before the recent introduction of the *'ūd* (also called *kabānj* in South Arabia), the favoured instrumental accompaniment to popular art music was apparently the 4-stringed skin bellied lute.
3. Turkish melodies also survive in the sung poetry of the Tihāmah.
4. It has been suggested by Dr. Yūsuf 'Abdullāh that the word *shubbābah* may be derived from *tashbīb*, the praise verse (2nd part) of the *qaṣīdah* (in communication with the author).
5. The melody generally follows a pentatonic system.
6. Other dances, reported but not seen, include the *zaḥfah* (serpent dance), *ḥaqfah* (sp.?), and *tuways*.
7. See Stone, p. 122.

upon to accompany a dance that includes the ritual stabbing procedure with a rhythm called *taḥḍirah* ("preparation"?), perhaps referring to its power to induce the state of mind and body necessary for the ritualistic ascent of the greased pole. It appears that the rhythmic formulae provided by the drummers both set off and maintain these states.

The special relationship of the drums to the dancer is once again demonstrated in the *zār*, a ceremony for the purpose of expelling a spirit that causes sickness and mental distress. The process involves prolonged and cathartic singing and dancing, and the more elaborate *zār* ceremonies are supported by ensembles of *muṭabbil* consisting of lyre *(ṭumbarah)*, *mizmār* and the *ṣaḥfah, marfa'*, and *madiff* drums. Here the orchestra fulfills an almost purely rhythmic function, with the *ṭumbarah*, and even the *mizmār*, subordinate to the drums. To the drums are attributed special powers to influence the *zār* spirit, and the afflicted are sometimes held against them as they are being played.[8]

The musicians performing for the *zār* are under the direction of a *muzawwir*, or master of ceremonies, who serves as intermediary between the spirit and the possessed. He himself does not play an instrument, but controls the dynamics of the music with abrupt commands and initiates the chants.[9] These follow a call-and-response pattern where the dancers and musicians answer in unison, which ultimately leads into an extended repetitive instrumental section, marked by syncopated rhythm patterns from the strummed *ṭumbarah*[10] until brought to a sudden conclusion.

But *muṭabbil* do not confine their activities to festivals and ceremonies. They can, and do, perform at any public gathering, entertaining at tea houses *(maqhā)* and *qāt* parties. Now, with more efficient transport available, they even make regular forays to "Yemen" (as the highlands are sometimes referred to) and can arrange to perform almost daily in a different *sūq*. In this setting a *mizmār* might accompany a woman singer, providing the musical support for an energetic boy dancing in the midst of a crowded throng of onlookers.[11]

Fees for this type of entertainment are casually paid as baksheesh, in contrast to the payment at more formalised occasions, where fees are highly negotiable. The better known musicians can demand considerable sums (several thousand riyals), but theirs is nearly always on a scale lower than that paid to the *fannān*, imported from the larger towns to play at weddings of wealthier families.

It is interesting to note the role that social standing plays in the composition of the *ṭibbāl* ensembles. Drumming, considered by the Tihāmah Arab to have strong associations with Africa, is generally the domain of the Akhdām,[12] while is it acceptable that other instruments – the reed pipes, flute, and lyres – are taken up by a former slave *('abd)* or even a tribesman *(qabīlī)*.[13] But the tradition of entertaining seems so central to the life of the Akhdām (and indeed one of the only professions open to them) that virtually everyone in their community is capable of performing to some degree. To the Tihāmah Arab, the Akhdām are entertainers.

It is encouraging to note in the survey that, despite greatly improved communications in recent years, there still exist on the Tihāmah distinct regional styles, dances, and even instruments. The *ṣaḥfah*, for instance, a feature of the *ṭibbāl* ensembles in the northern Tihāmah, is rarely encountered south of Bājil. The *farasānī* dance is unknown in al-Manṣūrīyah and the *sharaḥ* is quite foreign to al-Luḥayyah.[14]

Music on the Tihāmah does incorporate extra-Arabian elements, but African influences are perhaps overemphasised by listeners struck by its intriguing contrasts to highland Yemeni music. Questions of geographical origins of instruments, forms, or styles become tedious, or even irrelevant, in the face of the Tihāmah's history. Centuries of contact with Africa in the form of migration, invasion, and trade; mercantile activity with the Far East via the Indian Ocean trade routes; occupation by the Ottoman Turks have all contributed to the formation of the region's music, and like the architecture that flowered in the ports of Mocha, al-Luḥayyah, and Hodeida, it owes much to a geographical and cultural sphere that extends beyond the frontiers of the Yemen. It is perhaps best described as "Red Sea music", a term that has even more relevant and specific application to the *ṭibbāl* music, which performed by musicians who are obliged socially and economically to be itinerant, would naturally be less bound by any local convention.

---

8. Drums have historically played a role in all public events of importance on the Tihāmah, from military campaigns to celebrations. See references to kettle-drum ensemble (*ṭabalkhānah*) throughout al-Khazrajī, *The Pearl Strings; a history of The Rasúliyy dynasty of Yemen*, trans. J.W. Redhouse, Leiden-London, 1906-18. Charles Crane (*Journal of the Central Asian Society*, Vol. XV, Part 1, 1928) witnessed a punishment for drinking alcohol where the miscreant was paraded through the streets of Hodeida with a drum strapped to his back, the instrument beaten by an official. For a description of the *zār* ceremony see Stone, p. 119.
9. Often in a falsetto voice, reportedly to communicate with female *zār* spirits.
10. In contrast to the use of the *ṭumbarah* as a solo instrument, its function with the ensemble in the *zār* ceremony is essentially rhythmic. The instrument's close and long-standing connection with the ceremony is stressed by Tihāmah musicians and its identical role on the African Red Sea coast should not be surprising when considering the apparent African origin of the *zār*. That the ceremony is African is not questioned by the Tihāmah musicians and there are constant references to Ethiopia (Ḥabashah) and Sudan in the *zār* songs.
11. Integrated groups of male and female musicians were never found outside this context of the itinerant performers.
12. Variously called *ḥabashī*, or simply *aswad*, the Akhdām are spread throughout the Yemen, where they live very much outside the traditional tribal structure. Not allowed to marry into the tribes, nor own land, they dwell in isolated quarters outside the walls of most large Tihāmah towns, where they are engaged as entertainers, porters in the *sūq*, and street sweepers. The origins of the Akhdām are the subject of much speculation by both Arab and European observers. They casually trace their own ancestry to Africa, but Professor Serjeant has hazarded that they may be indigenous to Arabia and a remnant of some aboriginal population (R.B. Serjeant, "South Arabia," *Studies in Arabian History and Civilization*, London, 1981). Whatever the case, itinerant groups of a similar social status exist in Ethiopia and the Sudan (see J. Spencer Trimingham, *Islam in Ethiopia*, London 1952). Perhaps only a linguistic study will shed light on the history of the Akhdām. See also Stone, p. 132, n. 149.
13. There are exceptions to this, most notably amongst the Zarānīq tribe, who perform on drums at festivals to celebrate the date harvest in villages along the coast.
14. Regrettably, time did not permit investigation of reports that music in the Ḥaraḍ district exhibited a greater "African" influence.

INSTRUMENTS

Discussion

Lyres were almost certainly played in ancient South Arabia,[15] and they continue to be a feature of music on the Tihāmah, where their role is an interesting one. The *ṭumbarah* is used exclusively for the *zār* ceremony, either as a solo instrument accompanying a singer (See Plate 7.1), or as a member of an ensemble. Though found as far afield as Iraq, and even India,[16] the *ṭumbarah* is generally agreed to have originated in the Red Sea area.

The *simsimīyah*[17] seems also to have a long-standing connection with the Yemen, where on the Tihāmah it accompanies a type of ballad called *nabyah*. Associated with seamen, the instrument, with slight variations, is played throughout the Red Sea area and the Arabian Gulf (where it is called *ṭambūrāyah*). Interestingly, on the Sinai peninsula, where it is played by fishermen, its repertoire includes a class of songs called *yamanīyah*.[18]

The lyres are not now played in the Yemen highlands and many of the drums featured on the Tihāmah differ, in name or form, from those in the interior. The clay *marfa'*, for example, is considerably deeper than the highland copper *marfa'*. The *madiff*, an integral part of the ensemble that accompanies the *zār* ceremony, and the *ṣaḥfah*, are to my knowledge unknown beyond the Tihāmah.

Other instruments – the simple flutes and reed pipes – differ little from those played throughout the Islamic world. All of them, however, are played on the Tihāmah with the continuous circular-breathing technique which, in the case of the flutes, seems a quite rare and demanding exercise.

Annotated list

Madiff (or ***Madīf***). A large, free-standing wooden drum (about a metre high) played with one stick and one hand. It is an integral part of the ensemble that accompanies the *zār* ceremony. The name *madiff* is probably cognate with *duff/daff*, a tambourine.

Manqar. A smaller *marfa'* (see below). The name presumably derives from the same root as *naqqārah*, the kettledrum common to much of the Arab world.

Marfa'. A kettledrum made of clay with a head of calfskin. Played with two sticks *(khayzurān)*,[19] it is deeper (in shape) than the highland copper *marfa'*. (See Figure 7.1, Plate XXX.)

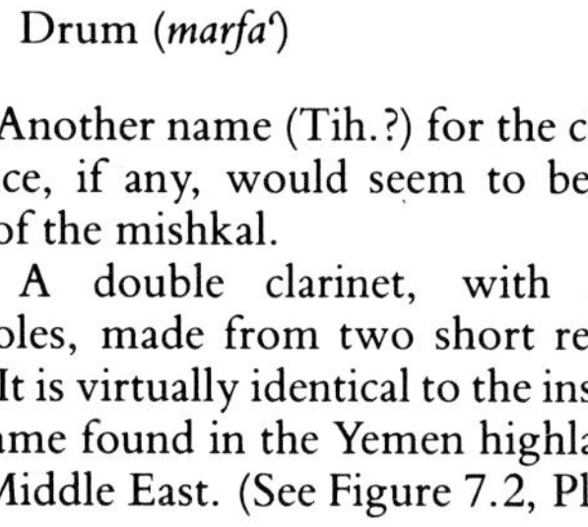

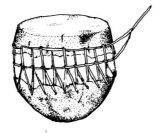

Figure 7.1 Drum (*marfa'*)

Mishkal. Another name (Tih.?) for the clay *marfa'*. The difference, if any, would seem to be in the higher tuning of the mishkal.

Mizmār. A double clarinet, with five pairs of fingerholes, made from two short reeds bound together. It is virtually identical to the instrument of the same name found in the Yemen highlands and much of the Middle East. (See Figure 7.2, Plate XXXI.)

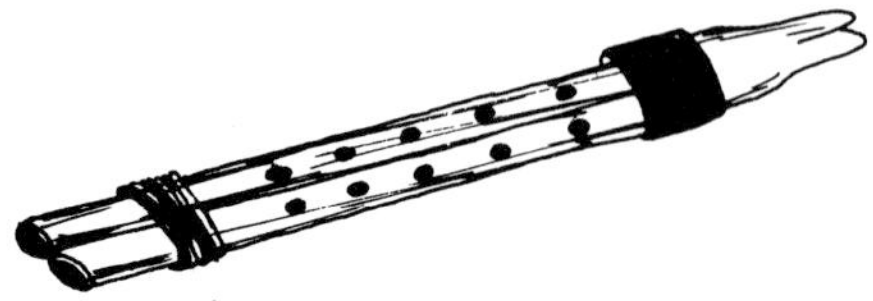

Figure 7.2 Reed pipes (*mizmār*)

Qaṣabah. A simple end-blown flute made from a reed.

Qulqulah. A small, double-headed wooden hand-drum (also called *ṭubaylah*). It is played by twisting the attached wooden handle, causing two wooden pellets on strings to strike the faces in rapid succession. On the Tihāmah it is carried by those called *jadhab*, (dervishes, snake-charmers, and contortionists) and sounded to announce their presence. Variations of the drum, associated with religious ritual, are common in many parts of Asia. (See Figure 7.3.)

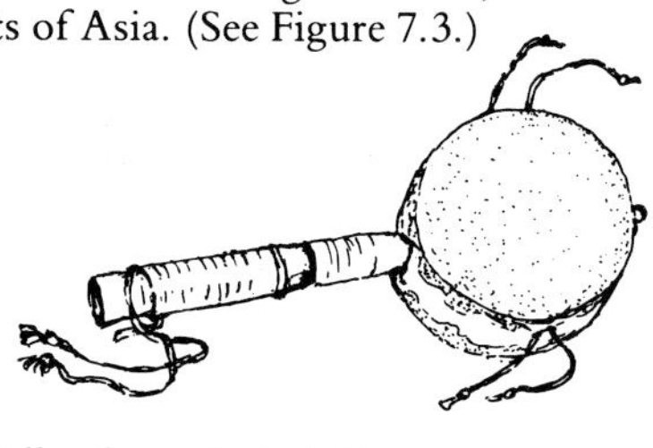

Figure 7.3 Pellet drum (*qulqulah*)

Rabāb. A single-stringed spike fiddle, played with a bow by itinerant entertainers. The soundbox can either be fashioned from wood or a metal container *(tanakah)*.

Ṣaḥfah. A flattened, single-headed clay drum with a sheepskin head attached by a metal band. The drum has a cylindrical wooden piece inserted through the length of the body, protruding out either end. The drummer secures his wrist around this 'handle' and alternately presses the partially open end against his chest for a muted effect.

Simsimīyah. A small box lyre made of wood with five wire strings. Its players favour a plectrum made from the bands of a tea crate.

Ṭablah. A cylindrical two-headed drum made of either wood[20] or metal. It is normally hung from the waist and played with the hands. (See Plate XXIX.)

Ṭār. A single-headed frame drum used to accompany religious songs.

Ṭumbarah. A large bowl-lyre consisting of a hollow gourd covered with skin as a resonator and two wooden cylindrical arms joined by a third.[21] As played on the Tihāmah, it has five strings of either gut or nylon. The plectrum is fashioned from a cow's horn.

Zīr. A clay drum (reported but not seen).

---

15. Two ancient South Arabian alabaster fragments (Marib/Sabaean?) showing depictions of lyres, are housed at the National Museum, Ṣan'ā'.
16. Jean Jenkins and Poul Rovsing Olsen, *Music in the World of Islam*, London, 1976.
17. I have not heard it referred to as *zamzamīyah* as mentioned by R.B. Serjeant (*Prose and Poetry from the Ḥaḍramawt*, London, 1951).
18. Amnon Shiloah, "The Simsimiyyah: A stringed instrument from the Red Sea area," *Asian Music* IV-1, 1972.
19. Made of *nasham* (GREWIA BICOLOR) wood.
20. Commonly from the *ẓūbah* tree (ACACIA MELLIFERA) or *sīsum* (mahogany).
21. From the *arj* tree (ZIZYPHUS SPINA-CHRISTI).

PROFILES OF SELECTED MUSICIANS

'Umar Yūsuf al-Turaybī. A performer on the *ṭumbarah* who worked much of his life as a blacksmith in Zabīd. He learnt the instrument from his father, but now has no pupils to pass on his ancient art. He lives exclusively off income from the *zār* ceremony. (See Plate 7.1.)

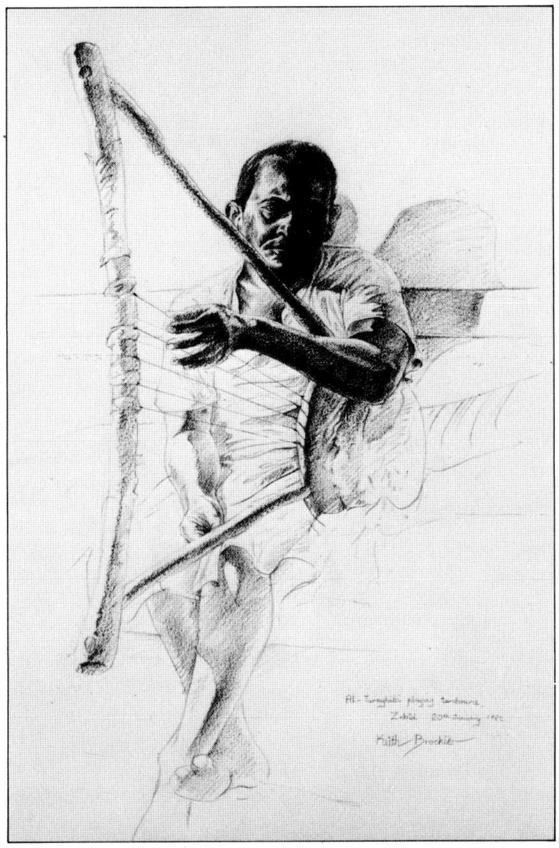

Plate 7.1 Al-Turaybī playing the lyre (*ṭumbarah*) [See *Plate XXXII*]

Kaḥtāl. A well-known, blind itinerant singer who resides in al-Quṭay'. He travels to weekly *sūqs* and entertains with his companion, a blind *shubbābah* player, singing topical songs and accompanying himself on a drum made from a polish confectionery tin.

'Ayāsh Ḥasan. A *mizmār* player of the Akhdām community settled in Wādī Zabīd. He travels considerable distances to perform at weddings and festivals, sometimes with members of his family, who are all musicians.

Nājī. Another *mizmār* player who lives in the Akhdām compounds of Hodeida and plays at *sūqs* and weddings in the central Tihāmah. He refers to himself as *"ṣāḥib al-mizmār"*.

'Ubayd Sālim. A musician who travels between Bājil and Hodeida entertaining on the *simsimīyah*. Though it is a traditional fisherman's instrument, the *simsimīyah* is used interchangeably with the modern *'ūd* to accompany popular music. Like many popular musicians, he considers himself an artist *(fannān)*.

'Umar Barakāt. A well-respected poet and singer *(musamma')* from Bayt al-Faqīh, living for the past 30 years in Hodeida. He served as personal poet to the Imām and, more recently, to the governor of Hodeida. He embodies the ideal qualities of the traditional poets: combining within one person lyricist, singer, and melodist *(shā'ir, mughannī, mulaḥḥin)*.

DISCOGRAPHY

The Afro-Arabian Crossroad, Music of the Tihama in North Yemen, Lyrichord LLST 7384. (professional musicians)

North Yemen, Unesco Collection – Musical Atlas, Odeon-EMI 3C 064 18352 (survey of highland and Tihāmah music)

Zaidi and Shafi'i, Islamic Religious Chanting from North Yemen, Unesco Collection – Musical Sources, Phillips 6586 040. (includes recording from Zabīd)

Music of South Arabia, Ethnic Folkways FE 4421. (Arab and Jewish songs from Aden and the Western Protectorate, 1951)

Music from Yemen Arabia – Samar, Lyrichord LLST 7284. (popular music)

Music from Yemen Arabia – Sanaani and Laheji, Lyrichord LLST 7283 (popular music)

Beduin Music from the Southern Sinai, Ethnic Folkways FE 4202. (includes "Yamania" songs accompanied by *simsimīyah*)

Ethiopia, Vol. 3 – Music of Eritrea, Tangent TGM 103. (includes a *zār* ceremony recorded in Massawa)

Music in the World of Islam, Vol. 3 – Strings, Tangent TGS 133. (includes "tambura music" recorded in Bahrain)

Pêcheurs de Perles et Musiciens du Golfe Persique, Ocora OCR 42. (includes lyre song from Bahrain)

ILLUSTRATIONS

Plate 7.1 Brockie, 380 × 280mm, conté pencil, courtesy of Private Collection; *Figures 7.1-7.2* Yamini Patel; Figure 7.3 Elinor Jones.

GLOSSARY

'abd	slave
arj	a tree (ZIZYPHUS SPINA-CHRISTI)
aswad	black
'awwād	lute player
fannān	artist
farasānī	a dance
ḥabashī	Ethiopian
ḥakamī	classical Yemeni verse
ḥaqfah	a dance
ḥumaynī	colloquial Yemeni verse
'īd	feast, festival
jadhab	dervish, exhibitionist
kabānj	*'ūd* (in South Arabia)
khayzurān	(drum)stick
khitān	circumcision
khudāmī	a dance
laḥn	melody
madiff	a drum
malḥūn	colloquial
manqar	a drum
maqhā	tea/coffee house
marfa'	a drum
marīsī	a dance
mishkal	a drum (Tih?)
mizmār	reed pipes
mughannī	singer
mulaḥḥin	composer
musamma'	singer of *samā'* (sufi ritual music)
muṭabbil	musician/drummer
muwwāl	secular, non-rhymed sung poetry
muzawwir	leader of *zār* ceremony

nabyah	sea shanty, ballad
naqqārah	a drum
nasham	a wood (GREWIA BICOLOR)
qabīlī	tribesman
qaṣabah	a flute
qaṣīdah	non-strophic poem, ode
qāt	a narcotic leaf (CATHA EDULIS)
qulqulah	a drum (Tih?)
rabābah	spike fiddle
ṣaḥfah	a drum
ṣāḥib	master
shā'ir	poet
sharaḥ	a dance
sharqī	a dance
shubbābah	a flute
simsimīyah	a lyre
sīsum	mahogany
sūq	market
ṭabalkhānah	drum ensemble
taḥḍirah	a dance
ṭambūrāyah	*simsimīyah* (in the Arabian Gulf)
tanakah	metal container
ṭār	a drum
ṭāriq	*muwwāl* (in northern Tihāmah)
ṭarīqah	religious (*sūfī*) brotherhood
tashbīb	verse of *qaṣīdah*
ṭibbāl	ensemble of professional itinerant musicians
ṭubaylah	*qulqulah*
ṭumbarah	a lyre (var. of *ṭambūrah*)
tuways	a dance
'ūd	short-necked lute
zaḥfah	a dance
zār	a spirit, exorcism ceremony
zīr	a drum
ziyārah	saint's day festival, pilgrimage
ẓūbah	a tree (ACACIA MELLIFERA)

ETHNOGRAPHY

8:1 NOTES ON THE CRAFTS, CUSTOMS AND LOCAL INDUSTRIES OF THE NORTH YEMEN TIHĀMAH 1982

Francine Stone

INTRODUCTION

In this paper, I offer observations made on certain crafts, customs and local industries of the North Yemen Tihāmah as they were being practised in 1982. Because my primary function during the fieldwork was that of Expedition coordinator and not that of a researcher, I only gathered information when the opportunity arose. Therefore the following notes were made without a systematic methodology that allowed me to carry out comparative enquiries across the entire region, or to check and countercheck my data. While this is regrettable, I have striven to augment the field notes with post factum research in order to place the observations in an historical context and to give reference to other related studies. In so doing, I would hope to point the way to more sustained and specialised research into the wealth of ethnographic and cultural material present on the Tihāmah.

I wish to acknowledge Robert Wilson for his countless suggestions regarding etymological, historical and geographical points in my paper, and for gently steering the manuscript toward a goal of accuracy and felicity of expression. To John Wood I am grateful for identifications of many of the plants, woods and natural substances mentioned herein. Equally valuable have been the contributions of Martha Mundy, John Baldry, Sayyid Maḥmūd al-Ahdal, Claudie Fayein, Dominique Champault, Cynthia Myntti, Aḥmad al-Shāmī and Etienne Renaud in reviewing and amplifying aspects of my material. Others who have participated in the challenge of this study are acknowledged for their assistance in specific footnotes. Whatever errors may occur in this paper, they are due entirely to my own shortcomings as an observer and a researcher; and I would apologise to all the above-mentioned individuals who deserve a flawless performance in return for their good offices.

Before commencing, a word or two is in order regarding the logic of presentation: I have more or less arbitrarily grouped my notes under the three main headings of the title, although many of the subjects could just as well have been treated otherwise. The point was to present the subject matter in such a way as to make it readily accessible to a variety of interests, be they ethnographic, social, economic or technological. Lastly, the bibliographic references for each section are presented in a block at the very end of the text, for ease of reading.

CRAFTS

BASKETRY

Palm fronds, grasses and straw are used widely on the Tihāmah to produce an assortment of utilitarian objects. The appearance of these articles, as one descends the escarpment from the highlands, marks the beginning of the Tihāmah, ethnographically speaking. In this respect, the basketry is an ethno-geographical indicator of primary importance.

The inhabitants of the date palm groves on the coast harvest the fronds, fibres and leaves of suitable trees and shrubs, and sell these in bulk at the major weekly *sūqs*. This raw material is then bought and made up into basketry articles either for household use or for sale in the *sūq*. Alternatively, local material is gathered from the scrub and the fields by those dwelling inland. In some instances it seems that material is even being imported for use in the manufacture of special basketry, as with the *kūfīyah*, pronounced *kūfiyah* (see below).

Basketry is a cottage industry carried on mostly by the women, who also market their own wares in the weekly *sūqs*. I was not able to ascertain the degree of specialisation involved,[1] but it certainly appears that basket making is a commonplace accomplishment amongst the women of the plain. Certain items are manufactured and marketed by men, and these will be noted in the subsections below.

Baskets (*zanbīl*)

Although baskets are perhaps the most common utilitarian item on the Tihāmah, available in great numbers in the *sūqs*, their variety is limited. Two basic shapes can readily be found – the carrying basket and the serving basket. The first is a deep, circular basket on a round base widening at the mouth. Opposing handles of wound vegetable fibre are tied into the rim. Baskets of this sort can be found in graduated sizes from as little as 30cm deep to over 150cm. The largest ones are used for storing grains, pulses or dates, the smaller ones for everyday domestic and agricultural purposes.

The basic construction technique in these baskets, and in many other basketry items (see below) is a form of plaiting, found from Kenya to Lebanon. It is an ancient technique whereby

> one plait, usually of nine weavers, but sometimes of thirteen, wind(s) from the centre or

1. For comments on the absence of specialisation in Wādī Mawr craftsmanship, as well as for village names where hats, "rattanware" and other craft items are made in the Wādī, see Mitchell-Escher-Mundy, *Yemen Arab Republic Feeder Road Study; A Baseline Socio-Economic Survey of the Wadi Mawr Region*, p. 21n.

base outwards to the rim. Each round is joined to the next by a cord which is enclosed in the outside edge of the plait; the inner edge of the next plait is woven round the cord of the last. The cord is invisible except for a ridge running between the plaits, and if the cord is withdrawn the whole basket unwinds in one long plait.[2]

As a rule these baskets are made from undecorated palm fronds (*ṭāfī*, Tih.?)[3] that are woven when green or wet.

The serving basket is a round, shallow platter shape, constructed by coiling and stitching together a tube core of frond spines which is wrapped in grass. Geometric designs are worked into the floor and the rim of the basket, using banana leaves or purple dye for contrast. Another basket type, normally associated with the Tihāmah but not in evidence this trip, is a hanging food container with a domed lid; it is plaited and decorated with geometric designs sewn onto the exterior in purple or brown threads.

Mats

Mats on the Tihāmah perform a wide range of functions. The largest mats (*hidmah*) are used as sacking, or siding and roofing in house construction[4] or they are erected over poles to provide tent-like shelters (*khidr*) for herders or migrant harvesters (*makhāḍirah*)[5] in the *khabt* zones. They are made by plaiting broad strips of palm fronds on a diagonal, following the basic technique described above in the Baskets section. Mats of this type can be cut into varying sizes according to need, the edges stitched down along the cut.

A round eating mat serves as both plate and table, being laid on the ground and the food placed on top of it. Those partaking of the meal seat themselves around the mat. Thus, it is made in a range of sizes to accommodate anywhere from one to over a dozen persons. The plaited stripping is strung together (as described in the Baskets section above) in a spiral, sometimes with the aid of a round wooden frame cross-braced through the diameter with two sticks which form a clamp. The mat rim is provided with a handle of the same material or of cord, for hanging when not in use. Geometric patterns, in concentric circles, are sometimes worked into the plaiting, but as a rule these mats are unadorned. We collected three different terms for them: *nakhal* (Bayt al-Faqīh), *muṣrafah* (al-Durayhimī) and *ṭabaqah* (Hodeida).[6]

Hats

It is in the design and the construction of "straw" hats that the Tihāmī craftsmen and craftswomen show their greatest inventiveness and skill. I made note of six distinct shapes of hat, between Zabīd and Wādī Mawr.[7]

This section deals specifically with the craft of hat making, whereas fuller descriptions of the hats, where and how and by whom they are worn, as well as notes on their names, are given in the Costume section (see below).

To those interested primarily in the technology of Tihāmah hat craft, I have to state that a study of their manufacture has yet to be done. I did not have the opportunity to document artisans at work. Women are probably responsible for most hat manufacture on the Tihāmah plain, as a cottage industry. However, without first-hand observation, I generalise with caution. What is clear is that men and women alike sell the hats in the market place, with women predominant. The exception to this is the *kūfīyah* (see below) which is merchandised by men exclusively.

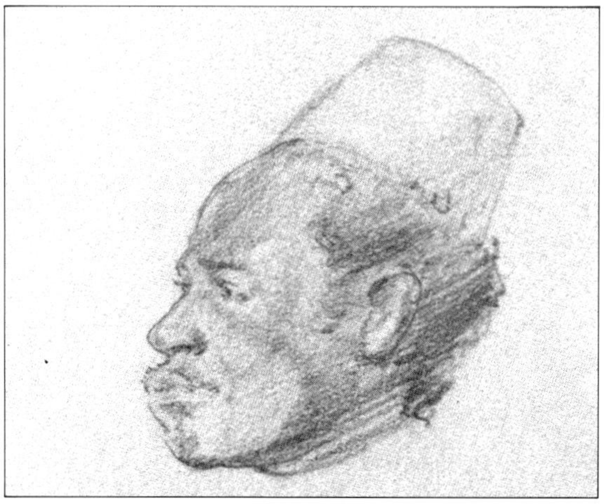

Plate 8.1 **Ḥasan Yaḥyā al-Qadirī**

It seems that the basic construction technique in all but the *kūfīyah* utilises the plaiting with cord joinery described in the Baskets section above. Again, the *kūfīyah* is the exception as it exhibits a radically different technique. What follows are descriptions of the salient construction features of each hat type:

***qubbah*, Bayt al-Faqīh.** (Two shapes: conical with brim; domed beehive with brim) The standard material used is tender dom palm fronds, slit into narrow strips. The plaited strand descends in a spiral from the apex of the crown to the edge of the brim. The average plait measures 1cm. At the junction of the crown and the brim, a headband is created on the inside of the hat by leaving one edge of the plait free-standing. The end strand is tied off perfunctorily and lashed into the edge of the brim. The beehive *qubbah* is concave on the top of the crown with a tiny hole in the centre. The conical *qubbah* comes to a closed point at the top.

***ẓullah*, Bājil.** (Shape: miniature cone with brim and snood strap) I could not obtain an example of this hat, try as I might. Its workmanship was clearly superb. I was told it comes from al-ʿAyn in Wādī Sihām, although it seems that it is no longer being made.

---

2. Dorothy Wright analysed it from a mat discovered in the Dead Sea caves which was carbon-dated to 3000 B.C. See D. Wright, *The Complete Book of Baskets and Basketry*, Newton Abbot, 1977, p. 133.
3. *Ṭāfī* is probably cognate with *ṭufyah*, leaf of the Theban palm. See J.G. Hava, S.J., *Al-Fara'id al-Durrīyah Arabic-English Dictionary*, (3rd Printing), Beirut, 1970, p. 434. Doreen Ingrams records the word *saf* [sic] for palm leaf in the Aden Protectorate, see D. Ingrams, *A Survey of Social and Economic Conditions in the Aden Protectorate*, p. 119.
4. See Ehrlich, p. 81 et passim.
5. See Wilson, p. 35.
6. See the reference to *aṭbāq*, basket-trays, in *Ṣanʿāʾ an Arabian Islamic City*, p. 230.
7. Others may well exist in the northern and southern extremities of the plain, although on our brief forays into the ʿAbs and the Mawzaʿ regions, I found nothing exceptional. Wilfred Thesiger photographed several intriguing Tihāmī hats in the ʿAsīr region in 1947. See W. Thesiger, *Desert, Marsh and Mountain*, pp. 72-3.

northern hat, Wādī Mawr. (Two shapes: *shimālīyah* – tall chimney-top with broad brim; *aṣab* – short hood with broad brim) The basic technique is the same as that used in the *qubbah*, although the material looks more like straw than dom palm fibre. The brim ends in a stiff rim made by weaving into the edge a tube of grass-wrapped reeds. This feature is common to both the northern hat shapes, although I have seen *aṣabs* without it. Both crowns have slightly concave tops which are closed. The size of the plaited strand is larger than that used in the *qubbah*, being on average 1.5cm.

***kūfīyah*, ubiquitous.** (Shape: fez-like, of varying heights, see Plates 8.1, 8.5) The construction technique of this hat differs from that of the other Tihāmah hats studied. It is intricate and extremely fine, but without seeing one being made, it is difficult to ascertain exactly how the construction is achieved.[8] The basic technique appears to be a form of twining, from which the hat derives its suppleness. The weave has a vertical look to it, as if the warp is vertical.[9] The work begins, as with the other hats, on a spiral at the summit, where concentric and radiating designs are twined and overstitched onto the flat top. These designs add strength to the top so that the crown will hold its shape. A fine flour or powder is pressed in between the stitches.

The fibre used to make the *kūfīyah* has not been identified, as far as I know. It is finer than either the local straw or palm frond, and is possibly rattan. It could be that it is imported.[10] Dr. Gunther Schweitzer (in communication with the author) reports seeing it being sold in good quantity at the major weekly *sūq* near ʻAbs. The traditional *kūfīyah* is said to be made only in the Salam (var. of Aslam) region, one hour's drive above ʻAbs, and Dr. Schweitzer's observations would corroborate this. Nowadays, a short and crudely woven version of the *kūfīyah* is available at modest prices in many Yemeni *sūqs*; this is an import from Saudi Arabia. The traditional *kūfīyah* climbs in price the taller it is; and one that is approximately 24cm high can cost over 1000YR. At a stall in the Bājil *sūq*, a wearer can take his *kūfīyah* to have it refurbished. The shop is lined with wooden forms of varying sizes on which the repairs are carried out.

Ropes

Ropes play an important role in furniture-making and house construction,[11] domestic, agricultural and mercantile activities. Much cordage in use on the Tihāmah today consists of local fibre. Some of it is derived from palm stalks, which break into tough strands when beaten. The ropes of the Wādī Mawr region, however, are twined out of *ḥalāfī* (Desmostachya bipinnata), a large and coarse grass which grows only in Wādīs Mawr and Ḥaraḍ. The manufacture of these ropes is men's work, taking a day to produce a 50m length (*ṭūl*) which is expected to last some three years before needing to be replaced. They are sold in great coils at the local *sūqs*.[12]

Miscellanea

Broadly speaking, any object made of vegetable fibre can be classified under Basketry, and therefore mention should be made of the incidental articles in everyday use on the Tihāmah which are constructed from fronds and grasses. The pigeon or chicken cage (*qafaṣ*), latticed and pearlike in shape, is a handsome artifact (see Plate 8.2). Also in the basket family is a tall, bee-hive shaped clothes frame on which garments are draped and placed over an incense brazier to receive the aromatic fumes. Hoops made of grass-wrapped coils are joined and cross-braced with smaller coils to make the hollow structure stand firm. It stands about 1.5m high. Fans on stick handles are plaited on the diagonal to give a herring-bone effect. The fancier ones are covered with glittery, imported cloth and studded with sequins. Sieves (*mankhul*) for straining and sorting grains are made of reeds like bamboo and of dom palm and banana fibres. Muzzles (*fidāmah*) of plaited rope restrain the appetites of cows, camels and donkeys (see Plate 8.2). Bags for the standard load (*ḥaml*) of salt are constructed in the same manner as ordinary matting. Women in the palm oases near salt quarries (see Salt Production) plait the strips for these bags in their spare time. Spools of the stripping can be seen in their hut compounds, ready to be made up into sacking. Donkey girths are woven from fibres resembling cactus. Finally, the humblest artifact of all is the broom, a mere bundle of coarse palm frond spines which is bent in half and lashed together, handleless.

Plate 8.2 Camel with muzzle (*fidāmah*) by poultry cage (*qafaṣ*) [See Plate XXXIV]

8. I am grateful to Sandra Newman for examining this hat and offering her comments on its technology.
9. An interesting, conical *kūfīyah* in the Musée de l'Homme, collected by Henri de Montfried, catalogue no. 34.138.7, is analysed thus:

   vannerie fine en forme de cône, obtenu par une tresse large de 1cm, disposée en spirale; les loves sont réunies les unes aux autres par un lien de même matière pénétrant dans la tresse alternativement d'un bord à l'une love à celui de l'autre en prenant une maille, et laissant apparaître une nervure spirale.
10. Information given to Robert Wilson in the ʻAbs region would support this. He was told that the material is *khayzarān* (cane) and that it is imported from India.
11. See Ehrlich, p. 87 et passim.
12. See Mitchell-Escher-Mundy, op. cit. p. 121.

POTTERY

Local potters on the Tihāmah produce many of the ceramic items used in the household and the workplace. They make pots, bowls, cups, water jars (*qārūrah*, pronounced *gurrurah*),[13] griddles (*malaḥḥah*), waterpipe jars (*jaḥlah*, pronounced *gaḥlah*),[14] ovens (*tannūr*), incensors (*mabkharah*) and braziers, to name a few.

Ḥays is the "capital" of Tihāmī pottery, and has been active for at least four centuries.[15] The word *ḥaysī* means pottery. Here crockery is produced with distinctive shapes and a distinctive brown-green glaze made from copper and lead oxides obtained today from the pulverised plates of automobile batteries. Pottery making is by no means limited to Ḥays, however. Al-Marāwiʻah, al-Manṣūrīyah, al-Ḥusaynīyah, Mawr, al-Zuhrah, Maḥall 'Abs, Dayr al-Qawsh, Kabbat al-Shāwush (see below) are among the towns and villages noted for their potters.

Pottery techniques are simple, even primitive in some cases. Shelagh Weir[16] has described some of the standard methods she observed, namely the wheel and the paddle-and-anvil technique. I can only add two variations: at Kabbat al-Shāwush, the potter walks around a fixed pillar of columnar basalt[17] on which his clay sits. He gathers the clay from exposed seams on the hillside above the village, where it is dry and sandy-textured. He washes and reconstitutes it for use. His pots are fired for an hour and a half at evening, after having baked all day in the sun.[18] At al-Ḍaḥī, the potter sits on the ground with his legs in a pit, working a treadle which turns the wheel in front of him. His kiln is an open, earthen stack about 1m high with a firing chamber divided into three parts below, and a single opening at ground level for draught.[19]

In my experience, the potters of the Tihāmah are men, although women may participate in the decoration of the pots which today carry geometric designs in paint or incision or glaze.

TEXTILES

Of the long and at times illustrious textile tradition, admirably documented by John Baldry,[20] little can be found on the Tihāmah today. The craft, while certainly in decline, is not moribund however; cotton production on the Tihāmah has been promoted and despite unfavourable economic factors,[21] it is supplying the cotton factory in Ṣanʻā' with raw material for a reinvigorated textile industry, centred on the capital.

On the Tihāmah, weaving has been practised traditionally in Zabīd, Bayt al-Faqīh, al-Marāwiʻah, Hodeida, al-Durayhimī and al-Manẓar.[22] Baldry documents the numbers of small hand looms (*muḥāwakah*) in these various centres in 1978.[23] In 1982, we found no ready evidence of looms remaining in Bayt al-Faqīh or al-Marāwiʻah, one working loom in Zabīd, and twenty to thirty looms in al-Durayhimī and the same number in al-Manẓar, although we did not carry out a systematic search. The traditional weavers' quarter (*ḥārat al-ḥawak*) in Hodeida had been displaced by concrete-block houses, but whether or not it had been successfully relocated elsewhere in the town, we did not ascertain.

The Tihāmah weaver produces a multi-coloured length of cotton cloth which can be used as a shoulder cloth (*maṣnaf*), or a bedspread (*mafrashah*), or a sarong (*fūṭah*), or a multi-purpose cloth and carry-all called *liḥāf*. These differ from each other in length and border decoration, and it is not always clear which is which, since the terms are used somewhat interchangeably. The weavers themselves simply speak of a single unit of length and multiples of it. Shelagh Weir has described the techniques used on the two standard types of looms, the fixed heddle and the horizontal treadle loom, and the addition of the border, a specialised craft,[24] as well as the resist-dyeing of the distinctive red and black muslin headscarves (*maqramah*, pronounced *maghramah*) whose manufacture occurs in Hodeida. John Baldry completes the picture with his explanation of the entrepreneurial steps whereby the cloth progresses from weaver to market.[25]

13. Different names can be found for the different shapes, i.e. *kūz*, thin-necked; *qillah*, pronounced *jallah*, round-bodied; *kudān* (unconfirmed, possibly a variant pronunciation of *kīzān*, pl. of *kūz*) or *kuʻadah*, with handles.
14. Oliver Myers traces the word, which he gives as *ğaḥlah* [sic] or *qaḥlah*, meaning the egg-shaped water pots of the district around Aden, to the Mahri word for egg, *ğoḥol* [sic], citing as his source B. Thomas, "Four Strange Tongues from South Arabia, The Hadara Group," *Proceedings of the British Academy*, Vol. XXIII, 1937. See O. Myers, "Little Aden Folklore," *Bulletin de l'Institut Français d'Archéologie Orientale*, Vol. XLIV, Cairo, 1947, p. 226.
15. See E. Keall, "Zabid and its Hinterland: 1982 Report," *Proceedings of the Seminar for Arabian Studies*, Vol. 13, 1983; see also Al-Radi, p. 51 et passim (and Plate XIX).
16. S. Weir, "Some Observations on Pottery and Weaving in the Yemen Arab Republic," *Proceedings of the Seminar for Arabian Studies*, Vol. 5, 1975, pp. 65-69.
17. These columns look remarkably like ḥimyaritic building columns, so much so that they have attracted notice from archaeologically minded persons such as Niebuhr who noted their human-made appearance at a site near Lelue [sic], *Travels Through Arabia*, Vol. I, p. 288; and Muḥammad al-Shamīrī (see Al-Radi, p. 53) took Dr. Al-Radi to examine one in his village, Maḥall al-Shamīrī, thinking it might be an archaic artifact. (See also Al-Radi, p. 54.)
18. Niebuhr remarks upon the fact that "on cuit les briques et les pots, non dans un four, mais en plein campagne." C. Niebuhr, *Voyage en Arabie*, Vol. I, p. 251.
19. See C. Niebuhr, idem.
20. Baldry, "Textiles in Yemen; Historical references to trade and commerce in textiles in Yemen from antiquity to modern times," *British Museum Occasional Paper No. 27*, London, 1982.
21. These are cited as "low prices maintained by the Government, a shortage of agricultural credit facilities, lack of improved seeds and adverse weather conditions" by Europa Publications Ltd, *Middle East and North Africa 1982-3*, p. 880. Equally serious is the fact that cotton farming is labour intensive, and must compete with wage levels earned by emigrant workers.
22. Baldry, op. cit., p. 54.
23. Baldry, op. cit., p. 64.
24. Weir, op. cit., pp. 70-71. To Ms Weir's notes, I would like to add my observation of a lengthy process of preparation of the warp threads whereby they were brushed with a wheat-flour paste. This is done to reduce friction on the fibres and to add a form of sizing.
25. Baldry, op. cit., pp. 64-65.

The weavers of al-Durayhimī, where I made my notes, are buying cotton thread from the Ṣan'ā' textile factory and the dyes are purchased from outlets in Bājil. It was thought they were imported from India. To make one *liḥāf*, 20YR are spent on the materials and the finished cloth is sold to the middle man for 55YR. In the *sūq*, the same *liḥāf* costs 100YR.

The combinations of colours are seemingly endless, although the stripes invariably run lengthwise along the cloth. It would be interesting to study what governs the choice and the seriation of the colours from one weaver to the next.

Indigo (*nīl*), favoured by the highland tribesmen and women for their turbans and dresses,[26] has long been a major industry of the Tihāmah, particularly of Zabīd.[27] Here, indigo (INDIGOFERA TINCTORIA or I. ARRACTA)[28] was cultivated in great quantity in the medieval period.[29] Today indigo is no longer a domesticated plant; it has gone back to its wild state and natural spread.[30] One of the two remaining indigo dyeing ateliers in Zabīd, Bayt Ibrāhim Ṣālih 'Abūd,[31] imports chemical dyes from Germany. Nevertheless, traditional dyeing implements are still being used (see Plates 8.3, 8.4), including huge clay vats, mallets (*madaqqah*) made of wood (*ḥumar*, possibly TAMARINDUS INDICA) and wood block stamps with which the finished bolts are signed and certified thus: *māl al-'āl*.

The procedure of indigo dyeing has challenged dyers in the four corners of the world since antiquity. It is a painstaking and unpredictable process, the success of which depends on numerous variables. Each indigo atelier has its own techniques, even its own secrets. How a particular indigo dyeing tradition has solved the mysteries of the dye is of interest to other indigo dyers. For this reason, a proper study of the techniques employed in South Arabia would repay the trouble of the researcher.[32]

Plate 8.3 **Indigo Beaters, Zabīd**, pounding the cloth with mallets (*madaqqah*)

Plate 8.4 **Indigo Pots, Zabīd**, large clay dyeing vats

26. See *Ṣan'ā' an Arabian Islamic City*, p. 192n.
27. See al-Maqdisī, *Kitāb Aḥsan al-Taqāsīm fī Ma'rifat al-Aqālīm, Bibliotheca Geographorum Arabicorum*, ed. M.J. de Goeje, III, Leiden, 1906, p. 98.
28. Other plants used as sources of indigo dyes in South West Arabia are given by A. Grohmann, *Südarabien als Wirtschaftsgebiet*, pp. 262-266. The two Tihāmah species named here have been identified for me by John Wood.
29. See Wilson, p. 36.
30. John Wood has kindly supplied me with this information.
31. We did not locate the other atelier, Bayt 'Alī Sa'd, reported to us by Fr. Etienne Renaud in 1981.
32. As this paper is going to press, Jenny Balfour-Paul has received a grant from Elmgrant Trust, Elmhirst Centre, Dartington, Devon, to investigate the indigo dyeing techniques extant in the Yemen, including those of Zabīd. A paper is forthcoming.

Various indigo dyeing activities have received attention from casual observers.[33] Niebuhr mentions it being practised in al-Ḍaḥī as well as around Zabīd.[34] But none have documented the process in any technical detail, as far as I know. Nor can I rectify the situation beyond describing what I saw through one working day at Bayt 'Abūd in Zabīd.

The cotton cloth, from Ṣan'ā', is immersed in huge clay vats in the main courtyard of the atelier and hung on poles to react with the oxygen of the air, the step which activates the dye. Subsequent baths in successively hotter vats are carried out across the street in a walled annexe. Again, the cloths are hung in the air and dried before each successive plunge which imparts a deeper and deeper colour to the cloth. The constituents of the dyeing procedure were given as *nīl*, *qurqah* (identity unknown)[35] and *tizīn* (identity unknown). The bolts are brushed with a flour paste (*nisha'*) in the main atelier and hung on poles to dry during the midday break. In the afternoon, the bolts are folded and laid over half-buried logs and beaten with mallets until shiny. The finished bolts are stacked around an impressive, high-tiered *dīwān* on the ground floor of the atelier. With fine wood carving, this room had been used by the workers and patrons as a place to smoke and to chew in grander days. It was now abandoned to cobwebs and bats.

Four or five labourers as well as the owner and his son are now employed at the atelier, where a generation ago, it had been the workplace of over twenty men. The men actually processing the cloth appeared to be ex-slaves, their fingers, lips and hands all a Berber blue from handling the dye.

A length of cloth is sold for 40YR wholesale. And 25 kilos of imported synthetic dye costs 4000YR today, whereas in 1974 a barrel weighing 56 kilos cost 1000YR.[36] The market for this cloth today comprises a mere handful of tribespeople in the northern highlands, or so we are told.

CUSTOMS

COSMETICS

With one exception, the elements of female maquillage and cosmetics on the Tihāmah do not differ strikingly from those used in other parts of the Yemen, that I know. The hair and body are anointed with imported coconut oils, colognes and essences (*'anbarī*) by those who can afford them. Incense (*bakhūr*), derived from local gum arabic (*salām*, ACACIA EHRENBERGERIANA or A. ARABICA) or more often imported (such as *lubān dhakar*, olibanum, BOSWELLIA CARTERIA) from Somalia, Ḥaḍramawt and Dhofar, is burned and the smoke wafted into the hair and under clothing from a small incensor (*mabkharah*). Henna (*ḥinnā*, LAWSONIA INERMIS) is applied to the hands and feet; black antimony (*kuḥl*) painted on the eyelids. Turmeric (*hurud*, CURCUMA LONGA) is used as a sun-block, and to soften the skin and remove blemishes. Similarly, cardamom (*hayl*, ELETTARIA CARDAMOMUM) is used as a pomade on the head and face, the paste being prepared by steeping the seeds in water and then crushing them up with the pods. *Ḥām*, a lava-like ash substance, is ground into black powder and used to paint the body with designs (*khiḍāb*).

The feature of female beautification which is singular to the Tihāmah consists of a vermilion paint prepared from red antimony and sweet-smelling spices and applied to the centre parting of a woman's hair as when worn in plaits (*zarr*). This crimson streak (*ḥusn*, pronounced *ḥūsn*) is seen in the northern Tihāmah only. The effect is reminiscent of Hindu women's make-up.[37]

Finally, a small black mollusc shell is sold in fair quantities amongst the perfumes and unguents at Sūq al-Khamīs. I was told women use it "on the head", but could gather no further information. It would seem specific to the Tihāmah.

COSTUMES

Traditional dress on the Tihāmah varies considerably from place to place, with the most marked change occurring north to south rather than east to west. After a brief description of typical male attire, which is on the whole less differentiated than female dress, I will present my observations on certain women's costumes in four main regions: Zabīd, Bayt al-Faqīh, Bājil, and Wādī Mawr and its environs.

Men's apparel

If there can be said to be a quintessentially Tihāmī man's costume, it is that of the farmer/villager who wears a white *fūṭah* (a wrapped skirt similar to a sarong),[38] and a white or striped cotton jacket with long fitted sleeves, a V-neck, and cut just below the waist. The neckline exposes a bare chest, and the ensemble is accompanied by a fez-shaped "straw" hat (*kūfīyah*) which is either nestled in a turban, generally white, or it stands alone, at

33. See J.T. & M.V.A. Bent, *Southern Arabia*, p. 144; D. Ingrams, op. cit., pp. 136-137; F.M. Hunter, *An Account of the British Settlement of Aden in Arabia*, p. 105, and R. Manzoni, *El Yemen*, pp. 55-57.
34. C. Niebuhr, *Travels through Arabia*, Vol. I p. 268, 286.
35. John Wood suggests this might be *qawqa'* caucanthus which grows in the foothills and has a bark but he does not know its function in this instance. John Baldry (op. cit., p. 63) cites a safflower dye called *qurtum* CORTHAMNUS TINCTORIUS used traditionally, but this does not seem to have bearing on the identity of *qurqah*.
36. See Musée de l'Homme, Département d'Afrique Blanche et Proche Orient, Mission Champault, catalogue no. 74.182.65.
37. Compare with the "bright saffron coloured streak half an inch wide down the centre parting of her hair, perhaps made with a strong solution of henna" of the Sulubba woman in Kuwait. See H.R.P. Dickson, *The Arab of the Desert*, ed. R. Wilson and Z. Freeth, London, 1983. p. 53. W. Thesiger observed in the Tihāmat al-'Asīr in 1947 that "the young men and children have long hair, parted in the centre and anointed along the parting with a paste of crushed 'labab' seeds." He does not state the colour. See W. Thesiger, "A Journey Through the Tihama, the 'Asir, and the Hijaz Mountains," *Geographical Journal*, p. 192.
38. See Textiles above.

Plate 8.5 **Hodeida Man Smoking**, wearing a (*kūfīyah*) hat, the mouthpiece (*qaṣabah*) of the waterpipe (*madā'ah*) in his hand

a back-sloping angle on the head, accentuating the typical pointed ears and heart-shaped face of the "Red Sea" Tihāmī (see Plate 8.5).

The *kūfīyah* is an expensive and prized item, by tradition very finely made (see Basketry). It comes in a range of heights from squat to towering. Some say it is associated with the Zarānīq tribesmen, others ascribe it to peoples of Danakil descent.[39] I could see no demarcation in its use, either socially or regionally, although it is rather more frequently worn on the coast.[40]

The Zarānīq do have a distinctive item of dress worth mentioning, even though it is now only worn ceremonially, and that is the headband (*ikāwah*, Tih.?)[41] which circles the bare forehead. It can be made of leather or copper or even silver.[42]

Modern tastes have led to the introduction of the shirt, tee-shirt and trousers, particularly in the ports and roadside towns. A white, crochet skull cap also called *kūfīyah* or *ṭāqīyah* (the finest being made in Zabīd) is often worn by middle class men. The *qamīṣ*, a floor-length shirt, is favoured by men of wealth or position. Lime and mauve were two colours I noted as examples of the alternatives to the conventional white.

39. The Zarānīq established trade relations with the Danakil, a fact documented by the Portuguese in the Middle Ages, I am told by John Baldry. This could well explain the confusion evidenced by the *kūfīyah* associations.
40. This hat is popular well up the escarpment, not just on the Tihāmah.
41. Compare with the "*aqal*" (presumably *'aqāl*) in the Musée de l'Homme, Mission Champault, catalogue no. 72.49.76 worn over the Zarānīq headcloth and traditionally made in Hodeida by Jews.
42. In addition, a small hand shield (*radād*) of leather, some 20cm in diameter, can still be found, i.e. in the Zabīd *sūq*, a relic of the days of Zarānīq bellicosity (see Baldry, p. 47).

Women's dress

Zabīd. A dress style common to the area is a sleeved tabard with a panel inset on the bodice which is decorated with vertical crimping. The sleeves are elbow length, and the dress fabric features bright patterns, the inset sporting an even more raucous design. *Ḥabashī* women (Akhdām) favour this dress (*thawb*, a general term for dress), which they cut rather low in front and wear with a scarf on the head. This might be a square scarf tied in a bow on the crown, or a long headscarf (*maqramah*, see Textiles) wound into two snoods over the ears, the ends tied at the temples, with one end often left hanging down on the shoulder. I never saw this particular type of dress worn with a hat (nor in fact did I ever see an Akhdām woman wearing a hat).

Bayt al-Faqīh. Here, the farmer women who come into public adopt a dress which is fitted at the waist and ornately decorated with silver thread appliqué on the sleeves, the bodice, the back and side panels and the hem (see Figures 8.2-8.3). This trim is traditionally applied to a basic black cotton; a flash of colour shows at the throat where a strip of brightly coloured cloth is sewn to the underside of the plunging neck opening. On the head, it is customary to wear a headscarf topped by a medium-sized hat called *qubbah* (see Basketry). Women generally wear a domed, beehive shaped *qubbah*, and men prefer the one which is conical.

Bājil. Again regarding women seen in public, a variation of the Bayt al-Faqīh dress exists which carries similar appliqué work on black cotton, but which is cut in a wide poncho shape, with front and back panels of heavy decoration and narrow bands of trim at the hem and sleeve borders (see Figure 8.1). The front panel does not open as deeply at the throat as does that of the Bayt al-Faqīh dress. The headwear for

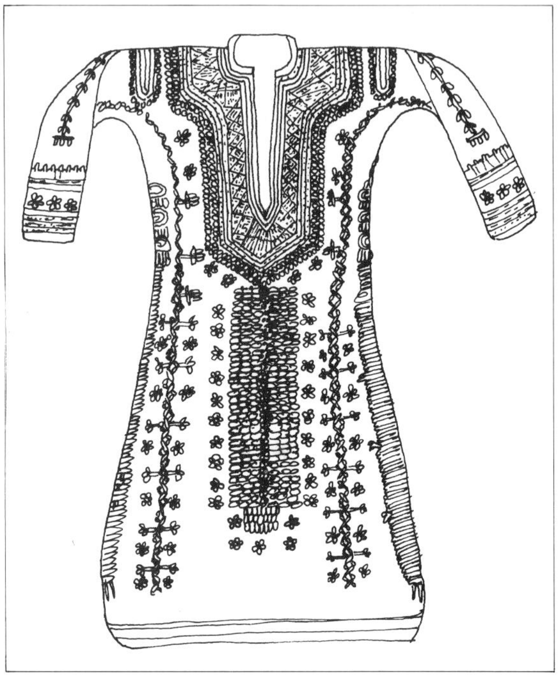

Figure 8.2 Bayt al-Faqīh dress, front

this dress (which is called *durrī*, Tih.?) consists of the standard headscarf on top of which is perched a tiny straw hat called *ẓullah*[43] and held on by a snood strap (see Basketry). For sale in the Bājil *sūq* was an interesting type of garment in the shape of a jacket with short sleeves and cut to the knee. Of basic black cotton, this bolero-style jacket is elaborately machine-stitched in glittery gold and red appliqué. It has the look of a modern rendition of an older style, but I did not

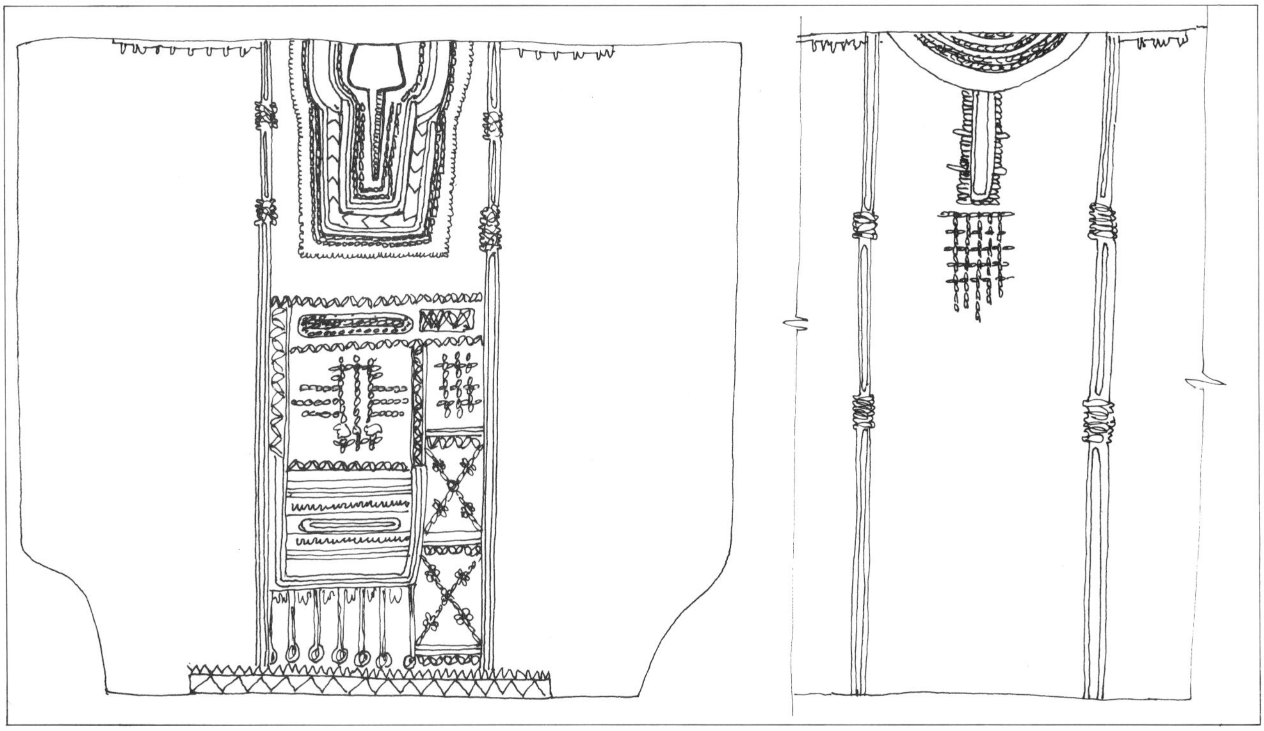

Figure 8.1 Bājil dress, full front and back centre panel

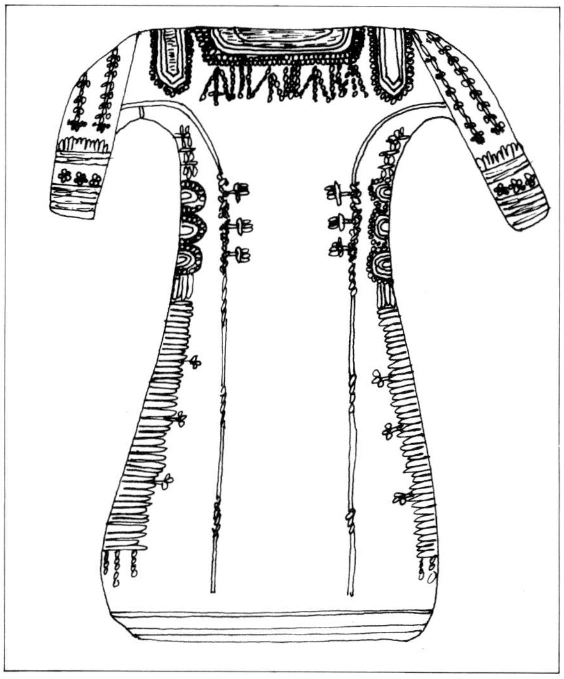

Figure 8.3 Bayt al-Faqīh dress, back

find its traditional prototype, nor did I see this jacket being worn locally. Also for sale were poncho-cut dresses of light, transparent nylons, black or white, and decorated with tinsel-thread embroidery depicting flowers, minarets, aeroplanes, stars in irrepressibly garish motifs, obviously items of harem apparel (see below).

Wādī Mawr and environs. North of Wādī Surdud at approximately al-Ḍaḥī, one begins to encounter the elements of dress which are entirely characteristic of the northern Tihāmah. These are the "ten gallon" straw hat and the gauzy muslin *qamīṣ* (a general term meaning dress) for women.

The hat is worn by men and women alike, and regrettably the only name I recorded for it (*shimālīyah*) was collected in the south and reflects an outsider's terminology.[44] A cousin to this sombrero is called *aṣab* (*'aṣab*?) and has a shorter, broader crown (see Basketry). A gathering of northern Tihāmīs is a bobbing sea of these Oz-like hats.

Women here are clad in long, flowing garments, cut in the same poncho shape as the Bājil dress, but made of very light muslin which renders them see-through. They are generally bright monochromes – scarlet, cobalt, saffron, magenta. Some have simple embroidered trim at the neck which is slit open to the bustline. Younger women wear this *qamīṣ* over a skirt or petticoat and a "sari" top; old women will dispense with the top and go bare-breasted. When a woman is out-of-doors working, her head is covered with a headscarf and a hat. Armlets (*malāquf*, Tih.?) grace the bare upper arms. She may wear multiple bracelets of plastic (or, formerly, of glass), or thick bands of silver alloy, either hollow or solid, which are worn in pairs. These metal ones might be chased or filigreed or threaded, or stamped and hatched, with coins soldered on at the join.[45]

Harem attire. Indoors, or in the privacy of their compounds, the women of the Tihāmah choose to wear the diaphanous, glittery frocks favoured by women all over the Yemen. Due to the heat, however, the throat, chest and midriff are usually bare, and a skirt and blouse are worn as often as a dress. Young girls wear pantaloons under their skirts. Mature women generally prefer to be free of undergarments except for a slip.

CIRCUMCISION

Circumcision (*khitān*), the only rite of passage about which we made specific enquiries, deserves special attention on the Tihāmah because this is the only place in North Yemen where female circumcision is practised[46] and because the ceremony of male circumcision as a boy's initiation into manhood has been an occasion for remarkable festivities.[47]

The response to our questioning indicated that adolescent male circumcision is no longer practised, and certainly we did not encounter a ceremony. However,

43. It is likely that this is the general term for a hat, or for that which gives shade, such as an umbrella. The Bājil hat, in fact, is far too diminutive to provide shade, and I suspect it has another name of its own which I did not obtain. *Ẓullah* is pronounced *dullah* in Bājil, as well as in Wādī Mawr, where Martha Mundy (in communication) recalls hearing it used. It is also recorded by Ḥ. al-Waysī, *Al-Yaman al-Kubrā* as "head coverings called in the Tihāmah *al-ẓulāl*, sing. *ẓullah* (p. 98). Compare with *miẓullah* mentioned by R.B. Serjeant as a hat worn by Ḥaḍramī women, *Studies in Arabian History and Civilisation*, London, 1981, I, p. 137. He notes the pronunciation as *midhullah* on the catalogue card no. 48.149 detailing a Tarīm hat collected by him, University Museum, Cambridge. J. Chelhod also heard the "m" prefix, as a Bājil hat he collected for the Musée de l'Homme, (Mission Chelhod, catalogue no. 70.90.49) is listed as "*mdal*". This discrepancy between *ẓullah* and *miẓullah*, while quite plausible in standard Arabic, is perhaps evidence of the substitution of "*m*" for the definite article "*al*" in the Tihāmī dialect. For this and other aspects of the dialect in the central Tihāmah, see J. Greenman, "A Sketch of the Arabic Dialect of the Central Yamani Tihāmah," *Journal of the American Association of Teachers of Arabic, al-'Arabiyya*, University of Michigan, 11 (1978), Nos. 1 & 2.
44. As indicated in the preceding note, a general term for this hat is *ẓullah*.
45. For photographs of similar examples collected in Saudi Arabia, see J. Topham, *Traditional Crafts of Saudia Arabia*, pp. 78-83.
46. See C. Myntti, *Women and Development in Yemen Arab Republic*, p. 81; see also, R.B. Serjeant, *Ṣan'ā'*, p. 558n. Niebuhr refers to female circumcision being practised at Mocha in the mid-eighteenth century. He specifically states that it did not occur in Ṣan'ā'. See C. Niebuhr, *Description de l'Arabie*, p. 70.
47. Alain Saint-Hilaire has filmed and photographed a male circumcision ceremony in al-Qathan (presumably a variant pronunciation of al-Kadan), in Wādī Surdud. See A. Saint-Hilaire, *Je Reviens du Yémen*, p. 96.

the subject is naturally a delicate one. The law forbids post-infantile circumcision, and it may well be that the custom has not died out but is just not flaunted. We were told that boys are now circumcised at seven days of age. And females undergo a modified clitoridectomy at infant age as well, receiving little more than a ritual "nick", according to Dr. Claudie Fayein (in communication).

However, it is said that in Salam (var. of Aslam) above 'Abs young men are still circumcised on their wedding day in front of their intended bride, and if the youth flinches, she has the right to refuse him. Although our source for this information was considered quite reliable, it has to be put down as hearsay since our stay in the 'Abs region was too short to permit investigation. G. Wyman Bury[48] describes an 'Asīrī circumcision which closely parallels that reported still to exist above 'Abs.

HEALING

Westernised medical facilities are still few on the Tihāmah. To our knowledge, there is al-'Ulufī Hospital in Hodeida, a French medical team at Yakhtul, a village north of Mocha, and a clinic at al-Zaydīyah and one at al-Muḥarraq founded by the Red Sea Mission.[49] In addition, Catholic Relief Services runs a USAID-funded health programme for the Tihāmah which is responsible, along with other governmental programmes, for providing local areas with doctors and nurses. Many villages now have a Sudanese or Egyptian general practitioner in residence. Nevertheless, the facilities are barely adequate, and this is one of the many reasons why local "healers" are still quite common and their advice regularly sought by the Tihāmīs.

Home-remedies are, of course, the first resort for family ills. Those which we observed were not particular to the Tihāmah and are practised widely in the Yemen.[50] They included the use of costus wood (*'ūd qust*) the smoke of which will draw off fever and is good for intestinal troubles; incense (*lubān dhakar*, BOSWELLIA CARTERIA) which is inhaled for coughs and used as a dehumidifier.[51] Turmeric (*hurud*, CURCUMA LONGA) applied to the face (and other parts of the body) acts as a sun block and treats afflictions which require "cooling".[52] Cautery, *mīsam* (pronounced *māsam* in Wādī Mawr) is another very common method for dealing with sickness or pain. The head of a heated nail (*mismār*) is held against the flesh, raising on it a large round blister which then is sometimes rubbed with ashes.[53] It creates a mark, a considerable scar, termed *wasm*, which can be seen most readily on the forehead between the eyes or on the cheek but which is also burned onto the sole of the foot, on the heel or wherever the source of the affliction is deemed to be. It is said that *jinn* dislike iron.

One medicinal plant not mentioned by Myntti, *muraymirā'*, relieves discomfort from "cold" ailments when infused in a tisane. It is also called *sakarah* on the Tihāmah, and Lane describes it as an anaesthetic herb;[54] and Dozy lists it as *murmayrān* which he gives as *éclaire*, greater celandine in English.[55] Finally, oils are used to promote health by strengthening the body and protecting against the sun. On the Tihāmah, sesame oil (*zayt simsim*) is traditionally recommended.

In the case of infants and children, extra measures are taken to ensure health. These include the wearing of amulets (which I observed most frequently amongst Akhdām babies), generally in the form of a thong or string tied around the neck or hips or ankle or wrist. Occasionally a silver ring is threaded onto the strip, or leather pouches containing talismans are hung from it. In addition, male children might have their heads shaved or the hair closely cropped with a long wisp left on the crown. Mrs. Ingrams reported that such tufts, called *qunza'ah* in Aden, have an apotropaic function.[56]

Another private form of healing available to a Tihāmī is to go to the shrine of a local saint (*walī*) (see Saints and Saints' Days below). Cynthia Myntti speaking from her experience in al-Ḥujarīyah, describes this option for local people in Lower Yemen: "The shrines are said to radiate the *baraka* of the saint and healing rituals are based on the transfer of this *baraka* to the sick person through use of water, earth or leaves from near the grave. Candles and incense may also be burned."[57]

The healing powers of the saint are sometimes passed on to his descendants, the men or women charged with keeping his shrine. Such a person is called *manṣab* or *manṣabah*, which according to Muḥammad al-'Uqaylī "is a dialect term which is applied in the Tihāmah to any sufi *shaykh* who is set up as a leader (*ra'īs*) and a spiritual authority (*marji' rūḥī*) whom they acknowledge to be a stronghold of beliefs and a source of blessing."[58] Al-'Uqaylī traces this term back only to the 4th century A.H.

Thus, when ailments are chronic or complicated by psychological factors, and when home remedies have proven ineffective, the afflicted person can seek out an individual who is empowered with the skill of healing. This could be a *manṣab*, as at al-Marāwi'ah where the *manṣab* Ahdal (see Saints and Saints' Days below) is renowned for his treatment of female infertility. But more often, it is a "professional healer" knowledgeable in natural and/or supernatural remedies. The professional healer may claim religious authority for his or her ministrations, although such claims are frequently manufactured to impart an air of respectability to an otherwise dubious profession. The titles they assume imply such religious credentials: *shaykh*, *shaykhah* or *sharīfah*.

The generic terms for these professional healers vary according to the attitude of the speaker toward their practices, as in English the word could be naturopath or shaman or quack. In the region of al-Marāwi'ah,

48. G.W. Bury, *Arabia Infelix*, p. 33.
49. Also in Hodeida is a hospice for lepers and the insane; it is run by the Sisters of Mercy.
50. See C. Myntti with J. Fleurentin, "Medicinal Plants in Yemen: A Preliminary List," (unpublished).
51. Other incenses used on the Tihāmah but not necessarily as medicine include gum arabic (*salam*, ACACIA EHRENBERGERIANA and A. ARABICA) and balsam (*bisham*, COMMIFORA GILEADENSIS, also referred to as *murr*).
52. In al-Manārah, a woman doing poorly in her pregnancy was painted on her face and arms with *hurud*.
53. Niebuhr recounts seeing the *mismār* applied to the flesh of a cabin boy who complained of a gut ache en route from Jeddah to al-Luḥayyah. C. Niebuhr, *Description de l'Arabie*, p. 115.
54. E.W. Lane, *Arabic-English Lexicon*, London, 1863-74, pp. 1391, 3018.
55. R. Dozy, *Supplément aux dictionnaires arabes*, Leiden, 1881, repr. Beirut, 1968, Part II, p. 593. Dr. Myntti believes it to be a sage, and says it is sold only on the Tihāmah.
56. See D. Ingrams, *A Survey of Social and Economic Conditions in the Aden Protectorate*, p. 100.
57. She goes on to say, "Visible skin disorders are the most common ailments taken to the saints' shrines with which I am familiar." (in communication)
58. M. al-'Uqaylī, *Al-Taṣawwuf fī Tihāmah*, p. 36. Robert Wilson has very kindly supplied me with the translation of this and other excerpts from al-'Uqaylī's text.

marwā'ī means healer, due presumably to the fame of the *manṣabs* of the Ahdal family (see above). The most neutral term we found was simply *duktūr baladī*. Another word which was unverified was *wutāf*, reported in al-Ḍaḥī where the Sudanese doctor estimated they number some 50 in the village.

The healer, however, who works his cure primarily by ridding the patient of evil spirits is called *muzawwir*, and the healing session at which the exorcism is performed is a *zār*, and in it the spirit is named and expelled or propitiated.[59] *Zār* is a common practice in Afro-Islamic communities. It can be found in Egypt, Ethiopia and the Sudan, for instance. It occurs in the Gulf and other parts of the Arabian peninsula. In Aden, Oliver Myers relates that the *zār* is "locally believed to have been introduced from Ancient Egypt."[60]

In North Yemen, the *zār* ceremony is considered unique to the Tihāmah. It is not condoned by the State or by the tenets of Islam, and although we encountered no resistance to our interest in the *zār*, we did not press our enquiries and confined our objectives to recording the music of a *zār* ceremony.[61] In the following notes, I shall describe what we saw and heard in an anecdotal fashion, and hope that an anthropologist will have the opportunity to gather more substantive information on Tihāmah *zār* practices.[62]

We were taken by a local informant in al-Zuhrah to a hamlet on the southern side of Wādī Mawr at ten in the evening on the chance of finding a *zār* happening that night. One indeed was about to take place and we were admitted to the *muzawwir's* hut where those seeking cures were beginning to assemble. The first two hours were spent there; *qāt* was chewed and negotiations were carried out with the *muzawwir* who came and went constantly. At midnight the musicians had gathered in the forecourt of the hut, an open area shared with several other huts of the hamlet and surrounded by a thicket wall. The ground sloped slightly, and the musicians took their place at the top of the slope. With one notable exception, there was little variation in the format during the two and one-half hours that we watched: the musicians played, the "patients" danced and sang, and the healer presided, calling encouragement to the "patients" and instructions to the musicians.

Men, women, and an infant, took part in the healing. The onlookers, some twenty or thirty people, were both men and women, boys and girls. I would describe all the participants (with the exception of the musicians) as local, farmer people by their appearance. Some of the onlookers joined in the dancing from time to time. The "patients", however, six in all, stayed on their feet throughout, dancing without let-up. Near the end of our stay, one man reached what might be described as the climax of his cure, and was carried into a nearby hut in a swoon. In the case of the infant, the *muzawwir* was asked to allay his discomfort from teething. He brought the babe up to the musicians, holding it above his head. He then returned the child to its mother and went into a large round hut on the fringe of the courtyard and carried on a dialogue with the spirit to be exorcised, shouting at it and answering himself in a falsetto shriek, speaking for the spirit which was angry and unwilling to quit its victim. The music and dancing continued all the while.

The dancing itself was most remarkable, consisting of a combination of shoulder-shimmeying and a backward-leaning shuffle performed most often by a line of people who advanced and retreated from the musicians, arms linked or independently. Both kinds of movement involved considerable agility; the shimmey was done so fast that the shoulders became a blur, and the shuffle posture was slanted sharply backward on the verge of a fall. Only one old woman maintained anything like a moderate pace, which she kept up without pause for the entire time we watched. When we left at two in the morning, one had the feeling that all concerned were just beginning to warm up.

Mocha and its environs are known for their local healers. We did not witness a *zār* here, but we met with a healer of high repute and one of his musicians, a butcher by trade, who had conducted a session the night before our visit. The healer's sister also commands a considerable following among women, who bring to this *sharīfah* their fertility problems. Cynthia Myntti has attended one such women's *zār* in Mocha, and from her we understand that in Mocha at least it is customary to segregate the *zārs* by sexes, unlike the Wādī Mawr *zār* where both sexes participated. Lastly, we were given the name of a famous healer in Hodeida, but did not contact him.[63]

LOCAL FOODS

The diet of the Tihāmī includes items which differ from the standard food of the highlands, due in part to the hotter climate and the proximity of the sea, and to foreign influence. *Ḥilbah*, the mainstay of the highlander's diet, is less important on the Tihāmah; whereas fish make up a substantial portion of the lowlander's nourishment. Taboos against eating seafood are not in evidence, although shellfish is far less popular (and far more expensive) than fish. Away from the immediate coast, the fish that is consumed must be smoked or dried in order to be preserved (see Fish Curing below). The dried fish, usually a sprat or a sardine (*wazīf*, pronounced *wasif*) is prepared in a spicy tomato sauce. The smoked fish (*ḥanīdh*, pronounced *ḥanīd*), normally a mullet, can be fried or boiled or eaten as is. *Ḥanīdh* is also the name for a smoked meat dish. Mutton is wrapped in banana leaves and left to cook in its juices overnight buried in a bed of ashes. It is eaten as a speciality on Fridays.[64] Another major distinction between highland and

59. In the absence of published material on Tihāmah *zār* practices, I am adhering to terms collected by myself and Anderson Bakewell in the field. O. Myers in his excellent paper, "Little Aden Folklore," (see Bibliography) records other variations. He indicates that *muzawwirīn* or *muzawwirāt* are the patients and initiates of the healer or healeress who he terms *'arif* [sic] (p. 225) or *zār* (p. 204) while the ceremony can be a *zār*, *mazār* (p. 204) or *ism* (p. 225).

60. Ibid.

61. See Bakewell, p. 104 et passim.

62. For instance, the names of the jinn implicated in the disorders require study, as do the physical objects, dances, foods, abstentions and other therapies involved in the healing. Furthermore, the question whether Akhdām practice *zār* healing amongst themselves and if so, how, deserves investigation. And lastly, what if anything can be added to Oliver Myers' assessment of the pre-Islamic and pre-Ḥimyaritic, that is to say the Neolithic, vestiges in elements of such folk rites. See O. Myers, op. cit., p. 218 et infra.

63. For reasons of tact, I have omitted all personal names and placenames which we collected relevant to the *zār*.

64. I understand from John Baldry that the best meat *ḥanīdh* can be had in al-Marāwi'ah, although it is also highly touted in Zabīd.

Tihāmah foods are the deep-fried batter savouries available in many large *sūqs* on the plain. These have strong affinities with Indian street food of the "bhaji" variety – onions, green chillis, onion tops, sorghum-flour batter, etc. Melons, papaya, limes and, of course, local dates[65] are commonplace, whereas in the highlands they appear only occasionally.[66]

Local bakeries of a rather ad hoc nature[67] are catering to an appetite for pastries. At al-Luḥayyah, the daily selection in the *sūq* included ginger muffins, pink-iced cupcakes, drop-scones and macaroons. These can be found alongside the more traditional jelly sweets, syrup-coated bars and batters and sesame balls which are sold in pyramidal mounds in the large *sūqs* such as Bayt al-Faqīh. Fresh cheese seems to be another innovation as a market commodity, but it can only be bought in areas which have access to Saudi Arabian imports, such as at al-Luḥayyah and 'Abs.

Breakfast on the Tihāmah (*qura'*, Tih.) is taken around 10 a.m. and includes fish, thin griddlecakes (*laḥūḥ*) which can be fried on clay griddles (*malaḥḥah*), or metal ones (*ṭāwah*) and a bread (*dajurrah*, pronounced *degurrah*, Tih.) or a roll (*bājīyah*, Tih?, pronounced *bāgīyah*) made from black millet and baked in the ashes. This is washed down with fresh buttermilk (*rayb*) or tea or a ginger-coffee infusion made with coffee husks (*qishr*) and sweetened with sugar (*miraysī*, pronounced *marīsī*).[68] In the towns, bakery bread (*rūtī*, pronounced *rōtī*) and broad beans (*fūl*) are often substituted for these humble rural foods. Lunch (*buddā'*, Tih. dialect for *ghadā'*?) is eaten between 12 noon and 2 p.m. by the townsfolk. A typical meal in al-Luḥayyah featured crumbled sorghum bread mashed with banana and honey,[69] fried fish served whole, and rice topped with a spicy tomato sauce. Supper (also called *buddā'*) was not a meal of which we had occasion to partake in Tihāmī homes, and therefore cannot describe.

SAINTS AND SAINTS' DAYS

Sufism on the Tihāmah is an absorbing subject. It has given rise to devotional poetry and music[70] such as the *dīwān* cycle of the sufi poet, 'Abd al-Raḥīm ibn 'Alī al-Bura'ī.[71] It has produced holy men of great stature, such as Shaykh 'Alī ibn 'Umar al-Shādhilī of Mocha,[72] and it has been responsible for the development of many of the Tihāmah's towns and villages. Running parallel with sufi teachings is a marginal-sufism, studded with shamans and folk heros of dubious connection to orthodox Islam. Sufism and marginal-sufism are intertwined in Tihāmah history and in present-day practice, as can be seen from my notes on the saints' day festival below. This fact makes any discussion of saint (*walī*) worship and saints' day rituals (*ziyārah*) hazardous, especially for one as inexperienced in this field as I am. I present my notes, therefore, with the following elementary remarks.

The vogue for sufi teachings seems to have flowered on the Tihāmah with the Ayyūbids. Before this, however, the influence of Iraqi sufism was felt, as the historian 'Umārah indicates in his description of 'Alī ibn Mahdī who came to power in 1156 A.D.:[73]

> After a time, 'Aly went on the pilgrimage. (...) He met with pilgrims, the doctors and the preacher of 'Irāk and he became filled with the knowledge they imparted. On his return to Yaman he led a life of retirement, but he exhorted the people, warning them against soldiery. (...) He possessed a well-stored memory, was constant in...the teaching of the Sūfis. He used to speak of things that were revealed to him in the future, and the accurate fulfilment of his predictions became one of the most powerful means by which he won the hearts of the people.[74]

Whatever the precise beginnings of sufi teachings on the Tihāmah, they were adopted by a people susceptible to the allure of magic, predisposed to superstition. To such a populace the holy men who embodied the teachings were capable of superhuman acts, of miracles. Thus the cult of saint worship arose, as it has done in many other regions of the Islamic world.[75] Whether the predisposition to such cults amongst Tihāmah people was introduced by Indian example or injected from African animist strains, or if it lingered from pre-Islamic times, is unclear. There are indications that pre-Islamic vestiges cling to at least one saints' day ritual on the Tihāmah (see below), but what makes the Tihāmah customs distinctive are not their origins, nor yet their main features which do not differ from other cults of saint worship, but the mere fact that they survive and thrive on the Tihāmah plain today; whereas such customs have ceased to play a role in the social life of most other regions of the Yemen where they have existed.[76]

Saint worship in the mediaeval period played a role in the geographical structuring of the Tihāmah. It was responsible for the development of many towns and

65. Those at the best stage of ripeness are called *munāṣif* (*Ṣan'ā' an Arabian Islamic City*, p. 543). Even on the Tihāmah, though, dates imported from Saudi Arabia are more highly favoured than the local varieties.
66. With the discussion of foods in *Ṣan'ā' an Arabian Islamic City*, mention is made of other Tihāmah specialities such as *mashabbak*, a criss-crossed pretzel-shaped sweet made in Hodeida (p. 556) and *qalīyah*, fried/toasted grain (p. 555n). Also cited is the medieval Rasūlid treatise, *Bughyat al-fallāḥīn* which concerns itself with Tihāmah foods (p. 542).
67. At one in al-Ḍaḥī, a hemp-strung funeral bier had been pressed into service as a giant cooling rack for freshly baked muffins.
68. See *Ṣan'ā' an Arabian Islamic City*, p. 555, for the possible origins of the word, either meaning sugar coming from Mauritius or from Marseilles. Robert Wilson adds that he was told sugar was called *muraysī* because it was first imported by a man from Bayt al-Muraysī, near Ṣan'ā'. He judges the story to be apochryphal, and tends toward Mauritius as the likely source (in communication).
69. A dish known all over the Yemen as *fatūt*.
70. See Bakewell, p. 104.
71. He died in 803 A.H. (A.D. 1401).
72. Credited with the introduction of coffee.
73. See Wilson, p. 32.
74. Henry Cassels Kay, *Yaman Its Early Medieval History*, London, 1892, p. 124.
75. See, for instance, Toufik Canaan, *Mohammaden Saints and Sanctuaries in Palestine*, London, 1927; Dale F. Eickelman, *Moroccan Islam*, Austin, Texas, 1976.
76. This disappearance of saint cults is due largely to the Revolutions which have altered the social orders of both North and South Yemen. The *sayyid* class, from which many *manṣabs* hailed, fell into disfavour, and the shrines were looked upon with similar distaste. See Abdulla Said Bujra, *The Politics of Stratification*, Oxford, 1971.

Plate 8.6 **Al-Ḥabīl near Bājil, Jabal Dihnah and Jabal Jamā' in the background**

villages. Followers would collect around a given holy man and settle near the site of his tomb to partake of the blessings (*barakah*) attributed to him. In this way, it is said the towns of Mocha (see Plate 4.2), Bayt al-Faqīh, Ibn 'Abbās (see Figure 6.25) and al-Luḥayyah were founded.[77] Perhaps settlements existed on these sites prior to the life of the patron saints in question,[78] but only archaeological investigation will produce evidence to rewrite the accepted legends.

Visitation (*ziyārah*) to the tomb of a saint, which is thought to impart blessings, takes on a ritual nature in the cult of saint worship. Once a year, pilgrims congregate on a given saints' day and festivities take place. Nevertheless it is important to point out, before we proceed to an account of one Tihāmah *ziyārah*, that a *ziyārah* need not be ritualised and can consist of a simple visit to the saint's tomb for any number of personal reasons. One can find scattered about the Tihāmah isolated tomb sites (see Figures 6.21-6.24) where local men and women come to burn incense and lay sprigs of basil or plant small flags, in an act of supplication or of gratitude, often connected with the reputed healing powers of the holy man (see Healing above). The line here between devotion and superstition is fine, and much more study needs to be done before we can presume to understand the motivations and the practices of the people who visit these graves. Near the coast, for instance, it is customary to stack sawfish snouts against certain tombs (as in other parts of the Red Sea and Indian Ocean littoral),[79] and at a derelict graveyard in the scrub east of Bayt al-Faqīh, women come to burn incense on top of the graves of dead persons that are unknown to them, seeking fulfilment for their wishes from the powers of the Beyond. There seems to be little or no reference to Islam in these practices.[80]

The account which follows of the annual festivities at the tomb of Walī al-Shamsī Ahdal near Bājil describes one particular *ziyārah* of the many which take place on the Tihāmah throughout the year. It should by no means be taken as typical. Indeed, it seems to include some exceptional elements. However, an assessment of the typical and atypical features of Tihāmah *ziyārahs* must be held in abeyance until documentation of many such festivals can be accumulated.

77. The saints connected with each are: Mocha – 'Alī ibn 'Umar al-Shādhilī, d. A.D. 1418; Bayt al-Faqīh – Aḥmad ibn Mūsā ibn 'Alī ibn 'Umar ibn 'Ujayl, d. A.D. 1291; Ibn 'Abbās – Ma'mūn ibn 'Abbās, d. A.D. 929; al-Luḥayyah – Aḥmad ibn 'Alī al-Zayla'ī, early fifteenth century. See Wilson p. 36.

78. Al-Hamdānī knew of Mocha in the eleventh century, Eric Macro tells us, "The Topography of Mocha", *Proceedings of the Seminar for Arabian Studies*, Vol. 10, 1980, p. 55.

79. Outside the tomb of Ibn 'Abbās, where this is the case, the story is related by the *faqīh*, Muḥammad Aḥmad Suwayd, that the snouts are to thank the saint for introducing the skill of net fishing, thereby unlocking the riches of the sea.

80. Fr. Etienne Renaud (in communication) has noted the presence of "curious cemeteries" throughout the Tihāmah, especially on the al-Haqah to Ḥays road.

Observations at the ziyārah of Walī al-Shamsī Ahdal

The *ziyārah* took place on the first Thursday and Friday of *Rabī' al-Thānī* at a hamlet named Dayr al-Khadāmah some 4km WSW of Bājil in the lee of a rock outcrop which is quarried by the Bājil Cement Factory. This village is referred to locally as al-Shamsī, after the saint who is buried there.

The tomb of the *walī* in its walled enclosure stands a short distance from the village to the east. It is surrounded by nearly half a kilometre of lesser graves, which are made of river stone apparently taken from the walls of a site which stood where the graveyard now rests. Sherding by Dr. Selma Al-Radi established dates for this site from the early Islamic period to the 13th or 14th century.[81]

The village itself is a small collection of stone and thatch huts and concrete buildings which are clustered on the apex of what appears to be an earlier habitation mound. It was not possible to gather sherds here due to the festival crowds.

For the occasion, foodstalls, trinket stands, swings and a wooden ferris wheel had been erected on the open ground to the south of the village. From here, a well-trodden path led over the boulders out into the acacia scrub to the tomb of the saint.

On the afternoon of the first day of the *ziyārah*, pilgrims and pleasure seekers milled about the fairgrounds and visited the tomb enclosure which had a multicoloured canopy (*maḥmal*) erected over it for the occasion. Within the tomb precinct, men of the *sayyid* class sat against the enclosure walls, reading from illuminated editions of the *Qur'ān*. Pilgrims, entering from the west, circumambulated the tomb itself, moving counter-clockwise to reach the entrance of the tomb which faces east. Here the gap between the tomb and the enclosure walls was narrowest, obliging the pilgrims to pass single-file before the tomb opening. This aperture is not more than 100cm high and 75cm wide. In the dark recess, a man squatted, chanting and passing out earth from the tomb floor to each pilgrim. Crowded around the tomb were also many beggars, young and old alike, seeking alms.

By the late afternoon, musicians[82] had gathered and were performing in a tight circle amid the foodstalls. Through the throng of onlookers we saw some five or six dancers apparently inserting knives into their sides and cheeks, in time to the drumming.

The *sayyids* began their *mawlid* (recital of the Prophet's life) at sunset, holding it in one of the two principal huts of the village. From here to the tomb and back, they strode three at a time back and forth, back and forth, arms linked and chanting in unison.

By nine o'clock in the evening, the *mawlid* was in full voice, some 15 men congregated in the bare, stone hut. Next to this hut was another identical one, and leaning against its front wall were two long poles, termed *sirū*. One was approximately 7m high, the other more than 8m, both of unplaned wood. Inside this hut, a woman was preparing ghee, creaming it with her hands in a wooden bowl. Other women were roasting melon seeds. This building, referred to as *bayt al-sayyid*, did not appear to house a working family. Its contents were largely unused and cobwebbed. From the rafters hung pots in rope halters, blackened with age. People wandered in and out with no apparent function, yet it was clear that this was the centre of the ritual preparations, headquarters of the principal *sayyid*, a formidable man in his sixties.

Outside in the open space in front of these two huts, one of the two poles was taken and set horizontally on trestles, and the work of anointing it began, with 3 or 4 men performing the ritual. First these attendants washed it down with water, then they applied a mixture of henna and attar, then a coat of the creamed ghee. After each application, the pole was buffed with a soft cloth. Finally, the pole was bathed in billows of incense. Next a bundle of rags, tied together in rope fashion and wound in the shape of a huge egg, was produced from the main hut. Also brought out were an iron sockle for planting the pole in the ground and a pronged spike of iron to crown the pike. The prongs of this spike formed a parabola, suggesting stylised bull horns or the crescent moon. The spike was embedded in the rags as the rope was painstakingly wound around the head of the pole, until the original egg shape was recreated. The *sayyid* himself directed this procedure, chanting prayers and assisting with the swaddling.

At this point, we were removed by the local police, ostensibly to check our papers. When we managed to return an hour later, the second pole had been completed to look like the first, and the two of them were upright in the courtyard, being braced from below by men with arms stretched over their heads. A boy was suspended by his waist over the prongs at the summit of one pole. Drumming accompanied him. He lowered himself to full arm's length, hanging by his hands from the spike. Finally he slithered down. We had been told he would hang by his neck on the prongs but did not see this. Another boy shinned up the second pole, grasped onto the prongs and hung there motionless. He did not surmount the spike. Eventually he spiralled back down the pole and fell backwards in a stiff swoon, into the arms of waiting men who carried him into the *sayyid's* hut.[83] The music stepped up in intensity and dancers gathered around the drummers. Some 15 of them. They stripped to the waist and bared their thighs. In time to the music, they inserted *jambīyahs* (daggers) into their ribs and abdomens and thighs, sometimes two at a time held together, and one man worked a blade into his cheek. We witnessed these acts from a distance of less than a foot. The men did not bleed and no wounds were visible, although we could discern blood on the knives up to the hilt as they were extracted. The men danced all the while. We were told that these men were local, that they did this for the *walī* and were protected from injury by him on this one occasion annually. They did not do this for payment.

The story we were told by the *shaykh* of Bājil, Muḥammad 'Alī al-Muzarīyah, and amplified by his brother and retainers went this way:[84] Al-Shamsī, the

81. See Al-Radi, p. 51.
82. See Bakewell, p. 104.
83. John Baldry, who has witnessed this *ziyārah* twice, saw 15-20 men climb the poles on each occasion. Presumably we missed many while we were replying to police enquiries. Baldry also offers (in communication) the information he was given that "62 pilgrims came from Saudi Arabia and even the Ḥaḍramawt" to attend the *ziyārah*. During the 2 day long festivities we observed over a score of Pakistanis in the crowd; they had come from the Cement Factory, presumably as onlookers, not as faithful.
84. See Al-Radi, p. 51.

saint, had come to the village long ago and found its people in the thrall of a monster who lived on the ridge above the settlement.[85] This monster exacted one or more virgins a year as his due and devoured them. Al-Shamsī slew the monster and liberated the village from its terrible fealty. Every year at the *ziyārah*, the elders of the community require the younger men to climb the pronged poles and to perform miraculous feats to commemorate the slaying of the monster as they themselves can no longer do, being old.

No further explanation was offered for the details of the rite which we saw take place.

Discussion

The primary questions which arise regarding this *ziyārah* are: who was al-Shamsī, and what is the significance of the pole. Since neither issues were satisfactorily explained by our informants, what I have to add is drawn from subsequent research, and is offered very much as "working" notes.

The Ahdal family, as Dr. Al-Radi points out,[86] are a famous Tihāmah family, counting among their members the historian Abū 'Abdullāh al-Ḥusayn ibn 'Abd al-Raḥmān al-Ahdal al-Ḥusaynī (born about 779 A.H., 1377 A.D.) and the jurist Yaḥyā ibn 'Umar al-Ahdal. They trace their lineage to a son of Fāṭimah, and branches of the family settled in Iraq, Syria,[87] the Ḥaḍramawt and the Tihāmah, notably at Zabīd. More relevant to Walī al-Shamsī is the branch of the Ahdal family seated at al-Marāwi'ah, a major village 20km SW of Bājil. Here the Ahdals have long held the title of *manṣab*, meaning in this case the descendants of a saint entrusted with keeping his shrine and distributing his blessing. The present day *manṣab*, al-Ahdal, is credited with working miracles on barren women (see Healing above). We did not meet the man.

Al-'Uqaylī in his account of sufism on the Tihāmah speaks of Shaykh 'Alī ibn 'Umar al-Ahdal, using as his source the history written by Ḥusayn ibn 'Abd al-Raḥmān al-Ahdal, *Tuḥfat al-Zaman fī tārīkh sādāt al-Yaman*. We learn that the Shaykh 'Alī al-Ahdal was the religious master of Balghayth ibn Jamīl, the saint of Bayt 'Aṭā', whose dates were 556-651 A.H., A.D. 1161-1253 This is the only information I can locate from available sources regarding the possible identity of Walī al-Shamsī Ahdal.[88]

As for the pole and the rituals connected with it, parallels can be found in the folk practices of the western Aden Protectorate, documented by Oliver Myers in 1947. He relates how, at the winter festival at al-Duraymīyah devoted doubly to Ma'agiz [sic] and Am-Shaybah [sic], two *'ūds* or poles of unplaned wood were "dressed", that is to say wound round with bits of cloth, which in the eyes of the faithful were turban and *fūṭah*.[89] He repeatedly speaks of a standard or flag called *bayraq* associated with rituals for both saints and spirits. Such a *bayraq* is paraded to the tomb of Walī al-Ghadīr at Burayqah during the *ziyārah*.[90] Even more pertinent is the *bayraq* which figures into the *ziyārah* of Sīd 'Umar near Bīr Aḥmad. Myers recounts that "another *sīd*, a living one, comes to the *ziarah* and climbs to the top [of] Sīd 'Umar's *bairaq* while it is held and, standing on the points of the crescent, waves another flag."[91] He includes several photographs of *bayraqs* in his paper, but unfortunately none shows such a crescent nor seems to be dressed in a manner that closely resembles the *sirū* of Walī al-Shamsī.

The pole, its use and its symbolism, raises the issue of pre-Islamic rites retained in this *ziyārah*.[92] One cannot avoid the parallels with the ancient South Arabian Moon god, symbolised by the crescent shape of the bull's horns. And once this echo has been sounded, it seems to resonate that the saint should bear the name al-Shamsī – the Sun. Indeed, the story given for the villagers' gratitude to the hero-saint seems altogether too mythological to date from the era of Islam. But returning to the pole with its crown of rags and crescent-shaped prongs, there are definite affinities with two, possibly pre-Islamic emblems discussed by Prof. Serjeant, the *bayraq* and the *quba'*. He explains the *quba'* as an object the shape of a hat (*miẓallah*) worn by Ḥaḍramī women and stuffed with rags from the clothing of the departed saint. It is used in the pilgrimage to the sanctuary of al-Ḥāwī in Tarīm:

> I cannot but wonder if it [the *quba'*] is an ancient cult symbol surviving into Islam with which some phallic significance was at one time associated. I feel inclined to see resemblances and dissimilarities between the *ḳuba'* and *bairaḳ* of the western areas of the Aden Protectorate. The *bairaḳ* which is a pole surmounted by a crescent in brass and provided with a circle of jingling bells below is undoubtedly a God-symbol, now transmuted into a saint symbol which can move from place to place.[93]

85. Without making too much of this topographical feature, it is interesting to note J.S. Trimingham's comments about the function of a certain kind of hill in pagan cults which have been absorbed into *ziyārah* rites in Ethiopia. (*Islam in Ethiopia*, Oxford, 1952, pp. 247-253). Furthermore, O. Myers gives a detailed list of hills and stone out-crops (with photographs) in Little Aden which have magical and spiritual associations. O. Myers, op. cit., p. 197 et infra.
86. See Al-Radi, p. 51.
87. Where John Baldry tells me the family has written a history of al-Ahdals.
88. See M. al-'Uqaylī, op. cit., p. 32. In a confusing passage regarding the tomb of Shaykh 'Alī ibn 'Umar al-Ahdal, and presumably quoting from the *Tuḥfat*, it seems that this important site could not be located satisfactorily by Ḥusayn ibn 'Abd al-Raḥmān al-Ahdal who says, "but I saw someone from that region who wrote history who said 'His tomb is at Kadaf [read *kidf*, shoulder, or hill] al-Sawdā' and it is known by many people of al-Marāwi'ah.' Perhaps he is referring to the place known as al-Maḍmūnī in the district of al-Rumāh on the right side of Wādī Sihām. ...but it is more generally understood among the inhabitants of that place that the person buried there is the grandfather of the *shaykh*...." Idem.
89. O. Myers, op. cit., p. 227.
90. This saint has strong connections with the North Yemen Tihāmah since he is known as Aḥmad ibn Aḥmad al-Za'īlīya [sic] whose father was the founder of al-Luḥayyah. O. Myers, ibid., p. 191 et infra. (See Wilson, p. 36.)
91. Ibid., p. 228.
92. See R.B. Serjeant, "Hūd and Other Pre-Islamic Prophets of Ḥaḍramawt," *Studies in Arabian History and Civilisation*, London, 1981, for a most elucidating article about the great south Arabian prophet, al-Hūd, and others, and about the survival of pre-Islamic practices in contemporary rites.
93. Ibid., pp. 136-7.

It is as if the Walī al-Shamsī pole, *sirū*,[94] somehow combines aspects of these two ritual objects and makes them giant-size to fit the story.

Regarding the "miracle" of the daggers – the repeated and vigorous self-stabbing without apparent injury – nothing can deny the powerful effect of this display. I personally am in no doubt that the incisions were genuine. Nevertheless, such ecstatic violence can be found in numerous rites elsewhere in the Oriental world, in Islamic, Hindu and Christian contexts. The dagger dancing at the *ziyārah* of Hāshim Bahr, Shaykh 'Uthmān in Aden,[95] the piercing and self-flagellation at the Hindu festival of Kataragama in Sri Lanka, and the fire walkers at the Anastenaria of Kosti in Northern Greece are three such examples.[96] How one chooses to explain these phenomena depends on one's attitude to faith and to science.

What is telling in al-Shamsī's *ziyārah* is the attitude of the Tihāmīs themselves to this event. The onlookers at this ritual did not question that the participants (with the exception of the musicians) were ordinary villagers, and that one way or another they were protected from harm by the *walī*. Although there exist Akhdām (the pariah class of menials, mendicants and entertainers) who earn their living by public displays of self-mutilation and contortionism,[97] the individuals at the *ziyārah* were not professionals and allegedly not Akhdām.[98] It may be, of course, that they were practised in the skill of inserting blades into abdominal muscles without causing harm to the organs (as for the thighs and cheeks, this is not so easily explained). It still takes transports of faith, or at the least great courage, to skewer oneself on the prongs of the pole and to thrust knives up to the hilt into one's anatomy.

I feel obliged to close these comments with a warning to curiosity seekers who would witness this *ziyārah*. Inappropriate conduct and unseemly attention will not only mar this festival, but might bring about its ban by authorities. And this would mean the extinction of something as rare as the gazelle and the Arabian bustard on the Tihāmah. Therefore I would ask that these notes not be misused.

WEEKLY MARKETS

The system of weekly markets is common throughout the Tihāmah.[99] One day a week in each given locality, goods are bought and sold in an open-air market which serves the villages and farms in the surrounding area. Sometimes the marketplace is within a settlement (as at al-Rāfi'ī, Wādī Mawr) or in towns like Bājil or Bayt al-Faqīh, but it can just as well stand on its own, accessible to the spread of settlements it serves (as at Sūq al-Khamīs[100] and al-Ẓāhir, Wādī Mawr).

Many of the merchants are itinerant and they rent a stall at a string of markets, going from one to the next throughout the week. There are occasional vendors too, or ones who sell only at their neighbourhood market. These are generally farmers or women who sell the products of their cottage industry.

It used to be that the day before a large weekly market such as that at Bayt al-Faqīh or Sūq al-Khamīs, the goods would begin arriving on camelback and by donkey. Now with the advent of the small truck, market activity begins at dawn on the day and by the late afternoon, when the buying and selling is over, the market place and environs are deserted.

How a weekly *sūq* is administered and policed is a fascinating study, but one well beyond the scope of our enquiries.[101]

It is hardly an exaggeration to say that life on the Tihāmah is organised around the weekly event of the *sūq* – the majority of villages having few or no shopping facilities on a daily basis. The *sūq* is far more than a mercantile operation; socialising takes place, meetings are held, news is exchanged. Entertainment can be had in the form of games of chance (played with dice on numbered boards), or from contortionists, snake charmers, sword swallowers, musicians and storytellers[102] who can be found circulating through the crowds. Local *shaykhs* make themselves available to tribesmen for consultation and arbitration on the *sūq* day. Medical problems are attended to, hair cut, individuals contacted. The market place is a clearing house for the affairs of an entire neighbourhood. It is an exceedingly healthy social arrangement and one of the ingredients of the present-day tranquility of the Tihāmah.

---

94. This word, *sirū*, may also provide a clue to the pre-Islamic nature of the rite, since, according to Dr. Al-Radi, it appears to be an ancient South Arabian word form. Even so, I am grateful to Prof. S.D. Goitein for calling my attention to the standard Arabic word, *sarw*, meaning evergreen cypress, CUPRESSUS SEMPERVIRENS (see H. Wehr, *Arabic-English Dictionary*, New York, 3rd edition, 1976, p. 408). This tree does not grow on the Tihāmah to my knowledge.
95. See A. Rihani, *Around the Coasts of Arabia*, p. 330.
96. O. Myers mentions dagger dancing at the *ziyārahs* of Walī Daūd [sic] at Dār al-Amīr and of Walī al-Ghadīr at Burayqah, which he describes in some detail. (Op. cit., p. 224.)
97. We encountered such entertainers at Sūq al-Khamīs and al-Khawbah during our fieldwork. See n. 102 below.
98. One team member, Dr. Al-Radi, was under the impression that they were indeed Akhdām. O. Myers reported that the dagger dance of Walī al-Ghadīr he saw was performed by Ḥajjūr, a slave group. (Op. cit.)
99. For reference to the medieval weekly market at al-Jurayb, see Wilson, p. 35.
100. This important market is known under several names. Written Arabic sources such as Ḥ. al-Waysī (op. cit.), and the British maps use Khamīs al-Wā'iẓāt. It also takes the name of the powerful *sayyid* family, al-Hayj, of al-Kāmalīyah in Wādī Mawr, under whose jurisdiction it falls, thus Khamīs al-Hayj. Colloquially however it is referred to simply as Sūq al-Khamīs, and although there are numerous Thursday *sūqs*, no further qualification is needed when this *sūq* is meant.
101. An extensive analysis of the market system can be found in *Ṣan'ā' an Arabian Islamic City*, Chapters 12, 14 et passim. Although these studies pertain mainly to the Ṣan'ā' market, which is permanent, chapter 14 includes a useful comparison with the weekly *sūq* system researched on the Tihāmah by Hermann Escher.
102. We were unsuccessful in obtaining a word or words for this kind of entertainer. *Majdhūb* (possessed) is perhaps the most suitable but it is not heard in common parlance on the Tihāmah. *Ibn 'alwān* is given, although this has been taken over from the term used to describe the followers of the saint in Yifrus. For further reference to these entertainers as musicians, see Bakewell, p. 104, 106. See also Saints and Saints' Days above.

LOCAL INDUSTRIES

BEE KEEPING

Honey (*'asal*) has been a commercial item in the Tihāmah for centuries. Al-Hamdānī writing in the tenth century singled out the region between Wādī Zabīd and Wādī Rima' as being particularly rich in honey.[103] It is still farmed around al-Ḍaḥī and al-Zaydīyah, by local reports. In Zabīd, where we made enquiries, bees are kept for family use, and the honey for sale in the *sūq* is imported. This statement must be qualified, however, since it was the dry season during our fieldwork, and the bees were not producing in quantity.

One bee keeper had 3 hives in his yard, 2 of which were active. Long, terracotta tubes resting on cement blocks served as the hives. The ends were plugged with perforated metal discs (cut from vegetable oil tins) and the edges sealed with mud. Charcoal had been burned near the hives. The bees were happy enough with this arrangement to contribute some 5-6 kilos to the family larder. Hives are customarily kept in the fields, but we did not encounter them.

BOAT MAKING AND FISHING[104]

The livelihoods of local fishermen and boatwrights on the Tihāmah coast at the present time seem less under threat than are other traditional professions. They are benefiting from the very changes which are causing other local industries to disappear, namely mechanisation and better communications. The catch that once could only be bought or eaten locally (unless preserved by some form of curing, see below) can now reach Hodeida within a matter of hours and be frozen and trucked to the highlands, where a taste for Red Sea fish and shrimp is gradually developing. Furthermore, the outboard motor has freed the fisherman from the whims of wind and currents, increasing the number of hauls he can make when the fish are running. Thus we found both fishing and boat making, within reach of Hodeida, to be viable pursuits in 1982.

Boat Making

In both al-Luḥayyah and al-Khawbah, we observed aspects of construction of the common, open-hulled, rib-and-plank type of fishing vessel called *hūrī* on the Tihāmah (see Figure 8.4).[105] A large *hūrī* holds ten men; the smaller one seats six men. We also found the term *sanbūq* being used to refer to the larger *hūrī*, although the word was generally taken to mean the ocean-going trading vessel with high poop deck, which is a cousin to the dhow.[106]

A boatwright in al-Luḥayyah takes one month to build a small *hūrī*. The boat will sell for 6000-8000YR. The larger *hūrī* represents 2 months' work and will sell for 30,000YR. The boatwrights we questioned were constructing 4-5 *hūrīs* at a time in their open sheds on the waterfront. The side planks of a newly constructed *hūrī* hull are of planed wood that is imported. Singapore and Italy were mentioned as sources of these planks; the kinds of wood were given as *zinjīl* (identity unknown)[107] and teak (*sāj*). The ribs are unplaned and of local wood, *arj* (ZIZYPHUS SPINA-CHRISTI, known in upper Yemen as *'ilb* or *sidr*) being the most preferred. Pitch (*ḥumar*, pronounced *ḥamūr*) is used to caulk the ribs. Projecting from the stern are two long poles by which the captain leans out over the side.

103. Al-Hamdānī, *Ṣifat Jazīrat al-'Arab*, p. 103, l.16.
104. These field notes were compiled in conjunction with Anderson Bakewell and Steven D. Ehrlich.
105. Prof. Serjeant translates *hūrī* as "dug-out canoe", see R.B. Serjeant *The Portuguese of the South Arabian Coast*, as does D. Ingrams, *A Survey of the Social and Economic Conditions of the Aden Protectorate*, p. 132. Both are speaking of a vessel of the Indian Ocean waters.
106. C.W. Hawkins gives a good technical definition of a *sanbūq* as "an Arabian or Somali dhow recognized by its curved stemhead and carved quarter strakes. (. . .) It has a transom stern." (C. Hawkins, *The Dhow*, Lymington, Hampshire, 1977, p. 136.) He attributes the word *sanbūq* to the Portuguese *sambuco*, but R.B. Serjeant disputes this, tracing its origin to an early South Arabian word. (R.B. Serjeant, "Sailing the Indian Ocean," *Gazelle Review*, Vol. 4, London, 1978, p. 6.) G. Percival-Kaye describes the common *sanbūq* of 20-50 tonnes burden as "the 'Cinderella' of the Arab sailing world, nothing comes amiss to her, coal, sand, timber, dates, all are accepted." (G. Percival-Kaye "The Red Sea Slave Trade," *The Anti-Slavery Reporter*, Vol. 10, 1955, p. 51.) For a good representative sketch, see H.R.P. Dickson, op. cit., p. 216. The *sanbūqs* we visited moored off al-Luḥayyah were from Jīzān; they were carrying sand, barrels of oil, tins of pineapple, biscuits and other food-stuffs.
107. R. Dozy gives *zinjīl* as "sorte d'olive longue (LECHIN AZEYTUNA)," op. cit., p. 606.

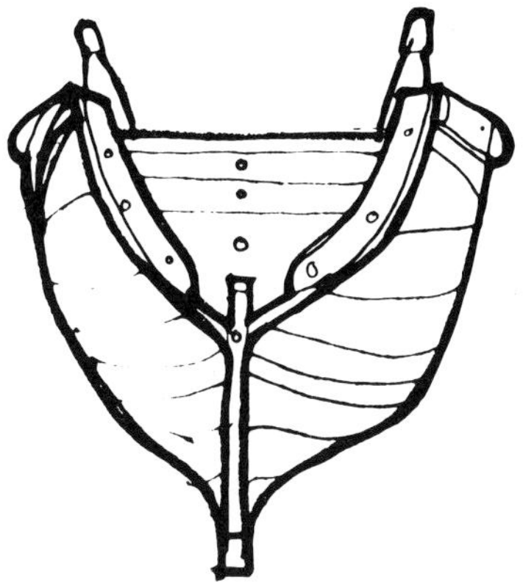

Figure 8.4 Fishing vessel (*hūrī*) and cross section

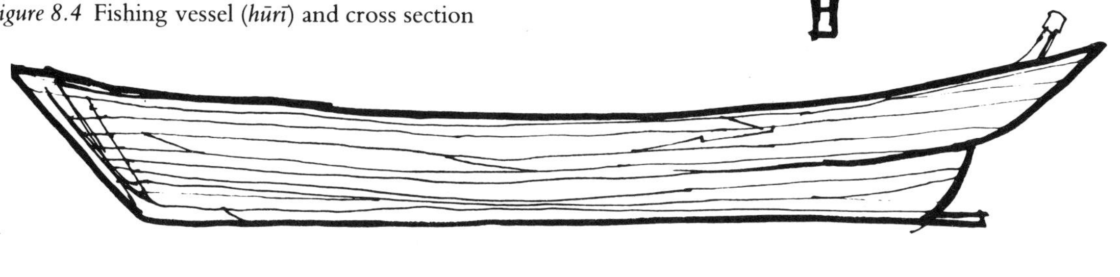

The traditional tools used by the boatwrights are fine specimens of vernacular implements, the most notable being wooden drills operated by a bow and string, and scoops (for the pitch) which are also wooden and shaped like fish.

The fishermen maintain their *hūrīs* by coating them every month or two with a preparation called *shaḥm*, a grease made of a mixture of lime and animal fat, usually cow or camel.[108] The properties of *shaḥm* are such as to prevent against worms and to provide waterproofing. It is white and is applied with the hand to the hulls. The fat costs 150YR per *tanakah*, an 8-litre tin, and it takes about two tins to coat a 10m long *hūrī*.

As mentioned above, the *hūrīs* have been motorised in the last 4 or 5 years, and a sail is now a rare sight. We saw only one of the three sails said to be left in al-Luḥayyah. Nevertheless the waterfront at al-Khawbah was thick with *hūrīs*, some 150 to 200 of them at anchor or pulled up on the beach at the time of our visit. Such a fleet represents a thriving industry for this coastal village.

Fishing

While there are numerous traditional methods of fishing off the Tihāmah coast,[109] I am offering notes on a form of off-shore net fishing which we observed at al-Marāziqah, south of Hodeida. The process makes use of a primitive craft which has not heretofore been discussed, to the best of my knowledge, as an Arabian boat.

The boat in question (see Plates 8.7, XXXIII) is in the nature of a raft. It seems to be made of either balsa wood or palm trunks (an abundant local material). The rafts are constructed with 8 to 12 trunks depending on their thickness. These are stripped and lashed together with cordage, the tapering ends of each log laid together to form a slightly upward bent prow. In all, an average craft measures approximately 3m in length. A thin plank is lashed athwart the stern. Here the fisherman (one per craft) sits, facing away from the prow when working the net (see below). He faces the prow to paddle, which he does with a double-headed paddle. He also stands and poles along with a 6 or 7m pole made of wood as he manoeuvres near the shore. The pole tip, 15cm, is pointed and capped with metal. The raft rides partly submerged in the water and is therefore remarkably stable at the surf line where it does its work.

While this craft is neglected in studies of Arabian boats, Alan Moore in 1925 noted at Massawa the presence of:

> a small raft of three or four logs. The fore ends of the largest logs are slightly turned up, and generally the logs forming the sides are stouter than those in the middle, so that the craft is a little hollowed amidships. A light piece of wood is laid athwartships near each end and lashed. They use a double-bladed paddle with round blades. (...) The raft shows little above the water but the upturned ends of the logs.[110]

From his description, it would seem to be identical with that of the Tihāmah south of Hodeida. Richard LeBaron Bowen, in his article "Primitive Watercraft of Arabia",[111] calls attention to rafts of Indian origin which have disappeared from the Oman area but which survive in the Red Sea, and he cites this very passage from Moore as evidence. Furthermore, Eric Kentley of the National Maritime Museum, who has examined our visual documentation of the Tihāmah raft, notes its resemblance to the *kattumarams*[112] of South India, although these have no cross timbers and have stem pieces

108. D. Ingrams indicates that in Aden, shark oil was used as well. (D. Ingrams op. cit., p. 133.) And from H.R.P. Dickson comes the further observation of Gulf vessels that above the waterline shark oil was used, whereas lime and sheep fat served below. (H.R.P. Dickson, op. cit., p. 213.)
109. For descriptions of analogous methods in Aden, see D. Ingrams, op. cit., pp. 131-135 and her bibliography, p. 139. Also Mitchell et al, op. cit., p. 205.
110. A. Moore, *Last Days of Mast and Sail*, Oxford, 1925, p. 138.
111. In *American Neptune*, Vol. 12, 1952, pp. 186-221.
112. *Kattumaram* means "lashed logs" in Tamil. Rupert Kirk who made watercolour studies of Mocha in the early 1830s did several drawings of this raft, which he too labelled a "catamaran". This portfolio is housed at The Royal Geographical Society, cat. no. X228. An even earlier reference to catamarans at Mocha is made by Prof. H. Cleghorn in his diaries of 1795-1796 (see *The Cleghorn Papers*, ed. Rev. Wm. Neil, London, 1927, p. 136).

Plate 8.7 Fishing raft near al-Marāziqah [See Plate XXXIII]

to accentuate the upturn of the bow.[113] On the basis of the physical evidence, then, it is possible that the boat was imported into the Red Sea from India, possibly via Oman.

The linguistic evidence does not inform us further, I fear. The word we collected for the pole, *majarrah*, seems to be standard Arabic. The term taken down for the raft, however, is more puzzling: "*chasabo*". Either the word is dialect or it is non-Arabic. Or it was simply misheard. Assuming for the moment, that the word is bona fide, one's first inclination is to seek an African origin, but no material has come to light that would support this.[114]

Among primitive crafts found on the eastern side of the Arabian peninsula, the *shāshah* and the "*chalabīyah*" invite consideration, although on the physical evidence alone, they do not seem to be related to the "*chasabo*". The *shāshah* or *kellek* (Turkish, *çiliç*)[115] is a reed boat, described by S.B. Miles in 1919 thus:

> On the Batineh coast...we find a primitive kind of surf-boat. This boat is called "shasha".... It is made solely of date sticks, two bunches of which are tied together at the small end to form the stem, the thick ends being joined to form the skeleton of the boat, which is filled up with palm bark and coconut fibre; they are about 12 feet [3.66m] long and can only hold one or two men, who sit in it half immersed in the water.[116]

It survives today in Oman.[117] "*Chalabīyah*" is a term used for the reed bundle rafts of the Iraqi marshes, as recorded by James Hornell.[118] As with the *shāshah* it is not sufficiently similar to the "*chasabo*" to constitute a true kinship. For the moment, the matter remains unresolved, and the word "*chasabo*" unconfirmed. It may be simply a variant of *khashab*, meaning wood in Arabic.

Fishing with the raft involves a collective effort between the lone boatsman and a team of fishermen on the shore. A net (*shabakah*) made of local fibres or of nylon or both, is played out in a semi-circular sweep beyond the surfline by the boat, while 3 or 4 men hold its on-shore end. Once the net is laid, the raft returns to shore bringing the other end to another 3 or 4 men and boys, some 15m further along the beach. Together the teams of men pull in the net, letting it drag the bottom which is relatively deep here, over 3m at the surf line. The process of hauling in the net takes nearly an hour, and the entire procedure is repeated two or three times in a morning.

Regarding the catch obtained by this method, the smaller fish (*ḥūt*, pronounced *ḥūth*, used for fish in general) are divided amongst the fishermen, who string them through the gills on circlets of dune grass and take them home for their midday meal.[119] The more lucrative elements of the catch are sold to the Hodeida truck, an open-backed Suzuki that skims along the beach, stopping only long enough to buy up the haul if the price is right. The fish that can be netted in this manner include mullet, hind, grouper, needlefish, crab and shrimp (*qubqab* or *jumbarī*, pronounced *gumbarī*). Occasionally, bonito, red tuna, dogshark and skate are brought in like this, but not the prized kingfish, as far as I am aware.[120] Every so often, a sea tortoise (*zukr*, Tih?, unconfirmed) is caught inadvertently in the net. These are not eaten, nor are their shells taken, to my knowledge. They become the children's plaything, leashed by a front flipper and led around until, hapless creatures, they die and their carcasses are abandoned to the birds.

Fish curing

At al-Khawbah and al-Luḥayyah, the main income from fishing results from the sale of cured rather than fresh fish. Neither community has easy access to the new Hodeida-Jīzān road,[121] cut off as they both are by stretches of treacherous *sabkhah* (pronounced *subkhah*) or deep sand; thus they maintain their traditional practice of curing their catches and selling them at the weekly markets of the interior, al-Luḥayyah community trucking its fish to the *sūqs* of Wādī Mawr, and that of al-Khawbah going further south to al-Zaydīyah, al-Qanāwiṣ and al-Ḍaḥī. Both fisheries compete for sales at Sūq al-Khamīs, the largest *sūq* of the northern Tihāmah (see Weekly Markets).

At al-Khawbah, some 10,000-20,000 fish are cured a day, considerably more than at al-Luḥayyah, where I made notes on the curing procedure. The process, which utilises a smoking technique, takes place on the shore to the north of the town centre. Some 3 men work over piles of freshly caught fish, mostly varieties of mullet; one gouges the eyes and guts the belly with a knife, another salts the cavity with rock salt crystals; the third rams a slender cane stalk (*qaṣab*) down the throat to the full length of the fish. This keeps it from curling as it is smoked. While the fish is being prepared in this way, a woman readies the ovens (*mawfā*, pronounced *mawfah*). These stand in rows perpendicular to the shore, oriented east-west (see Figure 8.5). They are roughly 60cm high and an equal diameter at the base, being bee-hive shaped

113. I am entirely grateful to Eric Kentley, the ethnographer of the Archaeological Research Centre of the National Maritime Museum, for having supplied me with the relevant references in Moore and Bowen, and for having contributed his own informed analysis of the craft in question.
114. The *mtumbui* (Swahili), while equally primitive, is a dug out long boat of the Kenyan coast, and therefore not relevant either physically or linguistically. In the Sudan, there are no coastal rafts Eric Kentley tells me, and the small, flat bottomed, sea fishing, plank boat there carries the name *ramas*, which is presumably derived from the Arabic for raft (*ramath*). Known Arabic words for rafts (*ramath*, *ṭūf*, and *'āmah*) provide no clues. (See H. Kindermann, *'Schiff' im Arabischen*, p. 60).
115. Ibid. *Kellek* is a "native raft of timber and brushwood supported on skin bladders", according to the Naval Intelligence Division, *Iraq and the Persian Gulf*, U.K., 1944, p. 558.
116. S.B. Miles, *The Countries and Tribes of the Persian Gulf*, London, 1919, p. 413.
117. For a photograph of the craft, see W.H.D. Facey and E.B. Martin, *Oman – A Seafaring Nation*, Muscat, 1979.
118. J. Hornell, *Watertransport*, Cambridge, 1946, repr. Newton Abbott, Devon, 1970. See also Buxton and Dawson, "The Marsh Arabs of Lower Mesopotamia," *Indian Antiquities*, Vol. I, pp. 289-97; H.H. Brindley, "The Sailing Balsa of Lake Titicaca and Other Reed Bundle Craft," *Mariner's Mirror*, Vol. 17, 1931, pp. 7-19; W. Thesiger, "The Marshmen of South Iraq," *Geographical Magazine*, Vol. 120, 1954, pp. 272-281. A notable variant spelling for this boat is *chelabiza*.
119. The fishermen at al-Marāziqah live with their families in very simple huts just behind the dunes. Brackish wells afford them their independence from the village in the palm groves. They are shy and solitary people.
120. See A. Rouaud, *Les Yemen et Leurs Populations*, pp. 128-9.
121. Completed in 1981 with Saudi funds and Korean labour.

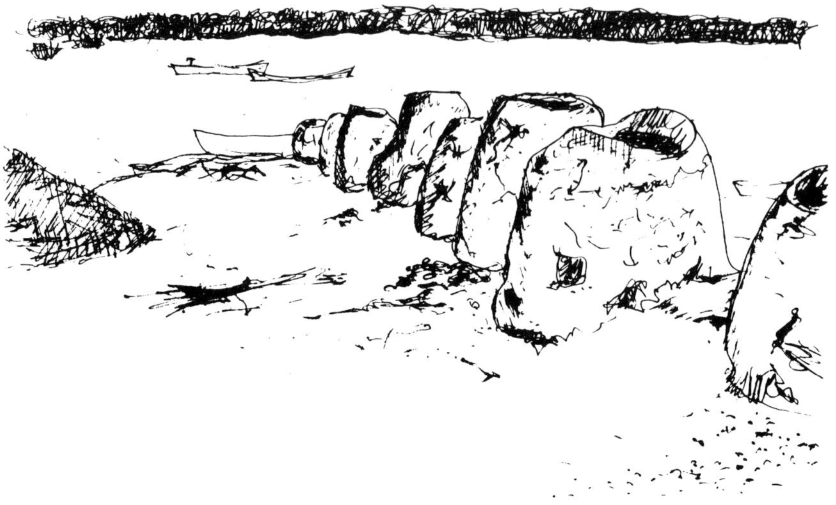

Figure 8.5 Fish smoking ovens, al-Luḥayyah

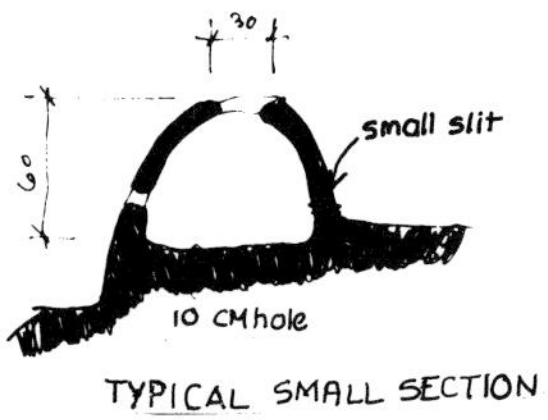

Figure 8.6 Oven cross section

with a 30cm opening at the top. The typical oven is vented with a 10cm hole on the north side and one access to the fire chamber at ground level on the south side (see Figure 8.6). Into these chambers the woman inserts stalks and brush. The fish are stacked upright in each oven, and the opening at the top is covered with a clay jar or a bucket and further blocked up with dampened rags. The fish are left to smoke over a bed of embers for an hour and a half. The curing takes place in the early afternoon, following the morning's fishing which brings the catch to shore between 10 and 11 a.m. The smoking produces a fish of moist, flaky meat still clinging to the bone, that will last for several days without spoiling. This smoked fish is called *ḥanīdh* (pronounced *ḥanīd*, see Local Foods), as opposed to dried sprats or sardines (*wazīf*). We did not find any fish drying activities during our fieldwork, although the *wazīf* were being sold at the Bayt al-Faqīh *sūq*.

BRICK MAKING

Brick making has been a vital industry on the Tihāmah at least since the Middle Ages. The forts of al-Ḍaḥī (see Plate 6.6), al-Zaydīyah, al-Ḥusaynīyah, Bājil, al-Zuhrah, al-Muʻtariḍ (see Plates XXVII-VIII) al-Rāfiʻ ī (see Plate 6.5), to name just a few of those standing today, as well as the mosques and houses made of permanent materials in the centre of the Tihāmah[122] have been constructed from locally made bricks. It is the fabric of the Rasūlid minaret at al-Mahjam (see Plate 4.1)[123] and of monuments in Zabīd still standing from that period, and it is almost assuredly the major fabric of earlier Islamic structures at sites such as al-Kadrā',[124] where the absence of any visible masonry suggests the use of brick rather than stone, since brick does not long withstand the ravages of man and sand characteristic of the Tihāmah, and since stone is not readily available in the centre of the Tihāmah plain.[125]

Two principal kinds of brick (*ṭūb*) can be found in use on the Tihāmah. The first is made of a mixture of straw and clay, and can be of varying sizes. It is the "half-brick" of this variety[126] which has given rise to the elaborate facades of the houses of Zabīd (see Plate 6.13), where the geometric designs are devised from low-relief brickwork. Similarly, some of the interior decoration results from patterning of these small bricks (see Plate 6.14). We did not encounter working factories making this brick during our fieldwork.

The other kind of brick is a poorer sort and is made entirely from clay (*ṭīn*). Its manufacture was observed at al-Durayhimī, a village on the coast at the mouth of Wādī Kuway. This brick is used in the construction of the narrow irrigation channels that snake along the peripheries of the fields, and it is also still employed in house construction by those not wealthy enough to afford the newly-introduced cement blocks.[127]

The manufacture of these crude bricks takes place, from start to finish, in the *wādī* bed itself, with quarry and kilns both contained within an irregular gully covering roughly half a hectare, which had been created by the

122. See references to Zabīd domestic architecture, Chapter 6.
123. See Wilson, p. 32.
124. See Wilson, p. 31, and Al-Radi, p. 53 et passim.
125. See references to the thick alluvial deposits overlaying basement rocks, Chapter 1.
126. See *Ṣanʻā' an Arabian Islamic City*, p. 227n.
127. In 1977, I was shown the first local factory in Zabīd making these cement blocks. In 1982, we found no substantial village on the plain which did not have cement block structures mixed in among the daub-and-wattle huts and the brick houses.

process of excavating the moist clay. At this westernmost section of the *wādī*, although there is no surface water, except at times of unusual spate, the clay beds retain water all year round. Extra water is brought up from temporary wells dug in the quarry floor; these, like the quarry pits, are abandoned as they run dry or become too deep for easy access.

The raw clay is smeared in a 5cm thick layer over burlap sacking, where it is fashioned into roughly 15-20cm long bricks with the aid of a rectangular wooden mould. The bricks are then laid out to dry. This initial portion of the work is done from sunset until 9 or 10 o'clock in the evening, the men working by moonlight whenever feasible. I did not ascertain whether these hours were kept because the men worked as farmers during the day or whether it was to avoid evaporation that would make the clay difficult to spread and to mould. I suspect both. During the summer, the bricks are left to dry in the sun for 3 days. In the wintertime the drying period is increased to 5 days. Then the bricks are ready to fire. This is accomplished in a pit kiln, which is bedded with dom palm trunks and dom palm fruit (*bāsh*, Tih.?) scavenged from the nearby groves. The bricks are stacked inside the kiln, which can hold several thousand at a time, and then they are overlaid with underbrush and palm fronds (*ṭāfī*). Once the fires are lit, the bricks are left to bake for 4 days; thus it takes 7 to 9 days, depending on the season, to produce finished bricks.

The price of 1000 bricks is 150YR. The cost, since nearly all the materials are to be had from nature's bounty, is nil. However, due to the crude method of firing, there is much wastage, many of the bricks fusing in the uneven temperatures, or curling too badly to be usable. Two men worked the quarry and kilns I visited, a young adult and an adolescent. I was told that there are 20 brickmakers left in the area of al-Durayhimī. Here a farmer realises some 20YR a day from his labours, while a brickmaker barely does better at 30YR a day. In Bājil as little as 6-7 years ago, more than 50 brickmakers made their living; today the trade has shifted entirely to concrete block manufacture.

MODERN INDUSTRIES[128]

The notable modern industries on the Tihāmah in 1982, either extant or in the planning stages, include brick factories at al-Manṣūrīyah (under local management with German machinery) and at Ḥays (Italian management), cement factories at Bājil (Soviet built) and al-Mafraq (in planning), power plants at Mocha (in planning, Saudi Arabian backing) and at Hodeida (British management), rock salt mining at al-Ṣalīf (backed by the Yemen Bank for Reconstruction and Development with a grant from the Kuwait Fund for Arab Economic Development, and managed by the Ministry of Economy), cotton ginning at Zabīd (local management) and at Hodeida (also privately owned), an oil refinery at Hodeida (under construction to be jointly run by Mobil International Petroleum Corporation and Yemen Oil and Mineral Resources) and one in planning for al-Ṣalīf.

Other light industries centred at Hodeida feature a tobacco factory (British management), a soft drinks factory, the Yemen Dairy (local management with an IFC grant), an oxygen plant (set up with USSR funds and State run), and an aluminium products plant.

Mocha, al-Ṣalīf and Hodeida maintain the three commercial ports of Yemen, the largest being at Hodeida (managed by the Yemen Port Corporation backed by the International Development Association among others). There is an airport at Hodeida and another on Kamarān Island (to which place access is restricted). Telephonic communications link Hodeida to the limited national grid and to INTELSAT (operated by the British).

The Tihāmah Development Authority coordinates a major agricultural development scheme vital to the Yemen. This is financed by the United Nations, IDA, KFAED and others. It is currently emplacing a land improvement project in Wādī Mawr due for completion in 1984. The target of the scheme is large-scale output of cotton, vegetables, cereals and oilseeds as well as expanded livestock farming in the arable *wādīs* of the Tihāmah.

PEARL DIVING

Pearl diving for profit in the Yemeni waters of the Red Sea is no more. That being said, the lore remains. A 75 year-old, former pearl diver (*ghawwāṣ*, pronounced *ghawṣ*) in al-Luḥayyah, Aḥmad 'Abdullāh al-Mukhayī, took us in a *hūrī*[129] to pearl beds on the far side of an offshore sand bar to the south west of town. This was far more an occasion to reminisce about the industry than to obtain pearls, since the season for pearling is July not January.[130] The pearls of the Arabian seas have been coveted luxuries since antiquity[131] and those of al-Luḥayyah rated foremost for their beauty and abundance. Yet it has been 20 years since the beds were worked actively. The reasons given for the cessation are that, with the Revolution, money could be made faster in other commodities which were not as labour-intensive or as subject to competition from the Gulf. The beds, we were assured, are as pearl-bearing as ever, even though our septegenarian guide failed to wrest one oyster shell (*ṣudaf ḥaqq al-lu'lu'*) from the sea bottom for us. He would have had to dive some 4-5 metres, something better left to younger men.

At other places on the Tihāmah shore we encountered youths and fishermen clearly unable and unwilling to swim. In al-Luḥayyah, however, the ability to swim and dive is relatively common among the menfolk, young and old alike. With the current fashion for pearls in Ṣan'ā', one wonders why the pearl diving of al-Luḥayyah cannot be revived.

SALT PRODUCTION

The history of salt (*milḥ*) production on the Tihāmah, either by panning at the sea's edge or by quarrying rock salt deposits, could well start in antiquity, but it is not until the 18th century that references to salt production

128. I am grateful to Irena Knehtl for providing much of the information for this summary.
129. See Boat Making. Also Mitchell et al, op. cit., p. 205.
130. See H. de Montfried, "Red Sea Pearl Fishing", *National Geographic Magazine*, p. 611. De Montfried gives *sadaf* [sic] as the mother-of-pearl bearing shell, and *bilbil* [sic] as the pearl bearing shell, a distinction which I am unable to verify.
131. See Pliny the Elder, *Natural History*, XII, 18, par. 84.

and trade begin to proliferate. Nowhere in the relevant passages of *The Periplus of the Erythraean Sea*[132] is salt specifically mentioned, although it was known to be an important additive to the foods and the dyes of the peoples of Classical times. In the tenth century A.D., the salt deposits of the Tihāmah are mentioned by al-Hamdānī as being "in the region of Mawr and al-Mahjam".[133] By this he presumably means the salt hills in eastern Wādī Mawr known as Jabal al-Milḥ (see below) and the two deposits around al-Ṣalīf, one on the peninsula itself and another on the mainland at the base of a gypsum outcrop called Jabal al-Qumah. While the salt resources of the Tihāmah were probably exploited for local use all through the Middle Ages, it is not documented as a commercial commodity until relatively recently. Niebuhr records seeing the sea salt extraction process at Ghulayfiqah and near Mawshij en route to Mocha.[134] The salt pans still visible at Mocha today were noted by both Dela Garde-Jazier (1738) and Bellin (1764).[135] The Turks at the turn of this century[136] lined their pockets with profits derived from the salt mines of al-Ṣalīf and environs.[137] In the 1920s, the salt mines of al-Zaydīyah and al-Luḥayyah (read al-Ṣalīf and Jabal al-Milḥ) were active according to al-Washalī.[138] And in the 1960s, salt was being shipped from al-Ṭāyif,[139] north west of Bayt al-Faqīh. Today salt is the only mineral of economic significance exploited in Yemen (see Modern Industries).

The rock salt deposits at Jabal al-Milḥ[140] some 12.5km east of al-Luḥayyah, where I made my notes, are quarried manually, with dynamite the only modern technology in an otherwise traditional procedure. An average of 15 men work the quarry (possibly *qumah*, pronounced *gumah*)[141] itself, laying sticks of dynamite into crude bores, detonating them and then prying up the loosened slabs of salt with pick-axes and adzes (*qadūm*, pronounced *guddum*). They load the salt chunks into burlap sacks on the back of a donkey which ferries them out of the quarry bed to a palm-trunk work house half-way out of the pit area (see Plate 8.8). Today this area extends over some 3 square kilometres at the western base of the *jabal*, a cluster of gypsum outcrops.

The workhouse is a rectangular structure constructed of palm trunks and thatch. It has one wide portal without doors in the centre of its south wall, and a centrepole supporting the roof. Into this enclosure, the donkey is driven to be off-loaded, the salt chunks poured into piles around the room. These piles are set upon by labourers who crack the larger chunks into crystals. Others scoop the crystals into palm-frond bags (see Basketry). These are stitched closed with a large needle and palm fibre, and stacked around the walls in neat rows. Some ten men are employed in the workhouse sector of the operation. Camels are used to transport the bagged salt, some 20-25 bags per beast, to local weekly markets and across the *sabkhah* to al-Luḥayyah.

The salt, I understood, is sold in pairs of bags. Thus one *ḥaml*, or standard load of salt, is two-bags full. Each bag weighs 6 kilos, and the *ḥaml* sells for 14YR. It was claimed that 6,000-10,000YR are made each week at the Jabal al-Milḥ quarry (amounting to some 8-9 camel loads a day), but it was not clear whether the concern was owned privately or cooperatively).

The current *ḥākim* of al-Luḥayyah, Sayyid Ḥasan al-Daylamī from Dhamār, asserted that the quarries at Jabal al-Milḥ were worked in Ḥimyaritic times. As far as I know, there have been no archaeological investigations in the area that shed light on the issue. It is worthwhile to note, however, that the only known pre-Islamic inscription blocks in the northern Tihāmah were sighted by Paolo Costa in a mosque at a place he gives as 'Alī Mahmūl, and locates east south east of al-Luḥayyah in the Wādī Mawr/Wādī 'Ayyān region.[142]

Plate 8.8 **Salt Quarries, Jabal al-Milḥ**, view over quarry from the abandoned Turkish (?) depot

132. See Al-Radi, p. 30.
133. Al-Hamdānī, *Ṣifat*, p. 155, ll.18-21.
134. Niebuhr, *Travels Through Arabia*, Vol. I, p. 316.
135. See E. Macro, op. cit., p. 61. Mr. Macro generously made his studies available to us before we went into the field. He has assembled a unique collection of early maps and drawings of the port which is of benefit to researchers and oriental art historians.
136. See Baldry, p. 46.
137. See G.W. Bury, *Arabia Infelix*, p. 125.
138. I. al-Washalī, *Dhayl Nashr al-Thanā' al-Ḥasan*, p. 225.
139. H. al-Waysī, op. cit., p. 90.
140. The village cluster which surrounds the quarry site is known locally as Jabal al-Milḥ, but other names are recorded for it. Al-Hamdānī says ". . . there is the salt of al-Qumah in the region of Mawr" (op. cit.), by which he certainly is referring to this site. Al-Washalī (op. cit.) gives al-Kasha'ah, and this is echoed by C. Ritter (op. cit., p. 887) as Koscha [sic]. He presumably took it from Niebuhr (*Description de l'Arabie*, p. 200). Al-Waysī (op. cit., p. 98) uses the plural, Jibāl al-Milḥ, and the British D.O.S. maps which were not finalised for this region at the time of our fieldwork, name the village both as Guma [sic] and as Jabal al-Milḥ, at the same time calling the elevation Jabal al-Milḥ and offering Jabal Kushah [sic] as an alternative (map sheet no. 1542 B4). The Swiss Technical Co-operation Service 1:500,000 map print still another possibility for the hills' name rendering it parenthetically and with a question mark as Jabal Qudmī; they too give Guma [sic] as the village name.
141. I cannot confirm from lexicographic sources this word *gumah* which I collected in the field. It is clear however, that Qumah is a placename closely associated with salt quarry sites, see above.
142. See the map on p. 175 of P. Costa and E. Vicario, *Arabia Felix A Land of Builders*, New York, 1977. See also Chapter 4, p. 30, n.5. Further details were supplied by Dr. Costa in communication.

Plate 8.9 **Camel pulling sesame oilpress, al-Manṣūrīyah, 10th February 1982**

SŪQ INDUSTRIES OF ZABĪD

The *sūq* of Zabīd, like most major town *sūqs*, is a place of manufacture as well as a place of sale. One can find iron and tin smithing, Tihāmah bed carpentry and assembly (although many Tihāmīs are capable of stringing their own furniture seats), and tailoring, to name the most obvious.[143] In addition, certain food stuffs and smoking products are produced within the *sūq*, as I shall describe.

Sesame oil (zayt simsim)

Sesame oil is pressed, traditionally, in a huge wooden mortar (*ma'ṣarah*, pronounced *maṣarah*, or *ṭāḥūn*) made of a wood named as *sawl* (ACACIA NILOTICA, subsp. INDICA). Into this mortar are placed 1½ baskets (approx. 2 kilos) of raw sesame (*simsim* or *juljulān*, SESAMUM INDICUM) seeds and two handfuls of water. A female camel is harnessed to the large pestle and she walks a circle around the mortar, pestling the seeds for 4 hours (see Plate 8.9). The oil is decanted and the grounds (*'uṣarah*, pronounced *uṣarah*) are fed to the camel, which then rests and another beast is roped up for the afternoon session, also 4 hours. The working camel is normally blindfolded to prevent her from getting dizzy or distracted as she turns. In Zabīd, there were 6 sesame presses 15 years ago. In 1982, we found 2.

Tobacco derivatives

The Tihāmīs are fond of a form of snuff they call *shammah*, which is an admixture of tobacco and potash (*karah*, Tih.?,[144] or *ramād* in modern Arabic). The tobacco leaves are dried and "aged" in the sun for 2-3 days, then ground to a powder on round grinding stones, and finally mixed with the potash in nearly 50-50 proportions. The snuff is then sold by weight. Those taking snuff place it inside their lower lip or onto the tongue in sizeable amounts, ingesting the juices slowly. It is not inhaled, as far as I observed.

Another tobacco product is called *malṭūṭ* (Tih.?)[145] and consists of tobacco mixed with date sugar to form

143. The two workshops which I noted that lay outside the confines of the *sūq* were the one for indigo dyeing (see Textiles) and one for the manufacture of waterpipe hoses (*ḥibil*), both of which require more room than is readily available in the warren of the *sūq*.

144. The additive to *shammah* is termed *dujduja* [sic] in the Miller-Escher-Mundy, op. cit., p. 135, where it is listed as imported from Aden. *Dujduja*, a variant form, can be compared to *duqduqah* cited in *Ṣan'ā' an Arabian Islamic City*, p. 177.

145. A classical origin for this word may be found in *maltūt*, implying crumbled or mixed, a suggestion made by Robert Wilson.

a sweet substance that is smoked in the waterpipe (*qaṣabah*[146] or *madā'ah*). The tobacco is shredded and rubbed with the sweetener (*qaṭārah*) which is prepared by caramalizing date sugar and simmering it with water for 4 hours. The mixture is then formed by hand into individual balls the size of golf balls and sold by the piece. It is, I must say, a most pleasant smoke.[147]

CONCLUSION

On the basis of random notes such as these, general conclusions are not justified. The most that should be said here of the crafts studied is that they do not reach great heights of artisanship, being of a functional nature. The customs of today pertain mostly to a rural society, and do not display the urban sophistication of the medieval Tihāmah. Lastly, the local industries represent pockets of self-sufficiency that are giving way to modern technologies and tastes, with the exception of fishing which is practised on a substantial scale along traditional lines.

These notes do not purport to give a comprehensive picture of life on the Tihāmah, yet I would not want to close without at least a mention of the important features which have not found a place in this paper. Either because of the season, or because our work did not bring us into contact with various pursuits, or because some practices are now rare or gone, certain information was not collected. Thus nothing has been said here about the history, the technologies and folk traditions associated with the major agricultural commodities of the Tihāmah – cotton, coffee,[148] dates and grain. Each of these deserves an extensive profile, if a balanced picture of Tihāmah traditions were to be given. Of the crafts which have been neglected, needlework and tanning have had particularly rich histories. Tanning was not found in practice in our 1982 survey. Horsemanship has played a significant role in the political and social affairs of the Tihāmah of the past, and deserves to be described. Tihāmah weddings are an occasion for distinctive dances and costumery and customs, none of which have been noted here. The tribal map of the plain merits documentation, particularly as it overlaps and interacts with highland tribal sway. The Akhdām groups, living on the fringes of Tihāmī society, have customs which set them apart in their eating habits, their superstitions, their religious practices, their tribal structure, nomenclature and skills, to mention a few.[149] Lastly, the dialects of the Tihāmah are a major differentiating factor which has not been adequately treated.[150] Still other aspects of traditional life vie for attention, and it is ultimately a matter of personal predilection which one singles out for study, such is the cultural richness of the Tihāmah.

146. While *qaṣabah*, meaning reed or cane, should only refer to the waterpipe stem, synecdoche is at work here in common Tihāmah usage. (See Plate 8.4.)

147. *Jirāk* is another sweetened tobacco that is highly prized on the Tihāmah. It is imported from India.

148. Coffee is not grown on the Tihāmah, but in the foothills overlooking it. In the past, however, virtually all the emporia through which the beans passed on their way to the coffee houses of the world were situated on the coastal plain.

149. Although references to the Akhdām are scant, the following sources contain useful information: T.J. Arnaud, "Les Akhdam de l'Yemen, leur origine probable, leurs moeurs," *Journal Asiatique*, Series 4, Vol. 15, Apr. 1850, pp. 376-87; T. Gerholm, *Market, Mosque and Mafraj*, Stockholm, 1977; J. Horgen, "Akhdam tribe in servitude," *Geographical Magazine*, Vol. 48 (9), 1976, pp. 533-8; A. Rouaud, op. cit., pp. 146-7 et passim; R.B. Serjeant, "South Arabia," *Studies in Arabian History and Civilisation*, IX, London, 1981, pp. 232-4; also R.B. Serjeant, "South Arabia and Ethiopia – African elements in the South Arabian population," *Proceedings of the 3rd International Conference of Ethiopian Studies*, 1966, pp. 25-33; Muḥ. 'Alī al-Shahārī, *Ṭarīq al-thawrah al-Yamanīyah*, Cairo, 1966. (The Horgen and Rouaud texts are not always reliable.) Delores Walters is currently engaged in studying the social structure of an Akhdām community for a PhD dissertation, New York University. See also Bakewell, p. 105, n. 12.

150. The only study of which I know is by J. Greenman, see note 43 above. University of Michigan, Vol. 11, nos. 1 and 2, 1978. However, Niebuhr includes a comparative glossary of Egyptian and Yemeni words that was compiled by Forsskål. In it are examples of Tihāmah dialect which make it an interesting document. See C. Niebuhr, *Description de l'Arabie*, pp. 74-78.

APPENDIX I

A partial list of saints' day festivals on the Tihāmah, given by village north to south.

Place	Date	Saint
Bayt 'Aṭā'	1st Friday of *Rajab*	Balghayth (or Abū'l-ghayth) ibn Jamīl (556-651 A.H., 1161-1253 A.D.)
Ibn 'Abbās	11th day of *Rajab*	Ibn 'Abbās
Al-Ḍaḥī	27th day of *Rajab*	Ismā'īl Muḥammad al-Ḥaḍramī (d. 676 A.H., 1277 A.D.)
Dayr al-Khadāmah	9th-10th day of *Rabī' al-Thānī*	Al-Shamsī Ahdal
Al-Quṭay'	2nd day of *'Īd al-Kabīr*	Al-Khazān
Al-Raws	Last Thursday of *Sha'bān*	Ibn Ghannī (?)
Bayt al-Faqīh	During *Rabī' al-Awwal*	Aḥmad ibn Mūsā ibn 'Ujayl (d. 690 A.H., 1291 A.D.)
Al-Tuḥaytā	1st Friday of *Sha'bān*	Al-Abqar

APPENDIX II

The Tihāmah Expedition collection of artifacts and ethnographic objects and their provenances:

Basketry

Basket (*zanbīl*), Bayt al-Faqīh.
Plaited dom palm, circular on round base, widening at brim, 2 handles. 62cm long at brim, 48cm wide at brim, 45cm high, 45cm diameter at base.

Eating Mat (*nakhal, muṣrafah, ṭabaqah*), Bayt al-Faqīh.
Plaited dom palm, round with handle. 83cm diameter.

Cow Muzzle (*fidāmah*), Sūq al-Khamīs.
Plaited cord of vegetable fibre. 18cm wide at rim, 17cm deep, 130cm strap.

Donkey Girth, Sūq al-Khamīs.
Plaited vegetable fibre. 110cm long, 7cm wide.

Broom, Bayt al-Faqīh.
Bound dom palm spines, handleless. 61cm long.

Salt Bag (*ḥaml*), Ṣan'ā'.
Plaited dom palm matting, cut and stitched with vegetable fibre. Made in Northern Tihāmah. 26cm wide, 39cm deep.

Fan, Bayt al-Faqīh.
Plaited dom palm on stick handle, the entirety covered with synthetic cloth and sewn with sequins. 23cm square, handle 41cm long.

See below for various hats.

Cosmetics

Black Antimony (*kuḥl*), Bayt al-Faqīh.
Imported

Red Antimony (*ḥusn*), Sūq al-Khamīs.
Imported

Cardamon Seeds (*hayl*), Bājil.

Costumes

Dress (*qamīṣ*), Bayt al-Faqīh.
Black muslin with silver-thread appliqué, tailored waist and sleeves, 120cm long, 41cm waist, 45cm sleeve length, 52cm hem width, 23cm collar.

Dress (*durrī?*), Bājil.
Black muslin with silver-thread appliqué, poncho shape. Two examples. 101cm long, 86cm wide at hem, 21cm wide under the arms.

Dress (*qamīṣ*), Bājil.
Synthetic black with glitter-thread appliqué, poncho shape. 108cm long, 94cm wide.

Dress (*qamīṣ*), Sūq al-Khamīs.
Synthetic red and glitter cloth, tailored waist, short sleeves, girl's size. 83cm long, 28cm waist, 50cm at hem, 13cm sleeves.

Dress (*qamīṣ*), Sūq al-Khamīs.
Sheer muslin, red, poncho shape. 120cm long, 76cm wide.

Dress (*qamīṣ*), Sūq al-Khamīs.
Sheer muslin, black with embroidered trim at neck, red lining, poncho shape. 122cm long, 81cm wide.

Dress (*qamīṣ*), Sūq al-Khamīs.
Synthetic, black gauze with red lining, poncho shape. 120cm long, 80cm wide.

Skirt, Bājil.
Synthetic, patterned, gathered on wide waist band. 97cm long, 36cm wide at waist, 66cm wide at hem.

Blouse (*ṣudayrīyah*, pronounced *sidayrīyah*), Bājil.
Synthetic, patterned, wide collar and deep open throat, short sleeves, bolero shape. 29cm long, 40cm waist, 21cm sleeves.

Jacket, female, Bājil.
Muslin, black with red lining, golden-thread appliqué, short sleeves, high collar, knee-length coat. Two examples. 92cm long, 44cm wide, 13cm long sleeves.

Headscarf (*maqramah*) female, Sūq al-Khamīs.
Muslin, black with red panels and paisley pattern from discharge dyeing. Made in Hodeida. 220cm long, 100cm wide.

Headscarf, female, Bājil.
Synthetic gauze, multicoloured. Imported. Two examples 68cm square.

Jewellery

Bracelets (*malāquf*), Sūq al-Khamīs.
Hollow silver-alloy, chased bands joined with Saudi Arabian coin. One pair. 7cm across, 1.5cm thick.

Hats

Hat, male (*kūfīyah*), Bājil.
Twined (?) vegetable fibre, natural with ochre trim at crown and rim, brimless, fez-shaped. Made in Aslam. 17cm tall, 17cm wide at base, 8cm wide at top.

Hat, female (*qubbah*), Bayt al-Faqīh.
Plaited dom palm, natural, narrow brim, bee-hive shaped crown. 13cm tall, 29cm wide at base, 5cm wide at top, 6cm wide brim.

Hat, male (*qubbah*), Bayt al-Faqīh.
Plaited dom palm, natural, conical with narrow brim. 22cm tall, 28.5cm wide at base, 6.5cm wide brim.

Hat, male and female (*shimālīyah, ẓullah*), al-Rāfi'ī.
Plaited dom palm, natural, tall chimney-top shape with broad brim, and handle in brim to hanging. 18cm tall, 38.5cm wide at base, 9cm wide at top, 11cm wide brim.

Pottery

Water Jar (*qārūrah*), Bayt al-Faqīh.
Terracotta, painted in gold, red, white and black geometric designs, long neck, two handles joined to body.

Cup, Ṣan'ā'.
Terracotta, yellow-green glaze, teacup size, handle. Made in Ḥays. 6cm high, 6.5cm diameter at rim, 4cm at toe.

Incensor (*mabkharah*), Bayt al-Faqīh.
Terracotta, painted with white, red and black geometric designs, bowl on small pedestal, arched superstructure over bowl of 4 arches joined by circlet at top for hanging. 20cm high, 10cm wide.

Textiles

Multi-purpose, male (*liḥāf*), Khalīfah.
Woven cotton, multicoloured with lengthwise strips, burgundy, gold, black and silver, borderless with tassled end strands. Made in al-Durayhimī. 200cm long, 150cm wide.

Bolt of Indigo cloth, Zabīd.
Cotton dyed with aniline and stamped with the mark of the dyer. Cloth made in Ṣan'ā', dyed in Zabīd. 300cm long, 80cm wide.

Miscellaneous

Pellet drum (*qulqulah*), al-Sukhnah.
Skin stretched on wood with wooden handle, beads on leather straps tied to either side of drum face, string loop on handle. 11cm in diameter, 6cm thick, 15cm long handle. (See Bakewell, p. 106 and figure 7.3).

Sickle (*miḥrāth*), al-Suwayq.
Iron piece comprising blade and handle. 31cm long. (The use of *miḥrāth* to mean sickle is unusual. Plough is its normal translation.)

Donkey Bit, al-Suwayq.
Iron bit, cross piece, cheek bars and rings. 23cm long, 12cm wide.

Door, al-Luḥayyah.
Carved wooden cupboard door, floral and tongue motif. 54.5cm high, 21cm wide.

APPENDIX III

A partial list of weekly markets, compiled during our fieldwork.

Sunday
Al-Ḥaddah Raqub, al-Ẓāhir (al-Luḥayyah's closest weekly *sūq*), 'Abs

Monday
Madan, al-Marāwi'ah, al-Ḍaḥī

Tuesday
Al-Jarrāḥī, al-Rāfi'ī (Wādī Mawr), al-Zaydīyah

Wednesday
Al-Manṣūrīyah, al-Tuḥaytā, Bājil (primary)

Thursday
Al-Turaybah, Sūq al-Khamīs, Khalīfah, al-Qanāwiṣ, Mawza'

Friday
Bayt al-Faqīh

Saturday
Al-Suwayq, Bājil (secondary), al-Sukhnah, Sabt al-Maḥrab, al-Mighlāf, al-Zuhrah

BIBLIOGRAPHIES

BASKETRY

Bibliography

Niebuhr, Carsten, *Description de l'Arabie*, Amsterdam, 1774.

———————, *Travels Through Arabia and Other Countries in the East*, 2 Vols., Edinburgh, 1792, repr. Beirut, 1965.

———————, *Voyage en Arabie & en d'autres pays circonvoisins*, 2 Vols., Amsterdam, 1774-1780.

Mitchell, B., H. Escher and M. Mundy, *A Baseline Socio-Economic Survey of the Wadi Mawr Region, Yemen Arab Republic Feeder Road Study*, The World Bank, Washington, D.C., May 1978.

Thesiger, W., "A Journey Through the Tihama, the 'Asir and the Hijaz Mountains," *Geographical Journal*, London, Vol. 110, 1947, pp. 188-200.

Further reading

Ingrams, Doreen, *A Survey of Social and Economic Conditions in the Aden Protectorate*, Eritrea (?), 1949.

Topham, John et al., *Traditional Crafts of Saudi Arabia*, London, 1981.

Further reference

Examples of Tihāmah basketry can be found in the following collections:
Musée de l'Homme, Paris.
Museum of Natural History, New York.
National Museum, Ṣan'ā'.
Tihāmah Expedition, London. (See Appendix II)
(University Museum, Cambridge University, Cambridge. The collections of South Arabian artifacts, while from the Aden Protectorate, offer useful comparisons. Those acquired and/or catalogued by R.B. Serjeant are superbly documented.)

POTTERY

Bibliography

Niebuhr, Carsten, *Description de l'Arabie*, Amsterdam, 1774.

———————, *Travels Through Arabia*, Edinburgh, 1792.

———————, *Voyage en Arabie*, Amsterdam 1774-1780.

Weir, Shelagh, "Some Observations on Pottery and Weaving in the Yemen Arab Republic," *Proceedings of the Seminar for Arabian Studies*, Vol. 5, 1975, pp. 65-69.

Further reading

Champault, Dominique, "Notes sur certains aspects de la céramique au Nord Yémen," *Objets et Mondes*, Paris, Summer 1974.

Ingrams, Doreen, *A Survey of the Social and Economic Conditions of the Aden Protectorate,* Eritrea (?), 1949.

Dostal, Walter, "Analysis of the Ṣan'ā' Market Today," *Ṣan'ā' an Arabian Islamic City*, eds. R.B. Serjeant and R. Lewcock, London, 1982, pp. 272-273.

Further reference

Examples of Tihāmah pottery can be found in the following collections:

Dr. Mark Littlewood, Gillingham, Kent. (A private collection)

Musée de l'Homme, Paris.

Museum of Mankind, British Museum, London.

Museum of Natural History, New York.

National Museum, Ṣan'ā'.

Tihāmah Expedition. (See Appendix II)

(University Museum, Cambridge University. See Basketry, Further reference.)

TEXTILES

Bibliography

Baldry, John, "Textiles in Yemen: Historical references of trade and commerce in textiles in Yemen from antiquity to modern times," *British Museum Occasional Paper No 27*, London, 1982.

Bent, James Theodore and Mabel Virginia Anna Bent, *Southern Arabia*, London, 1900.

Grohmann, Adolf, *Südarabien als Wirtschaftsgebiet*, Brünn, 1930.

Hunter, F.M., *An Account of the British Settlement of Aden Arabia*, London, 1877.

Manzoni, Renzo, *El Yemen*, Rome, 1884.

Al-Maqdisī, Shams al-Dīn, *Kitāb Ahṣan al-Taqāsīm fī Ma'rifat al-Aqālīm, Bibliotheca Geographorum Arabicorum*, ed. M.J. de Goeje, III, Leiden, 1906.

Middle East and North Africa 1982-3, 29th Edition, London, 1982.

Niebuhr, Carsten, *Description de l'Arabie,* Amsterdam, 1774.

____________, *Travels Through Arabia*, Edinburgh, 1792.

____________, *Voyage en Arabie*, Amsterdam 1774-1780.

Weir, Shelagh, "Some Observations on Pottery and Weaving in the Yemen Arab Republic", *Proceedings of the Seminar for Arabian Studies*, vol. 5., 1975, pp. 65-69.

Further reading

Ingrams, Doreen, *A Survey of the Social and Economic Conditions of the Aden Protectorate*, Eritrea (?), 1949.

Serjeant, R.B., *Islamic Textiles, Material for a History up to the Mongol Conquest*, Beirut, 1972.

____________, *Studies in Arabian History and Civilisation*, London, 1981.

Ṣan'ā' an Arabian Islamic City, ed. R.B. Serjeant and R. Lewcock, London, 1982.

Further reference

Examples of Tihāmah textiles can be found in the following collections:

Musée de l'Homme, Paris.

Museum of Mankind, British Museum, London.

Museum of Natural History, New York.

National Museum, Ṣan'ā'.

Tihāmah Expedition. (See Appendix II)

(University Museum, Cambridge University, Cambridge. See Basketry, Further reference)

COSMETICS

Bibliography

Ingrams, Doreen, *A Survey of Social and Economic Conditions in the Aden Protectorate*, Eritrea (?), 1949.

Grohmann, Adolf, *Südarabien als Wirtschaftsgebiet*, Brünn, 1930.

Niebuhr, Carsten, *Description de l'Arabie,* Amsterdam, 1774.

____________, *Travels Through Arabia*, Edinburgh, 1792.

____________, *Voyage en Arabie*, Vol. I, Amsterdam, 1774-1780.

Ṣan'ā' an Arabian Islamic City, ed. R.B. Serjeant and R. Lewcock, London, 1982.

Thesiger, W., "A Journey Through the Tihama, the 'Asir and the Hijaz Mountains," *Geographical Journal*, London, Vol. 110, 1947, pp. 188-200.

COSTUMES

Bibliography

Niebuhr, Carsten, *Description de l'Arabie,* Amsterdam, 1774.

____________, *Travels Through Arabia*, Edinburgh, 1792.

____________, *Voyage en Arabie*, Vol. I, Amsterdam, 1774-1780.

Thesiger, W., "A Journey Through the Tihama, the 'Asir and the Hijaz Mountains," *Geographical Journal*, London, Vol. 110, 1947, pp. 188-200.

Topham, John et al., *Traditional Crafts of Saudi Arabia*, London, 1981.

Further reference

Examples of Tihāmah costumes can be found in the following collections:

Tim Francis, Brook Green, London. (A private collection of jewellery)

Musée de l'Homme, Paris.

Museum of Mankind, British Museum, London.

National Museum, Ṣan'ā'.

Tihāmah Expedition. (See Appendix II)

(University Museum, Cambridge University, Cambridge. See Basketry, Further reference)

CIRCUMCISION

Bibliography

Bury, G. Wyman, *Arabia Infelix*, London, 1915.

Ingrams, Doreen, *A Survey of Social and Economic Conditions in the Aden Protectorate*, Eritrea (?), 1949.

Myntti, Cynthia, *Women and Development in Yemen Arab Republic*, Eschborn, 1979.

Saint-Hilaire, Alain, *Je Reviens du Yémen et T'en Rapporte des Nouvelles Vraies*, Paris, 1975.

Further reading

Fayein, Claudie, *Une Française Médecin au Yémen*, Paris, 1955.

Jargy, Simon and Alain Saint-Hilaire, *Yémen avec les Montagnards de la Mer Rouge*, Paris, 1982 (?).

Thesiger, W., "A Journey Through the Tihama, the 'Asir and the Hijaz Mountains," *Geographical Journal*, Vol. 110, 1947, pp. 188-200.

HEALING

Bibliography

Grohmann, Adolf, *Südarabien als Wirtschaftsgebiet*, Brünn, 1930.

Myers, Oliver H., "Little Aden Folklore", *Bulletin de l'Institut Français d'Archéologie Orientale*, Cairo, Vol. XLIV, 1947, pp. 177-233.

Myntti, Cynthia, "Changing Attitudes Toward Health: Some Observations from the Hugariyya," presented at the *Symposium on Contemporary Yemen*, Centre for Arab Gulf Studies, University of Exeter, 15-18 July, 1983.

——————— with J. Fleurentin, "Medicinal Plants in Yemen: A Preliminary List," (unpublished).

———————, "Women in Rural Yemen," *USAID*, Ṣan'ā', November 1978 (mimeo).

Niebuhr, Carsten, *Description de l'Arabie*, Amsterdam, 1774.

———————, *Travels Through Arabia*, Edinburgh, 1792.

———————, *Voyage en Arabie*, Vol. I, Amsterdam, 1774-1780.

Thomas, Bertram, *Alarms and Excursions in Arabia*, London, 1931.

Further reading

Constantinides, Pamela Maureen, "Sickness and the spirits: a study of the *zaar* spirit possession cult in the northern Sudan," *PhD thesis (LSE)*, University of London, 1972 (unpublished).

Fayein, Dr. Claudie, *Une Française Médecin au Yemen*, Paris, 1955.

Johnstone, P., "Tradition in Arabic Medicine," *Palestine Exploration Quarterly*, London, 1975, pp. 23-37.

Ingrams, Doreen, *A Survey of Social and Economic Conditions in the Aden Protectorate*, Eritrea (?), 1949.

Lewis, I.M., *Ecstatic Religion; an anthropological study of spirit possession and shamanism*, Harmondsworth, 1971.

Naval Intelligence Division, *Western Arabia and the Red Sea*, U.K., 1946.

Schopen, Armin, *Traditionelle Heilmittel in Jemen*, Weisbaden, 1983.

Serjeant, R.B., "Folk Remedies from the Hadhramawt," *Bulletin of the School of Oriental and African Studies*, London 1956.

Stark, Freya, *A Winter in Arabia*, London, 1940.

Trimingham, J.S., *Islam in Ethiopia*, Oxford, 1952.

———————, *Islam in the Sudan*, Oxford, 1949.

Vaughan, James, "Notes Upon the Drugs Observed at Aden, Arabia," *Pharmaceutical Journal and Transactions*, London, Vol. 12, 1852-1853, pp. 226-228, 268-271, 385-388.

LOCAL FOODS

Bibliography

Grohmann, Adolf, *Südarabien als Wirtschaftsgebiet*, Brünn, 1930.

Ingrams, Doreen, *A Survey of Social and Economic Conditions in the Aden Protectorate*, Eritrea (?), 1949.

Niebuhr, Carsten, *Description de l'Arabie*, Amsterdam, 1774.

———————, *Travels Through Arabia*, Edinburgh, 1792.

———————, *Voyage en Arabie*, Vol. I, Amsterdam, 1774-1780.

Ṣan'ā' an Arabian Islamic City, ed. R.B. Serjeant and R. Lewcock, London, 1982.

Further reading

Bornstein, Annika, *Food and Society in the Yemen Arab Republic*, FAO, Rome, 1974.

Bury G. Wyman, *Arabia Infelix*, London, 1915.

Mitchell, B., H. Escher and M. Mundy, *A Baseline Socio-Economic Survey of the Wadi Mawr Region, Yemen Arab Republic Feeder Road Study*, The World Bank, Washington, D.C., May 1978.

SAINTS AND SAINTS' DAYS

Bibliography

Manzoni, Renzo, *El Yemen*, Rome, 1884.

Myers, Oliver H., "Little Aden Folklore," *Bulletin de l'Institut Français d'Archéologie Orientale*, Cairo, Vol. XLIV, 1947, pp. 177-233.

Niebuhr, Carsten, *Description de l'Arabie*, Amsterdam, 1774.

———————, *Travels Through Arabia*, Edinburgh, 1792.

———————, *Voyage en Arabie*, Amsterdam, 1774-1780.

Serjeant, R.B., "Hūd and Other Pre-Islamic Prophets of Hadramawt," *Studies in Arabian History and Civilisation*, London, 1981.

Al-'Uqaylī, Muḥammad ibn Aḥmad 'Isā, *Al-Taṣawwuf fī Tihāmah*, ?, 1964.

Further reading

Al-Ḥabshī, 'Abdullāh Muḥammad, *Al-Ṣūfiyyah wa'l-Fuqahā' fī'l-Yaman*, Ṣan'ā', 1976.

Hunter, Capt. F.M., *An Account of the British Settlement of Aden in Arabia*, London, 1977.

Lewis, I.M., *Ecstatic Religion; an anthropological study of spirit possession and shamanism*, Harmondsworth, 1971.

Rihani, Ameen, *Around the Coasts of Arabia*, London, 1930.

Smith, W. Robertson, *The Religion of the Semites*, London, 1914.

Wastermarck, E., *Pagan Survivals in Mohammaden Civilisation*, London, 1933.

Further reference

The *faqīh* of Ibn 'Abbās, Muḥammad Aḥmad Suwayd

The *faqīh* of al-Ḍaḥī, 'Umar Ya'anī.

WEEKLY MARKETS

Bibliography

Escher, Hermann, A., *Wirtschafts und sozialgeographische Untersuchungen in der Wādī Mawr Region (Arabische Republik Jemen)*, Wiesbaden, 1976.

Mitchell, B., H. Escher and M. Mundy, *A Baseline Socio-Economic Survey of the Wadi Mawr Region, Yemen Arab Republic Feeder Road Study*, The World Bank, Washington, D.C., May 1978.
Ṣan'ā' an Arabian Islamic City, ed. R.B. Serjeant and R. Lewcock, London, 1982.
Schweitzer, Dr. Günter, "Social and Economic Change of the Rural Distribution System: Weekly Markets in the Yemen Arab Republic (Abstract)," presented at the *Symposium on Contemporary Yemen*, Centre for Arab Gulf Studies, University of Exeter, 15-18 July, 1983.
Steffen, Hans, *Final Report – on the Airphoto Interpretation Project of the Swiss Technical Co-operation Service, Berne, carried out for the CPO, San'ā'. The Major Findings of the Population and Housing Census of February 1975 and the Results of Supplementary Demographic and Cartographic Surveys done in the districts of Turbah, Jabal 'Iyal Yazid, Al-Luḥayyah and in the Mashriq of Yemen*, Zurich, 1977.

BEE KEEPING

Bibliography

Grohmann, Adolf, *Südarabien als Wirtschaftsgebiet*, Brünn, 1930.
Al-Hamdānī, al-Ḥasan ibn Aḥmad, *Ṣifat Jazīrat al-'Arab*, ed. D.H. Müller, Leiden, 1884-1891.
Ingrams, Doreen, *A Survey of Social and Economic Conditions in the Aden Protectorate*, Eritrea (?), 1949.

Further reading

Ingrams, W.H., "A Report of the Social, Economic, and Political Conditions of the Hadhramaut," *Colonial*, No. 123, pp. 52-54.
Naval Intelligence Division, *Western Arabia and the Red Sea*, U.K., 1946.

BOAT MAKING AND FISHING

Bibliography

Bowen, Richard LeBaron, "Primitive Watercraft of Arabia," *American Neptune*, Vol. 12, 1952, pp. 186-221.
Ingrams, Doreen, *A Survey of Social and Economic Conditions in the Aden Protectorate*, Eritrea (?), 1949.
Kindermann, Hans, *'Schiff' im Arabischen*, Zwickau, 1934.
Miles, S.B., *The Countries and Tribes of the Persian Gulf*, London, 1919.
Moore, Alan, *Last Days of Mast and Sail*, Oxford, 1925.
Percival-Kaye, G., "The Red Sea Slave Trade," *The Anti-Slavery Reporter*, Vol. 10, Series VI (1955), pp. 49-52.
Rouaud, Alain, *Les Yemen et Leurs Populations*, Brussels, 1979.
Serjeant, R.B., *The Portuguese off the south Arabian coast*, Oxford, 1963, repr. Beirut, 1974.
__________, "Fisher-folk and fish-traps in al-Bahrain," *Bulletin of the School of Oriental and African Studies*, XXXI, London, 1968.
__________, "Sailing the Indian Ocean," *Gazelle Review*, Vol. 4, London, 1978, p. 6.
UNDP/FAO Fisheries Development Project: YEM/74/003, *Newsletter and Information Paper* (mimeo), Vol. 1, #7, Oct 1975; Vol. 1, #8, Nov 1975; Vol. 1, #9, Dec 1975; Vol. 2, #2, Feb 1976; Vol. 2, #3, Mar 1976; Vol. 2, #4, Apr 1976; Vol. 2, #5, May 1976.

BRICK MAKING

Bibliography

Chelhod, J., "Introduction à l'histoire sociale et urbaine de Zabīd," *Arabica*, 25, i, Leiden, 1978.
Niebuhr, Carsten, *Description de l'Arabie,* Amsterdam, 1774.
__________, *Travels Through Arabia*, Edinburgh, 1792.
__________, *Voyage en Arabie*, Amsterdam, 1774-1780.
Ṣan'ā' an Arabian Islamic City, ed. R.B. Serjeant and R. Lewcock, London, 1982.
Varanda, Fernando, *Art of Building in Yemen*, London, 1981.

MODERN INDUSTRIES

Bibliography

Europa Publications Ltd, *Middle East and North Africa 1982-3*, London, 1982.

PEARL DIVING

Bibliography

Monfried, Henri de, "Red Sea Pearl Fishing," *National Geographic Magazine*, Vol. 72 (1937), pp. 597-626 (with photographs).
Grohmann, Adolf, *Südarabien als Wirtschaftsgebiet*, Brünn, 1930.
Pliny, the Elder, *Natural History*, XII, 18.

Further reading

Ritter, Carl, *Vergleichende Erdkunde von Arabien*, Berlin, 1846-47.
Villiers, Alan, *Sons of Sinbad*, London 1940.

SALT PRODUCTION

Bibliography

Bury, G.W., *Arabia Infelix*, London, 1915.
Grohmann, Adolf, *Südarabien als Wirtschaftsgebiet*, Brünn, 1930.
Al-Hamdānī, al-Ḥasan ibn Aḥmad, *Ṣifat Jazīrat al-'Arab*, ed. D.H. Müller, Leiden, 1884-91.
Macro, Eric, "The Topography of Mocha," *Proceedings of the Seminar for Arabian Studies*, Vol. 10, 1980, pp. 55-66.
Niebuhr, Carsten, *Description de l'Arabie*, Amsterdam, 1774.
__________, *Travels Through Arabia*, Edinburgh, 1792.
__________, *Voyage en Arabie*, Amsterdam, 1774-1780.
Al-Washalī, Ismā'īl ibn Muḥammad, *Dhayl Nashr al-Thanā' al-Ḥasan*, ed. M. al-Shu'aybī, Ṣan'ā', 1982.
Al-Waysī, Ḥusayn, *Al-Yaman al-Kubrā*, Cairo, 1962.

Further reading

Glaser, E., *Skizze der Geschichte*, Vol. II, Berlin, 1890.

Ingrams, Doreen, *A Survey of Social Conditions in the Aden Protectorate*, Eritrea (?), 1949.

Ritter, Carl, *Vergleichende Erdkunde von Arabien*, Berlin, 1846-47.

SŪQ INDUSTRIES OF ZABĪD

Bibliography

Grohmann, Adolf, *Südarabien als Wirtschaftsgebiet*, Brünn, 1930.

Mitchell, B., H. Escher and M. Mundy, *A Baseline Socio-Economic Survey of the Wadi Mawr Region, Yemen Arab Republic Feeder Road Study*, The World Bank, Washington, D.C., May 1978.

Further reading

Ingrams, Doreen, *A Survey of Social and Economic Conditions in the Aden Protectorate*, Eritrea (?), 1949.

ILLUSTRATIONS

Plate 8.1 Bream, 175 × 125mm, pencil; *Plate 8.2* Brockie, 380 × 280mm, watercolour, courtesy of Rothmans of Pall Mall (Overseas) Ltd; *Plate 8.3* Bream, 380 × 255mm, charcoal; *Plate 8.4* Bream, 380 × 255mm, charcoal (study for etching); *Plate 8.5* Bream, 255 × 125mm, pencil (study for etching), courtesy of John Shipman; *Plate 8.6* Brockie, 280 × 380mm, watercolour; *Plate 8.7* Brockie, 265 × 370mm, watercolour, courtesy of George and Jill Kassis; *Plate 8.8* Nankivell, 530 × 405mm, pencil drawing; *Plate 8.9* Brockie, 305 × 280mm, ink, courtesy of Abdul Rahman Shukri; *Figures 8.1-8.3* Yamini Patel; *Figure 8.4* Ehrlich; *Figures 8.5-8.6* Ehrlich.

GLOSSARY

Notes on pronunciations that are given within the text of this paper may not apply outside the context and the locality where they were collected.

'āmah	a raft
'anbarī	perfumed, essence of perfume
'aqāl	headband
'ārif	person who performs the *zār* ceremony (Aden), knower
arj	a wood (ZIZYPHUS SPINA-CHIRSTI), also known as *'ilb* and *sidr*
aṣab	a northern Tihāmah hat, possibly *'aṣab*
'asal	honey
bājīyah	a roll made of black millet
bakhūr	incense, see *mabkharah*
barakah	blessing
bāsh	fruit of the dom palm tree (HYPHAENE spp., see Plate 2.1)
bayt	house
bayraq	a ritual pole (Aden)
bisham	balsam (COMMIPHORA GILEADENSIS)
buddā'	lunch, lunch time, var. of *ghadā'*?
chalabīyah	a raft
dajurrah	a bread, millet possibly with cowpea
dīwān	reception room, collection of poems
duktūr baladī	local healer
duqduqah	a tobacco additive, identity unknown, see *karah*
durrī	a Bājil dress
faqīh	village historian, learned person
fatūt	bread pudding
fidāmah	muzzle
fūl	broad beans
fūṭah	a sarong-like cloth
ghawwāṣ	diver
ḥabashī	Ethiopian
ḥākim	a judge
ḥalāfī	a grass (DESMOSTACHYA BIPINNATA)
ḥām	ashes, lava
ḥaml	load
ḥanīdh	smoked meat or fish
ḥārah	quarter, section of a town
ḥaysī	pottery, from Ḥays
ḥawak	weaver
hayl	cardamom (ELETTARIA CARDAMOMUM)
ḥibil	waterpipe hose, rope
hidmah	a large grass mat
ḥinnā	henna (LAWSONIA INERMIS)
ḥumar	a wood (possibly TAMARINDUS INDICA)
ḥumar	pitch
hūrī	a boat
hurud	turmeric (CURCUMA LONGA)
ḥusn	a crimson streak, beautification
ḥūt	fish
ibn 'alwān	follower of the Yifrus saint, an ecstatic
ikāwah	Zarānīq headband
ism	exorcism ceremony (Aden), name
jabal	mountain, hill
jaḥlah	a clay waterpipe jar
jambīyah	a dagger
jirāk	a sweetened tobacco
juljulān	sesame (SESAMUM INDICUM)
jumbarī	shrimp
karah	a tobacco additive, possibly potash, see *duqduqah*
khabt	desert zone
khashab	wood
khayzarān	cane, bamboo
khiḍāb	painted body decoration

khidr	tent(s)
khitān	circumcision
kidf	shoulder, hill
ku'adah	a water jar
kūfīyah	a fez-shaped hat, skull cap
kuḥl	kohl, black antimony
kūz	a water jar
laḥūḥ	griddle cake, see *malaḥḥah*
liḥāf	a multi-purpose cloth
lubān dhakar	an incense, olibanum (BOSWELLIA CARTERIA)
mabkharah	incensor, see *bakhūr*
mafrashah	bedspread
madā'ah	waterpipe
madaqqah	mallet
majarrah	a boat pole
majdhūb	possessed, ecstatic (also *jadhab*)
maḥmal	canopy
makhāḍirah	migrant harvester(s)
malaḥḥah	a clay griddle, see *laḥūḥ*
malāquf	bracelets
malṭūṭ	a sweetened tobacco
mankhul	a grain sieve
manṣab, manṣabah (f)	a title denoting a sufi *shaykh* possessing certain authority
maqramah	a headscarf
marji' rūḥī	one with spiritual authority
marwā'ī	a local healer, from al-Marāwi'ah
ma'ṣarah	(sesame) press, see *'uṣarah*
mashabbak	a grid-shaped sweet, see *shabakah*
maṣnaf	a shoulder cloth
mawfā	oven
mazar	person who performs the *zār* ceremony (Aden)
miḥrāth	a sickle, plough (a far more common meaning)
milḥ	salt
miraysī	sugar
mīsam	cautery
mismār	nail
muḥāwakah	loom, see *ḥawak*
munāṣif	a stage of ripeness of dates
muraymirā'	a plant, great celandine, see *sakarah*
murr	an incense, myrrh
muṣrafah	an eating mat
muzawwir	a local healer, exorcist, the patient of an exorcist (Aden)
nakhal	an eating mat, palm tree
nīl	indigo
nisha'	flour paste, starch
qadūm	adze
qafaṣ	poultry cage
qalīyah	a fried or toasted grain
qamīṣ	long shirt (m), dress (f)
qārūrah	water jar
qaṣab	cane stalk, see *qaṣabah*
qaṣabah	waterpipe, (waterpipe) stem, see *qaṣab*
qaṭārah	a date sugar
qāt	a narcotic leaf (CATHA EDULIS)
qawqa'	a plant, caucanthus
qillah	a water jar
qishr	husk, shell
quba'	a ritual object (Tarīm)
qubbah	a hat of the central Tihāmah
qubqab	shrimp
qulqulah	pellet drum
qumah	a word associated with salt quarries
qunza'ah	tuft of hair left on a tonsured boy's head (Aden)
qura'	breakfast, breakfast time
qurtum	a plant, safflower (CORTHAMNUS TINCTORIUS), safflower dye
radād	a hand shield (Zarānīq)
ra'īs	leader
ramād	ash
ramath	raft
rayb	buttermilk, curds
rūtī	a white bakery bread
sabkhah	salt marsh
saf	palm leaf (Aden)
sakarah	a plant, greater celandine, see *muraymirā'*
salam	an incense, gum arabic (ACACIA EHRENBERGERIANA or A. ARABICA)
sanbūq	a boat
sarw	a tree, evergreen cypress (CUPRESSUS SEMPERVIRENS)
sawl	a wood (ACACIA NILOTICA spp. INDICA)
sayyid	title denoting a member of the highest social class, see *sīd*
shabakah	net, see *mashabbak*
shaḥm	grease
shammah	a snuff
sharīfah (f)	title denoting spiritual leadership
shāshah	a raft
shaykh, shaykhah (f)	title denoting tribal or spiritual leadership
shimālīyah	a hat of the northern Tihāmah, something northern
sīd	lord, see *sayyid*
simsim	sesame (SESAMUM INDICUM)
sirū	a ritual pole (*ziyārah* of Walī al-Shamsī)
ṣudaf	sea-shell
ṣudaf ḥaqq al-lu'lu'	pearl-bearing shell
ṣudayrīyah	blouse
sūq	market
ṭabaqah	a basket, platter
ṭāfī	palm frond (possibly a cognate of *ṭufyah*)
ṭāḥūn	mortar, mill
ṭāqīyah	a skull cap
tanakah	vegetable oil tin
tannūr	oven
ṭāwah	a metal griddle
thawb	dress (f)
ṭīn	clay
ṭūb	a brick
ṭūf	a raft
ṭufyah	a tree, theban palm, see *ṭāfī*
ṭūl	length (of rope)
'ūd	wood
'ūd qust	a wood, costus
'uṣarah	grounds, see *ma'ṣarah*
walī	saint
wādī	seasonal river bed
wasm	cautery scar
wazīf	dried sprats or sardines
zanbīl	basket
zār	an exorcism ceremony, the person who performs the ceremony (Aden), see *mazar*
zarr	plait of hair
zayt	oil
zinjīl	a wood, identity unknown
ziyārah	ritual visit to a saint's tomb, visitation
ẓullah	hat, that which gives shade

EXPEDITION

INTRODUCTION

The activities of the Tihāmah Expedition included certain work, both of a research and an artistic nature, which has been largely untried, in recent times at least, on the Tihāmah. Where the archaeological, architectural and ethnographical surveys did not require techniques specific to the Tihāmah, the work which pertained to the music, the wildlife and the artistic documentation broke fresh ground, so to speak. The persons engaged in these disciplines had to suit their methods to the circumstances and conditions they found on the Tihāmah. Therefore the procedures they used represent acquired experience which might prove valuable to others, amateurs or professionals, wishing to pursue similar work. In the hopes that they may be of use, the field techniques of the Naturalist, the Music Recordist and the three Artists are described below.

For those who have a further interest in the technical aspects of the Expedition, there is housed at the Royal Geographical Society, London, a 24-page "Tihāmah Expedition Report". In it are summarised the aims, financing, administration and field logistics of the Expedition. Details are given pertaining to catering, equipment, transport, guides, fuel, weather, weapons, water, medical kit, personal kits, money exchange, contacts, maps and diplomatic clearances. The "Tihāmah Expedition Report" is available to fellows and non-fellows alike by application to the Map Room, Royal Geographical Society, 1 Kensington Gore, London SW7 2AR. [Ed.]

9.1: NATURALIST'S REPORT

Keith Brockie

For observation of the wildlife I used an Optolyth 30×75 telescope and a Leitz Tinivoid 10×40B binoculars. A blow-lens brush was essential to keep the lenses dust-free and sand-free without scratching the lens.

I used fine Japanese mist nets for catching the birds, two 12.2m × 2.7m and one 18.3m × 1.5m. These were strung between lightweight, aluminium sectional poles. One of the bats I caught by mist net, one in a butterfly net and the others by hand in their daytime, minaret roosts. These were put down with a rag soaked in chloroform. The rodents collected were caught in break-back traps baited with jam or peanut butter. Both the bats and the rodents were soaked in a jar full of a 10% solution of formaldehyde before being stored in plastic bags with cotton wool soaked in the solution and the bags labelled. The specimens were made up into study skins upon our return to Britain.

For general night use and for dazzling birds such as the Nubian Nightjar, I used an Ever-ready, power beam, 6 volt torch. This had a kryptonite bulb to intensify and concentrate the beam. The plastic construction and screw-on, metal battery make it a very robust torch, able to withstand much ill treatment.

Butterflies were collected using a standard lightweight butterfly net with detachable handle and collapsable net for ease of packing. The specimens, once gassed in a wide-mouthed jar fitted with a cork top and false bottom impregnated with chloroform, were transferred to triangle envelopes, labelled and stored in a cotton-padded carton. Care had to be taken to keep the carton free from ants which eat the butterfly carcasses. Moths were collected, already dead, from around the camping lamps and stove each morning, and stored in the same way as the butterflies. [Ed.]

9.2: MUSIC RECORDIST'S REPORT

Anderson Bakewell

For music recording I chose the Uher 4200 Report Monitor stereo tape recorder, a lightweight and relatively inexpensive machine. With it I used AKG 224E microphones and 5″ BASF LP 35 recording tape. Accessories such as nickel cadmium battery, headphones, leads, cables and a telescopic camera tripod converted to hold microphones were packed into a single canvas camera bag.

Whether the process of field recording was a welcome diversion or a burdensome interruption of the lives of the musicians on the Tihāmah depended very much on the amount of time spent with them beforehand. An intimate and convivial atmosphere nearly always produced the best quality music. Fees were, of course, agreed upon before recording, and were normally commensurate with the musician's professional entertaining fees for a corresponding amount of time.

I generally found it preferable, in terms of sound quality and comfort, to record in the open air. Private compounds, where the mud walls act as a partial barrier to the sand and wind, were ideal. Wind baffles on the microphones were needed in any case. The recording event, wherever it occurred, inevitably attracted attention, and curious and often noisy crowds were almost unavoidable. On one memorable occasion in Wādī Mawr, I evacuated musicians from an overly agitated village scene and resettled them under an acacia tree in the desert about 5km distant. But the villagers found our tracks and within minutes were descending upon us by every conceivable means of transport, from camels to donkeys and Toyotas. Only the action of the local *shaykh*, who took it upon himself to fire warning gunshots, turned back the horde.

Recording indoors presented a different set of problems. Settings varied greatly, and thatched huts, mud forts and cement bunkers all served. In acoustically "live" rooms, I found it particularly useful to hang long bolts of cloth (carried expressly for the purpose) from the walls to absorb the excessive "ring". When recording at night in huts not provided with electricity, the hissing of pressure lamps was an intolerable distraction, and candles were carried as an alternative.

Careful storage of tapes is particularly important in the hot and humid conditions on the Tihāmah. I placed all tapes, once recorded, in a series of plastic bags containing muslin sacks of silica gel to absorb moisture. These were then transferred as often as logistically possible to our air-cooled depot point in Hodeida.

9.3: ARTIST'S REPORT

Antony Bream

The original intention of this trip was to make studies and sketches of a topographical nature, landscapes and people, to amplify the work of the other artists on the trip. The stylistic basis for myself was very much in the British 19th-century School ranging from Roberts and Lear and Leighton to Seago via Brangwyn and Arthur Melville. The format was to be small; particularly colour work, and to be supported by larger drawings – black and white. Due to my passion for Frank Brangwyn and Melville I was anxious to prepare some work that would be adaptable in both the direct visual sense, i.e. "plein air", and drawings having a potential for graphic illustration.

Having worked in similar climatic conditions and terrain in Morocco, Italy and Spain, I have long established that which I consider a satisfactory working procedure. The difference on this trip was the availability of transport. In the last few years I have pursued the "preferable" mode of foot, bus and train. (This allows, as the Indian bearers put it, time for your soul to catch up with you.)

On this trip I decided to take my oil paints and panels as an auxiliary. Due to storage problems of wet pictures and dust and time factors these were abandoned and I returned to my original plan of making watercolours.

My equipment consists of:

one ½ imperial portfolio
one aluminium camp stool
one canvas back-pack, containing:
one ¼ imperial portfolio
one 25.5cm×20.5cm×6.5cm cigar box for brushes/pencils
one water jar
charcoal and fixative

Notes on materials are as follows:

My basic kit, which enables me to walk hands free for as long as possible, is restricted which is essential if one is to be free from exhaustion. There is often a tendency when working in the field to draw or paint a subject discovered at a time when one is tired. This is unsatisfactory – and to be avoided! My drawing materials are drawn from my large portfolio and main baggage containing extra pencils and watercolours. My ¼ imperial portfolio has heavy paper clips on it, four in all – kept rather in a book fashion.

I use three main types of paper:

Firstly – white watercolour – the best! Preferably made by Barcham Green England, handmade in one of last mills left over from the 19th century – Hayle Mill, Maidstone, Kent. Ninety pounds is satisfactory and doesn't need to be stretched. Effectively I use the strong paper clips for this. Continental paper or mould-made would have to be one hundred and forty pounds. My paper is cut with a knife to ¼ and ⅛ imperial and put in the (book) portfolio. R.W.S. Barcham Green is handmade and flexible – not too hard sized. This is used for pure watercolour work and the scale would be reminiscent of Turner – many would be sketch book size about 25.4cm × 17.78cm.

Secondly I use a toned paper – a difficulty outside of England. Preferably "Turner Grey" by Barcham Green which is handmade about one hundred and forty pounds on good grey or brown mould-made cover paper or cartridge. Roberts drawings of the Holy Land were made on a beautiful toned cartridge paper made from best rags – buff or blue grey – ideal for a mixed technique.

This is very suitable for the strong light condition of the Orient, the opaque light conveyable by gouache rendered with zinc white.

Thirdly a paper of a cheaper nature often Sugar paper – grey or brown which can be used for pencil or charcoal sketching – perhaps heightened with body colours.

The object of the papers is this:

First a pure watercolour drawing designed perhaps as an object in its own right.

Secondly a concept of making a drawing on toned paper – perhaps in pencil (graphite) or charcoal pencil – or charcoal (subsequently fixed) and depending on time, to elaborate with watercolours and body colour – very much the process favoured by Roberts and Brangwyn.

Thirdly uncoloured drawings made on the cheaper paper might well be useful to make etchings from. I try to make sketches that in fact have a dual purpose or role. One is to establish something of the colour values of my subjects – either in watercolour or body colour. Secondly drawings allied to these which are more concerned with the structure of my subjects. These might not seem at first connected but will support each other and cross fertilize if I decide to make oils – graphics or further watercolours in the studio – which is often my practice.

Paints are as follows:

Watercolours *in tubes* not pans. I prefer the Winsor & Newton Cotman colours – slightly second grade watercolour – which favourably mix with zinc white to make gouache (body colour). I carry in my luggage a larger cigar box filled with half a dozen tubes of each colour that I use. These are: zinc white in pots or tubes, cadmium yellow or lemon yellow, yellow ochre, light red, Indian red (which I like very much), cadmium red or vermillion, ivory black and ultramarine – sometimes viridian, burnt umber and cobalt blue. I try to avoid extraordinary pallettes for outdoor work – this is essentially the same as for oils – which gives me a similar colour reference – very important when changing from one medium to the next! I use a small plastic pallette about 25.5cm long and white – hat tins or pans. The tubes are kept in a small cigar box about 25.5cm×20.5cm and 6.5cm deep – packed with pencils –

all hardnesses, some charcoal, some lead – putty rubber, pencil sharpener and blades. I also carry a box of willow charcoal and fixative – with diffuser.

Working methods are as follows:

I use the aluminium camp stool which is carried in the back-pack. I sit to draw – in extreme cases – in crowds I draw standing up – which in some ways gives you more authority.

I sometimes carry the ½ imperial portfolio and drawing board – (light plywood) to make larger charcoal drawings. I would advise a light easel for watercolours of this scale with perhaps stretched watercolour paper damp on board. Again another headache and best avoided if speed and output are essential. Also weight problems are paramount again when scouting on foot for material.

I do however carry an umbrella or parasol in these climates. I remove the handle and affix it in an aluminium pole. Also a water bottle is pretty well essential. These two articles extend the kit and make the extra conventional portfolio a headache – best avoided!

I generally approach my subject in two ways:

Either as an observer or participant. This is rather difficult to explain to non-artists. Particularly in the Third World as an outsider one arouses so much attention that the scene is affected by your presence and is modified. Better therefore to make headlong for the fray and master the crowd by whatever resources you have. Needless to say misadventure is often the name of the game but can reveal anecdotal material.

Due to an essentially retiring nature I prefer to be an observer and am at pains not to be flushed from cover by jubilant natives until I too have my quarry in the bag!

Reflections on this trip:

Technically my reflections underline only one real failure – not enough gouache paint – that is zinc white. The six or seven-week trip required less watercolour worked than expected and more body work – and I was down to my last pot of white paint by week three – major mistake!! Next time take more jars – even poster paint will do – as this is cheap and due to climatic conditions is a major saving – that is, the paint dries very fast and would make pure zinc white an extravagance.

Perhaps also small bound sketchbooks instead of clip pads are preferable and contain one's subject matter in a coherent form.

The only confusing factor for me was that in working on my own I am essentially a morning person. I usually attempt to get my best work done by noon – travelling if necessary in the afternoon and work in the evening. Due to logistics, this was usually reversed. Most painters rise early and in the atelier tradition work in the studio was structured to end by 11 am. Also in topography, energy is a serious factor and distracted nerves and mind make for uninspired and laboured work.

9.4: ARTIST'S REPORT

Keith Brockie

Plate 9.1 **Keith Brockie**

Part of my work on the expedition during the five weeks fieldwork was to sketch and paint the wildlife, domestic livestock and landscape whenever possible. However, most of my time was taken up with observation and documentation of the wildlife.

To enable me to sketch wildlife from a distance I used an optolyth 30×75 telescope mounted on a fully adjustable tripod. This allowed me to draw with both hands free compared to the constant lifting of binoculars and subsequent loss in time and concentration. 30× magnification proved to be ideal, any larger magnification would have been useless in the constant heat haze conditions. On other occasions I used my Leitz Trinovid 10×40 binoculars as an aid to sketching.

My sketching and painting equipment had to be kept light and compact to enable me to carry it with all my other equipment. I used a variety of pencils, Caran d'Ache coloured pencils, conté pencils, watercolours and gouache. These were used singly or in a variety of combinations. I sketched and painted on a variety of watercolour papers usually tinted with a wash to combat the glare of the sun.

The problems I encountered were manifold. Getting started drawing in a country which was so vastly different from anything I had experienced before was difficult for the first week or so. It takes time, art-wise as well as climate-wise, to get used to the working conditions where everything is so new and exciting, making it difficult to concentrate for long on one subject. The hot climate was a problem; luckily we had a few days to acclimatise in the cooler mountain air of the capital, Ṣan'ā'. To go from the rigours of a Scottish winter where I had been skiing outside my cottage door the day before leaving for the hot arid deserts of the Tihāmah was an experience, to say the least. Shade was essential when sitting and sketching, except on the coastline where there was usually a refreshing onshore breeze blowing. One of the most useful items I acquired was a wide brimmed straw Tihāmah hat which provided shade in more open situations.

The local people were by far my greatest problem with regard to drawing wild animals and birds. Their insatiable curiosity caused me no end of troubles. Regardless of where I was drawing, individuals would appear as if from nowhere gradually increasing in number. This inevitably scared away the wildlife I was attempting to draw. On occasions no amount of gesticulations or relevant remarks would make them go away. Young children whom I chased off retaliated by throwing stones at a relatively tame flamingo I was sketching. This resulted in its immediate departure into the hazy horizon. Whilst attempting to draw birds on the seashore I was more often than not plagued by boys showing off on motorbikes, buzzing up and down the beach scattering the flocks of gulls and terns to the wind. Then they would follow me offering lifts, despite explanations to the contrary. Even trying to use the vehicle as a hide from both wildlife and people proved useless at times. Once whilst trying to draw vultures feeding on a dead donkey a van-load of natives drew up between me and the carcase. Despite my pointing my telescope straight at them and gesticulating to move aside they just sat there motionless for what seemed like hours. In the end I had to settle for a drawing of cattle egrets feeding off flies from the carcase. In contrast, whilst drawing at Shibām in the mountains an old woman came out from a nearby cave dwelling and sat beside me. The pleasurable expression on her face as she watched me drawing spoke volumes despite our inability to communicate verbally. She even gently wiped the remains of my rubber eraser from the paper each time I rubbed something out. In the animal markets people gave me no real problems provided I positioned myself so that a crowd could not accumulate behind me.

On a survey expedition, travelling inevitably takes up a great deal of time and is uncomfortable in the hot and dusty conditions when covering rough terrain. Getting stuck in sand dunes and *sabkhah* added to the experience of the expedition but ate up valuable field time. To get a lot of meaningful drawing done one really has to spend a long time in an area to get to know it rather than new areas all the time. Working with upwards of five people specializing in different subjects also meant compromise situations where one could not stop at any given time when an interesting subject appeared. The ideal position would have been one's own transport and a flexible schedule which was not possible with this expedition.

There is infinite scope for any artist interested in the wildlife and landscape of the Yemen. With wildlife it was a case of finding the best areas, which took up much time. The lack of published material on good wildlife habitats did not help, but with sketching it is mostly a case of finding areas to suit one's own requirements. Most of the coastal birds were very approachable but inland they were generally more wary. This was very much the case for wild animals such as the baboons which were extremely wary due to persecution. The few other animals seen only afforded fleeting glimpses often at long range. I hope the information given in the Fauna chapter will be of some use to anyone interested in the wildlife and in sketching and painting.

9.5: ARTIST'S REPORT

John Nankivell

Plate 9.2 **John "concentrating" drawing Selma by Jabal Jamā' camp site, 14th February 1982**

Preparation for any unknown area is always difficult given that the bane of every traveller is an encumbrance of luggage, therefore really careful thought and research into the conditions and problems to be encountered is imperative. Besides of course the usual baggage necessary for travel – clothes, supplies etc., a great deal depends on what the "creative" traveller does. Is he loaded with cameras and heavy photographic equipment? wet suits and oxygen? Does he wish to paint vast canvasses from the tops of obscure mountain peaks or observe the varied life of local swamps through delicate but heavy instruments?

In my own case, to draw was often quite enough, and that in planning always entails as much paper as possible in varied thicknesses and quality (humidity can render some papers useless) with a large stock of rough paper to protect the work while at work – all in a wooden/metal hollow drawing board box for protection not too large or heavy as to be impossible to carry (shoulder straps here were a good thing). Stores of necessary pencils, rubber erasers, knives, crayons, etc., according to needs and tastes, but even these certain things refuse to function in certain climates.

It was in carrying all this that I found I had problems and thus will need to be far better prepared in future. For example, a waistcoat such as was sported (from fishing) by the Bird Artist, Keith Brockie, which compartmentalised every object necessary for art work would have been a great help, providing of course one's memory could cope with what had been put into thirteen separate pockets. I myself use Staedtler, Mars Luminograph pencils, ranging from 4B to 2H. When these pencils were made solely in Germany, instead of under patent in England, they were a good deal more consistent in quality. It is very unsettling to begin work with an HB pencil which suddenly changes to a B or an H. I have often bought complete sets of pencils in other makes to find them useless when I came to work with them.

Because of this, I also never take such things as fixative with me, as I rarely feel I have finished a drawing enough to set it forever. Fixative allows no change of mind or correction of poor pencil quality, and, although in theory it stops damage, it never suffices on its own anyway.

I found that looking in my one bursting, small poacher's bag each day for one object in my cake-mix of pencils, food, tablets, papers, clothes, sweets and money extremely frustrating – a better situation must be in a heavily divided bag as well.

Sketch books etc., provided they are expensively boxed to protect them, are sound – except that if one is working for say three months, then everyday all one's work travels, is used, and put out, and inevitably becomes soiled. For me finishing a piece on a sheet and storing it as soon as possible was a better solution. Some damage in travel is always a risk and to be expected, nonetheless careful steps must be made to protect the work as soon as it is done. To make working more comfortable, such things as folding stools with backs, cushions and protection from the sun by umbrella, hat and glasses can often be essential. Again all this must needs be carried at times.

It is only possible to advise on conditions of work in the Yemen for the area which the expedition covered; climate and environment in other areas of that wild Republic will make certain advice invalid and need new answers for others. Suffice to say that as most things that move on the Tihāmah also bite – day and night repellant in the form of medicines and clothing are always necessary. In the Tihāmah climate too, all effort tends to be demanding and sapping of energy so that the traveller who is to undertake any research work etc., must allow the needs of that to take precedence over every other. If a climb to the top of a nearby hill to see the view destroys one for the rest of the day, don't undertake the exercise.

In my experience I find it very necessary to protect myself as much from cold as from heat. To sit in the sun for any length of time is of course not advisable; nonetheless one will inevitably often get too hot at work – on one side only, and it is extremely necessary to protect the sunless side from chill and cold. For this I take extra rugs or shawls to wrap carefully around my middle. The British Raj in India made compulsory for all, the wearing of padded wide cummerbunds to protect the internal organs and despite the nuisance of this, one should never ignore its good sense.

Each day then if possible must be thought out and planned. The way not to begin a day as I so often found is a long personally loaded trek to the vague site of some work, exhausting and time consuming and then to wander around with strange people being attracted to one, giving rise to hassle and complications and a long time before a suitable view, spot or site for the work is finally chosen. A bad time here can totally ruin several days work.

Wherever possible the ground should have been previously explored for permission from the people, a protected site chosen, and one's arrival arranged early before the heat and action of the day. When this was done things had a chance of going well. Sometimes even when it was not done and there were appalling hassles (such as for me at the mud-fort in al-Rāfiʿī village, which area unknown to me was a strictly private harem and where I was thrown off one spot and constantly aggravated in another), the drawing ended up well – but at what cost of nerves and energy.

This has always been a critical area for my work. The arriving, the sorting, the view-choosing and the first half hour must be as calm and uncomplicated as possible. If it's not, then (unless real inspiration takes over regardless – as it does occasionally) whatever the circumstances, there is little hope for a really elating day.

So often conditions of work will be bad and difficult to start with that it becomes only sensible to advance as many positive factors on the creative side as possible and not needlessly place the odds against success.

There will be times when whatever the preparation, the time spent will be full of tension and strain. The interior of the mosque at al-Durayhimī was one such; in theory, cool, quiet, clean and calm, in reality, stiflingly hot, dirty, smelly and full of people all eager to see the work. If one had a bad time getting there first, any work would have been totally impossible.

It is of course important to notice the social and cultural way of life of the peoples in the region, not only to have them as allies rather than enemies, but to understand how they cope with their climate. If they respect the heat and power of the midday sun and work early with a rest in the middle of the day, it is only wise to do the same.

I found myself in the first two weeks ignoring these facts and working all day, paying for it eventually in strain and overtiredness. Sometimes this is inevitable, when time was limited at certain places, one was forced to work through the day. I can only now feel that unless one is in a singularly peaceful, cool and attractive spot – such as the pavilion room at the Wāqidī house in Zabīd, one should not make a habit of very long hours.

Much of this advice is fairly commonsense, and circumstances in each expedition will necessitate many variations on behaviour and activity. Nonetheless if it's staying power one wants, care is essential. Friends of mine in the Diplomatic Service in Java pointed out to me forcefully that in that humid and dangerous climate they never attempted to do more than two separate things each day – i.e., work at the office and one other modest occasion and never overdo it. If the creative traveller has to do all his organising and preparation himself, then he must expect a definite reduction in the amount of quality work he can do and survive.

For my own part my main problems were ones of basic organisation, settling to work, choice of site and care not to try to do too much in difficult conditions.

The great trouble with finding a new and wonderfully existing visual world as the Yemen is that if one tried to see and record everything then total collapse would be inevitable.

For this reason, although we were firmly discouraged on this expedition from taking photographs (and I agree that casual, ubiquitous "tripper" photography – including my own – is disruptive), I later found that the results of my architectural photography were essential to reinforce my memory on certain aspects of unfinished work when approached later away from its source.

I remain, however, at least at the distance of several thousand miles, enthusiastic about the Yemen, the areas I have seen and those I longed to see. Aware that despite the, at times lethal and treacherous climate, the incredibly hospitable people, and their rich, if vanishing culture were a marvellous reward for any risks encountered.

ILLUSTRATIONS

Plate 9.1 Nankivell, 205 × 240mm, pencil drawing; *Plate 9.2* Brockie, 280 × 380mm, pencil.

INDEX

Abbreviations used in the Index are as follows: *c* = city, *t* = town, *v* = village, corr. = correspondences. Tihāmah placenames appearing in the lists of bird observations and lists of fauna collections in Chapter 3 are not indexed. Colour plates are indicated by bold page numbers.